A short history of colonialism

Wolfgang Reinhard

Translated by Kate Sturge

D0792744

Manchester University Press
Manchester and New York

Distributed in the United States exclusively
by Palgrave Macmillan

The translation of this work was funded by Geisteswissenschaften International – Translation Funding for Humanities and Social Sciences from Germany, a joint initiative of the Fritz Thyssen Foundation, the German Federal Foreign Office, the collecting society VG WORT and the Börsenverein des Deutschen Buchhandels (German Publishers & Booksellers Association)

Published by Manchester University Press
Oxford Road, Manchester M13 9NR, UK
and Room 400, 175 Fifth Avenue, New York, NY 10010, USA
www.manchesteruniversitypress.co.uk

Distributed in the United States exclusively by
Palgrave Macmillan, 175 Fifth Avenue, New York,
NY 10010, USA

Distributed in Canada exclusively by
UBC Press, University of British Columbia, 2029 West Mall,
Vancouver, BC, Canada V6T 1Z2

British Library Cataloguing-in-Publication Data
A catalogue record for this book is available from the British Library

Library of Congress Cataloging-in-Publication Data applied for

ISBN   978 0 7190 8327 3 hardback

ISBN   978 0 7190 8328 0 paperback

First published 2011

The publisher has no responsibility for the persistence or accuracy of URLs for any external or third-party internet websites referred to in this book, and does not guarantee that any content on such websites is, or will remain, accurate or appropriate.

Typeset
by 4word Ltd, Bristol, UK
Printed in Great Britain
by CPI Antony Rowe Ltd, Chippenham, Wiltshire

A short history of colonialism

WITHDRAWN
UTSA LIBRARIES

MANCHESTER
1824

Manchester University Press

Contents

List of maps

Acknowledgements

The maps are reproduced from Wolfgang Reinhard's *Kleine Geschichte des Kolonialismus* (2008) with the kind permission of Alfred Kröner Verlag, Stuttgart. Maps 1, 2, 3, 4, 6, 7, 12, 13, 14, 15, 16 and 17 were previously adapted from Wolfgang Reinhard's *Geschichte der europäischen Expansion*, 4 vols (1983–90) with the kind permission of W. Kohlhammer Verlag, Stuttgart; Maps 10, 11 and 20 were previously adapted from *Fischer Weltgeschichte*, vols 19, 20 and 33 (1968, 1969) with the kind permission of S. Fischer Verlag, Frankfurt.

Every effort has been made to contact the copyright holders and to obtain permission to reproduce copyright material, but if for any reason a request has not been received, the copyright holders are invited to contact the publisher.

1   Colonies and colonialism

The term 'colonialism' became a political slogan in the twentieth century, but in this book it will be used without implying a value judgement – similarly to the word's use in the nineteenth century, when it simply described the circumstances in the colonies. I will use 'colonialism' to mean one people's control over another people through the economic, political and ideological exploitation of a development gap between the two. Closely related to 'colonialism' is the term 'imperialism'. Now emotionally loaded to the point of being unusable, its narrowest definition is as the Marxist-Leninist designation for the final stage of capitalism since around 1900, while the widest definition embraces every form of a polity's will to expand and dominate. I will use the term as a dynamic complement to the more static 'colonialism': 'imperialism' will refer to the measures undertaken in order to establish colonialism. If imperialism emanates not from a colonial power, like Britain, but from a colony, like Australia, we may speak of 'sub-imperialism', and its outcome will be a formal or informal 'sub-colony'. For a long time the Philippines was a formal sub-colony of Mexico, while the slave trade made Angola an informal sub-colony of Brazil. If, in turn, imperialism and colonialism proceed from a former European colony such as the United States, we can (from a European perspective) speak of 'secondary imperialism' and 'secondary colonialism'.

Extremely important for a definition of colonialism are the components of alterity and differential development. To be colonialist, rule must be experienced as alien rule; complete assimilation ends its colonialist character, as in the case of England and Wales. A consciousness of alterity may be reawakened later, for example by highlighting linguistic difference – again as in the case of Wales. But not all rule, and not all foreign rule, is colonialist, and the notion of the 'development gap' enables us to distinguish conceptually between a colonialist and a non-colonialist exercise of power. The rule of the Romans over the Greeks was not colonialist, nor was the Russians' control over the German Democratic Republic – but the Romans' rule over the Germanic tribes was, and so was the Russians' control over the Kazakhs. This last example, like the Welsh case, constitutes 'internal colonialism': a colonialism that occurs inside the borders of a unified polity, here the

Russian Empire or the kingdom of England. Today, 'colonial empires' are increasingly being viewed as only a special case of 'empires' in general. In contrast to modern nation states, empires are comparatively heterogeneous formations composed of unequal parts with unequal status. From the perspective of world history, they are the older, 'normal' format of larger polities, from the Chinese Empire to the Kingdom of Great Britain, that predominated before Europe invented and implemented the 'modern state' and exported it across the world. To this extent, in formal terms and on a global scale, political decolonisation may be regarded as the process by which that pre-modern form of rule was irreversibly superseded by the modern state.

In the context of this definition, the idea of 'development gaps' gains important, though not absolute, discriminatory power. Clearly, it is susceptible to causing offence and being misunderstood as racist, but the term is used here in a primarily descriptive and strictly value-free way. It claims neither that there is a generally binding route of development travelled by humanity, towards a pinnacle of modernity where the West sits enthroned, nor that it is more fully human to possess nuclear bombs than bows and arrows, but only that differences of this kind have brought about particular historical consequences. Neither does the concept imply a clear-cut distinction between active colonisers and passive colonised. Rather, both are agents in the process of colonialism, if with different and variable roles. The colonised may have accepted colonialism with resignation, violently resisted it or ingeniously subverted it; they may have collaborated with the colonial rulers or even enthusiastically taken up stimuli for sociocultural transformation – either way, they actively joined in shaping colonialism and thus also the postcolonial world. The victims and perpetrators of colonialism can be sharply distinguished in many cases, but not all. As a result, it is not enough for a history of colonialism simply to record the pertinent activities of the colonial powers; it must focus too on the rise and fall of colonial and postcolonial societies and polities. Although the momentum for change may have issued largely from the colonial powers, its subsequent development occurred, to a more or less far-reaching extent, upon conditions set by the indigenous cultures. Japan probably exemplifies this most clearly, but it is certainly not the only case, and on closer examination proves to be the rule rather than the exception. This is why, despite cultural features shared all over the world, there is ultimately no single modernity of a purely western kind, but rather a plurality of modernities with specific characters. The course of historical events reveals four distinct paths of modernisation: Europe's own modernisation; that of its settlement colonies, the new Europes of the northern and southern hemisphere; modernisation that is instigated exogenetically but implemented autonomously, like Japan's; and the more or less enforced modernisation in the colonies under foreign rule. Of course, it must be borne in mind that existing power relations have led to an imbalance in the state of research and historical sources regarding the activities of the colonial rulers and those of the colonised, so that a dominance of the western perspective remains inevitable for the time being.

Colonialism logically implies the terms 'colony' (from the Latin *colonia*) and 'colonisation', the latter simply meaning the establishment of colonies. Strictly speaking, 'colony' itself originally means a newly created settlement, which may be independent or controlled by the polity from which the settlers have come. In a figurative sense, however, the term is used to describe any territory that is geographically separated from the originating polity, especially one overseas. The minimal content of the term 'colony' is thus settlement *or* rule, whereas the maximal content is settlement *and* rule. Based on this, we can distinguish three fundamental types of colonies, each of which has a series of variants.

1. *Trading-base or military-base colonies* are intended to serve either economic purposes such as commerce, or the securing of a military presence, or both. They may be subsidiary branches of a foreign polity, like the Italian merchants' colonies in the oriental cities of the Middle Ages, or even today the 'British colony in Rome'. Alternatively, they may be autonomous entities constructed on foreign soil. This is how the Macedonians and the Romans once built settlements, how the western European naval powers, beginning with Portugal, later established networks of bases around the Indian Ocean, and how the British stretched their web of naval outposts across the world. As a rule, economic and military goals were inseparable.

2. *Settlement colonies* may be considered the prototype of the colony, to the extent that colonisation has been seen as the epitome of 'history' – colonisation as the progressive settling and cultivating of the earth through increasingly numerous humanity, in fulfilment of the Biblical command to procreate: 'Be fruitful, and multiply, and replenish the earth, and subdue it' (Gen. 1: 28). However, this ignores the fact that few of the newly settled lands, whether in America, Australia or Palestine, were uninhabited before the founding of the colony; rather, they were already inhabited by other, less 'developed' people who now had to either leave or serve. In most cases this involved the displacement of hunters, gatherers and nomads by sedentary crop-growers – the spread of *cultura*, the highly developed economic form of agriculture and the private land ownership associated with it. Where crop-growers were already living on the land, such as in Algeria or Palestine, settlement colonisation meant imposing superior forms of agriculture. This

might result in (a) the previous inhabitants being completely driven out, as in British North America and Australia, or (b) those inhabitants being turned more or less fully into dependent labourers, as in Algeria and Israel, or (c) the existing population being replaced with imported labour, as in the American slave plantations. Historically, then, colonisation has rarely been possible without colonialism.

3. *Colonies of rule* are not restricted to trading and military bases but control the entire country without subjecting it to comprehensive new settlement. The older, Hispano-American type of settlement colony immediately comes to mind: a large number of immigrants settle permanently in the colony, but base their subsistence primarily on the domination of an indigenous majority which is, for this purpose, usually left largely alone to pursue its own economic way of life. The characteristic feature of the more recent, Asian-African type, the pattern being British India, is the domination of a huge majority of indigenous people by a tiny minority of colonial rulers, who are not even permanently resident in the colony. Both variants depend on the collaboration of indigenous helpers to survive.

Finally, the term 'decolonisation', coined in 1932, will be used in this book to designate a colony's attainment of political independence. Recent research on colonial history has made increasing use of the category of 'informal control', whereby a polity or its members are caused to carry out actions that would not otherwise have occurred, but without that polity being subject to a legal form of dependency on the source of the influence. This situation need not disappear with the onset of decolonisation, and it has not done so.

It will already have become clear that colonialism and imperialism overlap considerably with two other phenomena of great significance in global history: migration and the formation of empires. In colonialism, migration rarely occurs in the form of the movement of entire peoples, but has been crucially important as a more or less mass relocation of individuals. Such migration took place voluntarily in settlement colonies and colonies of rule, but was not necessarily limited to these types. Most migrants from Europe went to the already independent United States, which itself was a product of colonialism. At times, the enforced migration of workers has been hardly less important, in the shape of the Atlantic slave trade and also, semi-voluntarily, as indentured labour.

Although the 'development gap' criterion allows us to distinguish colonial empires from other empires with reasonable clarity, they still remain members of the wider genre. Empires differ from modern states in not being nationally homogeneous and frequently also in having a looser political structure. In most cases they have arisen through war and violence, but peaceful empire-building has also been possible, in the past often through dynastic marriage and succession, as in the case of Spain and Austria. The looser political structure of empires frequently resulted in concentric zones of declining political power, with semi-autonomous client states as the outermost ring. Apart from the clear geographical order, a broadly similar arrangement can also be found in colonial empires, such as the British Empire's distinction between Crown colonies, protectorates, more or less independent Dominions and countries that were, like Egypt, 'only' under British influence. Despite the continued existence of Chinese and Russian exceptions, the empire as a form of political organisation seems obsolete in today's era of the democratic nation state. If so, the disappearance of the colonial empires would be part of a more general trend – unless we regard the global power of the United States as a new empire in view of the many analogies with colonialism, just as for the Chinese and Russian cases.

In the definition I have set out here, colonialism is evidently a widespread historical phenomenon. However, the present study restricts itself to its most recent and most extensive case: European colonialism from the fifteenth century onwards. I nevertheless draw on relevant aspects of the historical environment, beginning with the precursor forms that were really colonisation rather than colonialism – in particular the early modern trading empires around the Indian Ocean, where the leading role was held by Asians, not by Europeans, but where the foundations were laid for the later European colonies of rule. A further complex is the secondary colonialism and internal colonialism of European colonies like the United States, Australia or South Africa, closely tied to European colonialism if only because the role of 'men on the spot' in European expansion was often greater than that of the metropolitan political centre. The third aspect is the non-western colonialism of Egypt, Japan and China, since this was prompted and enabled by, or at least had to respond to, western colonialism: Russian and Chinese imperialism were clashing in East Asia as early as the seventeenth and eighteenth centuries. But this leaves open the question of whether 600 years of western colonialism should really even be thought of as a unified historical period.

Today it is clearer than ever before that there is not, and probably cannot be, a serviceable 'total' theory of European colonialism. Everything offered under that heading so far has proved either one-sided and incomplete, or impossible to apply in the practice of research. However, this does not mean that western colonialism necessarily dissolves into a chaos of disjointed individual events. If its components cannot be translated by theory into a systematically ordered totality, they can nevertheless be shown to be concatenated temporally and spatially. The Russian advance into Central

Asia in the eighteenth century has nothing to do with the British occupation of Uganda in the twentieth, but it does have something to do with the established Chinese interests in the region. Furthermore, it is perfectly possible to draw meaningful generalisations out of individual research cases; the typology of colonies I presented above is an example of just that. There are also typical patterns of behaviour that recur again and again, such as the pre-emptive occupation of colonies, a phenomenon of both sixteenth-century Brazil and twentieth-century Africa. Above all, most chains of events in the history of European colonialism were not planned, at least not in the form that they eventually took, but followed the principle of unintended consequences. This was often exacerbated by the fact that the participants knew so little about each other. Thus, during high imperialism in Africa there were a surprising number of cases where European military interventions did not intend to seize possession permanently: permanent seizure came in reaction to the Africans' violent resistance, which made it impossible for the Europeans to withdraw without losing national prestige. The Africans were not familiar enough with European politicians to identify the mechanisms behind such reactions, while ambitious colonisers on the spot knew how to exploit them to the full, presenting their governments with faits accomplis in pursuit of their own interests.

Because of the limited degree of central planning, the role of specific, individual motivations is particularly significant for colonisation and colonialism. Here, too, broadly three groups of motives can be identified, sometimes but by no means always associated with different groups of actors. Heading the list are socio-economic motivations, generally aiming for the acquisition of profits and thus of enhanced social status. Although these are certainly not the sole forces behind colonialism, as was long claimed, they are never really absent. Of course, the form of profit and status will change over time, and priorities will shift. Momentum might, for example, arise from the social pressures of overpopulation, or from the capitalist striving for profit as an end in itself. Occasionally, a desire for modernisation has prompted the colonised themselves to draw the colonisers to their shores. Secondly, political motives are usually present, even if only in the shape of the ambition of power-hungry military men. Although the political centres seldom plan, they frequently feel obliged to react, often due to a defensive image of themselves: it is no coincidence that the ideologues of the Roman or the British Empire interpreted those formations as the products of long-term, pre-emptive defence. Thirdly, ideological, religious and cultural motives are also crucial. At stake was often a desire to bring true faith to the heathens, true culture to the barbarians. Such missionary aspirations were ideologically instrumentalised, but they must nevertheless be taken seriously and cannot be dismissed as mere smokescreens. At times political ideologies played a role, first and foremost the virtually obsessive nineteenth- and twentieth-century notion that capitalism must expand outward if it is to avoid perishing due to overproduction and underconsumption. That culminated in the social Darwinist credo of the nations' struggle for survival in the arena of global economics and politics. In each individual case, the specific combination of old and new motivations did not tip the balance alone: it was the context of the source and target regions in which those motives were embedded, including the actions of indigenous people, that gave rise to the particular event in line with the principle of unintended consequences.

While the scale of European colonialism is historically unparalleled, there can be no doubt that comparable phenomena existed much earlier. I will return in particular to the subject of Chinese colonialism, impressive in its continuity, but there are also grounds to claim that in Mexico and Peru, the Spaniards' colonialism really only replaced that of the Aztecs and Incas. Classical antiquity saw Phoenician, Greek and Roman colonisation, though probably not colonialism to any great extent, since the factor of alterity will have receded very fast due to assimilation. Most relevantly, in medieval European history we can identify phenomena that are not only structurally related to the European colonialism of the modern era but form part of its prehistory. Lands previously colonised themselves, such as England, Spain or Portugal, pursued colonisation in Wales and Ireland or in the reconquered south of the Iberian Peninsula; they then consciously drew on these experiences to become the most successful colonial powers overseas. The eastwards colonisation emanating from medieval Central Europe was continued in the modern period by Russian imperialism right up to the Pacific Ocean. Excluded from this movement, France resorted instead to the Crusades, which, although they failed to create colonies, stimulated developments (especially among the Italians) that helped to lay the foundations of Iberian expansionism.

2 The European Atlantic

The Florentine poet Dante Alighieri had foolhardy mariners banished to hell
for their presumption in daring to advance beyond the boundaries of the
oecumene, the known and inhabited world. Yet in Dante's time, the Middle
Ages, Europeans had long been pressing forward from their continent's
northern and southern seas – the North Sea and the Baltic on the one hand,
the Mediterranean and Black Sea on the other – into the Atlantic Ocean. In
the early modern period they made the Atlantic into a new 'Medi-terranean'
joining Europe and its colonies. The Europeans were never able to control
either the Indian Ocean or the Pacific with the same exclusivity as they did
the Atlantic. The explanation for their success to the west lies in particular
achievements in the spheres of economic life and navigation. A key example
of these is the 'mercantile revolution' led by the Italian cities of the High
Middle Ages, which introduced new forms of monetary transaction and the
capital company, the *societas* or *compagnia*, with their system of banking,
credit and insurance and with trading interests that reached across the world
as far as East Asia. It was against this backdrop that the eastern
Mediterranean region saw the emergence of what must be described not as
mere trading posts but as colonies. They produced commodities such as
mastic on the Genoese-controlled island of Chios, or sugar on the Venetian
islands of Cyprus and Crete, where slave labour seems already to have been
used. In the area of shipbuilding, the galley was joined by a more highly
developed 'round' ship, the 'cog' also common in northern Europe. By the
fifteenth century the round ship's bent keel had been replaced with a straight
design and its steering oar with a stern rudder, while mixed rigging was used
on three masts (a square sail at the forecastle and mainmast, a lateen on the
stern castle); these innovations made it easier to sail under strong winds and
to tack against the wind. In addition, the existing coastal navigation, based
on accumulated practical experience, was gradually supplemented by 'scientific' ocean navigation, using the compass, equipment to track the altitude of
sun and stars and determine latitude, and mathematical tables to convert the
findings. Only the precise determination of geographical longitude was miss-
ing until the eighteenth century, so that for many centuries it was impossible
to fully monitor compliance with the spheres of interest demarcated by lines

of longitude, such as the meridian agreed in 1494 between Spain and Portugal.

However, it would be wrong to conclude that such advances were 'causes' of the European expansion into the Atlantic. Neither was the allegedly unprecedented individualism of the 'Renaissance Man' so frequently invoked by idealist historiography, or the insatiable hunger for surplus value that its materialist opponents have habitually brought to bear. Nor will we find the 'cause' in specific key events of a specific national history, such as the year 1492, when Spain captured Granada, thus vanquishing the last bastion of the Muslims on the Iberian Peninsula; drove the remaining Jews from the country; and 'discovered' America – a seamless segue from reconquest in the *reconquista* of Spain into new conquest, the *conquista* of the New World. The process of European expansion in general, and Iberian expansion in particular, cannot be explained by means of this kind of isolated cause, or indeed by the clusters of causes that some historians assemble in its place. If expansion had begun at a specific moment in time, simply analysing the forces effective at that moment would allow us to trace its 'causes'. But in fact the process of expansion was a long-term interweaving of structures and developments, marked by changing configurations and thus by contingent events to a greater extent than historiography has, until very recently, been willing to accept. This is not to deny that, in any given case, certain conditions had to be fulfilled for the process to continue on its way, but the necessity of these conditions is something that the historian can often only identify in retrospect. In other words, European expansion as a process was seldom planned and mostly improvised. That makes it all the more difficult to discover today which conditions made this or that particular improvisation possible, and why this or that particular result emerged.

The Atlantic itself set conditions, ones that remained in force for as long as seafaring continued to depend on the wind and the ocean currents. Winds and currents favourable to a European discovery of America existed only in the far north and in the trade-wind zone between the Tropics; everywhere else, the wind blew into the faces of would-be explorers. In fact, the first Europeans to set foot on America were Vikings, who had arrived via Iceland and Greenland around the year 1000. The event had little impact on Europe because the surrounding conditions were unfavourable. The second, and definitive, European discovery of America could only take place when mariners had travelled far enough south to pick up the trade winds which would drive them effortlessly west. Columbus's initial crossing was calm and smooth. It was only the journey back that caused difficulties, as the Portuguese and Spanish navigators were still only just learning that for both outward and return journey to be made comfortably, a loop known as the *volta* had to be followed in the mid-Atlantic: clockwise in the North Atlantic between southern Europe and the Caribbean, anticlockwise in the South Atlantic between South America and Africa. That way, the sailors could exploit the trade winds on the way out and the prevailing northern and southern westerlies with their corresponding currents on the way back. The routes later followed between north-western Europe and North America were in principle similar, if more complicated: ships had to sail northwards to get west and southwards to get east.

The fact that the discoverer of the New World for Europe was a Genoese man who had switched his allegiance from Portugal to Spain, Cristoforo Colombo, and the fact that this New World was named by German humanists, Martin Waldseemüller or Matthias Ringmann, in honour of a Florentine businessman working in Seville, Amerigo Vespucci, may be coincidences in terms of the precise individuals involved. But in terms of the political configurations that they express, these 'coincidences' are highly significant. Genoa, competing with Venice to control trade in the eastern Mediterranean, had been able to secure the slave trade from the Black Sea area, but Venice had forced the Genoese out of the commerce in spices and other Asian luxury goods that could still be obtained, via Egypt, even after the collapse of the Crusader States. It was also certainly relevant that the year the final Crusader stronghold of Acre fell to the Muslims, 1291, was also the year the Vivaldi brothers sailed west, possibly already hoping to find a route to India and thus to break the monopoly of Egypt and Venice. Although all sorts of legends still circulated about the terrible sights to be expected in unknown lands and seas, in the High Middle Ages it had long been common knowledge that the earth was round. After the Vivaldis' disappearance at sea, the Genoese continued to engage in the up-and-coming countries of the Iberian Peninsula, their nearer neighbours, which is not to say that the Peninsula saw no activity from the Venetians (whose galleys were sailing via Lisbon to England), the Florentines or other Italians. In 1317, a Genoese was made hereditary admiral of the Portuguese fleet.

Evidently, the inhabitants of the Iberian Peninsula were fully aware of the value of Italian capital and Italian know-how, even if the empires of Aragon, Castile and Portugal had already developed seagoing activity on their own account. Once again, it would be beside the point to apply a national-history perspective and weigh up the Italian against the Spanish and Portuguese contribution or vice versa, especially since such distinctions were of little interest to contemporaries – as long, that is, as there were no business opportunities which were worth reserving for their own compatriots. Aside from the 'straggler' Granada, the *reconquista* had already been completed by the mid thirteenth century. The kings of the Aragonese confederation now established their empire in the western Mediterranean, which by the end of the fifteenth century would encompass the Balearic islands, Sicily, Sardinia and Naples. Portugal and Castile, as well, had built up a navy by the twelfth and thirteenth centuries and developed trading contacts with Flanders and England. For Castile, the Basque and Cantabrian coastline and western Andalusia offered convenient points of departure for the north and south. In 1184, Portugal became the first of the three kingdoms to establish a foreign trading post or 'factory' in the trading hub of Bruges, and in 1203 it was granted the right to pursue trade in England. The wars of the fourteenth century showed that the Castilian navy was superior not only to its Muslim counterparts but also to the English fleet.

In 1312, while searching for the lost Vivaldi brothers, the Genoese sailor Lancelotto Malocello rediscovered the Canary Islands, known to classical antiquity. This opened the door for repeated visits from Italians, Portuguese, Andalusians, Catalans and Majorcans, although it seems that the inhabitants' resistance prevented the seafarers from managing to take possession of the islands. Nevertheless, the Canaries became a diplomatic bone of contention between Castile and Portugal. The Pope was brought into the argument, and announced both the missionary idea and his own claim to suzerainty. In the second half of the fourteenth century, however, calm returned to the Canaries, interrupted only by isolated slave-hunting expeditions. The Iberian powers seem to have been hamstrung by the general crisis arising from the Black Death; later, Castile and Portugal were fully occupied with internal conflicts over succession and civil wars. Only in the fifteenth century were renewed attempts launched to carry the war against the Muslims to Africa. Castile and Aragon having divided up the north African coast into spheres of interest in 1291, the Portuguese felt excluded, and tried to acquire a base in North Africa through the coup-style capture of Ceuta in 1415. The sources tell of a crusading spirit and a thirst for fame, but while these motivations must certainly be taken seriously, a role will also have been played by economic factors: Ceuta was one of the terminal points of the trans-Saharan caravan routes along which the gold of Guinea (urgently required again from the thirteenth century on to make coins), black slaves and other commodities reached the Mediterranean.

The Portuguese plans for Ceuta failed to bear fruit, as the caravan routes were diverted. In response, Portugal now tried to bypass the North African Muslims by establishing direct contact with the producers of the sought-after merchandise and, they hoped, finding new allies against the Moors. Since the appearance of the supposed Letter of Prester John in the mid twelfth century, the notion had been stalking Europe that a powerful Christian ruler was to be found beyond the realm of the Muslims, 'in India'. At this time, the label

'India' might cover any number of locations, even Ethiopia, where there really was a Christian prince. But the quest for a sea passage to India – whatever 'India' was – is mentioned in Portuguese sources only after the middle of the fifteenth century. The initiator and organiser of the subsequent Portuguese forays was Prince Henry 'The Navigator', who had fought at the battle of Ceuta. From his base in Sagres and the port of Lagos in southern Portugal, Henry sent ever new expeditions south. Despite his sobriquet, Henry himself never set sail, and neither did he run a nautical academy in Sagres to furnish his expansionist endeavours with a scientific basis. Stories to that effect first surfaced in the seventeenth century, and have persisted stubbornly until the present day.

Between 1419 and 1425, the Prince's men, thrown off course by storms, discovered the uninhabited islands of the Madeira group, which were immediately settled and transformed into a centre of cane sugar production and viniculture. The discovery of the Azores between 1427 and 1452 probably occurred in a similar way, given that they lie in the middle of the Atlantic, far away from the African coast that was the sailors' objective. Only a *volta*, no doubt an unintentional one this time, could have led seafarers there, as it did Columbus on the way back from his first expedition. The case of the Canary Islands was different. There had been Castilian bases on the islands since the beginning of the fifteenth century, and by 1425 Portugal too had made a further vain attempt to subdue the indigenous population. In 1433, one of Henry's ships managed to overcome the dangers of the treacherous coastal waters of Cape Bojador, discovering that neither land nor seas south of that point in fact held any of the legendary terrors which had hitherto aroused such fear. After interruption by a fresh Portuguese attack on Tangiers, once again doomed to failure, the 1440s and 1450s finally brought maritime gains. Portuguese navigators reached Rio de Oro, Senegal, Cape Verde and Sierra Leone, and the first African slaves were imported. This made the voyages interesting for Portuguese and foreign – especially Italian – capital. In 1456 a Venetian and a Genoese discovered the Cape Verde Islands. A monopoly over the African trade was now established. It was held initially by Henry personally and then, after his death in 1460, by the Portuguese Crown, and was backed up internationally through papal bulls. The Crown leased out its monopoly while it turned its attention to new conquests in Morocco, but despite this change of focus, in the following twenty years Portuguese traders reached the coast of Gabon.

The Castilians did not allow themselves to be edged out without protest. In 1474 war erupted when the Portuguese king intervened in the new round of conflicts over the Castilian succession. After his defeat in 1479, the Treaty of Alcáçovas was signed, on the one hand laying down the succession of Isabella

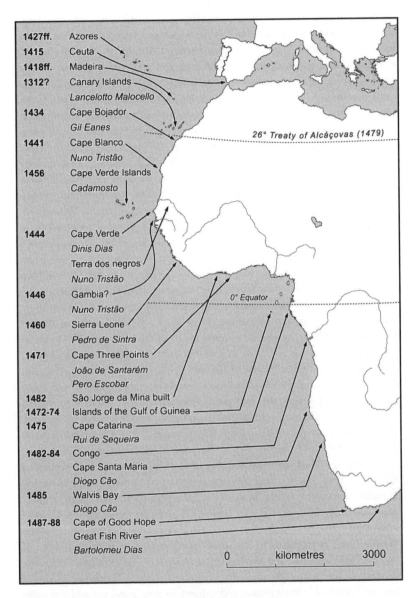

1427ff.	Azores
1415	Ceuta
1418ff.	Madeira
1312?	Canary Islands
	Lancelotto Malocello
1434	Cape Bojador
	Gil Eanes
1441	Cape Blanco
	Nuno Tristão
1456	Cape Verde Islands
	Cadamosto
1444	Cape Verde
	Dinis Dias
	Terra dos negros
	Nuno Tristão
1446	Gambia?
	Nuno Tristão
1460	Sierra Leone
	Pedro de Sintra
1471	Cape Three Points
	Joâo de Santarém
	Pero Escobar
1482	Sâo Jorge da Mina built
1472-74	Islands of the Gulf of Guinea
1475	Cape Catarina
	Rui de Sequeira
1482-84	Congo
	Cape Santa Maria
	Diogo Cão
1485	Walvis Bay
	Diogo Cão
1487-88	Cape of Good Hope
	Great Fish River
	Bartolomeu Dias

26° Treaty of Alcáçovas (1479)

0° Equator

0   kilometres   3000

Map 1   The Portuguese advance along the African coast

of Castile, and on the other recognising the Portuguese hold on all of Africa south of the 26th parallel. The Canary Islands lay north of this line, and were thus once and for all assigned to Castile, which proceeded energetically with its conquest until well into the 1490s. For the first time, the *reconquista* was being extended overseas, and adapted modes of action were developed that would provide the template for *conquista* in the New World. The social stratum most important to this process, both in the Canaries and in the New World, was the lower-ranking nobility. The *hidalgos* were driven by a will to upwards mobility through plunder and conquest, settlement and the founding of cities in the name of God and the king. This group was largely urban, and closely aligned with the 'bourgeois' zeal for acquisition. To this extent, the frequently asked question of whether the *reconquista* and, especially, the *conquista* were actually feudal and medieval in character or, rather, capitalist and modern starts from the wrong premise. The opposition is irrelevant in this binary form, because both components were present and inextricably interconnected. From a political point of view, as well, one should beware of taking the period's feudal language at face value. In Castile – and also in Portugal – a monarchy with absolutist claims was in fact drawing on the support of the cities and the rising group of the lawyers to fend off the higher nobility. The Crown was at the heart of all the Castilian ventures; it granted legal status to the discoverers and their new enterprises by issuing privileges. Even the Church was subject to the Crown. Finally, it would be wrong to attach the label 'crusade' to either the *reconquista* or the *conquista* as a whole: here, too, there is a risk of being misled by the religious jargon of the day. Although individual *reconquista* campaigns occasionally had elements of a crusade, and religion did constitute the chief dividing line, the real issue was nevertheless one of bounty and conquest, and switching sides across the religious divide was not uncommon. This is not to say that religious equality prevailed. The Christians initially respected the independence of the defeated Muslim communities just as, conversely, the Muslims respected that of the Christians and both respected that of the Jews, but this acceptance was never unqualified: it always carried the proviso of good conduct. To this extent, the period's limited religious tolerance can justly be regarded as a colonialist prefiguration of apartheid. Most importantly, a shift towards rigorous intolerance occurred in the course of the Middle Ages, culminating in the late fifteenth century with the expulsion of the Jews and Muslims and the Inquisition's persecution of suspect converts. And when the Spaniards were first faced with actual heathens, as in the Canary Islands, Christianisation and subjection went hand in hand – despite the fact that as early as 1434 the Pope had forbidden the Spanish to enslave Canary Island natives who peacefully accepted conversion. The Castilian Crown signed contracts, known as *capitulaciones*, with private military 'companies', offering the entrepreneurs royal authorisation in return for a commitment to take possession of the islands and settle them. The indigenous population was soon wiped out.

On the Portuguese side, the new king, John II (1481–95), took overseas expansion in hand more systematically than ever before. In 1481, in what is now Ghana, prefabricated components were used to build the fortress São Jorge da Mina, later called Elmina, as the hub of the gold trade, which had by now grown substantially. Between 1482 and 1484 the Portuguese discovered the Congo Empire in the north of today's Angola. Its African rulers wanted to carry out a missionary and development programme with Portuguese help over the decades to come. However, the interests of the Portuguese slave traders and the sugar planters now established on the island of São Tomé proved stronger, and Africa was anyway soon to be relegated to secondary importance for Portugal by the lucrative new trade with East India.

Some time around 1483, the Genoese Cristoforo Colombo (1451–1506) came to Elmina as a Portuguese captain. Already familiar with other Atlantic routes, in 1484 Columbus presented King John with his project of reaching the Indies by circumnavigating the globe westwards. The plan was not completely original: there are indications that the existence of, at least, additional islands west of the Azores was assumed at the time – though no solid evidence supports the romantic tale according to which Columbus had received reliable reports of land to the west. On the other hand, the realisation had not yet dawned that India could be reached via the southern tip of Africa, the classical authority Ptolemy having postulated a continuous southern land-mass that would have made the Indian Ocean an inland sea. The phantom of that southern continent, later in the shape of 'Terra Australis Incognita', continued to haunt geography for many years, until James Cook's circumnavigation of the globe in 1772–75 finally disproved its existence and Antarctic exploration in the nineteenth and twentieth centuries revealed the reality behind the notion. In spite of these assumptions, however, the scientific experts of the Portuguese Crown rejected Columbus's westwards plan. Deceived by an accumulation of traditional and more recent errors, he had wrongly calculated the distance and expected to find Japan where in fact the as yet unknown New World lay. As it turned out, this miscalculation was a stroke of luck for Columbus, but it did mean that, despite an occasional use of the term 'mundus novus', he remained convinced till the very end that he had landed in unknown parts of East Asia. In 1485 he applied to the Spanish, but found their experts no less sceptical; his project was turned down again in 1486.

In the meantime, John II of Portugal had not been idle. In 1487 he sent out spies to Egypt, disguised as Muslims, to reconnoitre the route to India, and had navigators search for a passage not only along the African coast but also up the Niger through the Guinea hinterland, where it was thought that the river might flow into the Nile. John even appears to have shown interest in a renewed offer by the frustrated Columbus when, in 1488, the news finally arrived that Bartolomeu Dias had rounded the southern tip of Africa for Portugal. Now that Portuguese success was imminent, the Spanish monarchs realised that Columbus's project might be their sole remaining chance of winning the race for a sea route to East India. The battle for Granada had been brought to a successful conclusion, and the cost of the new venture could be kept low. On 17 April 1492 the Spanish monarchs therefore agreed to Columbus's ambitious demands. He was given a loan, three ships and a contract guaranteeing him a hereditary aristocratic title, the position of admiral and governor, and a proportion of the profits. After thirty-six days of uneventful sailing from the Canaries, he reached an island of the Bahamas group on 12 October 1492. Columbus explored the north-eastern coast of Cuba and the northern coast of Haiti, then began what would prove a stormy passage back to Spain via the Azores and Portugal. Columbus's log, preserved in the form of an abstract by Bartholomé de las Casas, describes not only the magic of the New World and the conversion of its inhabitants, but also their labour, commodities and, especially, gold. The pattern of the Portuguese experience in Africa is impossible to miss.

Because the new-found islands lay south of the Alcáçovas line, a conflict with Portugal was inevitable. The Spanish monarchs took care to arrange a head start for their position by acquiring papal bulls in which the Aragonese pope Alexander VI, ever eager to oblige, granted them all the lands beyond a line 100 leagues west of the Azores. The important aspect of this move is not the implication that the Pope had the right to dispose of the world as he saw fit, nor the momentous use of the Christian mission to legitimise territorial acquisition, but the instrumental character of the papal documents as a diplomatic manoeuvre against Portugal – which itself had worked with papal bulls in the past and could thus hardly afford to ignore them now. On 7 June 1494, the parties signed the Treaty of Tordesillas, agreeing a line of demarcation 370 leagues west of the Cape Verde Islands at 46°37' W. This meant a partial revision of the Treaty of Alcáçovas, felt by the Spaniards to be disadvantageous, and secured Castilian participation in control of the Atlantic. At the time the Catholic monarchs' attention was focused on the Italian theatre of war, but nonetheless, even before the treaty with Portugal was signed, Columbus was sent out with a fleet of seventeen ships and around 1,400 men to put a definitive seal on the matter. During this and two further voyages between 1493 and 1504, Columbus explored the Greater and Lesser Antilles, the coast of mainland South America north of the Orinoco estuary, and the Central American coast between Honduras and Panama. As a coloniser he was less successful. The indigenous population's subsistence economy collapsed under the pressure of the Spanish demands and especially of forced labour for gold extraction, while the disappointed Spanish colonists rebelled. The trade in 'Indian' slaves that Columbus had begun was now foundering on the Indians' lack of aptitude for the work and a prohibition by the Spanish Crown, which did not want to lose its newly won subjects. As early as 1500, Columbus was replaced as governor by a trusted agent of the court. The monopoly enterprise named Crown & Columbus had fallen prey to the increasing pressure to succeed in the face of Portuguese triumphs.

Almost ten years after the Cape of Good Hope was first rounded, the Portuguese explorer Vasco da Gama (1459–1524) had now completed the first successful voyage to the East Indies. Leaving the Cape Verde Islands on 3 August 1497, he followed the trade winds west into the open Atlantic. On 4 November the west winds brought him to the coast of south-western Africa after three months with no sight of land – until then, nobody had dared to undertake such a lengthy voyage on the high seas, not even Columbus. Now the Portuguese felt their way laboriously along the coast, until in March they reached the Muslim principalities on the Swahili coast and with them the trading world of the Indian Ocean. After initial conflicts, in Malindi they found a pilot willing to guide them with the south-west monsoon to the spice-trading port of Calicut on the Kerala coast, where they arrived on 20 May 1498. Despite friction with the Muslim competition, the Portuguese started doing business with the Hindus, and in 1499, after a return voyage made more arduous by the fact that da Gama had not yet grasped the monsoon system, they succeeded in bringing their first cargo of spices home to Lisbon. That same year the Portuguese monarch made a high-flown addition to his royal style, thenceforth calling himself 'King of Portugal and Algarves of either side of the sea in Africa, Lord of Guinea and of the Conquest, Navigation and Commerce of Ethiopia, Arabia, Persia and India'.

In comparison to this, Columbus's West Indies seemed a poor affair; they could not possibly be the miraculous land whose discovery remained the prime objective of the Spanish Crown. It was imperative to find a passage to the wonderful East as soon as possible. To that end, the Crown dissolved its monopoly contract with Columbus and, from 1498, permitted other voyages of exploration and barter, to be carried out at the venturer's own cost but only under authorisation through a *capitulación* with the expedition leader and a 20 per cent share of the profits for the Crown. This was a throwback to the organisational models of the *reconquista*, and meant that it was now no longer only mariners and merchants who participated in the processes of exploration, but increasingly also battle-hardened members of the *reconquista* milieu. The transition from discovery to conquest began to take shape. In the years 1498–1503, the coast of South America was the main focus of exploration. The Portuguese were also part of this after 1500, when Cabral's Indian fleet, on its westbound *volta*, made landfall on the coast of Brazil – which, according to the (perfectly correct) Portuguese interpretation, lay east of the Tordesillas meridian. It quickly became clear that this must be an unknown continent. In 1507 the 'new' landmass was finally named by German scholars after the controversial Italian Amerigo Vespucci (1451– 1512), whose work *Mundus Novus* had been the first to market that insight successfully using print technology.

From now on, discovery rapidly turned into *conquista*, the exceptions being cases where resources were inadequate or the land did not seem worth the effort of conquering. The latter applied especially to North America, where the Spanish claims were challenged by Portuguese, English and French activity. The ubiquitous Italian experts played their role as well. The Venetian Giovanni Caboto (John Cabot), who received a royal patent from Henry VII of England in 1496, became the official discoverer of the fishing grounds off Newfoundland; the Tuscan aristocrat Giovanni da Verazzano, on a French commission, in 1524 explored the eastern coast of today's USA and later became interested in Brazil, as was common in France at the time. In 1533 the Francophile pope Clement VII granted Francis I a favourable interpretation of the bulls of Alexander VI, ruling that these applied only to the lands already discovered at the time, not to new ones. In 1534–42 Jacques Cartier undertook three voyages to the St Lawrence based on this ruling, exploring the river far into the area now Quebec. His venture makes it very clear what goal was in the minds of most of these explorers: they were hoping to find the stubbornly elusive westward route to India. The Venetian John Cabot had hoped to steal a march on Columbus in this respect, while Cartier thought the St Lawrence might prove to be the waterway that Verazzano had failed to find further south. After Vasco Núñez de Balboa's 1513 crossing of the isthmus of Panama from north to south, where he found the 'South Sea' (that is, the Pacific), the status of America began to change. From being considered a part of Asia, it became a barrier to the miracle lands of the east.

Columbus's dream was ultimately realised by a Portuguese sailor in the service of Spain, returning dissatisfied from India: Fernão de Magalhães, or in the Spanish form Fernando de Magallanes (*c.* 1480–1521). In 1518 Emperor Charles V gave him five ships with around 250 men. The Crown provided one quarter of the funding and the merchant Cristóbal de Haro from Burgos the other three quarters, possibly as a front for the Fuggers, Welsers and other southern German families who were hoping to get themselves a more cost-effective foothold in the spice business. Magalhães set sail in

1519, in 1520 passing the strait in the south of America that would later take his name. He crossed the Pacific in two and a half months without sight of land, tormented by hunger, thirst and scurvy, from today's Valparaiso to Guam, and was killed in the Philippines in 1521 when he intervened in a local dispute. Two of his ships reached the Spice Islands, and one managed to escape Portuguese attacks to return to Spain in 1522 with a rich cargo of spices. However, the venture could not be repeated, so that in 1529 Charles V sold his artificially raised claims to the Spice Islands to Portugal for the sum of 350,000 ducats – a sensible move, since by that time Portugal had anyway taken possession of the islands. Only when a return route to Mexico was discovered in 1565, a wide curve across the North Pacific that again followed the *volta* principle, did it become possible for the Philippines to take on the role of a back door to commerce with Asia. The islands, which had been occupied in 1564 from Mexican bases in response to high spice prices, now developed into a sub-colony of Mexico. For almost 200 years, the convoy traffic between Acapulco and Manila remained virtually the only European activity in the Pacific.

As for the Atlantic, its coastal waters had already been more or less fully explored by the first third of the sixteenth century. Over the next hundred years, all regions of America were made colonies of the European powers, and the western coasts of Africa, too, were drawn into that system of control. The Atlantic became a European inland sea, the Atlantic area a European commercial and communications system and a battleground for European power politics. In the seventeenth century the Caribbean – the American 'Mediterranean' – grew to be a particularly important arena for dramatic political events. As long as we remember the limits of such generalisations, we could certainly describe the Atlantic as a 'European world system', the focal point of which lay in Seville in the sixteenth, in Amsterdam in the seventeenth and in London in the eighteenth century.

3   Europeans and Asians

Before the European discoveries, the Atlantic had seen no intercontinental traffic whatsoever, and it was only the Europeans who created a 'world system' there – but on the Indian Ocean and the seas between Australia and Japan the situation was almost the exact reverse. Although by no means all the lands bordering these oceans were interested in seaborne traffic and trade, the general picture certainly justifies the claim that an Asian world system existed from ancient times, a system incomparably more sophisticated than anything accomplished by the Europeans of the time. On closer inspection, Italy's thirteenth-century global trading system, even at its zenith, takes on the appearance of a mere offshoot and appendage of the Asian one. As we learn more about the earlier economic life of the Asian region, it becomes ever more obvious how highly developed the Asian economies were in comparison with their European counterparts. In the fifteenth century the Chinese had sent a series of expeditions west, with hundreds of ships and tens of thousands of soldiers, so that the idea of a Chinese 'discovery' of the West is a perfectly realistic alternative scenario. These expeditions were abandoned not because of external resistance, but due to internal Chinese misgivings. The Europeans' advance into the Indian Ocean may have been revolutionary in that they were initiating direct contact with the central zones of a system with which they had previously entertained only indirect connections, and in that they did so with a significant degree of violence. Yet despite their considerable successes, the European activities remained marginal from the Asian perspective, were subject to terms set by the Asians, and depended on finding niches within the Asian system – niches that often arose only through a lack of interest from the vastly superior Asian powers, as was the case in India. Japan and China, in contrast, had no difficulty in keeping the Europeans at arm's length for as long as they found appropriate, or alternatively in imposing humiliating conditions on their European partners. These 'terms of business' would not alter fundamentally until the eighteenth or even nineteenth century. To this extent, in the context of sixteenth- to eighteenth-century Asia we can only speak of European colonialism in certain, territorially restricted spheres of European influence, or to the degree that European activities in Asia were intertwined with colonialism in other parts of the world, especially America. Otherwise, these were not colonialist enterprises but European trading systems in which territorial acquisitions and political rule were always driven by sober calculation in the exclusive service of commerce. Nevertheless, it was on these foundations that the European colonialism of the nineteenth and twentieth centuries in Asia would be constructed.

Portuguese 'Crown capitalism'

Faced with the baffled question of two Spanish-speaking Muslims or Jews encountered in Calicut, 'What the devil brings you here?', the Portuguese answer was short and to the point: 'We're looking for Christians and spices.' The spices whose supply to Europe they hoped to control were chiefly pepper, secondarily cinnamon, nutmeg and cloves. Pepper was harvested in the mountainous hinterland of the Malabar coast and in Sumatra, while cinnamon came from Ceylon, nutmeg from the Banda Islands, and cloves from the Moluccas, especially Ternate and Tidore. These much-invoked 'Spice Islands' lie between Sulawesi (formerly Celebes) and New Guinea. A substantial portion of the spice production of these areas went to Asian purchasers. Spice supply to the West was at this time firmly in the hands of merchants from the Arab world and Gujarat, in north-western India. They loaded cloves and nutmeg in Malacca, the central, unimaginably wealthy hub of trade between the Indian Ocean and the eastern seas. Together with cinnamon and pepper, the spices were taken to Jeddah on the Red Sea and from there through Egypt to Alexandria, where the Venetians were buying. High customs duties, in particular, meant that the price of the spices had increased more than twentyfold by the time they arrived in Alexandria, so that despite the prodigious detour it seemed worthwhile to take the route around the African continent in order to get the spices onto the European market directly from the producers. The existing owners of the European trade, unsurprisingly, baulked at this prospect, and the Portuguese decided that violence was the simplest way forward. Conveniently, the Arabs and some of the Gujaratis were Muslims and thus, as *mouros* or Moors, traditional archenemies of the Portuguese against whom it was both legitimate and honourable to fight. Additionally, Jeddah is the port of the holy city of Mecca, so that the resulting, vicious trade-war could be cynically presented as 'pepper crusaders versus cinnamon hajjis'. However, the rivalry between the two proselytising and expansionist world religions Islam and Christianity in Asia was not – as is often considered self-evident today – a mere pretext, veiling what was essentially a conflict of economic interests. It did have a genuine basis in the history of ideas and culture. Islam was on the advance not only on the Indian subcontinent, where the northern sultanates and, since the mid sixteenth century, the Mughal Empire had been pushing south at the expense of the Hindu kingdoms, but equally in the island world east of Malacca, where merchants were its main disseminators. Islam was already successfully established on Java in the fifteenth century, although to the east, on the Spice Islands proper, it had only a few years' head start on the newly arriving Christianity.

From 1500 on, a Portuguese fleet went east every year with the calcu-lated objective, explicitly described as such in the sources, of using terror to destroy the Muslims' trade and replace it with a Portuguese monopoly. These annual expeditions soon proved inadequate to the task, and as early as 1505 the Portuguese Crown decided to establish a permanent presence in the area, with a viceroy and a carefully planned system of bases to be positioned around the Indian Ocean. The project was realised mainly during the 1509–15 incumbency of the governor general Alfonso de Albuquerque. Albuquerque was a combination of war hero, politician and businessman, the first representative of the European genre of the overseas 'empire builder' and, as so often with figures of this kind, a man whose deeds have aroused alternating admiration and abhorrence. He first secured control over the East African coastal towns, which was not only important for shipping in the area but also secured a supply of gold from the Zambezi region, assisting the balance of payments. On the western coast of the Indian subcontinent several bases were established in the pepper district and in Gujarat; in 1510 they were joined by the newly conquered Goa, one of India's best harbours, as the centre of the new network. Finally, in 1511, the Portuguese defeated forces twenty times their size to capture Malacca, the gateway to the east. In 1515 Ormuz on the Persian Gulf was taken, while on the opposite coast Persia, recently converted to Shia Islam, was interested in collaborating with the Portuguese against its hostile Sunni neighbours. The Portuguese themselves kept the passage through the Gulf open for spices to supply the Near East, and made a steady income from the customs duties it collected. Under these circumstances, the original plan to close off the Red Sea completely no longer made sense. Albuquerque himself, in 1513, had failed to capture Aden at the Red Sea's mouth, and the Christian Abyssinians, with whom the Portuguese had built up some contact, were facing difficulties of their own in fending off the Muslims. In 1517 Egypt had fallen to the Ottomans, who took up the battle against their Portuguese competitors with considerably more vigour than had the previous Egyptian sultan. The Ottoman fleet's expedition of 1538 put severe pressure on the Portuguese, and although the fleet was forced to retreat when the suspicious Indian Muslims failed to offer it adequate support, it was still able to capture Aden and to leave a governor on the other side of the sea at Zeila. The Red Sea had thus become Ottoman. From now on the Portuguese resorted to participating in the lucrative smuggling trade in spices along this route, so that by the mid sixteenth century spices imported via the Gulf could be bought in Aleppo, and those imported via the Red Sea in Alexandria, in quantities almost as large as the shipments arriving from the Cape of Good Hope – as long as political relations with the Ottoman Empire remained untroubled.

In 1518 the Portuguese were able to build a base on the cinnamon island of Ceylon, and later succeeded in winning over the island's most important ruler to Christianity. East of Malacca, however, their resources stretched only to isolated bursts of activity. From 1513 on, they visited the Moluccas regularly, supporting the Sultan of Ternate against the Sultan of Tidore and, in 1522, building a fortress on Ternate in addition to their *feitorias* – trading stations or 'factories' – on Amboina and the Banda Islands. The choice of location was prompted by the arrival in 1521 of Magellan's Spanish expedition, which kept to the island of Tidore. From 1514 repeated attempts were made to push forward to China, Chinese merchants having been encountered in Malacca. But the Middle Kingdom had no use for the presumptuous 'western barbarians'. It was only in 1557 that trading interests led the Chinese to tolerate the Portuguese settlement of Macao on the western edge of the Pearl River Delta, and only in 1582 that the settlement was recognised officially. In 1999 this last remnant of the former Portuguese Empire reverted to China, the People's Republic having rejected earlier Portuguese offers of restitution. Just as in the early days, the Chinese leadership found it highly useful to keep Macao as an unofficial back door to the West, if one that was officially disdained. In the sixteenth century, China began to take an interest in the Portuguese, mainly as middlemen in the trade with Japan, to which China had also officially prohibited direct contact. But wealthy Japanese preferred Chinese silk to the Japanese equivalent, while the Chinese appreciated the silver so richly mined in Japan. In 1543 Portuguese traders had landed in Japan by mistake, and from 1544 their ships visited the islands regularly, after 1571 landing at Nagasaki, where the ruler had called in the Jesuit missionaries who had been working successfully in Japan since 1549. The Jesuits' knowledge of the country made them useful agents for business both with their compatriots and with China. Indeed, for the Japanese this was the chief reason to keep them in the country, while the Jesuits themselves relied on the profits of such trade to help sustain their blossoming Japanese mission. However, when the Spanish took the Philippines, starting in 1565, Japan – where centralised power had only recently been established after a period of civil war – became increasingly suspicious of a possible 'fifth column' at home. The persecution of Christians began. From 1600 on, the Portuguese became dispensable due to the presence of the Dutch and English, who, in addition, worked energetically to undermine their competitors. This was the point at which the Christians were suppressed, the foreigners driven out, and the country closed off. From 1641 Japan's western contacts were limited to strictly regulated trade with a Dutch 'factory' on the artificial island of Dejima in Nagasaki's harbour.

Here, as in China, Portugal's remarkable train of victories came up against its limits. Yet even if Portugal's rule was only over markets, not territories, it is still perplexing that a few hundred – later a few thousand – people were able to impose their will on a 'world system', in the face of highly sophisticated empires each of whose rulers disposed over many times the number of subjects available to the king of the small and sparsely populated Portugal. Certainly, the audacity recorded in the sources should not be underestimated. It had been drummed into the Portuguese through centuries of war with the Muslims, a true 'school for cutthroats'. Except for the Ottomans and some East Asians, Asia had no warriors of comparable ferocity. An additional factor was Portugal's obvious superiority at sea. None of the Indian empires possessed a navy, and the great ships of the Muslim merchants were built without metal, leaving them less robust than the Portuguese vessels. They were also constructed specifically to sail before the monsoon, and were therefore less easy to manoeuvre; the merchant vessels were clearly outclassed by the Portuguese ships' stern rudder and combination of square and lateen rigging. The European naval artillery also played its part, but the Portuguese benefited most of all from the patchwork nature of the political map around the Indian Ocean and in the eastern islands. Collective terms like 'Philippines' (after Philip II of Spain) and 'Indonesia' ('Indian Islands') were only created by the Europeans, as indeed was the political unity of these island groups. In such a fragmented context it was not difficult to play off Malindi against Kilwa, Cochin against Calicut, Persia against the Ottomans, Hindus against Muslims – especially as the emerging Mughal Empire pursued no maritime interests. When it came to China and the reunited Japan, of course, such methods were ineffectual.

The well-established Portuguese trading empire was based on numerous trading posts, fortified wherever possible, between Mozambique and Nagasaki. The network of such bases was particularly dense in East Africa, at the entry to the Persian Gulf and on the western coast of India. In Goa, Cochin, Colombo, Malacca and Macao, the Portuguese population was so large that Lisbon accorded it municipal rights to self-government. On the Zambezi, on the Indian west coast and in Ceylon there were limited territorial possessions. Goa was the residence not only of the almost omnipotent viceroy but also of the highest fiscal and commercial authority and the high court. The trading posts each had a *capitão* as their governor, a *feitor* responsible for business and an *ouvidor* for judicial affairs. The Crown also controlled and funded the recently established ordinary church hierarchy and the missionaries. This pattern was not new: Henry the Navigator himself had gained control over the Order of Christ, a wealthy religious order of knights, as a way of financing and legitimising his various ventures. The ecclesiastical expansion that accompanied its secular equivalent was bound to remain dependent upon worldly developments; no other option yet existed. The Pope and king established a series of dioceses under the archbishopric of Goa in India, and another two in Macao and Funai, Japan. The Inquisition kept a close watch over orthodoxy and morals, but also over the observance of the royal patronage of the church, the *patronato real*. Indeed, missionaries travelling via Lisbon to Asia without a royal licence risked being persecuted as heretics on the grounds that they had cast doubt on the Portuguese faith in the *patronato*.

East of Malacca, imperialist structures were even less advanced. Instead, the key role was played by regular monopoly convoys to the Moluccas, the Banda Islands and Japan. The leader of such a convoy was a *capitão-mor* and competed with the local *capitãos* for authority on the ground. Wherever possible, foreign ships were forced to accept passes – *cartazes* – that protected them from attack by Portuguese patrols and obliged them to call at Portuguese ports, paying customs duties there; this served both to implement the monopoly and to fill the coffers of the self-funding system. More important for the latter purpose was, however, Portugal's own trade within the Asian region, later known as 'country trade'. This port-to-port trading remained within the 'country', that is, within the East Indies. Spices, Indian cotton and Chinese silk were exchanged for Japanese gold, silver and copper and Persian silver; Persian horses destined for the cavalry of the Hindu Vijayanagar Empire yielded especially high returns. The goods shipped to Portugal itself made up only a small fraction of turnover in this very profitable trading system. In the early sixteenth century a 273 kg bahar of cloves cost 1–2 cruzados on the Moluccas, 9–14 cruzados in Malacca and 30–42 cruzados on the Malabar coast (the bahar of Malacca actually weighed only 210 kg, that of Calicut just 207 kg). Colourful silks could be sold in Japan for three to four times the price paid for them in China. The command of a monopoly convoy of this kind, which included a fixed share of the profits, was a much sought-after privilege accorded to members of the nobility, though in the later period these commands were auctioned off to the highest bidders. The advantages were clear: if in 1610 the passage to Japan cost 27,000 xerafines, plus another 40,000 for the ship, crew and provisions, the voyage promised profits of 150,000 xerafines.

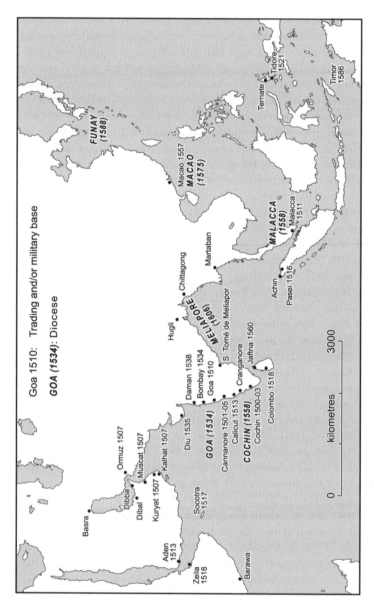

Goa 1510:   Trading and/or military base

GOA (1534): Diocese

Map 2   The Portuguese trading and missionary empire

The regular run between India and Portugal, known as the *Carreira da Índia*, was organised by the Crown through its *Casa da Índia* in Lisbon and its various factories in the Indies. In the sixteenth century four to eight ships of 400–2,000 tons travelled east once a year, following a timetable dictated by the Indian Ocean's monsoon winds. The voyage was extraordinarily arduous and often highly dramatic. It could take between four and a half and nine months in one direction, with losses of between 10 and 20 per cent of ships and probably between 40 and 50 per cent of human lives – that is, the voyagers were well aware that only every second man would reach his destination safely. The cargo was assembled by the factories in the Indies. For pepper, a 1558 calculation quoted a probable profit of 152 per cent, which after subtracting the infrastructural costs still came to 88 per cent. Much of the factories' purchasing was financed by Crown income from Asia, especially customs duties, and bills of exchange issued on the earnings from that trade; the fleets from Portugal initially also brought gold coin and copper, supplied in large part by the Fugger family via Antwerp, and from the mid sixteenth century onwards especially silver originating in Spanish America.

On the first voyages to the Indies, anyone could participate if they obtained a royal licence and paid a 5 per cent duty imposed on their goods. As well as the Italians, the Welsers and Fuggers of Augsburg and the Vöhlins of Memmingen took part on this basis: despite its economic muscle, the Portuguese Crown still needed additional capital from abroad. However, in 1506 a Crown monopoly was introduced to prevent the price of pepper crashing due to oversupply. The monopoly remained in force until 1570. It seems that the East India trade had boosted the Crown's creditworthiness to such an extent that it was now in a position to finance itself through loans. The Crown's monopoly only applied to spices and the means of payment necessary to purchase them; private entrepreneurs were still permitted to undertake trade in other commodities. This arrangement, along with the duty-free cargoes to which the participants in trade were entitled, opened the door to large-scale smuggling. The Crown monopoly was also being evaded via the Persian Gulf and the Red Sea, putting it at constant risk of rising supply and falling prices. Private participation in the spice trade under Crown control was therefore permitted again in 1570. Especially under Philip II of Spain, who from 1580 was simultaneously King of Portugal, the result was the practice of supply and distribution contracts with German-Italian consortia, designed to absorb the Crown's risks. The 'Asian contract' obliged financiers to buy the spices in the Indies and sell them to the Crown once back in Portugal. Since prices at both ends were fixed, profit could not be made through increasing quantity, but only through reducing the costs of the voyage (although, of course, the pepper could always be moistened,

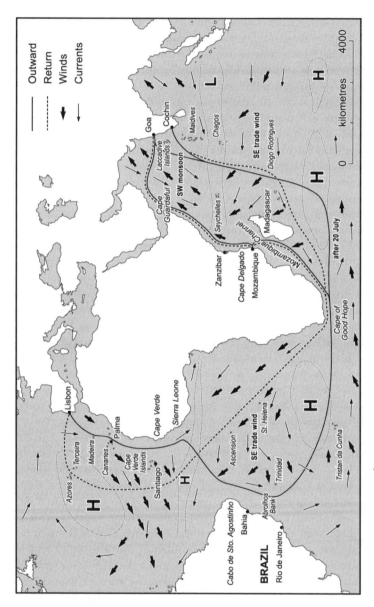

Map 3 The *Carreira da Índia*, 1589–1622

increasing its weight). In the 'European contract' the entrepreneurs agreed to purchase a certain volume at a fixed price and market it. Originally, the Crown had marketed the spices itself in Antwerp, the nerve centre of European commerce, and later in Lisbon. When the contracts expired in 1597, however, no new takers could be found for them; the political upheavals in both Asia and Europe meant that the risks involved had risen to an unacceptable degree. Of necessity, a kind of Crown monopoly was re-established, this time in a form that could only be sustained with the help, by no means voluntary, of Lisbon and other Portuguese cities. Portugal's Indian trading empire lost more and more of its stature, and even made a loss in the seventeenth century due to the costs of its defence. In the end the role of the East Indies for Portugal was completely eclipsed by Brazil.

The adult male population of Portuguese origin in Asia probably never numbered more than 14,000. Portuguese expansion cannot be explained by population pressure any more than can the *reconquista* or the Spanish *conquista* in America – on the contrary, the population of the Iberian empires was too small rather than too large. It was therefore rare for Portuguese women or entire families to come to India, so that even in Albuquerque's time relationships with high-caste, baptised Asian women were encouraged. This is how the mixed Eurasian population and culture arose, with pidgin Portuguese as the lingua franca of the East. The resulting milieu survived far longer than the Portuguese trading empire itself, and remnants exist even today. Its ethnic tolerance was greater than its religious tolerance, but was by no means as unlimited as the twentieth-century ideologues of 'Lusitanianism' would have us believe. Rather, the choice of indigenous wives and the recruitment of indigenous priests and members of religious orders was guided by a concern, if anything increasing in intensity, for a pale skin colour, 'because all these dark races are very stupid and vicious [...] and [...] the Portuguese treat them with the greatest contempt', in the view even of Alessandro Valignano, a Jesuit leader of Italian origins who was unusually open-minded in matters of intercultural contact. The Japanese, Chinese, Koreans and Vietnamese, in contrast, were accepted – for a long time they were considered 'white'.

Dutch mercantile capitalism

The Iberian powers had spearheaded European expansion in the sixteenth century, and their displacement by the Dutch in the seventeenth and the English in the eighteenth century may have surprised contemporaries mesmerised by the resplendence of the Spanish and Portuguese monarchy.

But the historian, that retrospective prophet, sees only a form of normalisation in this shift in the leadership of the mercantile-capitalist world towards the north-west of Europe, the region that was economically most highly developed and that lay at the heart of the European 'world system' of trade. Even in the Middle Ages, the Netherlands stood alongside northern Italy as one of Europe's two economic focal points and most strongly urbanised environments. At that time, the region's centre of gravity was in the south, in today's Belgium. Holland, between the Zuiderzee (then still open to the sea) and the North Sea, and its neighbour Zealand, the island world of the Rhine estuaries, were of little account compared to the medieval metropolis of Bruges and to Antwerp, which in the sixteenth century was the paramount commodity and money marketplace of Europe, where even the Portuguese initially chose to sell their spices. The Netherlands had long been connected with the Iberian Peninsula through commercial and political ties, and the northern territories formed the real heart of Charles V's Holy Roman Empire. Even the Eighty Years' War with Spain in 1568–1648 (interrupted by a temporary truce in 1609–21) did not immediately cause an economic rift, since Spain needed the grain and shipbuilding materials that the Netherlands could bring it from the Baltic, while the Netherlands needed silver from Spanish America. Business continued to thrive, if not strictly legally, but the main beneficiaries of the system were now Holland and Zealand, the south having been severely battered by its involvement in the war. Antwerp, especially, was lastingly blighted by the Spanish conquest in 1585 and the sealing of its port by its northern competitors. The city passed on its leadership to the blossoming Amsterdam, in part quite literally, through the northwards migration of its most economically powerful residents. Amsterdam's population grew from 30,000 to 105,000 between 1585 and 1622, and continued to rise. In the seventeenth century it was the hub of European shipping, Europe's largest commodity market and its controlling capital market. With the construction of the *fluyt*, a new ship specifically designed for the low-cost transportation of bulk goods, the Dutch secured the leading role in maritime traffic once and for all. Their business in credit at home and abroad flourished, and the Bank of Amsterdam, founded in 1609, played a role similar to that of Swiss banks today. It mediated international payment transactions and offered Europe's elite the opportunity to invest capital that needed to be discreetly tucked away.

It was natural that the Netherlands should enter the spice trade, just as it entered the American trade. At first its participation was indirect, leaving the risks and infrastructural costs to the Portuguese, but the succession of the Netherlands' arch-enemy Philip II of Spain to the throne of Portugal in 1580 placed this tidy arrangement in jeopardy – less through the threat of an embargo, as has been concluded in the past, than through Philip's new supply and distribution contracts with the Netherlands' German and Italian competitors. It now seemed far more worthwhile to establish direct contact with producers in the East. Confrontations with the Portuguese, likely to drive up costs, were to be avoided, initially by means of attempts in 1594–97 to find a northern passage to East India. Little came of these experiments apart from the discovery of Spitsbergen and Novaya Zemlya and an expansion of Dutch whaling. But the Catholic Dutchman Linschoten, who had become very familiar with the Portuguese Indies during the six years he spent there, but who evidently placed his patriotism above his religious loyalty, passed on the valuable information that Java, which lay outside the sphere of Portuguese power and could be reached via the Sunda Strait, bypassing Malacca, offered pepper and other spices in great quantities and at low prices. In response to this information, in 1594 Amsterdam merchants founded a company whose ships enjoyed only limited success but did manage to bring home a cargo of spices in 1597. Now fiercely competing enterprises began to mushroom; by 1601, eight different companies had sent fourteen fleets to Java with a total of sixty-five ships. One group even chose the passage via Cape Horn and ended up in Japan.

This degree of competition threatened to push up the price of buying in Asia, and might also offer the Iberian enemy a toehold for counterattack. Both political and economic reason prevailed in 1602, with the founding of a corporation that was to hold a monopoly for all the Netherlands, the *Vereenigde Oost-Indische Compagnie*, or Dutch East India Company (VOC). This chartered company was entrusted by the States-General – the ruling assembly of the Netherlands – with a monopoly on Dutch trade from the Cape of Good Hope eastwards to the Strait of Magellan, with additional political authorisations to wage war, close contracts, take possession of land and build fortifications. The VOC was divided into six chambers, based in Amsterdam, Middelburg, Delft, Rotterdam, Hoorn and Enkhuizen. By far the strongest of these was Amsterdam, holding 3.675 million guilders of the total capital of 6.425 million guilders. Of the numerous shareholders, only the *hooft-participanten*, or non-managing partners, investing more than 6,000 (in smaller chambers 3,000) guilders had some, albeit limited, control over the governors. The sixty *bewindhebbers*, or managing partners, could fill the vacancies in their ranks themselves, in cooperation with the relevant municipal authorities, and chose the seventeen delegates who made up the highest governing body, the *Heren Zeventien*. Eight of the seventeen 'lords' came from Amsterdam, four from Middelburg and one each from the remaining chambers; the seventeenth seat rotated in order to avoid an overall Amsterdam majority, although the influence of Amsterdam was in fact further strengthened by its investments in other chambers. The oligarchic nature of the leadership and its close integration with the Republic's most important political circles promoted a management style oriented primarily on the personal interests of the directors, who were the only ones to have a full overview of all the VOC's dealings. The shareholders were kept happy by the punctual and regular payment of dividends, at the expense of the formation of reserves. When bottlenecks arose, for example when large investments were required in Asia, instead of raising share capital the necessary funds were found from loans, the interest on which was paid using the stores of goods that had been kept in reserve to bolster prices. Because of their knowledge of the business, the directors themselves or their friends were able to act as creditors, thus further enriching themselves on the backs of the ordinary shareholders. During longer-term commercial downturns, however, these practices were bound to have dangerous consequences.

The path from the regionally based 'pre-companies' to the VOC meant a transition in business forms from the 'regulated company', as it was known in the English terminology that dominated at the time, via the joint-stock company, to a kind of stock corporation or public limited company in the modern sense. Regulated companies were partnerships with unlimited liability, bringing together merchants who operated independently and on their own account but following shared guidelines that were usually laid down by the authorities. In contrast, the joint-stock company was based on shareholders pooling their capital. This capital was, though, earmarked for a single venture, such as one voyage to the East Indies, or for a particular stretch of time, after which the accounts were settled and the company was dissolved or re-founded. The transition to the modern form occurred when capital was dedicated permanently and with liability limited to the amount paid in; when in theory anyone at all could participate directly; and when the shares began to be traded on the stock exchange – because since shares were constant, a change in ownership could only be achieved by trading them. The VOC had originally been obliged to buy out any shareholder whenever he might request, and to settle its accounts with all the shareholders after ten years, but these obligations proved obsolete and were abolished by the States-General as early as 1612. The VOC still differed from a modern public limited company, but less in the fact that it exercised a monopoly than in its semi-public character: it held a degree of political authority, even if this was exercised first and foremost in the interests of the business. Nevertheless, the financially more advanced business form generated by mercantile capitalism was capable of mobilising far more capital for a policy of colonialism than had the previous monarchical capitalism. Efficiency was also improved by a tighter and more rational setting of objectives. The Portuguese and

Spanish might be good businessmen, but they entwined the will to profit with the pursuit of quite different goals, based on aristocratic ideals of personal glory and service to the king through conquest, as well as the zealous urge to disseminate the faith. The Dutch merchants set little store by their reformed religion and nothing at all by the other noble impulses. Missionary activity must not break the bank, and was only tolerated when it posed no threat to business, as was the case with the anti-Christian Muslims and the Japanese. Discoveries that seemed unlikely to offer successful exploitation, like New Holland (that is, Australia) and New Zealand, may have received their names from the major provinces of the Netherlands, but they were otherwise ignored by their namesakes. If anything, the discoverers of these lands were lucky not to be reprimanded for having wasted valuable resources. And even on the existing field of VOC operations, expensive long-term projects like those proposed by the governors general Coen and van Diemen were rejected on the grounds of cost.

At the heart of the efforts in Asia stood the creation of a Dutch monopoly over the trade in spices. In 1605 the Dutch succeeded in establishing a fortress on the Moluccan island of Amboina (now Ambon) and signing a monopoly contract for spices with these Moluccans. The same applied for the Banda Islanders, although they turned out to be unreliable partners who did not hesitate to kill the occasional importunate Dutchman. In 1607, Ternate went over to Dutch protection and declared itself ready to sign a monopoly agreement as well. In 1609/10, the Dutch set up a factor's office in Hirado, Japan. Well aware of the importance of Indian textiles for the 'country trade', the Dutch on the subcontinent, too, immediately began to set up factories, although until 1605 this was only possible on the eastern coast. In 1609 the Seventeen decided to establish a long-term presence in Asia under a governor general, who was to build up a permanent fulcrum for the Netherlands' trade. The preferred location for the project was Java, as the Javanese port of Bantam housed the VOC's head office, though it was still under indigenous sovereignty; in addition, the English competition had also set up camp in the city. Jan Pieterszoon Coen, the governor general from 1619 to 1623 and again from 1627 to 1629, became a kind of Dutch Albuquerque. In 1614 he had written a memorandum calling for massive Dutch settlement combined with the complete monopolisation of the country trade, which was to be opened for Dutch traders as the basis of a system that would continue to pay for itself. It was on this solid foundation that the rigorous implementation of the spice monopoly and, after the expiry of the truce with Spain and Portugal in 1621, the capture of Portuguese trading posts, would build. But Coen was only permitted to realise the monopoly plan. He extended the 1611 factory in Jakarta into a fortress on his own initiative, successfully defending it against

attacks by the English and Javanese. In 1619 he made this coastal fortifica-
tion into the new capital of the VOC, named 'Batavia' in line with the
mythology of Dutch national origins current at the time. He managed to
thwart the 1619 treaty with the English that had been negotiated in Europe:
in 1623 the Dutch governor on Amboina had English 'conspirators' executed,
and that same year the English gave up the struggle, leaving Hirado and the
Japan trade to the Dutch and, in 1628, withdrawing to Bantam. In 1621 Coen
'pacified' the unreliable Banda Islands with the help of Japanese mercenaries. The inhabitants were tortured, slaughtered, sold as slaves and forced into
exile, and the nutmeg trees – their number carefully limited – were tended by
slaves under Dutch supervision. On the clove island of Amboina, in contrast,
it proved possible over the course of the seventeenth century to convert the
inhabitants to Calvinism, making them particularly reliable partners of the
Dutch and prompting them to flee to the Netherlands after decolonisation, as
'South Moluccans'. However, the production of cloves, unlike that of nutmeg,
was widely dispersed and could not be immediately subjected to monopoly,
despite Dutch expeditions dedicated to chopping down the competitors'
clove trees. The clove monopoly was only secured much later in the century,
thanks to two developments: in 1662 the Spanish were forced to abandon
Tidore, which they had taken in 1606, and in 1660–69 the Dutch succeeded
in gaining control over the Muslim clove market in Makassar, Sulawesi,
which had previously been openly accessible to the competition.

Coen's 1622 attack on Macao was repulsed; instead, the Dutch occupied
Formosa (Taiwan) from 1624 to 1661, using it as a base for their smuggling
operations with China until the island was captured by fugitive supporters of
the collapsing Ming dynasty. In its ventures into the China trade, the VOC
always had to share the field with other Europeans, but the Japan trade was a
different matter. After the Portuguese had been driven out by the Japanese
once and for all in 1639/40, the VOC managed to achieve a monopoly over
business with Japan – an extremely lucrative affair despite the many restrictions that were imposed. The Dutch factory on Dejima was set up in 1641.

In the west, the Dutch succeeded in building up a network of trade in
northern India, working from the north-western port of Surat, where a factory
had been established in 1616. The network included connections with coffee
production in Yemen and a factory in the new Persian port of Bandar Abbas.
Set up in 1623, this outpost took over the role of Portuguese-controlled
Ormuz, which was captured in 1622 by Persian and English forces. The
Dutch made respectable profits from, especially, the expanding trade in
Persian silk.

The smaller, more agile and better armed ships of the VOC, with their
highly disciplined crews, usually demonstrated their superiority in skirmishes

with the Portuguese. But it was only Coen's successors as governors general, particularly Antonio van Diemen from 1636 to 1645, who managed to penetrate the core of the system of Portuguese trading bases on the Indian subcontinent. In pursuit of an extension of the Dutch monopoly to cover cinnamon and pepper, an offensive against Ceylon was launched in 1636 and a fleet sent out every year to blockade Goa, until in 1643 the truce with Portugal – which had separated from Spain again in 1640 – at last began to show results in Asia. The truce also enabled the Dutch to establish their first factory on the pepper-producing Malabar coast. Malacca had already fallen in 1641, so that Portugal's presence in the eastern oceans was now limited to Macao. The Dutch no longer needed to use the Sunda Strait to bypass the Malaccan route to East Asia, as had previously been the case. After the truce with Portugal expired, the years 1654–63 saw the entire coast of Ceylon fall to the Dutch, along with all the Portuguese trading posts on the Malabar coast (this despite the fact that peace had already been made in Europe in 1662). In terms of marine supremacy, the Netherlands had ousted Portugal; only Goa and a few small bases remained as isolated pockets of Portuguese control.

Despite their very different driving forces, in structural terms the Dutch and Portuguese trading empires were strikingly similar. Where territorial possessions existed – around Batavia, on the Spice Islands, on Sulawesi and Ceylon – these were fully aligned with the requirements of the spice monopoly or with the security and supply of the head office. The same applied for the suzerainty over indigenous rulers that was established over time on Java, the Moluccas and Sulawesi. Permanent Dutch settlers in Asia remained rare, and were limited to the disregarded lower classes. True to their profit motivation, the shareholders and servants of the VOC aimed to get rich and then return home. Half of the 20,000 people in VOC pay in the eighteenth century were soldiers. And where relationships did arise between the Dutch and Asian and Eurasian women, the existing Luso-Asian culture prevailed: even children from entirely Dutch families are said to have sometimes spoken better Portuguese than Dutch.

Three fleets sailed from the Netherlands to Batavia every year and two back, as all business (with the occasional exception of coffee) had to be conducted via that hub. The fleets took to stopping off at the Cape of Good Hope, where from 1652 a station offered the mariners rest and food, a 'Tavern of the Seas' that would gradually grow into a settler colony. Between 1602 and 1750, the average number of outward-bound ships rose from ten to twenty-nine a year, with losses of 4.5 per cent. The low rate of losses compared to the Portuguese expeditions may be explained by the more businesslike administration of the Dutch and by technological advances. The VOC's chambers built ships that were standardised down to the last detail, as is shown by Pieter van Dam's internally circulated *Beschryvinge van de Oostindische Compagnie* (Description of the East India Company) of 1693–1703, around the time that profits appear to have been at their height. That period was followed by a decline which the VOC, thanks to its secretive structures, was able to conceal for a considerable time, until the 'patriots' intent on revolution liquidated this stronghold of conservatism in 1799 and nationalised its assets. However, the business policy of the Seventeen had already begun to show worrying cracks far earlier, when demand in Europe rocketed for Asian commodities not covered by the VOC monopolies. At the same time, the VOC could no longer finance its purchasing out of the profits of its Asian trading empire, because its monopoly on the country trade – which, unlike its Portuguese equivalent, aimed to be absolutely seamless – could no longer be sustained. Even the company's highest officers were working to the detriment of their employer by conducting their private business in questionable arrangements with the English, Asians or others. In fact, it has been suggested that up to three quarters of the Dutch country trade was accounted for by smuggling by this point. Finally, it is conspicuous that almost all the East Indies companies which sprang up in the course of the seventeenth century were established with the aid of Dutch expertise and Dutch capital. Often, they were nothing other than elements in a Dutch 'underground economy' made up of people excluded from the VOC's monopoly operations. The monopolist VOC had dug its own grave, destroyed by four weaknesses: its exclusivity, the management structure that this encouraged, its commitment to a fading pattern of demand for spices, and the unbending rigidity of its country-trade policy.

English mercantile capitalism, its European competitors and the Asian commodity cycles

The well-established English cloth trade of the Middle Ages, focused on Antwerp, collapsed in the sixteenth century, forcing the English merchants to diversify. Under Philip II they were more rigorously excluded from the Iberian markets than were the Dutch, who were necessary to Spain. However, the English made good use of the 'Levant Company' that was established in 1581 for the specific purpose of procuring spices, silk and other Asian luxury goods via Aleppo, along the Gulf route mentioned above. It was only with the start of Dutch voyages to the Indies that the Aleppo trade came under threat. This prompted London merchants to found an 'East India Company' with a royal charter, in practice a subsidiary of the Levant Company. Its starting capital was much smaller than that of the VOC, and until 1657 it remained a joint-stock company with a limited lifespan; in organisational terms, it thus lagged behind its more highly developed Dutch rival for many decades. However, by 1615 – partly with the help of its Dutch employees – the new Company had already managed to establish various factories on India's western and eastern coasts and in the Indian interior; in Malaya, Sumatra and Java; in Makassar on Sulawesi; and in Hirado, Japan. That year the trading posts were aggregated to form 'presidencies' based in Surat (Gujarat) and Bantam (Java). Especially notable is the establishment of the factory in Surat, which finally obtained its official permit from the Mughal emperor in 1613 after battles with the Portuguese. From 1616 the English traded with Persia, and in 1622 helped the Persians to capture the Portuguese-controlled town of Ormuz. In the East, though, the English made little headway against the Dutch. They were soon driven out of the Spice Islands, and in 1669 also from their substitute base in Makassar. They had already abandoned Japan in 1623, and in 1682 were even pushed out of Bantam, creating a rather modest substitute in the form of a pepper factory in Bencoolen, southern Sumatra, from 1685. Thus, although the English had originally targeted the Indian subcontinent only as a way of securing Indian goods for the country trade, the dominance of the Netherlands further east meant that the subcontinent gradually became the Company's main focus. It was not a voluntary move, but one that would have enormous consequences. On the eastern coast of India the English succeeded for the first time in capturing land for a fortified trading post: Fort St George, later Madras, today Chennai, was founded in 1641, and in 1651 the governor of Bengal, through the mediation of an English doctor, permitted the English to establish a factory in Hugli. Bombay, acquired as dowry in 1661 when Charles II married a Portuguese princess, was leased to the Company in 1668, but for the time being remained in the shade of Surat despite its reputation as the best harbour on the western coast.

The Company's relative lack of stature can be attributed in part to the constant challenges to its role in the English political context. Far from embodying a politically underwritten coordination of business and government, as in the Dutch case, the English Company was buffeted by conflicts that were fought out in Parliament between the Company, with its London backers, and other ports and interests. The Crown grasped every opportunity to extort loans and gifts from the interested parties, if necessary by issuing licences to their competitors. This was the context for the 'mercantilist' accusation that trade with the Indies was economically damaging because it promoted a deplorable outflow of bullion – European goods, and specifically English woollen cloth, being quite impossible to sell in Asia. This argument on the negative trade balance with the East was countered by the point that the imported goods did not remain in England, but were often re-exported at a profit, thus contributing to a positive balance of payments. The Glorious Revolution placed further severe pressure on the Company, traditionally aligned with the Stuarts, and a rival East India Company was created for the benefit of its competitors, which were offering cheaper credit in the wars against Louis XIV. However, the existing company wisely made substantial investments in its new rival, and was able to assert itself thanks not least to its ownership of the network of Indian trading posts. The two companies were amalgamated in 1709, forming the 'United Company of Merchants of England Trading to the East Indies'. Its total capital, now reaching £3.2 million, was put at the government's disposal in the form of loans at 5 per cent interest, in return for the granting of monopoly privileges. The English Company had finally caught up with – or even overtaken – its Dutch counterpart, although this did not mean an end to its political tribulations. The remarkable success of the Indies trade from the second half of the seventeenth century, after this hesitant start, rested less on spices than on the importation of Indian cotton goods, demand for which was rising fast. Because cotton imports were regarded as a form of competition for English textile manufacturing, a range of statutory restrictions were imposed in the period from 1700. These constraints did not apply to re-exportation or raw materials, and thus provided an effective stimulus to the processing of cotton within England. In this way, they contributed to the leading role that the cotton industry would later play in English industrialisation.

The management of the East India Company in London consisted of the Court of Directors, elected annually by the General Court of the shareholders, with a Governor and Deputy Governor. The crucial agents in everyday operations – especially making the annual orders for goods from the East, putting together the cargoes for export or procuring other means of payment, warehousing in order to steer prices, and sales – were the committees that reported to the twenty-four Directors and were effectively interlinked by the membership of the Governor or Deputy Governor in each one. Holders of at least £500 in stock were entitled to vote, and those holding £2,000 could stand for election as a Director. The Directors and the City of London milieu which associated with them made sizeable profits from re-selling imports and from the charter business in freight space. From the mid seventeenth century, the Company, unlike the Dutch VOC (and, incidentally, also its French equivalent), no longer built its own ships but rented shipping capacity. The ships' owners thus had to bear the risks of the voyages, though these were kept low through a complex system of spreading risk and distinguishing between different types of commodity. In the first half of the eighteenth century, the average number of traders bound for the Indies every year rose from eleven to twenty. The need to avoid the Cape of Good Hope, which was occupied by the

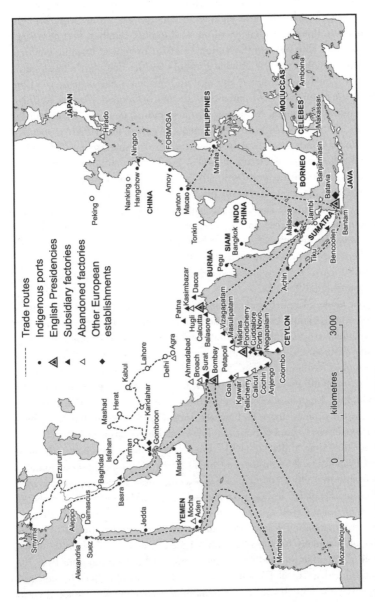

Map 4 East India Company bases up to 1760

Dutch competition, had led to the establishment of a stopover on the South Atlantic island of St Helena in 1659. In India, the number of stopping points had risen to 170 by the mid eighteenth century, when they were brought together into three Presidencies of equal standing: Bombay, Fort St George (Madras) and Fort William (Calcutta). In 1687, in view of looming conflicts with representatives of the Mughal Empire over the Company's legal status and levies, the headquarters of the western Presidency had been moved from Surat to the fortified city of Bombay, and the newly founded, likewise fortified, Fort William had taken the place of other trading posts as the centre for Bengal. The presidents were simultaneously governors of their respective residences, which were largely independent of Indian sovereignty. They headed a hierarchy of merchant ranks, but had no authority over Crown troops or ships. In the worldwide struggle against the French, the various interests were now no longer being pursued exclusively by trading companies with Crown privileges. The Company's officers in the Indies would have been perfectly willing to preserve the peace in the 1741–48 War of the Austrian Succession for the sake of an untroubled pursuit of their Company's profits and their own country-trade activities (the English country trade, unlike in the Dutch case, not being reserved for the company alone). The military, however, took a different view.

The peak of English trade in the East Indies, in the first half of the eighteenth century, should probably be seen in the context of a general economic upturn, since it was at this time that the establishment of similar companies became fashionable in many other countries and that the French company also enjoyed its highest profits. The first French voyages to the Indies, in the early seventeenth century, foundered on Dutch resistance even more rapidly than had the English ones. New initiatives under Richelieu culminated in a Madagascar project that was, however, soon abandoned and the naval base was moved to the island of Bourbon (known as Réunion from 1843). The next attempt, this time under Louis XIV, was – like Richelieu's – primarily motivated by politics. The minister of finance, Jean-Baptiste Colbert, found it intolerable that other countries were drawing profit from supplying France with 'colonial goods'. It was also a matter of national honour to drive back the dominance of the Netherlands and boost France's power on the high seas. Here, trading policy was a continuation of war by other means. But the monopoly company for the East Indies trade, formed in 1664 on the usual model of organisation and privileges, attracted little enthusiasm from the decentralised world of French commerce. It was established, funded and directed by the French Crown; the remaining investment was gathered virtually under coercion through loans from courtiers, the court bankers and the French trading ports. The company was staffed by Dutch experts. Although it proved possible to expand the trading posts of Pondicherry south of Madras and Chandernagore in Bengal, acquired in 1672 and 1674 respectively, into fortified bases, chronically inadequate resourcing meant that business was generally less than satisfactory. The French company also suffered from involvement in John Law's financial policy experiments, but in the eighteenth century its business finally began to pick up, and in 1736 its stock was quoted above face value for the first time. By 1755, however, this success was already beginning to ebb because of the war, and the company never fully recovered.

More or less all the East India companies established in the seventeenth and eighteenth centuries faced similar experiences or were even worse off than the French, although Denmark, Sweden, Brandenburg-Prussia and Austria were undaunted, repeatedly launching new ventures despite the failure of their companies. Apart from these countries, there was also short-term involvement by Portugal, Spain, Scotland, Genoa and even Poland. But in spite of participation by the almost ubiquitous Dutch monopoly-breakers, the newly founded companies suffered from a dearth of capital, making it very difficult for them to assert themselves in Asia against the Dutch and later the English. In most cases, too, they were hampered by military and political complications in their home countries. Denmark did manage to set up a colony in Tranquebar south of Madras, sold to the British only in 1845, but only the last of the three Danish companies flourished, thanks not least to its having entered a kind of symbiosis with British merchants, who carried out their private business under the Danish flag to the detriment of the East India Company. Another notable exception was the Austrian – or, in practice, Flemish – Ostend Company founded in 1719, which made a strong start but was sacrificed in 1727 in return for English and Dutch recognition of Maria Theresa's right to succession. For the Ostend Company, as for the Danes and various others, the extension of trade to China played an important role.

A wide range of commodities was exported from Asia; the cargo lists mention silk, porcelain, indigo, saltpetre and various metals. However, the most important goods were initially spices, then textiles, and later coffee and tea. The shift in preferences was naturally accompanied by a geographical shift based on the regions of production. The Dutch had originally been most interested in supplanting Portugal as Europe's key supplier of spices, but the fundamental lack of elasticity in demand for spices meant that by the eighteenth century pepper exports had settled at four to eight million pounds a year for the Dutch, two to four million pounds for the English. In the last third of the seventeenth century, the era of Indian cotton began. Cotton goods had originally been bought by the Dutch merely as a way of paying for spices, but they were then discovered by European fashion, which had long been moving towards lighter fabrics; cheap clothing was also required for the growing population of African slaves in America. The English now found themselves at an advantage, having focused their efforts on the Indian subcontinent – if only as a way of evading the Dutch hegemony over the areas further east. In 1684–89 the Dutch imported 1.1 million pieces of cotton fabric to Europe, the English 4.3 million. The rising demand for finer quality textiles resulted in a shift of production to Bengal. Because the finished products had to suit European tastes, the influence of the European clients made itself felt from the earliest stages of production.

However, by this time the third cycle, that of coffee and tea, had long since commenced. When Europeans first encountered the pleasures of coffee, around 1600, it was already a long-established drink in the Islamic world. In 1652 the first coffeehouse opened in London, and in 1661/62 coffee was marketed in Amsterdam as well. The year 1700 opened the era of elegant coffeehouses in Paris and other European cities. Rising prices in the coffee-producing area of Yemen led to experiments in coffee cultivation by the East India companies. In the end it was the Dutch who won the day with their Javanese-grown coffee, so that they only had to continue buying in the Yemeni port of Mocha as a way of keeping the world market price for coffee profitably high. In England, however, tea had by then taken the place of coffee and gin as the people's choice, and was becoming a crucial business sector. Because of the high import taxes imposed by the British, tea was also an important commodity for the non-British companies supplying the Europe-wide system of tea smuggling. At this time tea came only from China, which had been open to European commerce since 1685. Canton became a tea port, where from 1760 onwards a commercial organisation bearing the imperial privilege traded with the factories of the various European companies. British tea exports from Canton reached their peak only in the nineteenth century, when they were financed primarily by the profits from the Empire's territories on the Indian subcontinent, and later increasingly by the importation of Indian opium to China.

But even in the late eighteenth century, the Cantonese trade in European imports and bills of exchange was beginning to play a larger role than before on the Asian market, after the price of silver within China fell to match the European price. Up to this point, European exports to Asia had, just as in the Portuguese era, consisted mainly of silver, ultimately sourced from Spanish America (although the companies later began to mint their own coins out of the *reales de a ocho*, or pieces of eight). This outflow of bullion into Asia, so objectionable to the English mercantilists and others, did not arise simply from a failure to sell European goods – after all, why should Asians not be persuaded to buy European woollen cloth just as the Europeans had been to buy Asian cotton? The decisive point was the relative cost of quite another commodity, silver, which was highly sought after in China and, measured against its price in gold, was considerably more expensive in Asia than in Europe or the silver-producing countries of Mexico and Peru. For as long as this price differential continued to exist, silver therefore flowed into Asia. It fed into the Asian economic cycles and was by no means mainly stockpiled, as was once assumed. The significance of this outflow of silver should not be exaggerated in some now obsolete mercantilist style, and neither should the stimulus of European demand, apart from the case of the Indian regions producing textiles and the Chinese ones producing tea. In fact even in Bengal, European demand kept only 11 per cent of weavers busy in the eighteenth century. European colonialist exploitation in Asia thus initially remained within – quite literally – narrow boundaries, even if the terrorised inhabitants of the Spice Islands, the Indian weavers and the Javanese coffee farmers certainly had plenty of cause to complain.

European mission, mutual perceptions of Europeans and Asians, new discoveries

Alongside the trade in commodities, and often closely tied to it, Christian missionary work was the most notable European activity in Asia, not least because the missionaries took by far the most intense interest in the Asian cultures – if only as a way of 'knowing their enemy'. Considering the manner in which Islam and possibly also, in earlier centuries, Hindu culture spread so rapidly in Indonesia, it is fair to speak of a world-historical pattern of cultural expansion whereby merchants and missionaries join in introducing innovation. Clearly, the missionary efforts and achievements of Catholics and Protestants differed enormously, but this should be explained by variations in that pattern rather than by the much-invoked distinctions of theology. It is important to remember that at this time there were no international associations to support missionary work, of the kind that would arise in the late eighteenth and the nineteenth century, and the normal ecclesiastical machinery of all denominations was ill suited to sustaining a mission. Only the old Church with its religious orders – especially the highly qualified Jesuits – had access to specialised personnel and the necessary organisational structures, as long as the requisite funding could be secured. This was provided in part by the Catholic monarchs of Portugal, Spain and France, for whom the protection (and hence control) of the Church was an integrative component of their rule. The Lutheran King of Denmark pursued a similar path when he established a mission in Tranquebar, which, tellingly, was run by the Halle

Pietists, an organisation comparable to the Catholic orders in function. For the Dutch and English merchants, in contrast, the Christian mission was a cost factor that not only yielded no financial returns but in some cases even threatened to disrupt commercial relationships. Even so, in the early days, when the denominational conflict was still fresh and politically relevant, the Dutch did pursue missionary work, with little success in southern India and Ceylon but quite considerable gains on Amboina and Taiwan.

The mission of the Portuguese Jesuits, whose most important representatives – Alessandro Valignano, Matteo Ricci, Roberto de Nobili and Francis Xavier – came from Italy or Spain, was a very different matter. Its reach rapidly extended beyond the Portuguese sphere of power into south-eastern India, Japan, China and Vietnam, and it began to engage with foreign cultures to an unprecedented extent. The Jesuits made a habit of adapting their clothing and etiquette, manners and customs to those of their hosts. Among the Hindus this meant taking on the complicated rules of the caste system, so contradictory to Christian slogans of brotherhood. The indigenous languages and religious literature were studied in detail. Jesuits were the first European Indologists, Sinologists and Japanologists, even if their work soon fell into oblivion, and it was they who invented an alphabetical script for Vietnamese, still used today, to replace the Chinese characters. In China, Ricci went beyond these attempts at a religious dialogue in the medium of the Asian cultures: he tried to bolt the doctrinal system of Christianity onto the allegedly natural monotheism and high-minded morality of Confucius and the other classics, as the West had once done with Aristotelian thinking. Because this involved considerable concessions to Chinese 'ancestor rites' which were considered idolatrous, Ricci's programme faced fierce opposition from both inside and outside the Church. What Joseph Needham called the 'noble adventure' became mired in an emerging 'Chinese rites controversy', and the narrow-minded Europeanism of the subsequent imperialist era would anyway take no further interest in the issue. Within Asia, indigenous elites were only open to persuasion in cases where their own culture was under attack from within. It was no coincidence that the Jesuits were successful in Japan in the sixteenth century and China in the seventeenth, periods when these countries were in the throes of deep crisis. Their success evaporated later when political and cultural unity was restored.

In the Chinese rites controversy, French Jesuits played an important role. The appearance of French missionaries in Asia corresponded with the political expansion of France during the seventeenth century, but it also reflected the papacy's desire to curb the dominance of the Portuguese church. As it turned out, Rome's patronage of the French mission for this purpose would prove hardly less vexatious, right into the twentieth century.

Reports from French missionaries to Siam and Indochina in the seventeenth century are sometimes barely distinguishable from the reports sent by agents of Colbert's East India company, but in the course of the rites controversy, the French Jesuits in China produced a vast amount of literature to communicate to Europe their idealised image of China. This paved the way for a western craze for China that during the Enlightenment would tip over into a critique of the Church: what the Jesuits interpreted as natural foundations for Christianity, Enlightenment critics interpreted as a reason to find Christianity dispensable. Europe's interest in the foreign was always pursued in line with its own preoccupations, but whereas the missionaries were concerned with the alterity of the foreign, at least to the extent that was necessary for its intellectual subjection, the educated admired its similarity with Europe as a mirror held up to themselves. As early as 1701, Gottfried Wilhelm Leibniz had thought he recognised in the trigrams and hexagrams of the Chinese Book of Changes nothing other than his binary arithmetic of 1679, and saw the neo-Confucian Zhu Xi, considered a materialist, as an early proponent of his own concept of the relationship of spirit and matter. The figure that the later eighteenth century portrayed as a Chinese sage was little other than a fashionably disguised Enlightenment philosopher.

Europe was equipped with a hermeneutical model that enabled it to perceive the foreign in a factually accurate way while nevertheless appropriating it for European purposes. The Europeans were among the best philologists in the world, and were also practised in mastering foreign symbolism through understanding. Asia remained marginal for Europe, but sending European emissaries was part of the missionary manifesto of European culture, so that the information they brought back was studied by at least a certain segment of the European elites and thus bore long-term consequences.

Things were different in South and East Asia, where few documents before 1800 deal with Europe and its Christian culture, despite the fact that the cultural contact occurred primarily on Asian, not European, soil (at that time there was not yet any significant Asian presence in Europe). The self-assured Asian civilisations considered an encounter with Europe superfluous. For them, the European presence in Asia, and the cultural contact that seems so momentous from our perspective, remained an intellectually marginal affair, seldom arousing enough interest to merit any written record.

Here, a revealing difference emerges between East Asian and Indian perceptions of the Europeans and Christianity. In Japan and China, Christianity caused offence despite all its attempts at adaptation. Starting with the Confucians, the East Asians considered its strict sexual morality with obligatory monogamy liable to undermine the natural relationship of the sexes, the family with its respect for the ancestors, and thus the system of piety that underpinned society and the state. This critique must be seen in the context of a monistic world view that differed fundamentally from the western one and the chief proponents of which were the Buddhists – who, in turn, were in competition with the Christians in both Japan and China. The Buddhists' impersonal universe, developing in line with laws and recognising neither the general distinction between spirit and matter nor the essential personhood of God and the human being, had no space for a transcendental divine spirit supposed to have created the universe and human beings as unique individuals.

The contradictions in the Christian view were quickly recognised and attacked. If God is good, why did he create evil? If he is responsible for evil, how can he justify condemning human beings to hell? Why did he have to sacrifice his son to repair the damage? And how can that son be simultaneously in heaven and on earth? The Christian world view was regarded as intellectually inferior on account of its 'primitive' belief in personally active gods and the logical contradictions of its fundamental dualism. Because it seemed irreconcilable not only with Asia's world view but with its sociopolitical system, Christianity could not even be tolerated. Two claims to exclusive truth collided, resulting in persecutions of Christians in Japan, China and Vietnam in which ideological and political motivations were inextricably combined.

Such clashes were absent in non-Muslim India, where in place of the exclusivism of East Asia there was an inclusivism quite as objectionable to European minds. It was a strategy of incorporation that allowed western claims to exclusive truth simply to run into thin air. Of course there was only one God, as the missionaries preached – but the common people needed its many gods. Of course the message of the incarnation of God in Jesus Christ was very convincing – but it was just one of a long series of the divine incarnations or *avataras* in India's theologies. Ideas at the heart of the foreign understanding were briskly identified as components of India's own world view, with an underlying conviction that the foreign was ultimately inferior to the Indian way of thinking.

Unlike the Europeans, the Asians could only form an opinion of Europe's representatives, not of the region itself. Yet their perceptions were certainly both quite as accurate and quite as blinkered as those of their European counterparts. The Asians, just as the Europeans, were convinced of their own cultural and ideological superiority, and acted accordingly. Contrary to the claims of vulgar constructivism, this combination of perceptiveness and obliviousness did give rise to a substantial body of accurate knowledge by each side about the other, knowledge still sometimes drawn upon in Europe even today. This peculiar way of perceiving other cultures also underlay the exotic alternative ideals that flourished in Europe at the close of the eighteenth century. The emergence of the discipline of Indology around this time shifted European enthusiasm from the allegedly rationalist Chinese sage to the allegedly esoteric and mysterious sage of India and especially, thanks to a 'second age of discovery' in the Pacific, to the 'noble savage' of Tahiti. This natural man, with his naïve, innate virtue and sexual spontaneity, became the polemical antithesis to the European corrupted by Church and culture, even though travellers themselves had rather different tales to tell – the voyages of exploration now being accompanied by selected scholars, as part of the scientific methodology that had begun to motivate and drive the gathering of knowledge.

Enough progress had been made in navigation techniques over 300 years – nothing spectacular, but numerous small and cumulative steps – that seafarers could now expect to reach home safe and sound. The main momentum behind the new wave of discoveries was probably political, a surge of competing national ambition among the expanding European powers which began with the Russians' arrival in the North Pacific and continued with the race between England and France to find the fabled Southern Continent and the actual Australia. In 1728/29 Vitus Bering, a Dane in the service of the Russians, discovered the strait that now bears his name, and in 1741/42 he reached the southern coast of Alaska. Louis-Antoine de Bougainville's visit to Tahiti during his round-the-world voyage of 1766–69 was the source of the highly influential reports about the island. Above all, though, the three voyages of James Cook in 1768–71, 1772–75 and 1776–80 charted the coasts of New Zealand and eastern Australia, disproved the myths of the Southern Continent and the north-western passage past America, and discovered numerous island groups in the central and northern Pacific, including Hawaii, where Cook met his death. The exploration of the western coast of North America was completed by his successor, George Vancouver, in 1791–95. But this form of association between science and the politics of national prestige already belongs to a new era, one in which Asia too was to encounter fully developed colonialism.

4   The Iberian Atlantic

Especially in the highlands of Central and South America, the Europeans encountered highly sophisticated cultures that still fascinate us today – yet even in these regions there was a substantial development gap in terms of progress towards modern rationality and technology. It was a gap that would for the first time tip the scales in the power relations between human beings. The Europeans had a more efficient energy balance due to their deployment of animal power and its associated technologies, such as the wheel, the wagon and the plough. Their metal manufacturing techniques, including armaments, were far more advanced. And they had become accustomed to a more rational way of calculating cause and effect, means and ends, thanks to the Judeo-Christian 'disenchantment of the world': their transcendent God left plenty of space for an autonomous world of empirically knowable objects. Such distinctions meant that Latin America would become the first clear-cut, large-scale case of European colonialism. This is expressed in the nomenclature used even today. In the East, terms like 'the Philippines', 'Indonesia', even 'India' were imported European labels that themselves constructed the political and geographical entities they described. But the other half of the world is permeated with Eurocentric concepts to such a degree that it is still impossible to do without them. 'Discovery', 'conversion', 'western hemisphere', 'New World', 'America', 'West Indies', 'Indians' are among these more or less indispensable Eurocentric terms. In view of this terminology's ubiquity, contorted attempts to purify it in a politically correct way are unlikely to succeed, and anyway risk leading *ad absurdum* down an arbitrary number of paths. The historian is, I believe, better advised to trace Eurocentric terminology back to the constitutive circumstance that the matter itself, European colonialism, is Eurocentric and its history can thus legitimately – even to a certain extent necessarily – be discussed using Eurocentric language, each time with the implicit addition of the formula 'seen from the European perspective'. The very designation I have chosen for this chapter, the Iberian Atlantic, is 'seen from the European perspective', since it was the Spaniards and Portuguese who first made this ocean into a new 'Mediterranean' when they sailed to America in search of riches. For their monarchs, too, the New World existed primarily as a means of refilling the chronically leaking royal coffers. For this purpose, the treasures that the Indians had amassed over centuries, and that the conquerors squandered within a matter of years, were of only minor interest compared with the systematic exploitation of the silver deposits discovered in Mexico and Peru in the sixteenth century and the gold found in Brazil around 1700. That gold, together with the diamonds discovered shortly afterwards, was to bring Portugal revenues on a scale hitherto known only to Spain.

Spanish conquest and rule

At first, however, the region's power relations and economic opportunities were anything but clear, and the newcomers experimented with various options. Existing models played a role, but they had to be adapted to the specific conditions. Among these conditions was a strongly power-oriented and reasonably goal-oriented Castilian monarchy that invested only scant resources but aimed nevertheless to retain unqualified control.

Looking at the early days on Haiti, the influence of the Portuguese model is impossible to miss. The plan was clearly to build a system of bases for the procurement of gold, slaves and trading goods like the network the Portuguese had established on the Guinea coast. When it emerged that the gold had to be mined by the Spanish themselves, and that other commodities were almost non-existent, the resources of the Crown's monopolistic collaboration with Columbus did not allow the Spanish to enter quickly into the race with Portugal for contact with the Indian trading hubs or to tap into other lucrative opportunities. As a result, from 1498 the New World began to be opened up for private initiatives under royal licence, pushing a new group of people to centre stage: the seafarers backed by trading capital were now joined by members of the lower nobility and professional soldiers from the *reconquista* milieu. Spanish regions like Extremadura and New Castile, which had brought forth almost no explorers, contributed whole clans and clienteles of conquistadors. Close-knit insider networks of professional soldiers from the Italian wars of the Spanish Crown arrived in the New World. We might recall that Cortés and Pizarro were blood relations; that the conflict between the Pizarros and the Almagros in Peru amounted to a feud between Extremadura and New Castile; that the conqueror of Chile, Pedro de Valdivia, was a compatriot and client of the Pizarros, and so on. True to the style of the *reconquista* that had nurtured them, such men were interested in business opportunities of all kinds, but especially in looting and conquest – setting the scene for a seamless transition from discovery to *conquista*. Cortés, too, had set sail on a voyage of trade and discovery with rather vague objectives, yet ended up as the conqueror of the Aztec Empire. Battle was done with piety and loyalty for the honour of God and the king, but in return it was naturally expected that God would confer victory on His servants while the king would confer a generously dimensioned legitimation for rule over their spoils. For this reason, the idea of Christian mission, the salvation of the subjected heathens' souls, now came to the fore more strongly than it had done in the early years, and had to serve as a justification for the process of conquest. But whereas God and his saints were clearly ranged on the Spanish side – there was no shortage of apparitions of the Holy Virgin or St James to underline this point – the Crown often disappointed its champions. In contrast to the days of *reconquista*, it seemed that the Spanish monarchy would now refuse to tolerate a reproduction of feudal aristocratic rule in the New World, and was aiming instead for something more 'modern', a bureau-cratic empire controlled by lawyers that would also subject the Spaniards themselves to its discipline (if a rather rudimentary discipline in today's terms). Having risked their lives to capture new lands for the Crown at their own cost, the conquistadors felt offended in their feudal values by this policy, perhaps not without reason, and rebelled against it from time to time.

Legally, the conquistadors had put the seal on their own marginalisation when they signed their *capitulación* with the Crown for a planned campaign of *entrada* into America. These contracts made the adventurers commanders-in-chief, judges and governors, but they (or the instructions that often accompanied them) also defined the conquistadors' responsibilities in detailed terms. It was usually an easy matter for the Crown's lawyers to prove that a successful conquistador had in fact exceeded his mandate and author-ity, and use the contract to keep him in check. From 1498 on, the conquistadors normally had to fund and man their expeditions themselves, so that the procurement of the necessary capital was the first step for any venture. This was often done by setting up a *compañía*, which could grant a share in the profits to silent partners, as was the case in the contract for the conquest of Peru, signed by Pizarro, Almagro and a front man for the Espinosa bank. Agents recruiting the required troops stressed the fabulous riches to be found in the far-off destination and its similarity to Spanish landscapes. The partici-pants had to be able to fight, but knowledge of the manual trades and other professional skills were also in demand; priests and notaries were required, for instance. They had to provide their own equipment and were subject to martial law for the duration of the expedition, but afterwards were free to go wherever they wanted. This meant that the transition from capture to colonisa-tion was always a critical phase, although officially the founding of a town under Spanish law, including the allocation to the conquerors of Indian labour and urban plots on a grid plan, was supposed to be the pinnacle of the campaign and the moment of its transformation into colonisation. To ensure the success of an enterprise, the military ability of the conquistadors and their technological and ideological superiority was not the only factor. Indigenous allies and loyal concubines also played a role that should not be underestimated; without the assistance of the Tlaxcaltecs and his interpreter and lover Doña Marina (Malinche), for example, Cortés would probably not have been able to subjugate the Aztecs. Columbus, just as Cortés and Pizarro did later, took enemy rulers hostage, and their execution, along with other cruelties, helped to terrorise the indigenous opposition. Graves and sacred places were desecrated partly as a source of plunder, but also to display the power of the Christians and their God. Due not least to the financial structure of the expeditions, the invaders were under immense pressure to succeed, which added to the ruthlessness of their actions. The use of extreme cruelty was especially frequent in those cases where, outside the zones of 'high culture', the conquistadors encountered the unaccustomed tactic of ambush (at times using poisoned arrows) and genuine or supposed cannibalism.

Both politically and financially, the Crown's strategy paid off and the Conquest became a process that was controlled, yet essentially self-fuelling. Again and again immigrants gathered at particular locations and accumulated capital – through plunder, precious metals, native labour or trade in commodities and credit – that was then deployed for a further wave of expansion. The first such centre was Hispaniola (Haiti), occupied by Columbus, with Santo Domingo, the oldest Spanish city in America. It was from Santo Domingo that slave-hunters, then conquistadors, set out to attack the islands and mainland coasts of the Caribbean. In 1509 their targets were Puerto Rico and the coasts of Colombia and Panama, where gold and pearls were to be found, then in 1511 Cuba and in 1512 Jamaica. The Isthmus became a second centre with its city of Panama, founded in 1519. The expeditions from here out to the north-west, towards 'Golden Castile', were the first peak of Spanish atrocities. In 1526, Spaniards coming from Panama met up in Nicaragua with others coming from the north, where Hernán Cortés had entered the Aztec capital Tenochtitlán in 1519 and destroyed it in 1522. Straight away, in 1522, Cortés advanced northwards and southwards beyond the former Aztec sphere of power, subjugating Guatemala and Honduras; only the conquerors of the Mayan land of Yucatán in 1526 came directly from Spain. The south of today's United States was explored but judged of little interest, and the occupation of New Mexico occurred only around 1600, after the English had made an appearance on the Pacific coast, while California was not occupied until the end of the eighteenth century, in response to the English and Russian expeditions into the Pacific. San Francisco was founded only in 1776.

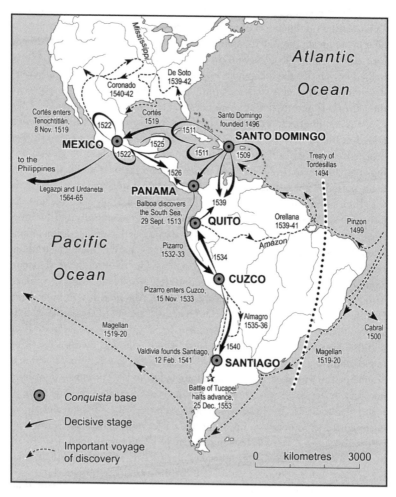

Map 5   The *conquista*

In the Panama centre, by 1522 attention had begun to turn to the 'golden land' of Peru. In 1531–34, after two attempts in the previous ten years and his appointment by the Empress personally in 1529, Francisco Pizarro conquered the heart of the Inca empire in the highlands, and in 1535 he founded today's Lima as the new capital – tellingly, a seaward-facing one. But civil wars erupted between the Pizarros and the rival Almagro family, then between disappointed conquistadors and representatives of the Crown. Only after 1550 did order return, and in 1572 the last stronghold of Inca rule was captured and the Inca emperor executed. The conquistadors immediately ploughed the resources they had looted during the Peruvian campaigns into further advances, beginning in the north with Ecuador in 1534. In 1538/39 three expeditions, from Ecuador, the north coast of Colombia and Venezuela, met in the highlands and reached agreement on the foundation of Bogotá. From 1529 to 1546, Venezuela was in the hands of a southern German business, the Augsburg house of Welser. As a direct investment by large-scale international capital, this arrangement was an exception to the usual financial arrangements, attracting opposition from the Spanish and ultimately failing due to inadequate profits. Otherwise, the German conquistadors in the service of the Welsers were little worse or better than their Spanish counterparts. Peru was the base from which Pedro de Valdivia launched the conquest of Chile in 1540 and founded Santiago de Chile in 1541. It was also the starting point for Gonzalo Pizarro to travel down into the Amazon rainforests; in 1541/42 a group of his men navigated the Amazon river all the way to the sea. Only the first expedition to the Río de la Plata was launched directly from Spain, after the Portuguese had posted claims in 1531. Buenos Aires was founded in 1535, abandoned in 1541 and re-founded, now permanently, around 1580. This time, the momentum came from the west, from Peru and Chile, and the same applies to other cities of the region that would later become Argentina. The focus of empire had long since shifted from the Caribbean to the more prosperous and densely populated highlands of Mexico and Peru. It would even be fair to say that the colonialism of the Spaniards was structured in advance by that of the Aztecs and Incas, whose subjugated peoples the conquistadors claimed to be liberating. In the south of Chile and in today's Argentina, around the Amazon region and in the north of Mexico, there was an Indian frontier which in some cases, like that of the Araucanians of Chile, remained a constant battle zone but more frequently was occupied by missionary districts. The typical 'frontiersman' of Spanish America was in fact not the trapper or cowboy, but the missionary.

The Spanish system of rule that was established in this manner crystallised around the Spanish cities, of which there are said to have been 331 by the year 1630, and the Indian communities, which were partially reorganised

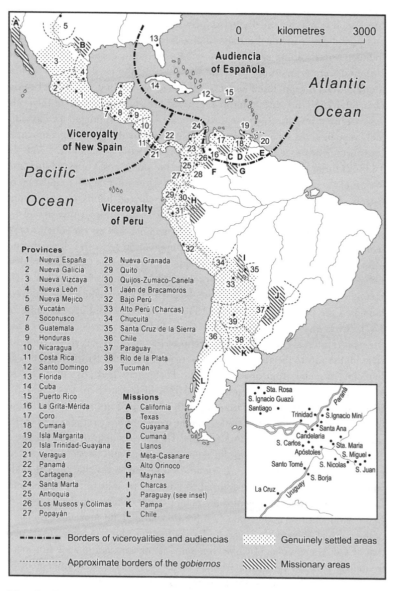

Provinces

1	Nueva España	28	Nueva Granada
2	Nueva Galicia	29	Quito
3	Nueva Vizcaya	30	Quijos-Zumaco-Canela
4	Nueva León	31	Jaén de Bracamoros
5	Nueva Mejico	32	Bajo Perú
6	Yucatán	33	Alto Perú (Charcas)
7	Soconusco	34	Chucuita
8	Guatemala	35	Santa Cruz de la Sierra
9	Honduras	36	Chile
10	Nicaragua	37	Paraguay
11	Costa Rica	38	Río de la Plata
12	Santo Domingo	39	Tucumán
13	Florida		
14	Cuba		
15	Puerto Rico	**Missions**	
16	La Grita-Mérida	A	California
17	Coro	B	Texas
18	Cumaná	C	Guayana
19	Isla Margarita	D	Cumaná
20	Isla Trinidad-Guayana	E	Llanos
21	Veragua	F	Meta-Casanare
22	Panamá	G	Alto Orinoco
23	Cartagena	H	Maynas
24	Santa Marta	I	Charcas
25	Antioquia	J	Paraguay (see inset)
26	Los Museos y Colimas	K	Pampa
27	Popayán	L	Chile

▬ ▪ ▬ ▪ ▬ ▪ ▬ Borders of viceroyalities and audiencias   ▦ Genuinely settled areas

┄┄┄┄┄┄ Approximate borders of the *gobiernos*   ⧄ Missionary areas

Map 6   Administrative divisions of Spanish America in the seventeenth century

following the pattern of municipalities in Spain – the Crown seems to have distilled its experiences at home into a consistent system for the new colonies. The Spanish cities had acquired considerable power in the course of the *reconquista*, and often controlled a large area of the surrounding countryside. Most importantly, they had proved their value to the Crown as allies in the restitution of royal power vis-à-vis the high nobility. In the New World, therefore, there were to be only municipalities, no more feudalism. To be sure, the American towns were prevented from forming municipal assemblies or *cortes* on the Castilian model, and neither were they permitted to participate in the Castilian *cortes* themselves. Because lower-class Spaniards on Hispaniola had often adopted an indigenous lifestyle and established themselves as virtual pashas among the Indians, it was decreed as early as 1502 that in future all Spaniards would be obliged to live in towns for the sake of improving cultural discipline. Likewise, the Indian tribal organisations were to be dissolved and the Indians gathered into communities for the purposes of Christianisation, hispanisation and control, a plan that was successfully realised in the areas of advanced civilisation during the sixteenth century, although without achieving the rigorous segregation from the Spanish that had always been intended. Despite the help of the missionaries, the process often took considerably longer in the case of the nomads of the frontier regions. The *reducciónes*, best known through the Jesuit missions of Paraguay, were settlements formed by this process of 'reduction' or concentration. The Spanish municipalities exercised self-government through an administrative council or *cabildo* and various elected offices, but it soon became a matter of course to inherit or buy the post of city councillor (*regidor*), so that a narrowly circumscribed oligarchy developed. Indian communities appear to have had a limited form of self-administration, under Spanish-style officials in combination with their own traditional chiefs. Both types of community, like the cities of Castile, came under the supervision of a royal official, the *corregidor*, who also held judicial and military powers. In Peru there were sixteen *corregidores de Españoles*, as against fifty-two *corregidores de Indios*, the latter having charge of several communities each. Because the *corregidores de Indios* were badly paid, they gradually took on the role of middlemen provisioning the Indians and selling their produce, and often became a thorn in the flesh of the people they were supposed to be protecting.

Such were the foundations of the five or six 'pillars' of the apparatus of colonial rule, which in principle were separate but in practice were interconnected in a multiplicity of ways. Nor was there an equal number of authorities of equal status. For administration there were thirty to forty *gobernadores*, while for justice there were ten collegiate courts, the *audiencias* of

Santo Domingo, Mexico, Panama, Guatemala, Lima, Bogotá, Guadalajara in northern Mexico, Charcas in Bolivia, Quito and Chile, as well as Manila on the Philippines, which were defined as part of Spanish America. The military reported to regional *capitanes generales*, and financial affairs were concentrated in the *cajas reales* or royal treasuries of the more important centres. The fifth pillar of rule was the Church, which since the papal grant in 1508 had been completely subject to the royal 'patronat' as implemented by the highest officers of the Crown. The thirty to forty dioceses that the Crown established were grouped into the five ecclesiastical provinces Santo Domingo, Mexico, Lima, Bogotá and Charcas. Enjoying a degree of independence that was substantial and, after the Council of Trent, not uncontroversial, the Indian missions operated by the mendicant orders and the Jesuits constituted a kind of sixth pillar. Between 1493 and 1822, the Crown sent at least 15,000 missionaries to America. Although the Crown had supported the bishops in their quarrel with the mendicant orders, after a promising start it suppressed the Council of Trent's proposal of a synodical system as furthering Church aspirations to autonomy just as, in the political arena, it suppressed attempts to establish representation of the estates.

An important role in the colonial system as a whole was played by the points of connection between different sets of authorities, which gave rise to a supplementary hierarchical order. Standard governors, for example, were dependent in military terms on certain other governors who combined the office of captain general with that of governor. Even more powerful were those governors who additionally presided over an *audencia*. At the top of the pile were the two viceroys in Mexico and Lima, who exercised these clusters of powers over particularly large provinces and furthermore, in analogy to the viceroys of Aragon or Naples in Europe, were the personal representatives of the monarchy for Central and South America respectively. However, this status included only a limited control over the other governors, who were able to communicate directly with the centre.

That centre consisted, from 1524, in the *Consejo de Indias* or Council of the Indies, a collegiate authority with comprehensive responsibility for all the 'pillars' of the system, including the Church. The proposals of the Council culminated in royal ordinances or *ordenanzas*, which, in line with the rescript procedure of early modern administration, usually decided individual cases from which general rules had to be derived. Still, they were codified in 1680 in the *Recopilación de las Leyes de Indias*. Below the Council was the *Casa de la Contratación*. Founded in 1503 on the model of the Portuguese *Casa da Índia* and based initially in Seville, from 1717 in Cadiz, the *Casa* was charged with handling the monopolistically organised maritime traffic and trade, levying the duties on that trade and supervising emigration. Its remit also included the collection of scientific data about the colonial empire by mariners and geographers.

In the course of intensifying state activity under the eighteenth-century 'enlightened absolutism' of the Bourbons, the Council of the Indies was replaced by a modern 'ministry'. In America the trend also resulted in the establishment of two additional viceroyalties, in Bogotá (1739) and Buenos Aires (1776), releasing the La Plata region from its absurd dependence on Peru. The pinnacle of this development was the introduction of the French intendant system towards the end of the eighteenth century. In place of the governors, parallel officeholders and the *corregidores* were to become reorganised administrative districts led by highly qualified intendants with wide-ranging responsibilities, highly detailed guidelines almost reminiscent of a welfare state, and local *subdelegados* who depended upon them. However, the primary purpose of the reforms was to increase revenue by reorganising and strengthening the fiscal system, especially in view of the rising cost of military operations. The tighter rein of the 'mother country' and higher levies unsurprisingly aroused resentment among the increasingly self-confident colonial elite. Significantly, it was only now that the term 'Spanish colonies' came into common use, the sixteenth and seventeenth centuries having always maintained the legal fiction of 'provinces' or even 'kingdoms' of the empire with rights equal to those in Europe – fictional on the one hand because of the political and economic discrimination against these regions, and on the other because of the general discrimination against their Indian majority population. Nevertheless, there was no appreciable impetus to dissolve the colonial relations of power, and even the frequent uprisings of the Indians rarely named such dissolution as their goal. The trigger for decolonisation came from outside: the collapse of the system of rule within Spain after the Napoleonic invasion, and the example offered by North America.

The economy and society of Spanish America

Hardly had the Crown made its hesitant transition from the notion of a trading empire to one of political rule than, in 1512, an insight found expression which would also be used to justify the change of course in German colonial policy in 1906: 'the entire riches of those regions are the Indians'. This was why, right from 1495, the enslavement of the Indians had been restricted to taking prisoners of war and in 1542, after massive abuse of this exception, was banned completely. But an unduly comprehensive protection of the Indian subjects was not in the interests of the Spanish immigrants, as Cortés is said to have pointed out succinctly in 1504: 'I came to win gold, not plough the fields like a peasant.' Although Spanish agriculturalists were to come to America, thus, there were to be no Spanish peasants or farm labourers; this lowest rung of society, as contemporaries saw it, was reserved for the Indians from the start. And the greater the importance of the production of precious metals, especially for the Crown, the more obvious it became that mining too was dependent on the use of Indian labour, in part even forced labour. There was thus a permanent contradiction between the Crown's interest in the welfare of its Indian subjects – itself, of course, dictated not by Christian charity alone but equally by political and economic reason – and the dual necessity of using those subjects' labour to placate the conquistadors and colonists and to produce the resources so urgently needed by the insatiable Spanish treasury.

To its credit, however, the Spanish Crown paid a surprising amount of heed to the missionaries critical of colonialism, critiques that started with the fierce advent-tide sermon of friar Antonio de Montesinos in 1511 and reached their crescendo with his fellow Dominican, Bartolomé de las Casas (1474–1566). Unlike his brother Dominicans, Las Casas did not stop at querying the accepted legal justifications for Conquest as set out in the *Requerimiento* of 1513: empowerment by the Pope and the mission to teach the faith. This proclamation and its associated declaration of war had to be read aloud to the Indians before opening hostilities in order to 'discharge the royal conscience', a procedure that even contemporaries regarded as a farce. But the *Requerimiento* did at least represent an attempt to create a legal basis for the Conquest, and to this extent it was – like the laws on the treatment of Indians codified as the *Leyes de Burgos* of 1512 – an initial response to the missionaries' protests. However, Las Casas went beyond this, disputing every inferiority of the Indians except for their lack of knowledge of the true faith. He was challenging an assumption of deficiency expressed at the time in the Aristotelian notion of the 'barbarian' and invoked countless times since then as a justification for colonialism, if only in the form of a paternalistic promotion of development in the interests of the colonised. True, nobody else wanted to take the argument as far as Las Casas. On the contrary, once the initial missionary euphoria had faded the Indians were kept in partial tutelage even in religious terms, so that for many centuries they were refused ordination as priests. Even so, in 1537 a papal bull was issued that expressly established the equal rationality of the Indians (who had formerly been regarded as semi-bestial); 1542 saw the *Leyes nuevas*, favourable to the Indians, and 1573 an ordinance that replaced the term *conquista* with *pacificación*, the practical consequences of which would be demonstrated in the less brutal procedures pursued during the occupation of the Philippines at this period. No comparably wide-ranging and effective self-criticism can be found in the history of colonialism until well into the twentieth century. It was eagerly deployed by Spain's colonial rivals, the French, Dutch and English, as ammunition for an over-dramatised defamation of the Spanish that persists to the present day and has now also engendered the fashionable accusation of genocide. Las Casas, as the originator of the 'Black Legend' of Spanish cruelty, received an undeservedly bad press in Spain until very recently.

It would, of course, be wrong to replace that *leyenda negra* with a 'White Legend' of Spanish colonialism. The interests at stake, in combination with the limited scope for implementation of laws from Europe, given that the Atlantic crossing took several months, meant that well-intentioned decrees often had little impact on the ground. For example, the system of *repartimiento* (later called *encomienda*), introduced in 1503, was originally designed to distribute Indian labour under coercion but in return for food, wages and instruction in Christianity, as a way of assuring the colonists' livelihood in an orderly manner – but it mutated into a brutal system of exploitation, threatening to become the nucleus of a new feudalism even though it was not actually linked to land titles and included a precautionary upper limit for Spanish ownership of land. At first the system seemed indispensable, and attempts to discontinue it led to a 1544 uprising by the Peruvian conquistadors. Rather than being abolished, therefore, the *encomienda* was transformed into a system whereby the tributes owed by a certain number of Indians (that is, the taxes that they would have owed the Crown) were assigned to the *encomendero* or trustee; all other authorisations ceased. This formed part of a policy to segregate the Indians from the Spanish settlers, a policy, finally enacted around the middle of the sixteenth century, that imposed a general ban on Spaniards and especially mestizos, mulattos and Africans taking up residence in Indian settlements. Separate development – a kind of 'apartheid' – was the goal, and a deceleration in the pace of hispanisation was accepted as a fair price to pay for it. This enabled the Indians to maintain a limited space of cultural freedom, reinforced by the missionaries through their cultivation of the indigenous languages. Nevertheless, in the long term it proved impossible to stem the flow of population into the cities and onto the now emerging large productive estates known as *haciendas*.

Clearly, many lives were lost to the cruelties of the Conquest and the more subtle consequences of the culture shock, slave hunts and slaveholding of the initial years, then the excesses of the *encomienda* system. But the mass death of Indians that rapidly commenced cannot be explained by these factors alone. After all, the slave hunts in the Caribbean were themselves a reaction to the catastrophic collapse in the working population of Hispaniola. The Indians of the Caribbean were soon largely wiped out. By around 1650, when a slow recuperation of population numbers began, a total of approximately four million Indians were living in Spanish America. The estimates for 1492 range between seven and 100 million, but thirty-five million is considered plausible. The Spanish would not have been capable of killing that number of people, quite apart from the fact that they were needed as labourers. The accusation of genocide thus dissolves into thin air. Instead, the main cause of the mass death of native Americans was the wave of infectious diseases introduced by the Europeans and Africans, diseases against which the indigenous population, isolated for thousands of years, had no immunity. Smallpox, plague, typhus, malaria, yellow fever, as well as influenza, measles, mumps and diphtheria, all claimed countless victims. A flu virus that arrived in 1493 is thought to have killed half the population of Haiti. In 1522, a smallpox epidemic resulted in the disintegration of Aztec resistance to Cortés. The Inca ruler Huanya Capac died in 1525 or 1527 in an epidemic that had already spread throughout his empire before the first Europeans arrived. Aside from the four million Indians, up to 1650 there were at most 440,000 European immigrants and around 300,000 African slaves brought in to replace lost Indian labour for those settlers who could afford such a purchase. In addition to these were growing numbers of mixed-race people of various origins.

The new economic interests of the Spanish rulers, combined with the changed demographic structure, made it necessary to restructure the economy. The 'fiscalist' Spanish economic policy was designed to supply the royal exchequer with income for the purposes of European power politics. This included Crown monopolies that could be passed on at a profit, especially mining rights and the mercury monopoly, but also the monopolies on salt and tobacco. The manufacturing of finished goods like wine, brandy and textiles was to be reserved for the mother country. 'Mercantilist' projects to develop the economy, in some cases using the monopoly companies that had proved so effective elsewhere, arose only under the enlightened absolutism of the eighteenth century. Although America imported wine and spirits, textiles and metal goods, it also developed a production and thriving interregional trade of its own. The demand coming from the large cities of Mexico and Lima was particularly important, as was that of the mining centres of Zacatecas and Potosí, a large city 4,000 m above sea level. Food was provided by the haciendas. Mexico and Ecuador saw the rise of large textile factories or *obrajes*, the workforce of which, like that of the mines, was procured in Mexico through the free market and in Ecuador through forced recruitment in the tradition of the *encomienda* and the related Inca system of *mita*.

The linchpin of the system was the silver-mining activity of Mexico and highland Peru. That included mercury from Peru and Europe used for the amalgam extraction of silver. The Crown leased its mining rights to entrepreneurs, and in Peru it also supplied them with forced labour. The situation of these labourers was atrocious, but many managed to escape through migration or even to enter the silver business on their own account. Apart from what was needed to administer the colonies, the Crown's share of the silver and the revenue from levies travelled to Spain as royal bullion, along with private bullion, payments for imports and other transfers. Other exports from America were of little significance in comparison.

Traffic with America was organised on the basis of convoys run by monopoly-privileged Spanish merchants under the supervision of the *Casa de la Contratación*. Once a year, the Mexico and Peru fleets crossed the Atlantic together under the protection of armed ships, the Mexico fleet heading for Veracruz and the Peru fleet for Nombre de Dios on the Isthmus of Panama; the two met up again in Havana, Cuba, for the return voyage. The journey west took eighty days, the journey east 120. On average, seventy-three ships a year sailed to America and fifty sailed back – silver took up less space. However, all estimates of the scale of the American trade must be viewed with caution because the system was so thoroughly undermined by smuggling (the La Plata estuary was particularly notorious in this respect). Similarly, to a very large extent the America merchants of Seville became fronts for foreign suppliers, at the outset mainly Dutch ones. The Spanish Crown spent its silver on war loans, so that the bullion flowed out of Spain into the international financial markets of Genoa and hostile Amsterdam. Even so, enough remained in the country for the inflation rate of the European 'price revolution' (a very modest one in present-day terms) to rise with every step closer to Seville. It was thus cheaper for the Spanish, and more profitable for the Dutch, French and others, to source goods destined for America from outside Spain rather than producing them at home. In combination with the excessive strains of power politics, the population losses caused by epidemics, and the Spanish aristocratic mentality, this economic mechanism contributed to the economic stagnation of a country that seemed at first sight to be in a privileged position due to its colonial riches. The bullion flowing out of Spain did not remain in the receiving countries, but was used to counteract their negative trade balance with the Baltic on the one hand, India and East Asia on the other. A world payments system arose in which silver from America was shipped via Europe and, on the annual Manila galleon, the Philippines into India and China, where the price of silver was highest. In Europe, contemporaries were already blaming the silver-induced increase in the money supply for the rise in prices. The reduction in silver imports, in turn, is supposed to have triggered the 'crisis of the seventeenth century'. However, it has now been established that silver imports were not so much reduced as concealed, and also that the European inflation had already taken shape before silver began to arrive from America. It would seem plausible to regard price trends not simply as a by-product of money supply but also as a consequence of population growth and the increased demand that this created. Another factor would be the less direct causes of the rise in money supply: a higher velocity of money circulation and an increase in credit volume, possibly as a result of the long-term fall in interest rates.

In America, Spanish colonialism gave rise to a multiethnic, racially stratified society, although the concept of race was at this stage defined not biologically but in relation partly to skin colour, partly to cultural (not least linguistic) affiliations. At the top of the hierarchy were the European Spaniards, followed by white people born in America, the 'creoles', the mestizos and the indigenous nobility, and finally the mass of the Indians and the imported Africans – bearing in mind that African slaves, because of the purchasing price invested in them, may still have been considered more valuable than ordinary 'Indios'. However, the relationship between colonial rulers and the colonised differed from the pictures presented by the models of class struggle and the new romanticisation of the Native Americans; it was neither socially nor culturally a fully dualistic and antagonistic one. The indigenous nobility, legally equal in status to the Spanish *hidalgos*, 'collaborated' with the Spanish in its own interest and mediated between the two worlds, often moving in each of these with the same assurance. More recent research has also shown very clearly that the encounter implied neither the annihilation of the Indian culture nor its continued existence beneath a thin European veneer, both of which claims are frequently made, but instead a productive appropriation that generated new cultures no less authentically 'Indian' than their pre-Columbian predecessors. This is perceptible even today in the fields of language and religion, which are interlinked to the extent that the missionaries, hoping to enhance the reach of their message, defied the official programme of Hispanisation to deliberately foster the indigenous languages. They systematically provided these languages with writing systems, at the same time reworking them lexically and grammatically with the help of state-of-the-art philology. That led not only to standardisation through the introduction of a written record, but also to innovation: the Indian loanwords in Spanish had to match up with a range of Spanish terms in the indigenous languages, and indigenous neologisms had to be created to describe things that had not existed in previous Indian cultures. This applied, for example, to most domestic animals and their associated vocabulary, and to religious life. Because the Indians were unfamiliar with the allegorical and metaphorical approach to religious texts that had been common practice in Europe for centuries, religion was an area where striking appropriations often took place. The metaphor of Christ as the 'sun of righteousness' became Jesus as a sun god, while the Virgin Mary on the crescent moon became the successor to the Moon Goddess and, like her, responsible for free love – another way of understanding the biblical story. No less tangible, but more theologically acceptable in European terms after the Church took early steps to steer its development, was the wonderful appropriation of the Virgin Mary into the Spanish Lady of Guadalupe through a Mexican apparition. She became the national icon of Mexico and ultimately the patroness of the whole of Catholic Latin America.

Brazil and its gold cycle

For many decades, Brazil played only a minor role for the Portuguese in comparison with their Indian trading empire. They limited themselves to harvesting and bringing back the dyewood after which the country was named. This was done via 'factories' in the accustomed Portuguese manner. Only when foreign competitors made an appearance, especially the French, who made repeated attempts to establish trading posts in Brazil right into the seventeenth century, did the Portuguese Crown in 1532 order the introduction of the system of land grants made to entrepreneurs, or *donatários*, that had proved so successful in the settlement of the Atlantic islands. The recipients of these grants were entrusted with comprehensive administrative, fiscal, judicial and military powers and with the task of distributing the land to other settlers. However, of the fifteen *donatária* divisions of Brazil, only Pernambuco in the centre and São Vicente in the south did well, in both cases due to the early introduction of sugar production and to successful cooperation with the Indians, which soon resulted in a large mixed-race population. Because the initial efforts had proved so unsuccessful apart from these exceptions, in 1549 royal administration under a *capitão-mor* was established on the model familiar from Asia. Bahia was made the capital and, from 1551, the see of a diocese. From 1621 to 1774, the area to the north of the bend in the Brazilian coastline at Cape São Roque became a colony of its own, the *Estado do Maranhão*, while until 1700 the south was divided into the three captaincies-general of Pernambuco, Bahia and Rio de Janeiro, bringing together self-governed towns and former *donatárias*. From 1577 there was a governor general, who for the first time in 1640 (and regularly from 1720) bore the title of viceroy. Furthermore, Bahia was given the status of an archdiocese, which in the eighteenth century held sway over six suffragan bishoprics in Brazil and two in Angola – the slave trade had made Angola a sub-colony of Brazil, just as the China trade had made the Philippines a sub-colony of Mexico.

The move of the Brazilian capital from Bahia to Rio de Janeiro in 1763 indicates a southward shift in focus that was part and parcel of a profound structural transformation during the eighteenth century. Well into the seventeenth century, Brazil's development had rested on the sugar business, which was focused on Pernambuco. Brazil was a part of the sugar-producing 'plantation America', and remained so even when the centre of that system had relocated to the Caribbean. But from 1695 onwards, new gold deposits were found in the south, apparently as a result of a determined search for an alternative to the stagnating sugar trade. The result was the first 'gold rush' in history. Adventurers streamed from the coast and from Portugal into the mining region, the focus of which was in Minas Gerais, soon to be part of the Rio de Janeiro hinterland. In 1711 the main mining camps were incorporated as Vila Rica de Ouro Preto, the Potosí of gold. The town turned into an inferno for the African slaves who extracted the gold, standing in water to pan the gold or working underground to dig out further seams. Because slaves were subject to tax, we have records to show that around 1740 there were 90,000–100,000 slaves in Minas Gerais, 18,000–20,000 of them in Vila Rica. The discoverers of a deposit had a claim on the exploitation of a certain area, but the rest belonged to the Crown, which was able to sell it piecemeal to other interested parties. Probably 80 per cent of the Brazilian gold came from Minas Gerais; the estimates of quantities vary considerably, and as in Spanish America a high level of unreported trade is likely due to smuggling and stealing. When the decline of gold extraction began in the 1760s, diamond mining, which had started in the same area in the 1720s, reached its peak. It was subjected to very rigorous control, over-production having initially resulted in a deterioration in prices.

The gold and diamond boom brought Brazil not only prosperity, but also a general structural change. The population grew substantially due to immigration and the rising importation of African slaves; the few remaining Indians were effectively irrelevant. In the area of São Paulo, the need to supply the mining districts gave rise not only to cattle farms, but also to iron-producing and manufacturing operations. The pull of demand reached further, too: peripheral areas in the north, west and south were invigorated by their role as suppliers of cattle. And Rio de Janeiro, as the port for the mining region, became the colony's prime city.

In Europe, the process that had occurred in Spain was now repeated with new actors. The gold came at just the right moment for Portugal, in a

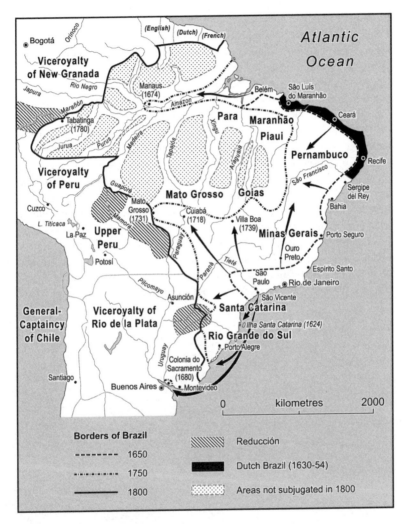

Map 7   The expansion of Brazil

phase of recession and suffering balance-of-payment problems after the 1703 Methuen Treaty with England, which laid down preferential treatment for English textiles in Portugal in return for similar conditions for port wine in England. The resulting lopsided trade balance could now be stabilised with the help of Brazilian gold, which after an initial ban soon flowed mainly into England. Just as previously in Spain, developing industry in Portugal did not seem worth the effort, since it was cheaper to import manufactured goods. Portugal became almost a kind of informal colony of Britain – in fact, England had exerted a strong political influence there even in the fourteenth century. Some commentators claim to have identified veritable cycles of industrialisation and deindustrialisation in Portugal, arguing that in times of crisis the Portuguese developed their own industry through protectionist measures, only to expose it to ruin in periods of prosperity through free trade with more powerful partners. More recent research suggests that these phenomena were limited to the Portuguese coastal areas. Nor are historians any longer quite so sure that the foundations for English industrialisation were built of Brazilian gold, the supposed parallelism between gold imports from Portugal and the development of the British gold standard now having been disproved. It is possible that the contribution of both Portuguese and Spanish colonialism to European development is more modest than the flows of precious metals would initially suggest. Apparently, being the proud possessor of a treasury packed with gold and silver is not everything.

5   Plantation America and the African Atlantic

Substantially more innovatory in economic terms than trade and mining was the plantation system of Brazil and the Caribbean, with its offshoots along the tropical coastlines of Spanish America and the south of today's United States. In the language of colonial policy, this was the first case of large-scale *mise en valeur*, the economic development and exploitation of colonies; in the language of economics it was the first case of dominance by an agroindustry. A plantation is a large agricultural enterprise that specialises in producing high-value agricultural merchandise for export, often by means of monoculture. It requires heavy capital investment, because the business needs not only a large amount of land and labour, but also technical plant for processing the produce. A rational management of production is therefore essential. In America, the most important plantation product was cane sugar, which commanded a price high enough to surmount the cost barrier of its long transport route to the buyers in Europe. Sugar cane thrives in a tropical climate, but it exhausts the soil, so that the production factor of land has to be available in unusual abundance. In this respect, America was at an advantage over the sugar-producing regions of the Old World – but when it came to the production factor of labour, the reverse applied. Because sugar cane has to be processed within twenty-four hours, an enormous amount of labour was needed, especially during harvest. The Indians of the highlands were accustomed to regular agricultural labour but ill-adapted to tropical lowland locations, whereas the indigenous population of the lowlands was not culturally attuned to labouring in the fields, and was anyway too small. The solution lay in the mass importation of African slaves, who were accustomed to both the climate and the type of work. The Portuguese had begun to trade in African slaves in the mid fifteenth century, and in 1479 the Treaty of Alcáçovas made them the first monopolists in the business. This development drew not only America but also Africa into modern colonialism: in the course of the slave trade – the first great enforced migration in history – parts of West Africa, such as the Guinea coast and Angola, became sub-colonies of America, while parts of the New World gradually acquired a population majority of African descent. Europe, too, was involved directly. For economic and navigational reasons, an economic system had developed by the eighteenth century that used to be given the rather schematic label 'triangular trade'. European ships took goods from Europe to Africa, slaves from there to America, and sugar from America to Europe, stimulating a surge of growth in the shipping activities of certain cities such as Nantes and Liverpool. It should be noted that not all ships sailed the triangle in this way, and there was considerable direct bilateral traffic in both directions, especially between Brazil and Africa. The production factor of capital was required not only for commerce but earlier on, during the production phase, since a sugar mill had to be built close to the fields. The mill crushed the cane between rotating rollers, yielding a syrup that then had to be purified and heated to thicken and crystallise it. Refined sugar suffered in the damp conditions of sea transportation, and this problem, along with the desire to spread the costs, meant that sugar refining was often carried out in the area of end use, in Europe or later North America.

Portuguese and Dutch Brazil in the sugar cycle

The America of the sugar plantations took shape in Brazil, bringing the country its first wave of prosperity and making it the world's largest sugar producer and exporter in the period from 1580 to 1680. Brazil's importance for Portugal now easily cast the waning East Indian trading empire into the shade. The key factor in its success was the abundant availability of suitable land in combination with favourable climatic conditions, especially around Bahia and Pernambuco. It is thought that between 1570 and 1629 the number of sugar mills, or *engenhos*, rose from sixty to 350, although their maximum capacity of 20,000 tons per year was not always fully exploited.

Labour was initially taken from Indian slaves, who appear to have still made up two thirds of the workers in Pernambuco in 1583. But escapes, population decline and a gradually more effective policy of protecting the Indians on the Spanish model (here too with important input from missionaries) combined to reduce their number during a period of rising demand, thus pushing up the price of slaves. This made it worthwhile to switch to the comparatively expensive but more productive slaves from Africa. In one *engenho*, 7 per cent of the workforce were Africans in 1574; that figure had already reached 37 per cent in 1591 and 100 per cent in 1638. In the period from 1570 to 1680, the number of Africans imported every year appears to have risen from around 4,000 to around 8,000. In some locations at this time, slaves already made up the majority of the population. According to Philip Curtin, during the sixteenth century the Portuguese probably took

100,000 Africans to Brazil, in the seventeenth 600,000, in the eighteenth –
prompted by the mining boom – 1.3 million, and in the nineteenth –
prompted by the coffee boom – a further 1.6 million. By 1818, the approximately 3.5 million inhabitants of Brazil were made up of around one million
white-skinned, half a million mulatto, and two million black people. The
indigenous Indians no longer even appear in the statistics. The African
slaves initially came from the hinterland of the Guinea coast, occasionally
also from Muslim pastoral tribes, and were widely considered recalcitrant.
The Angolan market, which opened up in 1575 when Luanda was founded,
offered access to the more tractable Bantus, and Angola became an indispensable sub-colony of Brazil when the Portuguese were driven out of the
Guinea coast by other powers.

At first, there was little natural reproduction of the slave population, due
to high mortality and a surplus of men. Because slaves had paid for their
purchase price in sugar after at most sixteen months, it was hardly worth the
effort of treating them with care. 'A sugar-mill is hell. Its masters are all
damned,' wrote a Jesuit in 1627. For the greater part of the year, the mills
operated from four in the afternoon to ten the following morning. The mills
were then cleaned and there were a few hours of rest. Apart from this there
were no breaks in the work of cutting the sugar cane, bundling it, transport-
ing to the mill and feeding it into the rollers. The worst task was the ceaseless
heating of the vats. The idyllic picture of Brazilian slavery painted by
Gilberto Freyre's book *The Masters and the Slaves*, first published in 1933,
has nowadays been largely discredited. Far from the kind of extended family
portrayed by Freyre, this was a tense and hostile relationship that oscillated
between the poles of enforcing labour and withholding labour – a dynamic
that slaves at times handled with some success.

In 1751, slaves made up 36 per cent of a plantation's value, the
'machines' 23 per cent, the land 19 per cent, the buildings 18 per cent and
the animals 4 per cent. The running costs of labour, at 58 per cent, fell to the
wages of the foremen and 'technicians' (23 per cent), replacing the one-in-
ten loss of slaves (19 per cent) and the slaves' upkeep (16 per cent).
Firewood accounted for between 12 and 21 per cent. Credit was obtained
from merchants or the Church. In the seventeenth century, the Brazilian
plantations were squeezed by a falling sugar price in combination with a
rising slave price: the Caribbean competition was producing more cheaply
and in greater quantities, and the demand generated by the mining sector
was making slaves more expensive. In 1710 four times as much sugar had to
be produced to replace one slave as had been the case in 1608. The experi-
ment of Dutch Brazil, too, came to grief because of these economic
difficulties rather than political problems.

The Portuguese merchants were in no more of a position than their Spanish colleagues to implement their claims to a monopoly on the Brazilian trade, as they lacked both shipping space and capital. Dutch and English traders saw their chance to fill the gap, aiming not least to keep the Spanish at bay at a time when Spain was, despite its limited resources, making a determined push for Brazil under the banner of the Spanish union with Portugal. It is thought that during the ceasefire of 1609–21, between half and one third of all the ships in Brazil were Dutch, while other sources suggest that the undoubtedly substantial Dutch share in the Brazilian trade was in fact carried out indirectly, via the Portuguese ports. Added to this was the usual smuggling activity. Sugar refineries were banned in Portugal in order to protect Brazilian processing, and the Dutch made good use of this niche. In 1622 there were twenty-nine sugar refineries in the Netherlands, twenty-five of them in Amsterdam. But when the war with Spain recommenced in 1621, Dutch business suffered much more than has previously been assumed. The Dutch saw the best solution as an expansion at the expense of Spain, or more specifically at the expense of the associated Portuguese empire, as in East India. To this end, the Netherlands chartered a West India Company (*Geoctroyeerde Westindische Compagnie* or WIC) with seven million guilders' capital. Its organisation resembled the East India Company, but with a guarantee and grant from the States-General, which was entitled to appoint one member of the nineteen-strong board, the *Heren Negentien*. The WIC was far more obviously intended as a political instrument than the VOC had been, and the flow of merchant capital was correspondingly hesitant. The renewed dominance of the merchant hubs of Amsterdam and Middelburg is deceptive: in fact, the WIC's capital was mobilised from the interior of the country, attracted by political and religious rather than commercial considerations. Strict Calvinists, especially wealthy religious refugees from Antwerp, played an important role.

Commercially, the WIC was not a great success. Its first attacks on Bahia and the Portuguese bases on the Guinea coast failed, and only the gold trade with Africa flourished. Not until the seizure of the Spanish silver fleet in 1628 and the successes of the 1630s and 1640s did the company enjoy a temporary boost in its share price. The sugar-producing region of Pernambuco was captured, and during the years 1630–54 a 'New Holland' existed in Brazil. The company controlled the world sugar business, including the slave trade. In 1637, the old Portuguese fortress of Elmina on the Guinea coast was seized; it would remain the Dutch focal point in Africa until 1871. In 1642 Angola and São Tomé also came under Dutch control. Between 1636 and 1645, the WIC sold 23,163 slaves in Brazil. Under the governor-general John Maurice of Nassau, New Holland experienced a short-lived upswing in 1637–44, including a cultural blossoming due to the artists and scientists in the governor's entourage. However, in 1641 the ceasefire with Portugal, now independent again, put a stop to the profitable Dutch business of privateering. In 1644 the Brazilians rebelled against the Dutch – so successfully that they were even able to recapture Angola for Portugal in 1648. In 1654 the last Dutch bases in Brazil were lost, and the peace of 1661 allowed the Netherlands only free trade with Brazil, in competition with the British, whose royal family was related by marriage to the new Portuguese monarchs. In 1664 the WIC also lost its North American colony New Netherland, today's New York, so that in 1674 it had to be rescued at a considerable loss and was restructured as a purely slave-trading concern. The sugar business in Brazil, too, was taking an unfavourable turn, until the colony experienced its new boom in the wake of the gold discoveries. The Dutch, and the Sephardic Jews of Portuguese descent who were strongly represented in their American trade, had by then made their decisive contribution to the establishment of plantation America's new and thriving hub in the Caribbean.

Sugar and new powers in the Caribbean

Originally the centre of the Spanish Empire, the Caribbean had long been supplanted in that role by the highlands of Mexico and Peru. These regions were more difficult to access for Spain's enemies, even if pirates like Francis Drake occasionally troubled the Pacific coasts. In contrast, the prevailing winds and currents meant that the Caribbean, like Brazil, lay open to Europe. Its islands were sparsely populated or even completely uninhabited. In short, it was an ideal gateway for anyone who wanted to smuggle goods – such as African slaves, demand for which was steady – into Spanish America or planned to launch expeditions of plunder, even conquest, from its shores. The French and English had already arrived there in the sixteenth century, leading to continual small-scale hostilities below the radar of official diplomatic relations. The diplomatic principle 'no peace beyond the line' was supposed to contain such conflicts and prevent them from escalating into full-scale war between the European powers. Often the boundary between low-level warfare and piracy was blurred, and by the mid seventeenth century autonomous communities of pirates, the legendary buccaneers, or *flibustiers*, had managed to establish themselves in the Caribbean, until the great powers found no further use for them and stamped them out. Power struggles in Europe habitually reverberated right into the Caribbean, and European wars with Spain had prompted the English and the French, as well as the Dutch and Danish, to occupy Caribbean islands. By establishing fixed trading posts, these countries would be able to carry out the usual operations and the acquisition of American goods such as salt or tobacco more easily and cheaply. The English occupied St Kitts and Barbados in the 1620s, and in the 1630s the French followed suit with Martinique and Guadeloupe, the Dutch with Curaçao. In 1655 the English took Jamaica, and in 1697 the French acquired the western part of the island of Hispaniola, or Haiti. Added to these were bases of all three powers on the coast of Guyana and British bases on the Honduran coast. Spain had little choice but to concur with these acquisitions. If the English and French first pitched camp on the Lesser Antilles, this was due not only to the fact that the Spanish had left the islands unoccupied but also to the location's potential advantages for shipping traffic, indicated by their Dutch sobriquet, the 'Islands Above the Wind'. Ships could be carried there by the trade winds, returning by a northwards route along the trade winds to catch the westerlies which would drive them on to Europe. In contrast, if they started out from Jamaica they were prevented by the trade winds from using the passage between Cuba and Haiti, and had instead to make a wide westward detour to pick up the Gulf Stream, which would carry them along the northern coast of Cuba into the west wind zone. This is why sugar from Jamaica was at times considerably more expensive than that from Barbados.

Initially, however, it was not sugar but tobacco, America's miracle plant, that enjoyed rising demand from Europe. Tobacco cultivation requires little capital but labour-intensive tending, and thus seemed perfectly suited to the settlers as free smallholders. If extra labour was required, here as in North America there was recourse to prisoners or to the indentured servants known in French as *engagés*: Europeans who entered a contract for a certain number of years' labour in return for their transatlantic passage, a kind of temporary enslavement. There was not yet widespread currency for the view, later taken for granted, that unlike people of colour and specifically Africans, whites were not capable of living in the tropics and certainly not of carrying out physical labour there. This topos of the later 'master-race' ideology arose from the observation that newly arrived Europeans suffered higher mortality than did the freshly imported Africans. The inference was based on a lack of understanding of the epidemiological causes. Africans and Europeans both possessed immunity against the Old World infections that had killed the Indians in such large numbers. But many of the Africans were also immune to particular tropical diseases that the Europeans faced without protection, especially yellow fever and certain forms of malaria. As usual, the racist conclusions drawn from this observation were not preconditions for the social transformation in the tropics, but followed that transformation as an ideology of legitimation.

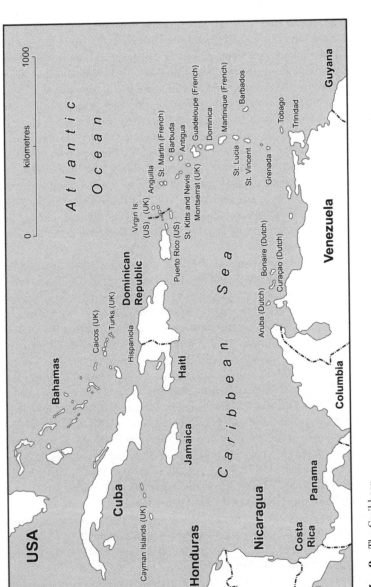

Map 8 The Caribbean

The expansion of tobacco production resulted in a drop in prices that hit the small cultivators hard, as did competition from the better varieties grown in Virginia. In the long run sugar prices declined as well, but smallholders did not have the same scope as large-scale farmers to exploit the elastic demand for the two items and absorb falling prices by increasing their production. That is to say, when sugar and tobacco became cheaper, more could be sold – but not everyone was in a position to produce that extra volume. In the short term, however, it was the temporary peak in sugar prices after the war in Brazil that made sugar an attractive option for better-off agriculturalists during the tobacco crisis. Dutch mariners, scenting their opportunity to do business without the burden of WIC monopolies and levies, offered their expertise and capital, procured slaves and equipment, and arranged for shipping and marketing. After its defeat the WIC itself took part in this business as well, and Jewish refugees from Brazil settled in the West Indies, bringing with them plentiful knowledge and connections. In fact, the Jewish community of Curaçao, founded in 1659, is the oldest in the whole of the Americas.

This was the prehistory of the 'sugar revolution' that occurred in Barbados between the 1630s and the 1660s. Other islands followed later, Saint Domingue not until the eighteenth century, giving it the advantage of unexhausted soil. This revolution was a victory for large-scale operations and entailed a significant shift in the demographic structure. Instead of 11,200 landowners with an average estate of 4 ha and 5,680 slaves, as was the case in 1645, by 1667 Barbados had only 745 landowners, their farms measuring between 80 and 400 ha, and 82,023 African slaves. Whereas in Brazil the sugar trade had included small-scale planters who supplied external mills, the West Indian business was dominated by large operations with their own processing facilities and an enormous demand for slaves. Of the £19,000 that a medium-sized Jamaican plantation of 240 ha and 200 slaves was worth around 1770, the slaves made up 37.5 per cent of the value, land 31.5 per cent and the sugar mill 20.8 per cent. It is thought that profits initially reached up to 50 per cent, though in the eighteenth century they levelled off at around 5–10 per cent. Even if these figures disregard the costs of replacement purchases, by the standards of the day sugar was a lucrative business. Despite claims to the contrary, it remained so in the British West Indies well into the 1820s; only then did competition from new cane-growing regions and sugar beet lead to its downfall.

Originally, sugar was bought up by European companies via their agents or captains on the ground. These merchants were often also the planters' creditors, so that payments for sugar were offset against payments for slaves and commodities and against interest and loan repayments, in a kind of barter arrangement. The French planters, who practised this system till the very end, had the French market to themselves thanks to the mercantilist policy of protectionism – yet in fact their sugar, the cheapest on the market, would surely have profited from free trade. Foodstuffs and slaves could also be bought from the English and North Americans more cheaply than in France. Like the rebellious colonists of British North America, the French settlers recognised that this colonial system benefited the mother country at their expense. They reacted in the wake of the French Revolution, though only to be pushed aside themselves by a slave revolution that would seal the fate of the French sugar island of Saint Domingue. The British planters, in contrast, shipped their sugar from the West Indies to England at their own risk and had it sold there on commission. Their agents also procured goods, credit and bills of exchange with which slaves could be bought. Because sugar prices were highest in Britain, under mercantilist conditions this set-up was to the advantage of those planters who could afford to live in England and there promote their involvements through the political lobby known as the 'West India interest'. Their political impact can be identified in the Seven Years' War of 1755–63, fought by the British in the West Indies as a chiefly economic conflict. Guadeloupe and Martinique were occupied and the maximum possible damage inflicted on the French slave trade. During the peace negotiations, the British rum-distiller and sugar-trade lobby demanded that Guadeloupe be annexed in order to expand production for re-export to the European continent. The planters' lobby, in contrast, feared competition and a resulting drop in prices. The government ultimately bowed to the City of London circles who were calling for control over the Canadian fishing grounds, and gave Guadeloupe back to the French even though, at the time, its value was calculated by both sides as being higher than that of the whole of Canada.

The African Atlantic

More than Brazil, and far more than Spanish America, the West Indian 'plantation America' and its population was a European colonial innovation without any precedent – the first artificial world of agribusiness. At 120–180 inhabitants per square kilometre, the settlement density was immense: for comparison, the highest settlement density in Mexico was thirty-six, in North America just twenty. The total population of the West Indies' plantation America, anything but extensive in area, is thought to have equated to one-seventh of Spanish America's total population and half of North America's. More than 85 per cent of that population were African slaves. Initially, just as in Brazil, the slave population did not reproduce itself but required a constant stream of imports. To raise its slave population from 45,000 to 324,000 between 1702 and 1808, Jamaica imported 659,000 people; Saint Domingue imported 864,000 Africans between 1680 and 1791 to raise its slave population from 4,000 to 480,000. Demand like this meant that the slave trade's core was in the Caribbean. Philip Curtin calculates that between the sixteenth century and the nineteenth century, when Spanish Cuba became the last hub of the sugar and slave economy, the West Indies and Guyana received 47.8 per cent of all African slaves, while Brazil received 38.1 per cent, the extensive Spanish American mainland only 7.8 per cent and what is today the United States even less, a mere 4.5 per cent.

These figures are deceptive in that they include slaves who were re-exported from the West Indies to Spanish America. Having lacked direct access to Africa since 1479, Spain was always dependent on others for its slave supplies. Since the sixteenth century, the Spanish Crown had been offering short-term contracts for the exclusive right to sell slaves to Hispanic America; until 1640, these concessions always went to Portuguese companies. In diplomatic language the term *asiento*, which originally covered a range of different contracts, eventually came to refer solely to this arrangement for slave supply. When Portugal regained independence from Spain, the *asiento* passed into Dutch hands (despite various front men), the Netherlands by then having pushed Portugal out of the trade with West Africa. The French did manage to acquire a foothold in the Senegal area, and the British possessed eighteen stations on the Guinea coast as early as 1665; when Angola was depopulated by an epidemic, the Portuguese too returned to the Guinea coast. After a short Franco-Portuguese intermezzo, the Bourbon succession in Spain meant that the Spanish *asiento* could be awarded to the French *Compagnie de l'Asiento* in 1703. However, in the 1713 Peace of Utrecht the British managed to acquire the contract as part of the spoils of victory. They had already established the South Sea Company in 1711 for the expected trade with Spanish America, planning among other things to use the slave business as a smokescreen for their clandestine trade in European finished goods. The Utrecht treaty only permitted them one cargo a year, but if the ship in question unloaded its cargo in the daytime at Portobelo, the port licensed for this purpose on the northern coast of Panama, during the night it could be reloaded with goods from Jamaica. The South Sea Company ceased its trading business in 1750: the *asiento* system had come to an end, though the European trade in African slaves had not.

An estimate dating from the American Civil War put the total number of African slaves sold to America at fifteen million. This number has persisted obstinately to the present day, despite Philip D. Curtin's 1969 publication of detailed results of his study of all the available data, *The Atlantic Slave Trade: A Census*. The book has, in Paul E. Lovejoy's view, proved its merit throughout all the subsequent discussions, even if other scholars, especially Joseph E. Inikori, have proposed higher numbers. Lovejoy puts the total number of slaves exported from Africa by Europeans and North Americans at 11,642,000, while Curtin's figure for the imports, at 9,566,000, is lower due to mortality during the transports. Although a surprisingly large number of slaves were still being transported during the nineteenth century, more than half of these totals were sold in the eighteenth century. The British accounted for 41 per cent of the eighteenth-century business, the Portuguese for 29 per cent, the French for 19 per cent, the Dutch for 6 per cent and the North Americans for 3 per cent. Of the smaller importers, which included Prussia and Courland, Denmark played the most important role, at times in cooperation with Schleswig-Holstein. According to Lovejoy, a further 5.15 million Africans were sold into the Islamic area in the sixteenth to nineteenth centuries. But Africa's loss of population cannot be established simply by adding these two figures, because of the extreme regional differences and gender distinctions. The preponderance of men among the people sold to America was by no means a factor only of demand in the colonies: it was due just as much to patterns of demand within Africa and the Arab world, where women and children were easier to sell. As a result, the reproductive capacity of African societies was not necessarily impaired in direct proportion to the number of human beings lost. In short, the shape of the African slave trade was determined not only by western demand, but also by African suppliers, who generally took good care to prevent the Europeans from buying directly at the slaves' places of origin and certainly from undertaking slave hunts on their own account. The existence of some West African 'military states', such as Dahomey (today's Benin), was connected with this African infrastructure of the slavery business.

In America, the slave price followed the economic cycle. In Brazil it rocketed during the gold boom after 1700 and the coffee boom after 1800, while its slower rise in the Caribbean will have been one more factor in that region's prosperity. In the United States, the complete ban on importing slaves from 1808 onward made it plainly worthwhile to treat the existing slaves more carefully and to move towards a system of slave breeding and domestic trade. It is for this reason that the African American population in today's United States is higher than would be suggested by the comparatively low numbers of slaves imported.

However, if the slave price in Brazil and the Caribbean doubled in the period 1700–1820, it quadrupled in Luanda and Senegal. This opened up a price gap which shrank the profits of slaving, so that at times European slave-trade profits were now ensured only by the sale of goods in Africa. The African suppliers, in contrast, were doing ever better business. Because it was now worth bringing slaves to the coast even from long distances, they were able to keep their supply flexible. It is said that during the eighteenth century the slavers increased the reach of their operations tenfold, to 1,500 kilometres. A considerable number of Africans thus profited from the slave trade. They were so well integrated into the Europe-oriented market economy that when the slave business was suppressed in the nineteenth century, they were able to readjust quickly and switch to supplying other products, especially palm oil, sometimes with the use of slave labour on the American model. In this way, the former slave-trading regions of today's Ghana and Nigeria became the forerunners of a western-style 'modernisation' and thus also of decolonisation. It also seems that Africans used the sale of slaves to rid themselves of extra mouths to feed during the frequent famines. From this point of view, the slave trade's enforced migration would have relieved the population pressure on Africa, not unlike the relief of eighteenth- and nineteenth-century Europe's population through 'voluntary' migration. Inikori's claim that the loss of population pressure entailed a loss of economic stimulus will not be easy to prove, but the population decline in some areas, such as Angola, certainly exceeded what could possibly have been economically beneficial, and had an injurious effect. A model proposed by Patrick Manning suggests that the population of Africa stagnated between 1700 and 1850, at a time when it was rising rapidly on other continents, so that Africa's share of the population of the Atlantic region fell from 30 per cent to 10 per cent between 1650 and 1850.

The higher slave price encouraged traders to act with more care, and mortality during the infamous 'Middle Passage' across the Atlantic fell in the course of the eighteenth century from 20 per cent to 10 per cent, then finally to 5 per cent. Those deaths not caused by the epidemics that spread rapidly in the densely packed transport ships were the result of bad nutrition and lack of clean water; dysentery played the largest part.

As for the slaveholders, for a long time historians insisted on the distinction between the Latin nations and the English. In this view, the Latins created legal regulation for slavery and within this framework (the French *Code Noir* of 1685, the Spanish *Código Negro* of 1789) recognised the slave's elementary human rights, whereas the English had no experience or regulations of this kind and allowed a brutal capitalist free-for-all, their Protestant indifference, furthermore, unmitigated by the softening influence of Catholicism. In reality, however, clerics of all the Christian denominations owned slaves perfectly officially, and the first protests of the Christian conscience came from the generally despised Quakers. Nor can much be surmised from the differences in the legal position, since this had more to do with the goals of the different systems of rule – bureaucratic centralism versus extensive self-administration – than with realities on the ground, where laws were flouted everywhere to an equal extent. At most, the practices for liberating slaves and the status of freedmen were more favourable among the Latins. Otherwise, the differences in the treatment of slaves are nowadays explained primarily along economic lines. The keeping of house slaves has always been considered more humane, and stagnating plantation systems would generally treat their slaves less harshly than prospering ones.

However, it would be hard to draw up a cost-benefit analysis for the different ways of treating slaves, whereas the sources do allow precise observation of the outcome of shipping and of the trade with Africa. The slave business was so attractive that in the course of the seventeenth century numerous monopoly companies on the Dutch model were founded to exploit it: in 1672 the Royal African Company, in 1673 the *Compagnie du Sénégal*, in 1685 the *Compagnie de Guinée*, in 1703 the *Compagnie de l'Asiento*, and so on. Just as had happened in the case of the East India companies, the efforts of smaller countries were often supported by Dutch traders looking for a chance to evade the monopoly held by their own WIC. This was true of the *Brandenburgisch-Africanische Compagnie* founded in 1682, which, however, was not able to assert itself against its competitors in the West Indies and was liquidated, as was the first German colonial possession in Africa. But between 1672 and 1730 free trade became the norm, and the companies were left only with the task of maintaining the bases.

Certain European ports were obvious beneficiaries of the triangular and slave trade, in France especially Nantes, then Bordeaux, La Rochelle, Le Havre, Saint Malo, Lorient, Honfleur and Marseilles. Nantes alone sent 1,400 slave transports, making up 45 per cent of the French trade, and the city's rising status was based largely on this sector, whereas in the other cities slavery generally remained just one of many branches of foreign trade. That was also the case for Liverpool, even though the city is said to have handled 85 per cent of the British and three sevenths of the European slave trade in the period 1795–1804. The port had supplanted Bristol as the leading slave-trading city in the eighteenth century just as Bristol had previously supplanted London, and at this time an average of 107 slave ships a year were leaving Liverpool, compared to eighteen from London and five from Bristol. But the slave trade constituted only one part of the city's American trade, and it has been claimed that Liverpool was more important for the slave trade than the slave trade was for Liverpool. Fabulous profits made the business as attractive as ever, but they alternated with much more modest returns and even losses. Of twenty-five voyages leaving Nantes in 1783–90, seventeen made profits of up to 57 per cent, but eight made losses of up to 42 per cent. The average was a 7.68 per cent profit. For all the shipments from Liverpool in 1761–1807, Roger Anstey has calculated an average profit of 9.5 per cent, although, as Inikori points out, the really substantial returns were garnered only by the few large companies capable of spreading their risks widely enough.

The multiplier effect of the slave trade should not be overlooked. It stimulated not only shipbuilding but also the East Indian trade and cotton manufacturing, because lightweight textiles were the most important of the goods used to buy slaves. Others included spirits, Irish linen and various metal goods from Birmingham, not least guns. The slave traders could not produce these goods themselves, unlike the German-Danish firm Schimmelmann: this company supplied its slave traders with spirits and textiles from its own estates and with guns from its own factory, then processed the imported sugar in its own refinery. The British slave traders stoked demand for goods from other companies, but was that momentum a factor in Britain's industrialisation? In his 1944 book *Capitalism and Slavery*, the African American Eric Williams, who became prime minister of independent Trinidad in 1956, attributed British industrialisation to the triangular trade, although he argued in terms not of demand effects but of the finances that the trading profits made available. Aside from a few individual cases, this claim cannot be upheld in general. The profits of trade were ploughed not into industry but straight back into commerce. In fact, even if they had flowed exclusively into the industrialisation process, they would have accounted for only 7.9 per cent of investment. More indirect effects can certainly be traced, for example the key role of trade in the emergence of the new 'country banks', which, in turn, were more important to industry than the traditional London banks. But while foreign trade tended to promote itself noisily and therefore left rich traces in the English sources, we should not overestimate its significance in comparison to the quietly effective and much further-reaching domestic preconditions for industrialisation.

In the same book, Eric Williams offered an even more politically charged thesis when he explained Britain's legal abolition of slave trading in 1807 and slaveholding in 1833 in strictly economic terms: 'Overproduction in 1807 demanded abolition; overproduction in 1833 demanded emancipation' (1944, 152). In fact, in 1776 Adam Smith had already declared slavery to be an outdated by-product of the mercantile system, and no less a figure than Johann Wolfgang von Goethe accused the British of pursuing economic motives with their abolition of slavery. Up to that point, European outrage had been expressed at the excesses of the slave system but rarely at the system itself, not even by committed Christians and proponents of the

Enlightenment. John Locke and Thomas Jefferson, among others, were involved in slavery. Only in the mid eighteenth century did widespread criticism begin, from Quakers and evangelicals on the one hand, Enlightenment thinkers like Montesquieu on the other. The Danish king became the first to ban slave trading in 1792, and a powerful movement with religious and humanitarian motivations – the first modern political mass movement in history – reached its goal in Britain in 1807 and 1833. In France the National Convention had hesitantly abolished slavery in 1794, but Napoleon, who was related by marriage to people in plantation circles, quickly re-introduced it. The need to maintain a distinction from Britain meant that France did not finally abolish slavery until 1848. Elsewhere, plantation America with its slave labour and slave trading persisted for much longer. The Spanish sugar island of Cuba did not reach its prime until the nineteenth century. In the south of the United States, British industrialisation led to a boom in the cotton plantations, and in Brazil a new upturn was prompted by coffee. Only in 1851 did Brazil, and in 1862 Spain (for Cuba), prohibit the further importation of slaves, which British navy patrols had long been trying to prevent with the help of a broad interpretation of international law. The United States' abolition of slaveholding in 1865 resulted in a civil war; in Cuba emancipation did not come until 1886 and in Brazil until 1888. We know today that Adam Smith and Eric Williams were both equally mistaken: at the time of the anti-slavery agitation the North American, Cuban and Brazilian plantations were working very profitably indeed, and Britain's West Indian sugar plantations continued to prosper after 1800. Their demise is likely to have been the consequence, not the cause, of the emancipation of the slaves. The success of the abolitionists in Britain can thus be explained by a rather chance historical configuration, and if they tried to promote their cause by offering 'modern' economic arguments for free trade and free labour, this should be seen as the veiling of philanthropic interests in economic garb rather than economic interests being disguised as philanthropy, as Williams claimed.

The African Atlantic was not a purely economic phenomenon; its lasting significance, at least, is sociocultural in nature. Although life on the plantations was no patriarchal idyll, as was once asserted, neither was it always a living hell, despite the excesses of exploitation. The notorious formula that a slave only had to live seven years, having then paid off the price of his or her purchase, has been disproved at least as a general rule. In fact, a slave who had survived the Middle Passage and succeeded in acclimatising to the new environment had a life expectancy of several more decades. The fact that the slave population was not initially able to reproduce itself is explained by its composition during the period when it depended on imports. A population of which just one-third were women was not sufficient for this purpose, especially as those women had passed part of their reproductive years, were accustomed to long intervals between births and often arrived without part-ners. As soon as imports ended and the gender ratio settled down, a normal population pyramid arose and the African American population reproduced itself or even increased, with particular success in the United States. That had less to do with improved treatment than with general improvements in living conditions, such as better nutrition, that also affected the white popu-lation. The Africans had often lacked vitamins and minerals even in their home countries, often quite simply common salt, with long-term conse-quences for their health. Investigations of the diet of slaves in the Caribbean, Brazil and North America show similar deficiencies there as well, but differ-ences in longitudinal growth also indicate that some slaves were better nourished than they had been in Africa, at least in terms of quantity. This could depend on the degree to which they were allowed to grow food for themselves: normally, plantation slaves were expected to provide at least some of their own food, although they were given little free time for cultiva-tion. Nevertheless, even under the conditions of the plantation economy, distinct African American societies and cultures were undoubtedly able to develop.

House slaves and slave craftsmen may have enjoyed greater freedom of movement and better chances of manumission. As for the majority of the plantation slaves, slave owners wanted to obtain from them the maximum output of labour, while the slaves' latent resistance contrived to keep this output as low as possible. Occasionally, such resistance became manifest, in the form of insubordination, sabotage, attempts on the owners' lives and revolts. Faced with an African majority, the white minority punished such actions with demonstrative brutality. But from the very beginning of the Spanish Empire, runaway slaves, or *cimarrones*, had been establishing and defending autonomous communities in the American wildernesses. Although there was hostility between Africans and Indians, sometimes deliberately inflamed by the Europeans, escaped slaves and indigenous Americans did also cooperate at times – a nightmare for the whites. In the hinterland of Ecuador's Pacific coast, for example, there was a 5,000-strong community of Africans and Indians known as the 'mulattos of Esmeraldas'; in his efforts to contain them, the governor of Quito was forced to conclude a treaty with their kings. Both Portuguese and Spanish settlers used Indian helpers to track down and destroy the *quilombos*, communities of fugitive slaves living in the rainforests, but there are plenty of indications that even the well-known African kingdom of Palmares, which survived in north-eastern Brazil until 1694, also had Indian inhabitants. On the Caribbean island of St Vincent, escaped slaves formed a group of several thousand 'black Caribs', the

Garifuna, a mixed Indian and African culture speaking the indigenous Aruak language, until the British deported them to Honduras in 1797.

In most cases, the slaves on a particular plantation were very diverse in terms of language and place of origin. It therefore made sense for them to adopt the language and religion of their masters to a greater or lesser extent. However, there was no Protestant slave apostle in the mould of the Jesuit Peter Claver, perhaps because British slaveholders, unlike their Latin counterparts, feared they would have to release any slave who was baptised. Additionally, popular Catholicism was easier to combine with an underlying African religiosity than was the more austere Protestant faith. The Old Testament, with its stories of the people of Israel enslaved in a foreign land and liberated by Moses, was most attractive, until the Anglo-American revivalist movement offered new, ecstatic forms of Protestantism more appealing to the Africans. In terms of religion the Africans in America showed great creativity, just as in general the cultural dynamism of the African Atlantic, persisting to the present day, should not be underestimated. Jazz has long been an accepted part of world cultural heritage, but the same creativity can be found in, among other things, the re-creation of African religion in a Catholic form.

Locally well-represented groups were able to spearhead this process, especially if they had already held cultural authority in Africa. Among the West African slaves of Bahia, the eighteenth-century Catholic sodalities formed the basis of new African temples, or *terreiros*, in the early nineteenth century, first associated with the name 'Candomblé' in 1826. Various groups brought their deities to this religion: Xangô came from Oyo, Yemanjá from the Egba, Oxum from the Ijesha, Oxalá from Ifé, and so on. Alongside these *orishas* of Yoruba theology it proved possible to integrate the *voduns* of the Jejé and the *minkisi* of the Angolans, since the differences were minor. In this way, despite the particular idiosyncrasies of Vodou and Santería, the West Indies saw the emergence of a 'common denominator' of African American religiosity in the cultural exuberance of plantation America. In Brazil Candomblé and, especially, Umbanda (a variation enriched by French Spiritism) still have millions of followers, who in the case of Umbanda increasingly include white Brazilians.

Across the Atlantic in Nigeria, the repercussions of the new African American cults appear to have acted as the catalyst for a common Yoruba identity to emerge. In fact, a high degree of creativity can already be seen in the manner by which Christianity was integrated into existing models of thought in the Kongo Empire of the sixteenth and seventeenth centuries. Christ was regarded as the great chief, the Virgin Mary as an African queen mother and thus Christ's co-regent following the pattern of African kingship.

The concepts of resurrection, heaven and hell were of little interest to the Africans, but all the more intriguing was the cult of the dead, especially that of the former kings. Sacraments and blessings, even wayside crosses, were considered especially powerful *minkisi*, while baptism served as a protection against witchcraft. In these forms, Christianity could be deployed as an additional source of legitimation for royal rule.

To be sure, cultural creativity does not preclude dehumanisation, and that applied to Africans as well. After all, there are indications that the growing demand for slaves emptied human beings of value despite their rising price by making them into commodities. Where manhunts and abduction are everyday practice, human sacrifices may descend into butchery, as was the case in Dahomey. And there is no doubt that the Africans expanded their traditional slave economy, adapting it to its white transatlantic counterpart. In the eighteenth century, there were as many slaves in Africa as there were in America, but by around 1850 there were many more, perhaps around ten million. In some countries there may indeed still be slaves – again a form of Atlantic commonality.

6   New Europes on the North Atlantic and the first decolonisation

For plantation America and the trading empires in Asia, the settlement of Europeans – colonisation in the narrower, traditional sense – played only an auxiliary and marginal role. That was not the case in Spanish America, where originally numerous names in the style of New Spain, New Castile, New Granada, New Extremadura and so on bore witness to a plan to attract European settlers and reproduce a cultural environment familiar to them. Indeed, there was no lack of Spanish immigrants, who brought their own lifestyles and settlement forms from home and radically transformed the cultivated landscape through livestock breeding, previously almost unknown in America, and the cultivation of characteristically Mediterranean crops like wheat and vines. Nevertheless, none of the country names based on the old homeland (city names were a different matter) survived. They were replaced either by earlier denominations, such as Mexico, Peru or Chile, or by new European coinages like Argentina, Brazil or Venezuela. We can take this as an indication that Spanish colonisation did not in fact ultimately create a New Europe, as had been intended, but entered into a symbiosis with the Indian majority population and the environmental conditions, frequently divergent from Europe, to create something new: a synthesis, in typological terms a hybrid between the settlement colony and the colony of rule. In North America, in contrast, although the name New France was fully eliminated by 1763 after the British conquest, 'New England' has remained robust as a culturally meaningful historical notion. Apart from New York and New Hampshire, almost all the names of former colonies are European neologisms, such as Virginia, Pennsylvania or Georgia. The indigenous elements were almost entirely suppressed in both name and fact. Instead, exclusively European settler communities arose that saw themselves not only as a new Europe, but in some cases even as a better one. If the sixteenth-century Spanish missionaries temporarily worked on the basis that the New World would allow a purer Christianity to replace the Old World's degenerate religion, similar notions can be found among the Puritans of New England, and they have persisted in a secularised form in the United States' self-image until the present day.

The New Europes are probably the most significant legacy of European colonialism. They are also radical colonialism, because here the development gap between colonists and the country's previous inhabitants led to those inhabitants' destruction, or at least their systematic marginalisation. In contrast to their Spanish American counterparts, the North American settlers wanted to cultivate the land themselves; its existing owners were therefore dispensable. The fact that New France did not experience the conflicts that New England did in this respect was due less to different models of colonisation than to the proportionate sizes of the groups concerned and the sparse Indian settlement of the lands around the St Lawrence River.

New France in Canada and New Netherland on the Hudson

Having failed to find either a passage to Asia or any attractive commodities apart from the fish of Newfoundland's Grand Banks, Europeans initially showed little interest in northern America. Instead, in the mid sixteenth century the French tried (in vain) to establish themselves in Brazil and Florida. Only when rich men in Europe took to wearing hats again, and Europeans had learned the technique of making felt for these out of beaver fur, did the north-east of America regain its attraction, this time as a source of beaver pelts. After various attempts, the French finally settled on the Atlantic from 1604 onwards, in the Bay of Fundy, the area that would later become New Brunswick and Nova Scotia and that the settlers named 'Acadie'. Acadia was to be harried from start to finish by its English neighbours. At the very beginning of the French colonisation process stood Samuel de Champlain (1567–1635), who would later initiate the colony on the St Lawrence River, Canada proper. In 1608 he founded Quebec City in a bid to pre-empt the Protestant English and Dutch and secure fishery and trade for France. In the course of several journeys of discovery, he advanced southwards as far as Lake Ontario and Lake Huron, still spurred in part by the hope of finding a route to the Pacific. These journeys were made possible by the friendly attitude of the Indians, but because these were Algonquin and Huron (Wendat), in 1609 the French clashed with their opponents, the Iroquois. It was the opening shot in an almost uninterrupted enmity between the French and the Iroquois, closely entwined with the two groups' competition for the fur-trading business and its geography.

In the north, on the St Lawrence, Algonquin joined forces with the French in the fur trade, while furs from the Great Lakes region and the adjacent area to the west fell to an Iroquoian trading people, the Huron, who lived between Lake Huron's Georgian Bay and Lake Simcoe. The Iroquois in the narrower sense, the league of the Five Nations – Seneca, Cayuga, Onondaga, Oneida and Mohawk (joined in 1722 by a sixth, the Tuscarora, immigrating from the south) – between Lake Ontario and the Hudson took up business with France's European rivals, first of all the Dutch, who had formed a colony on the Hudson River.

Still in the service of the Dutch East India Company, in 1609 Henry Hudson had discovered the river that would take his name. In 1614/15, merchants from Amsterdam created a company to handle the fur trade in this area, now known as 'New Netherland', and were granted a short-term monopoly for this purpose by the States-General. When it expired in 1618, there was no difficulty in transferring the claim on New Netherland to the Dutch West India Company, founded in 1621 with a monopoly for the whole of the western hemisphere, which despite its South Atlantic interests was very much aware of the opportunities offered by the fur trade. In 1624 the Company tried for the first time to establish settlers at various points between Connecticut and Delaware, in the hope of consolidating the claim that the English had been disputing since 1622 – in the English view, it was not the mere discovery of lands that justified their possession, but their effective settlement by at least fifty people and their economic exploitation. Among these new bases was the fur-trading station of Fort Orange, established in 1624 south of today's Albany, NY. However, the scattered outposts along the coast could not be sustained, and the Dutch presence was gradually concentrated on the island of Manhattan, which had been bought from Indians in 1626 for goods worth sixty guilders. There, New Amsterdam grew to be the central settlement of the colony. In 1653 it was granted a municipal charter and the right to self-administration. However, once again the costs initially outweighed the profits, so that in 1628/29 the WIC tried to turn the settlement over to private capital. Perhaps based on the model of the *donatários* of Portuguese Brazil, *patroon* landholders were to receive generous land allocations and privileges. In return they were required, at their own expense, to establish settlers, over whom they held manorial rights. Just as in Brazil, the system proved only intermittently effective, so that in 1639 independent settlers were also promised land and the WIC's fur-trade monopoly was abandoned in their favour. Gradually, more immigrants arrived, and in 1655 the energetic governor Pieter Stuyvesant (1647–64) captured the Swedish colony that had been founded on the Delaware in 1637. But New Netherland only just managed to escape disaster in the First Anglo-Dutch War of 1652–54, and in 1664 it was seized by an English fleet during the period of undeclared war at sea, finally being relinquished after the Second Anglo-Dutch War of 1665–67. Since then it has been called New York; a short Dutch occupation during the Third Anglo-Dutch War of 1672–74 remained an isolated episode. The stronger New England had absorbed the weaker New Netherland, a process that would be repeated for New France, although there in the face of far more vigorous resistance.

At first, the Dutch presented the main competition for the French in the fur business. For the Indian cultures, the exchange of furs for European goods held a somewhat different significance from its role among the Europeans, but it was the expansion of European mercantile capitalism that shaped the dynamics of the fur trade. The Europeans not only had an eager market for furs, but also owned the feared firearms, which the Iroquois were able to obtain more easily from the Dutch than their enemies could from the wary French. In 1626, the Iroquois defeated their competitors, the Mohicans, in the upper Hudson Valley, then turned against the Huron, supposedly because the beavers had by then been hunted largely to extinction in Iroquois grounds. The Huron are thought to have been more numerous than the Iroquois confederacy originally, but in 1634–39 they, like the Indians of Latin America, were demoralised and decimated by disease. This was the consequence of the missionaries' focus on the Huron, especially after 1625 when the Jesuits arrived in the area. The link between Christianity and death was evident to the Huron themselves. The better-armed Iroquois were able more or less to extinguish the Huron nation in 1648–50, in campaigns of destruction during which several Jesuits died at the stake. The Iroquois succeeded in securing access to the furs of the west.

With only around 300 inhabitants in 1645, New France was much too weak to halt this train of events. Even so, settlements were founded in Trois-Rivières and Montreal. In 1635 the Jesuits, who until 1659 dominated the Church in the region and also held strong political influence, established a college in Quebec and brought nuns across the Atlantic to educate girls and provide nursing care. This should be seen in the context of the attempts of a new monopoly company for Canada, founded under Richelieu, to create an unambiguously Catholic New France. A manorial system of *seigneuries* was established like that in the mother country, while the parent company left the colony's trade and administration to a subsidiary made up of the settlers under the governor and the Jesuit superior. However, New France was still not really capable of withstanding the attacks of the English or the Iroquois, and was additionally weakened by internal conflicts between the Jesuits and the regular Church hierarchy. Further factors were determined, though vain attempts by the Church leadership to block the sale of liquor to the Indians and limit its catastrophic consequences gained them only unpopularity.

Colbert's ascendancy from 1663 finally brought some consistency into France's colonial policy in general and its Canada policy in particular. The plan was to heap honour on the king and shame on his enemies by making his overseas territory of New France viable at last. The new West India company, which despite thorough propagandistic preparation had the same crypto-royal character as its East India counterpart, limited its efforts to the economy, while politics and administration were now to be placed in the hands of representatives of the Crown: the governor for political and military matters, the intendant for matters of administration, business and finance. New France was to be ruled like a French province, only better. That meant not only the strictest Catholicism and a more efficient, seemingly more humane judicial system, but also (and especially) absolutism. Local self-government was not tolerated even in its most rudimentary form, certainly not the claims of the estates to a political role like that in the mother country. Although the first intendant, Jean Talon (1665–68 and 1670–72), may fairly be regarded as the founder of the new Canada, the status of the governor was in fact far greater than his equivalent in France, especially because the country was constantly reliant on his military skill. The new regime sent a twenty-four-company regiment of regulars to Canada and solved the Iroquois problem by destroying the Indians' villages and stores. In 1667 the Iroquois, additionally afflicted by an outbreak of disease, were persuaded to make a peace that would last well into the 1680s. Four hundred former soldiers were subsequently deployed as peasants under the seigneurship of their officers – in theory, rural Canada was a feudal society. In the eighteenth century it had 180 seigneuries with 8,000 rent-paying peasants. However, the levies and other payments they made were negligible, so that in practice the seigneurs have been described as mere land and settlement agents. In fact, functionally similar institutions can be found both in the medieval German colonisation of central and eastern Europe and in Brazil and New Netherland.

Because the best land lay on the river banks, the seigneurial system gave rise to the typical settlement pattern of Old Canada: farms serried along the bank on narrow lots perpendicular to the river, at times with a second row behind them and manors and churches in between. As a military captain, the seigneur took up the key role in a community in both military and political terms, alongside the priest – for, to the disgust of visiting members of the Enlightenment milieu, the French Canadians had grown to be a closed society led by priests, a set-up that would facilitate their cultural survival under the later English rule. Colbert promoted immigration and sought to remedy the shortage of white housewives by sending poor but respectable girls to the colony. As a result of this policy, the population grew from 3,000 to 10,000 people between 1663 and 1685. Subsequently, in the absence of further significant immigration, it had to rely on its own reproduction. It did so very successfully, thanks to prosperity and favourable living conditions along with a state bonus paid to colonists who married and had several children, and is said to have sometimes reached among the highest net reproductive rates of whites in general. In 1763 there were already 85,000 French Canadians. In 1739, 72,000 ha of farmland was producing over 634,000 hl of grain and sustaining 39,000 head of livestock.

Colbert, a master of dispassionate calculation, had prohibited the colony from further expansion but immediately undermined that ban with an exception most revealing of European colonialism's rivalry for power: expansion was permitted if another power threatened to take possession of the land. In 1670 the English 'Hudson's Bay Company' had been formed and, defying French attacks, it began to build up its north Canadian fur-trading empire on the Bay, an empire that in the nineteenth century would form the core of Canada's northern territories. Unlike other colonial enterprises of the period, the Hudson's Bay Company still exists today, as a retail company operating department stores. More important for the French, however, was expansion in the region of the Great Lakes and points further south. This was propelled by missionaries and trappers until René-Robert Cavelier de la Salle navigated the Mississippi right to its estuary in 1682 and took possession of the land for Louis XIV, as 'Louisiana'. Starting from Canada, a chain of forts was established along the Mississippi and Ohio river systems. Biloxi was founded in 1699, and Mobile on the Gulf coast in 1711. To absorb the costs of these ventures, the new colony was transferred to a series of monopoly-holders from 1712. In 1722 the city of Nouvelle Orléans (founded in 1718) became the colony's heart, in practice independent of Canada.

Canadian expansion was driven by *coureurs de bois*, fur traders (later called *voyageurs*) searching for pelts, and missionaries, especially Jesuits. The Jesuits were pursuing similar goals to those of their colleagues in Iberian America: the Indians were to be made sedentary, 'civilised' and Christianised through the skilful integration of their own culture, which to this end was carefully studied by the missionaries. Sedentary Iroquois groups like the Huron were better suited to that project than the semi-nomadic Algonquin, but even among the Huron Jesuit success was limited, because whereas life in the Jesuit *reducciónes* of Spanish and Portuguese America offered an attractive alternative to serving white masters, the missions of the Canadian *patres* could offer the Indians little protection against their enemies, especially the Iroquois. The French colonial system was anyway not based on Indian servitude or segregation from the whites but, like the Spanish system in its early days, on the idea of assimilation through contact. To be sure, in reality such contact tended to take a negative course, perhaps due less to the lax principles of the *coureurs de bois* now fanning out across the whole of Indian North America, who were held in low moral esteem despite their impressive skill as explorers, than to the demoralising effects of the liquor trade that they and others continued to pursue. In 1724 the Canadian missionary Joseph François Lafitau's work *Mœurs des sauvages amériquains* injected new life into the myth of the Noble Savage, well before the discovery of the South Sea islands (traces can be found in Voltaire, among others), but this may have been only a propagandistically effective overcompensation for the far less rosy reality.

Eighteenth-century New France was in rather good shape. The colony was self-sufficient, building ships and exporting goods, especially furs and fish, to France. As long as it did not have to be defended, it had the further advantage of costing Paris nothing. But if the period between Henri IV and the early part of Louis XIV's reign was dominated by colonial policy goals in the Spanish mould, the conquest of new lands for God and the king and the reproduction of Europe overseas, under Colbert there was a shift in orientation towards the mercantilist goal of a colony from which the mother country could draw as valuable as possible a range of complementary goods for the benefit of its own economy. From this perspective, Canada had less and less to offer as time went on, and French politics and public opinion were increasingly inclined to leave the colony to its own devices and concentrate instead on the mercantilist colonial paragon, the flourishing plantation America of the Caribbean. As a supplier of foodstuffs and related goods to the sugar islands, Canada could not compete with its New England rivals. Its location put it at a serious disadvantage, but most importantly its population of just 85,000 was not enough to defend its enormous terrain against 1.5 million English North Americans, who had carried out no expansion of comparable audacity but who, when conflicts arose, enjoyed the advantage of the interior-line position.

Nevertheless, the French held out for a surprisingly long time when their always latent enmity with the British erupted into a series of wars prompted by European power struggles. It was a conflict that would last, with interruptions, from 1684 until 1763, the 'heroic' era of the Leatherstocking tales. Most of the Indians took the part of the French, with the important exception of the Iroquois, who during those decades often terrorised the larger part of the north-east. As a result of the English settlers' advance across the Appalachians, the focus of the conflict moved to the Ohio region in the eighteenth century, the confrontation over Fort Duquesne, later Fort Pitt (today's Pittsburgh), being particularly fierce. As prime minister, William Pitt the Elder sealed the matter with a massive deployment of regular troops; 1759 saw the fall of Quebec, and 1760 that of Montreal. In the 1763 Treaty of

Paris, France lost Canada (except two small islands off Newfoundland) to Great Britain and Louisiana to Spain as compensation for Florida, which Spain had been forced to cede to Britain. New France had become British. Would it now be swallowed up by New England as New Netherland had been before it, and as New Netherland itself had swallowed up New Sweden?

New England and the building of British North America

Just as the Spanish had their *reconquista*, so the English too had a kind of previous colonial experience upon which they could draw in the New World: the conquest of Ireland. Although Ireland had been made a kingdom, institutionally modelled on the kingdom of England, it remained subjected to its English neighbour. To an increasing extent as time went on, only its English inhabitants counted. Waves of them were settled in commercially organised 'plantations' after expropriations of the Irish, while the Irish themselves were regarded as inferior barbarians in need, first and foremost, of civilisation. Even their common religion ceased to be significant when the English adopted Protestantism and regarded papism as merely a further proof of Irish inferiority. More than a few of the first Englishmen to arrive in North America had accumulated experience in the battles and businesses of Ireland on how to handle on the one hand colonists, on the other a barbarian environment. At the same time, there was also no lack of English people who switched sides to join the Irish or Indians and felt perfectly at home in their new cultural surroundings. Despite – or perhaps because of – their background in Ireland, Raleigh and his kind were adventurers in the Spanish conquistador mould rather than Dutch-style, soberly calculating businessmen. Their aim was to get rich by plundering precious metals or seizing mastery over land, neither of which was feasible in North America. That did not prevent their propaganda deploying economic arguments as part of its wide spectrum of justifications for the colonial venture. Richard Hakluyt's 'A Discourse Concerning Western Planting' of 1584 argued, among other things, that America could provide England with a market for wool, supply cheaper ship-building materials, and above all offer tropical fruits, wines and other goods that England did not produce itself. Not only could the gospel be preached in America, but Protestant religious refugees from other countries could be lured there and England's own indigents transported out of harm's way. And in the case of war, English youth could use America to learn and hone their skills. These notions would recur again and again in the colonial discourse of subsequent centuries. Particularly noteworthy is the population policy argument, because this was the first case in which colonisation was driven by the idea of superfluous population – specifically, the poor, vagrant and criminal population, whose number had grown alarmingly. Over time, it became common practice for courts to pass the sentence of transportation to America. In the period 1718–75 alone, 50,000 convicts were sent to work on the tobacco plantations of Virginia and Maryland. For the better-off, it was dissatisfaction with the religious and state regime at home that occasioned emigration. A group of strict Calvinists, the Puritans, objected to the 'papist' line of the Anglican established church; rising taxes and the intervention of state authority caused unrest – but for emigration to start in earnest, further conditions were necessary: the peace with Spain in 1604 and the commercialisation of colonisation through the instrument of the joint-stock company. Within the sphere of interest to which it laid claim, Spain certainly did not recognise English colonisation, yet now had little choice but to accept it. And while the English had previously, like the Dutch and other nations, countered the wide-ranging claims of the Iberian powers by the right of de facto occupation and settlement, they now used theological and juridical exegesis to develop universalist ideas very similar to those of the Latins, presenting themselves as the new chosen people and America as the new Canaan, whose inhabitants – as heathen barbarians – had fundamentally no right to the land.

Soon after peace was concluded, merchants and politicians set up the Virginia Company for the colonisation of New England. In 1607 Jamestown was established on Chesapeake Bay, only to teeter constantly on the brink of collapse due to disease and hunger. A certain John Rolfe became the settlement's saviour when, in 1612, he introduced the West Indian variety of the tobacco plant, which would soon prove to be the colony's sole but prodigious economic success story, and in 1614 married Pocahontas, the daughter of the local chief, thus temporarily improving relations with the Indians. The Company's management in England, reorganised and restaffed on a number of occasions, additionally resolved to distribute private land on a generous scale and to attract potential immigrants – hitherto deterred by the draconian local criminal law – by promising them a right to participate in the settlement's legislation. In 1619 America's first 'representative assembly' met, in the Jamestown church. Because Pocahontas and her father had died, nothing now prevented the disappointed Indians from attacking the settlements, with great success, in 1622. The Company was bankrupt by then, and no longer capable of taking defensive action. As a result the colony was taken over by the Crown and placed in the hands of a governor and council; for the time being, there was no more talk of a house of representatives. However, the Crown too had little money to spare and thus remained dependent on the settlers' cooperation, so that the people's representation was convened again in 1627 and in 1639 received official recognition.

Attempts to settle the north failed at first, until in 1620 a group of 101 people, mainly radical separatist Puritans, arrived on the *Mayflower* carrying a patent from the Virginia Company. Before founding their colony, Plymouth near Cape Cod, they signed the 'Mayflower Compact', a kind of social contract that is regarded as the founding document of American democracy, even though it could equally well be read as an act of submission to the leadership of a few individuals. With help from the Indians, Plymouth survived, but not much more than that. The settlement of Salem was founded in 1626 by another group further north, but a real change in fortune only came with the subsequent establishment of the Massachusetts Bay Company, whose influential shareholders managed to secure it a royal charter of its own in 1629. The Company's shrewd Puritan members bought out the others and quietly moved the headquarters to America when, in 1630, they set off for the colony with around 1,000 people and founded Boston as the core of the new colony of Massachusetts. Over the following decade the colony received an average of 1,600 further immigrants every year, so that in 1640 it and its offshoots numbered 11,500 inhabitants, compared with 10,000 in Virginia and a mere 270 in New France at this time. In line with its charter, the colony, now identical with the Company, was administered by a governor and his assistants, elected by the General Court. This body, which met four times a year to make resolutions, rapidly evolved from a stockholders' meeting into an assembly of all the settlement's full citizens or 'freemen', later of their delegates. Only full members of a parish of the Congregational church, which held sole sway in the colony, could attain the status of full citizens – there was no question of democracy, let alone religious tolerance. Rather, the system of rule followed the republican 'mixed constitution' that was much advocated at the time, a combination of monarchical, aristocratic and democratic elements, while the Church made the most rigorous intolerance a matter of principle; after all, it argued, the immigrants had moved to the New World to establish a strict religious and political order in line with their own ideals. Dissidents like Roger Williams, a proponent of religious freedom, were banished. This state of affairs led to further settlements being founded in a matter of years, quickly giving rise to the independent colonies of Rhode Island and Connecticut, while Massachusetts first turned its attention to gaining control over the colonies to its north, New Hampshire and Maine.

However, refuge in America was sought not only by Puritans but also by Catholics, likewise suffering persecution in England in the early seventeenth century. The Catholic Lord Baltimore hoped to turn this fact to financial advantage through profitable colonial investments, but Virginia rejected a Catholic master. Instead, he used his good connections at court to procure a charter for the neighbouring territory in 1632, naming it Maryland – after the

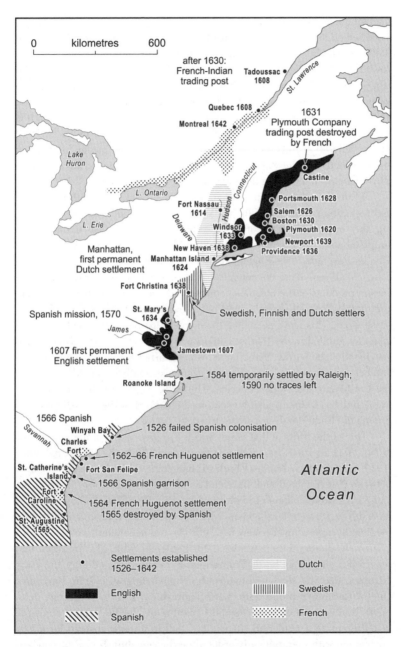

Map 9   European settlements in North America, 1526–1642

English queen but with Catholic overtones of Marian devotion. This charter, modelled on the privileges of the medieval county palatine of Durham, made Baltimore and his heirs the colony's 'absolute lords and proprietors' and laid down the establishment of a feudal system. But once Catholics ceased to be persecuted in England, the settlement process begun in 1634 could no longer get by without Protestants. This was already generating conflicts in the 1638 meeting of the assembly also established by the charter. The English Revolution intensified unrest, which the Proprietor tried to buffer in 1649 with a 'Toleration Act'. In vain: in 1651 he was driven out by his Puritan enemies, although he was reinstated in 1657 by the conservative dictator Oliver Cromwell, enabling the Toleration Act to come into force.

While the other colonies found a modus vivendi with both revolution and restoration, Massachusetts baulked at the latter, and also took to violating the navigation laws of 1660, 1663 and 1673 that updated and supplemented the English Commonwealth's first Navigation Act of 1651. This had excluded non-English ships from traffic between England and its colonies; all imports to the colonies had to be carried out via England, while certain products of the colonies, 'enumerated commodities' including sugar, cotton, tobacco and indigo, could only be exported to England or English possessions. This move cemented the mercantilist policy that had long been taken for granted in the Iberian nations and France, but it was also directed specifically against the Netherlands, which during the seventeenth century had become a kind of global shipping agent, especially as regards trade with the Caribbean and North America. The three Anglo-Dutch wars between 1652 and 1674 should also be seen in the context of the British policy of driving the Netherlands out of the American trade.

One of the fruits of that policy was the appropriation of the new colony of New York in 1664. Its owner was the Duke of York, the later King James II of England, whose brother Charles II had granted him Maine and the area between New England and Maryland as his property in 1663. In 1664 the Duke gave two members of his retinue land south of New York, which they named New Jersey after the home island of one of them. Resold many times, the land became a royal colony in 1702. The two beneficiaries of the Duke's grant were among the eight speculator noblemen who, also in 1663, had received a charter as Lords Proprietors of a colony named after the king, Carolina, that was designed to absorb colonists migrating from Barbados. One of Carolina's proprietors, Lord Shaftesbury, with his secretary John Locke drafted a set of 'Fundamental Constitutions' for the colony, aiming to 'avoid erecting a numerous democracy' and to provide instead for a new aristocracy with hierarchically ordered land ownership. It proved impossible to plan much more than the capital city, Charlestown; as so often, the free-for-all of a buyer's market prevailed, demand remaining stunted by a lack of profits. The north was settled primarily by migrants leaving Virginia, and in 1701 the colony had to be divided once and for all. By this time, the more usual system of government with a governor and assembly had long since become established in both North and South Carolina.

As one of the king's creditors, in 1681 the influential Quaker William Penn (1644–1718) was able to acquire a charter as the Proprietor of 'Pennsylvania'. It was designed to be a refuge for his persecuted co-religionists (who were still threatened by execution in Massachusetts) and a model Christian commonwealth, but also a good business opportunity. What had originally been an extremely egalitarian draft constitution was accordingly revised along more oligarchic and plutocratic lines. By this time print technology had made propaganda possible on an unprecedented scale, and the colony's success was considerable. In 1685 it already had 8,000 inhabitants – Massachusetts and Virginia by now had over 40,000 – and its capital, Philadelphia, soon began to compete with New York and Boston for the position of prime trading port. The land for the first settlements on the Delaware, which Penn, in contrast to other colonists, had bought from the Indians under proper contracts for the sum of £1,200, was among the most fertile on the eastern coast. To gain access to the sea, Penn acquired the area that is now Delaware from the Duke of York. Geographically separated from Pennsylvania, it was given a separate administration and in 1775 became independent.

In 1677 Massachusetts had been able to put a legal stamp on its takeover of Maine by buying the proprietary rights; Maine would only become an independent member of the United States in 1820. New Hampshire had been taken over by the Crown from the proprietor's heirs in 1679 and made into a separate royal colony. The new king, James II, also tried to gather all the colonies between Maine and New Jersey, especially the notoriously recalcitrant Massachusetts, into a 'Dominion of New England' that would be ruled by royal officers and a governor general, largely abolishing the existing self-administration. But the Glorious Revolution of 1688/89 in England thwarted this plan. The English developments reinforced stormy reactions to the project and even uprisings in the colony, for not only did the new measures smack of absolutism, but the Catholic James II was also open to accusations of colluding with the colony's arch-enemies, the Indians and the French. After all, it was only in 1675/76 that Massachusetts had weathered the last desperate rebellion of its region's Indians during 'King Philip's War', which ended with the Indians being more or less completely wiped out. Their leader, Metacomet, had received assistance from northern tribes, suspected by the colonists of having been backed by the French; the Iroquois had refused to offer their services. After skilful negotiations in London, Massachusetts obtained a compromise and in 1691 was given a new charter, William III's attention being absorbed with quite other concerns in the European arena. It became a 'normal' colony with a royal governor, a franchise based no longer on Puritan orthodoxy but on property, and a precept, albeit restricted, of religious freedom. In fact the theocratic mentality was anyway losing traction at this time; the 'Yankee' was replacing the 'Puritan' as the typical New Englander. In the other colonies of New England nothing changed, except that Massachusetts now incorporated the Pilgrim Fathers' bankrupt Plymouth.

New York was a different matter. Among a population still waiting for the assembly it had been promised in 1683, the fear of Indians and Catholics triggered a revolt headed by the merchant Jacob Leisler, whose 'committee of safety' took over the regiment. This development was not to the taste of the Anglo-Dutch landowners and commercial oligarchy, who were better connected in London. In 1691 the colony was given a 'charter of liberties' with an assembly, and Leisler was executed. In Maryland, the Catholic Proprietor was suspected of agitating against the new regime in England, and was deposed in an insurrection. The Crown's reaction was to confirm his economic authority, but not his political powers. In the Carolinas, too, the Proprietors' star was fading. Their right to govern was questioned by the assembly's call for the right of legislative initiative. The renewed requirement that all officers must be Anglicans was impossible to implement, and it also became clear that the Proprietors were no match for the external threat from Indians, Spaniards and French. In 1729 they were obliged to cede their rights to the Crown once and for all.

The colony of Georgia, bordering the Carolinas to the south, was created not only as a rampart against Indians and Spaniards, but above all as a 'philanthropical' political project. In 1732 the colony's trustees received a charter empowering them to settle released convicts. Parliament contributed financial grants, and in return the colony was to be passed over to the Crown in 1752. The original idea was to prevent large-scale landholding and slavery, liquor and democracy, but circumstances led, as usual, to a 'normalisation': in 1750 slavery was officially permitted and an assembly approved. Georgia had aligned itself with the general trend.

Normalisation meant first and foremost that all the colonies developed variations on the same political system. Certainly, at local level the institutions familiar from the mother country had been re-created in very divergent ways, depending not least on the respective population size and settlement density. In New England, for example, there were elected town councils, whereas elsewhere such councils were recruited by co-optation and the county officers generally appointed by the governor (in England itself the local government of the day was, if anything, even more oligarchic). At colony level, there were now always the central organs of a governor, a council and an assembly, the right to vote for which was based on a property qualification. It is probable that an average of at least 50 per cent of white men in the colonies had the right to vote, more than in Britain. The assembly was responsible for the colony's legislation and especially for approving taxation. These duties were uncontroversial under English legal principles, but the same could not be said of the assemblies' ambition to allocate and control spending, an aspiration that grew out of the right to approve taxation, as it has always done in the history of representative bodies. In this dispute the position of the assemblies was strengthened, and that of the governor weakened, by the arrangements for paying the governors' salaries: the Crown did not as a rule pay these salaries itself, but had them paid by the assemblies, which consistently refused to reserve a fixed amount of funding for the purpose. The governor was appointed by the Crown, or in the remaining two proprietary colonies, Pennsylvania and Maryland, by the Proprietor; only in Rhode Island and Connecticut was the governor elected by the assembly. Strictly speaking, the governor actually had a stronger role than the king in the mother country, since he was the Crown's representative, the head of the executive and the judiciary (which was less independent in the colonies than in England), the commander in chief and the vice-admiral. In practice, however, his apparently absolute power was restricted both by his financial dependence on the assembly and by the fact that he could not himself distribute the highest offices and the seats in his usually twelve-person council; these were granted directly by the Crown to the colonial oligarchy. Only in Rhode Island and Connecticut, again, were the councillors elected. This made it difficult for the governor to build up a body of reliable supporters, even if the oligarchy generally found cooperation with the Crown to be in its best interest. The council fulfilled the functions of the English upper house, the privy council and the cabinet all at once – it participated in government and formed the highest court (together with the governor) and the assembly's upper chamber (without the governor). Overall, it was thus a miniature and simplified reproduction of Great Britain's core political institutions, similar to the Irish version, though that was substantially more complete.

The economy and society of British North America

The New Europe in British North America was a great success, not only politically but also economically, socially and culturally. In 1760 the total colonial population numbered 1.6 million, of whom 1.3 million were white and 0.3 million were Africans; in 1780 the total was 2.7 million, including 2.15 million whites and 0.55 million Africans. An important factor in the population increase was lower mortality and thus high natural growth, thanks to improved living conditions and the absence of the demographic disasters caused by disease, but immigration was also crucial. Curiously, we know more about the forced migration from Africa than we do about white immigration, for which only rather dubious estimates are available. In both the seventeenth and the eighteenth centuries, refugees from religious persecution and economic misery moved to America. Originally, when New England saw a population growth of 600 per cent in 1660–1720, the emigration of surplus, potentially religiously and politically undesirable people had been supported in England, but emigration dropped in the eighteenth century. A large population was now regarded as a rich resource, religious persecution had eased and the standard of living was beginning to rise. It seems that only around 75,000 people left England for America between 1700 and 1760, but other sources of migration now came to the fore: 20,000 Scots, 10,000 Huguenots, and especially Germans, Swiss and Ulster Scots. In Germany there was systematic advertising for emigration, to the chagrin of the authorities. As well as general population pressure, it was the recatholicisation of the Palatinate and the effects of the wars with France that drove many Germans from the country. First came the members of sects, then large numbers of Lutherans and Reformed Protestants. By 1760 German emigrants are thought to have numbered 100,000, rising to 135,000 by 1775, mainly clustered in the middle colonies. The destitute could fund their passage as indentured servants. In 1760, one third of Pennsylvania's population was of German descent, and xenophobic reactions by the Anglo-Americans were not long in coming, despite the Germans' general eagerness to assimilate. No less a person than Benjamin Franklin asked: 'Why should the Palatine Boors be suffered to swarm into our settlements, and by herding together establish their language and manners to the exclusion of ours?' In the same period, around 100,000 formerly Scottish settlers from the north of Ireland arrived, under pressure equally from English economic policy and the Anglican church. They had high hopes of life in Massachusetts, but when the colony's Congregationalists discovered that the newcomers were Presbyterians, their church was burnt down and a law passed to discourage further immigrants. Only in Pennsylvania could the Ulster Scots expect to avoid discrimination, but there they had no chance of acquiring any land. They therefore moved to the frontier, together with German-speaking and other English-speaking outsiders, and in some cases later edged into the hinterland of Virginia and Carolina. Unlike the Quakers, they regarded the Indians as lawless and considered it disgraceful that such idle fellows had left so much good land unexploited for so long. It is little wonder that strained relations developed along the Indian frontier in the Appalachians, later in the region of the Ohio and its tributaries.

In any case the relationship of the settlers in British America with the Indians was generally anything but harmonious, even though – or precisely because – the English did not, like the Spanish, automatically regard the indigenous people as vassals but as standing outside the law, in extreme cases almost as autonomous subjects of international law. That implied not so much respect as antagonistic alterity. Despite grandiose declarations about spreading the gospel, missionary activity was in fact rare, few groups having the requisite money or inclination. It remained limited to isolated and ineffective, though in themselves remarkable, initiatives like that of the missionary John Eliot in Massachusetts or the Moravians in Pennsylvania. More widespread was the Puritan ideology that said the new 'chosen people' must take their 'promised land' from the 'new Canaanites'. The ideological agenda was dominated by the rapidly growing settler population's hunger for land. Because there was no comparable discourse among the few French settlers, the Indians understandably preferred to stick to these. But even where land acquisition proceeded peacefully, as in the case of William Penn, it was founded on a momentous sociocultural misunderstanding, one that reappears again and again in the history of colonialism: like other semi-nomads and small-scale planters, the North American Indians recognised only a more or less collective land ownership, certainly not the notion of private property as tied to a specific plot in the European sense. In New England, the fence thus became an emblem of the region's irreversible Europeanisation. When Indians let Europeans cultivate land, the two sides were working on different assumptions, and the Indians were justifiably outraged when they were subsequently confronted with the claim to exclusivity entailed by the European concept of property.

In these circumstances, the technological and logistical superiority of the whites meant that, unlike in Latin America, the demise of the Indians was a foregone conclusion. They might win a battle but never, except with the help of England's European foes, a war; when the English (later the Americans) had no more white opponents on the continent, the Indians' fate was sealed. It is possible that the implacable nature of this struggle gave rise to, or at least generalised, those cruel customs of war that lend the Wild West genre its excitement. Taking scalps, at least, was a custom of Indian origin, but it was taken over and encouraged by the whites.

The demographic structure, culture, society and economy of the colonies was anything but homogeneous. For example, the various new immigrant groups contributed additional nuances to an already disunified religious map. In 1750, there were 465 Congregationalist parishes, concentrated in New England; 289 Anglican ones concentrated in Virginia and Maryland; 233 Presbyterian ones clustering in Pennsylvania, New Jersey and New York; 138 Lutheran ones, over half of which were in Pennsylvania; 132 Baptist ones with focal points in Rhode Island and Pennsylvania. Then there were German Reformed in Pennsylvania, Dutch Reformed in New York, Catholics in Maryland and Pennsylvania, and many more. Even without the 'Great Awakening' led by eighteenth-century Protestants, religious pluralism and the centrality of the lay element – if only because of the lack of trained pastors – would have had their invigorating effect. American universities show the traces of this pluralism even today. The Congregationalists founded Harvard College in 1636, and the Anglicans followed in 1693 with William and Mary College, Williamsburg. Yale in New Haven, founded in 1701, was designed to train more orthodox Congregationalists than could be provided by the now liberal Harvard, while in 1746 Presbyterians created a college in New Jersey that would later become Princeton University. In New York, the paralysing deadlock of Anglicans and Presbyterians meant that King's College, founded in 1754 and the germ of the later Columbia University, remained non-sectarian, as did the Academy of Philadelphia (today's University of Pennsylvania), founded by the Enlightenment thinker Benjamin Franklin.

It is no coincidence that the south is absent from this list. It was sparsely populated and had a steeper social pyramid, due not least to its numerous black slaves, who endowed their owners not only with wealth but also with status. In 1770 the ratio of white to black in North Carolina was 2:1, in South Carolina 2:3, in Georgia 6:5. The south was part of plantation America – but the New Englanders, where the black population was only 1–3 per cent, were North America's slave traders. The slave business was only one component of their extensive trading activity, however. And if North America's New Europe was largely agrarian, neither in New England nor in the other colonies did it conform with the romantic image of the colonist as an independently self-sufficient tiller of the virgin soil. Rather, we see the colonists quickly integrating themselves into Europe's global trade, thus creating a major source of both American and British prosperity. By the end of the colonial period, the estimated average income of the Americans was already many times that of the developing nations today, and 10–20 per cent of it came from the profits of exports. On the other hand, the Americans spent an average of one third of their income on purchases from Britain, a substantial incentive for British manufacturing. But if North America's imports differed little across the board, its exports must be seen in terms of regional distinction, an overlapping categorisation into four groups having proved a useful framework: New England to Connecticut; the middle colonies from Connecticut to Maryland; the Chesapeake colonies or 'Upper South' from Maryland to North Carolina; and the 'Lower South' from North Carolina to Georgia.

New England required countless items from the mother country and produced nothing at home that would pay for them. The New Englanders thus firstly tried to manufacture the goods themselves; secondly managed to sell those export articles rejected by England in the West Indies and in southern Europe, earning money to pay for their imports; and thirdly focused on the service sector, specifically shipping. This structure made New England so similar to Old England that a tense relationship of latent competition was bound to arise. It is no accident that New England is where the War of Independence broke out, though the limited status of colonial manufacturing should be attributed less to mercantilist prohibitions by the mother country than to England's ability to supply the same goods more efficiently and cheaply. In the colonies the production factors of labour and capital were comparatively expensive, unlike land, which was cheap. As a result, the sectors that flourished were those exploiting the raw materials from that land: mills and, especially, timber processing. There was massive production of barrels, which were used at the time as transport containers for all sorts of goods, especially in the West Indies. In the eighteenth century shipbuilding blossomed, and in 1775 one third of England's 7,000 ships had been built in America. The New Englanders carried out 75 per cent of their English trade on their own ships. Added to this was the processing of iron ore and of West Indian imports. In 1770 the colonies had twenty-six sugar refineries and 140 rum distilleries. But New England's really big business went in the reverse direction, supplying the West Indies with fish, meat, grain and wood products; it was when the British authorities tried to squeeze more taxes out of these activities that the War of Independence erupted. Fish, especially cod, was also sold in southern Europe, and opened up channels for further business. Ironically enough, the arch-Protestant 'codfish aristocracy' of Boston supplied arch-Catholic southern Europe with its fasting staple, stockfish. However, this official trade probably accounted for only a third of revenue: another third came from coastal trade and smuggling, and the remaining third from the invisible profits of the service sector.

The middle colonies turned out to be successful imitators of New England, thanks especially to their fertile soil and the grain it yielded. The grain was likewise exported to the West Indies and southern Europe, although in this case American and British ships shared the transport business. On Chesapeake Bay the picture was different: its exports consisted mainly of tobacco that was shipped on British vessels by British merchants.

These merchants were often also the creditors of the tobacco plantations, operated with African slave labour, and it was from their ranks that some of the great bankers of the nineteenth century arose. The extensive credit system created additional purchasing power, and was necessary for as long as the mercantile system kept cash scarce in the colonies and London prohibited the issuing of paper money in its stead. The indebtedness of the Virginian elite, especially, may have further contributed to revolutionary resentment. In the Lower South, the main export articles were rice and indigo from the plantations of South Carolina; North Carolina and Georgia supplied South Carolina with foodstuffs and became almost its economic sub-colonies. As a whole, by the end of the colonial period the merchandise trade of British North America probably showed a substantial deficit, which was balanced out by earnings from the service sector and political, especially military, spending by Britain. British attempts to pass these costs on to the colonies themselves were at the root of the colonial independence movement. Nevertheless, the system worked to the benefit of both parties, for even after gaining independence the United States remained a good customer of its former mother country – if anything, the volume of such trade actually rose appreciably. On the other hand, American demand contributed substantially to Britain's prosperity, even if its scale was not large enough to have engendered industrialisation, as was once thought.

The first decolonisation

As early as 1748, the man who would later become the reforming controller general of France, Turgot, compared settlement colonies with fruits that cling to the tree of the mother country until they are ripe, when they will fall through their own weight or on being shaken. Evidently this ripeness consists, on the one hand, in the colonial community achieving dimensions sufficient for it to develop significant interests of its own and, on the other, in the existence of a sufficiently numerous political elite – an elite as defined by the mother country's sociocultural yardsticks, that is: one that that has become familiar with the mother country's instruments of power and learnt to wield them against it. The factor connecting these two aspects is the consciousness of a separate identity, an 'imagined' community that defines itself not least by delimiting itself from other communities, in the present case from the imagined alterity of the 'mother country'. In the decolonisations of the twentieth century, the model of the nation state was to play the crucial role in this process, accentuated by the racial element of national self-determination: the belief that it is self-evidently preferable to be ruled badly by people of the same skin colour and culture than to be ruled well by foreigners. In the late eighteenth century this was not yet an issue. The inhabitants of the American colonies were white people whose ancestors had come from the mother countries, or at least from Europe. Accordingly, the colonists saw themselves as American English, French, Spaniards or Portuguese with interests that deviated to only a limited extent from those of the European centres and that could, if those interests were taken adequately into consideration, easily continue to coexist with the mother countries under the same imperial roof. It was not only the colonies that did not yet have a sense of national identity: in Europe too such an identity was only just beginning to take shape. In both cases, the community that bestowed identity was as yet more regional in nature. Settlers in British and Spanish America alike identified with their individual colony, not with an overarching entity. It was thus pivotal to subsequent developments that in North America precisely this kind of overarching unity came into being and, after a bloody civil war, consolidated itself in the nineteenth century, whereas similar endeavours in Spanish America foundered on the greater force of regional identities. Even in British America it was by no means predictable that the conflict with the mother country would culminate in independence, certainly not in independence with a new nation, the first large-scale federal state in history. To reach such a point, the preconditions were those very specific, individual events and interests that distinguish the various decolonisation processes historically in spite of all their regularities and common ground.

In British North America, the issue at stake was initially a considerable tightening of political and fiscal control from the mother country during and after the Seven Years' War, in line with the mercantilist system now well established in Britain. When the emerging conflicts of interest were articulated politically, it became clear that the mother country and the colonies no longer shared the same political goals, making it impossible to retain a common basis of understanding. It was not the colonies that had changed, but the mother country, where new views of parliament and of the empire now prevailed. In France, Spain and Portugal, too, some decades later, innovations in the mother country would trigger events in the colonies. The first white decolonisation was certainly not initiated by an aggressive colonial desire for independence.

The disappearance of the French from North America in 1763 meant the loss of an external threat that had welded colonies and mother country together. However, the Crown, by taking control of the Indian and fur-trading country, inherited the role of the French and prevented the colonists from continuing their westwards advance. Although colonial self-government had gained confidence during the Seven Years' War, it was still not taken quite seriously by the British professional soldiers. After the war, London was inclined to ask the colonists to pay up, since they had benefited from the substantial sums of money that had been pumped into the defence of the colonies, to the detriment of Britain's national debt. It was British taxpayers who now had to bear the cost, while the tax burden was far lower in the colonies. In 1764 import duties on goods from the West Indies – raw materials for sugar and rum production – were halved, but at the same time a first campaign to control smuggling was launched, and vigorously implemented without trial by jury. This injured both the Americans' wallets and their sense of right and wrong: an explosive combination, as it turned out. In 1765 the stamp tax on printed matter and official documents was introduced, bringing the mother country rich returns, and in 1767 new duties were imposed on imports from Britain. After vehement protests both these measures were largely rescinded, but with an explicit note by the British Parliament that it possessed unlimited authority to legislate on the colonies, which were not represented in Westminster. However, the colonists' slogan 'No taxation without representation' was based on a different, and older, understanding of parliamentary representation, according to which the parliamentarian's task was to act specifically in line with the views of his electors – an idea at times not too far from the imperative mandate practised in earlier assemblies of estates. In mid-eighteenth-century Britain, the more 'modern' doctrine of virtual representation had taken hold, according to which Parliament, once elected, had no further direct reference to the electors but embodied the whole nation corporatively, and was indeed identical with the political nation. The 'Americans', like the Irish, were part of that body, but were counted as second-class citizens over whom Great Britain's political nation could, in line with its parliamentary theory, adjudicate without their participation. This political justification of the hated fiscal and political measures would rule out compromise and ultimately provoke the independence struggle.

In 1773 the East India Company, heading for crisis, obtained the right to ship its tea directly to America instead of having to take it via England. This change would have lowered prices to undercut not only the legal tea trade but even tea smuggling, and thus opened up the prospect, politically threatening for the colonists, that the population would accept the cheaper tea and with it the customs duties on tea that had been levied since 1767 as a way of symbolically underscoring British sovereignty. In protest, the tea was thrown into the sea by activists dressed, in an interesting symbolic statement of American identity, as Indians. From this point on, British criminal laws, along with American boycotts of British trade and administration, ushered in an escalation that led to the outbreak of war in 1775. The well-organised

'Patriots' systematically mobilised their forces and terrorised the pro-British 'Loyalists', who were ultimately driven out (many settled in Ontario, Canada). This did not, however, mean that the Continental Congress of representatives of all the colonies that assembled in 1775 immediately set independence as its goal, even though Thomas Paine's 1776 pamphlet *Common Sense* threw an incendiary spark into the decision-making process. It was the House of Commons' refusal to enter into dialogue, the necessity of setting up a new order in place of the disintegrating old one, and the hope of finding foreign-policy allies that paved the way for the 1776 Declaration of Independence, the text of which combined a medieval revocation of vassalage with an Enlightenment programme of human rights. The extensive and decentralised nature of the colonies made it difficult to defeat even these rather inefficient revolutionaries. In the end, France's entry into the war was what tipped the scales – incidentally also helping to trigger the French Revolution that would follow just a few years later by increasing the French national debt to a critical point. The Treaty of Paris in 1783 made the United States independent. Its borders were to be formed by the Mississippi and the Great Lakes; an attempt to conquer Canada had failed. Although Britain did not grant the French Canadians any representation, it had recently begun to respect their Catholic religion, so that they felt more comfortable under British rule than in the company of the anti-papist southerners.

By 1776–80 almost all the states had created new constitutions and bills of rights, and the Articles of Confederation ratified in 1777–81 thus created a confederacy rather than a federal state. The central administration was allowed to exercise only those rights expressly delegated to it, in particular foreign policy, Indian affairs and coinage standards. It had neither any tax income of its own nor the authority to implement central resolutions against the individual states. A new, more strongly unitary federal constitution was drawn up in 1787 and came into effect in 1788, under the impact of power-conscious nationalism (especially among the officers of the army), a need for a common foreign-trade policy in order to overcome the post-war depression, and the elites' fear of too much democracy, of the political influence of the masses threatening order and property. The system now involved a strict separation of powers, with a representative principle that accorded influence to the people, as the state's fictive sovereign, only at elections. The federation was supposed to take over the stabilising function previously fulfilled by the Crown. A new federal capital – belonging to none of the states, and designed from scratch on the drawing board – symbolised the new political system. After conflicts of interest and revolution, the Declaration of Independence, internal feuding and war, history's first decolonisation had been brought to a successful conclusion with the creation of a constitution, a state and a nation. It set the standard for all subsequent decolonisations and established the necessary phases once and for all. One of the lessons is that the success of decolonisation never depends solely on developments internal to the colony or the attitudes of its inhabitants. Rather, there is always a 'triangle' of forces, where a role is played secondly by political developments in the mother country and the attitude of its government, and thirdly by the specific configuration of international politics, not least the enemies of the relevant colonial power. The Americans of the eighteenth century received help from the French just as the Vietnamese of the twentieth century received help from the Russians.

The example of the United States, the 'leaven of freedom', thus did not immediately trigger revolutionary developments in the rest of America, even though those areas were by no means devoid of tension. In Spanish America, the economic upswing had fed a growing self-confidence among the American-born Spaniards, the 'creoles', or *criollos*, vis-à-vis the Spanish of the mother country; they now liked to call themselves 'Americans' rather than 'Spaniards'. However, the reforms introduced by enlightened absolutism had if anything increased the priority accorded to Europeans in appointments to administrative offices, a principle designed to strengthen the cohesion of the empire. It was suggested that criollos receive appointments in the mother country in compensation, but this idea failed to materialise, and the proposal – derived from developments in North America – to establish three American kingdoms under Spanish princes and imperial rule from Europe was, likewise, never a serious option. Frustration spread. Nevertheless, rebellions and attempted rebellions found little support among the criollos, who often regarded these as tantamount to a threat from the Indian underclass – in which case the criollos found it safer to combine forces with the mother country. In the end, the almost completely white Argentina was the most 'revolutionary' of the Latin American countries, while Peru, which had a large Indian population and had experienced a significant Indian uprising in 1780, was 'liberated' last. And in Mexico, popular rebellion ironically led to the establishment of a conservative regime that allied royalist and independence-minded elites. In other words, if Latin America did not become a New Europe in the narrow sense, this was precisely why its decolonisation proceeded largely without the participation of the Indian masses, or even against them, in a kind of civil war between factions of the white elite. Here as in North America, decolonisation remained a white affair. Although in theory the Indian even then served as an ideological figure emblematising Latin American identity, in practice Indians continued to be excluded from the political process for the long term. Indeed, those remnants of the Indian protection policy that the Enlightenment had left in place were to fall victim to the fashion of liberalism and the power politics of the new criollo elite.

There is, though, one exception in the context of this first white decolonisation. In the French western part of Haiti, Saint Domingue, the whites, 6 per cent of the population, had hardly staked their claim to emancipation within the French Revolution when they were swept away in 1791 by a great uprising of the African slaves, 88 per cent of the population. In 1799–1801 the slaves' leader, François Dominique Toussaint L'Ouverture, seemed on the point of realising a configuration still of interest today, the combination of an African regime with a European-style economy, across the whole of the island. Napoleon was able to eliminate him, but in practice did not succeed in reintroducing slavery. Left to itself, Haiti disposed of the remaining whites and its new population of smallholders pulled out from the world economy. Chronologically, the second case of decolonisation was actually not a white but an African American one, though this is often forgotten due to its limited success. The remaining plantation regimes were left traumatised, but in contrast to the United States the Haitian revolution appears not to have sent out wider political signals, not even to Africa in later years.

In Ibero-America, the first impulses for decolonisation came from Napoleon's activities on the Iberian Peninsula. Upon his invasion of Portugal, the Portuguese monarchy was transferred to Brazil in 1808 and the colony raised to a status equal with Portugal. British assistance in this move was rewarded with preferential tariffs in the new, generally free-trade economic system, securing Britain a dominant position on the market for many decades thanks to the superior range of goods it could supply. When the legitimate heir to the Spanish throne was displaced by Napoleon's brother Joseph, both Spain and America responded with the formation of legitimist provincial councils, *juntas*; in America the juntas additionally demanded increased autonomy from Spain, and were thus suppressed. These events were the fertile soil for the next surge of revolutionary movements, responding to the renewed French attacks on Spain in 1810. The liberal Constitution of Cadiz, created in 1812 by the Spanish resistance, was no longer capable of holding back the increasingly marked trend towards independence, and the harsh Spanish reaction after the fall of Napoleon only intensified that trend. Venezuela had already declared its independence in 1811, but the *liberador* Simón Bolívar (1783–1830), who had seized the reins of the movement, did not manage to push through his programme, despite support from Colombian parts of New Granada. In 1814/15 his plans were thwarted by the *llaneros*, the fierce herdsmen of the south, who had been won over to the royalists against the criollo elite, and then by the Spanish army, which the restored king had sent to America. In Mexico, a popular movement was unleashed in

1810 by the parish priests Miguel Hidalgo (1753–1811) and José Maria Morelos, but was put down by a coalition of conservative elites. Revolutionary Chile was overcome in 1814 by a counterattack from Peru, a stronghold of royalism. Only in the La Plata region did the independence movement enjoy long-term success: there, the movement's repulsion of two attempted British invasions in 1806/07 had given it an immense boost. However, it immediately became doubtful whether the group ruling in Buenos Aires would be able to preserve the former viceroyalty's unity in the face of conflicting interests. La Plata lost Upper Peru (today's Bolivia), previously part of its viceroyalty, and Paraguay too went its own way. In Uruguay the conflict between the revolutionary countryside and the capital, Montevideo, which had remained royalist out of rivalry with Buenos Aires, culminated in the country being occupied by Brazil. Only in 1829/30, after a war between Argentina and Brazil, did Uruguay become independent, as a buffer state between the warring parties.

The remainder of the former colonies had reverted to Spanish rule between 1814 and 1816. However, the king pursued policies that were so reactionary, and affronted the now well-articulated American interests so thoroughly, that the criollo elites were alienated from Spain once and for all. As a result, fresh campaigns for liberation successfully advanced both northwards and southwards until, in 1822, their protagonists were able to shake hands in Peru. José de San Martín (1778–1850) had been marching from Argentina through Chile and Peru from 1817, while Bolívar finally got his way in Venezuela in 1818 because the *llaneros* had now taken his side. Thanks to a rebellion in Spain, by 1822 Bolívar had managed to unite Colombia, Panama and Ecuador with Venezuela to create the republic of Greater Colombia. In 1824 the last royalists in Upper Peru were vanquished and in 1825 the independent nation of Bolivia was founded there. In Mexico, the successful liberal uprising of 1820 in Spain was a key factor in permanently turning the conservative elites against the mother country. A military dictatorship masked as an empire was established in 1822, then in 1824 a conservative federal republic. Central America, headed by Guatemala, first joined this federation but immediately separated off again. The fragmentation of Central America is perhaps the clearest indicator of how strongly regional interests dominated independent Latin America, with provinces or even smaller entities ultimately establishing themselves as new states. All Bolívar's grand plans for federation were doomed to failure; after his death even Greater Colombia, the old viceroyalty of New Granada, quickly broke apart into Venezuela, Colombia and Ecuador.

Only in Brazil did regional movements fail to take root. Here, too, independence was prompted by a reactionary turn in the mother country, though in this case one proceeding not from the Crown but from a constituent assembly that, formed in 1821 after a liberal putsch, planned to demote Brazil back to the status of a mere colony. The king had left an heir in Brazil for precisely such an eventuality, and in 1822, with the support of the planter aristocracy, he declared the country a hereditary empire – an arrangement that would remain in place until 1889.

In the 1820s and 1830s, the new states gradually gained recognition from the European powers, last of all from the Pope. The process was part of a wider agreement to forgo political interference in the western hemisphere, as called for by the United States in the Monroe Doctrine of 1823. To be sure, colonial rule continued in and around the Caribbean. Most important was the Spanish sugar island of Cuba, its slave plantations flourishing after the eradication of the French competition. The island's criollo elite knew their plantations would be safest under Spain. Cuba gained its independence in the wake of the Spanish-American War in 1898, the rest of the Caribbean only after the Second World War.

7   New Europes in the southern hemisphere and the second decolonisation

When settlement colonies gave rise to New Europes overseas, it was the result of mass emigration followed by a massive increase in the settler population due to the favourable conditions offered by the new environment. In the period from 1500 to 1800 probably two to three million Europeans emigrated, but between 1800 and 1960 there were at least 61 million Europeans participating in intercontinental migration. Whereas the very first colonial powers had too few rather than too many people to drive their expansion, England was already a different matter. And from the eighteenth century the population explosion in Europe began, increasing social pressure wherever there were too few industrial jobs to absorb the growing number of people. Mass emigration was not merely a remedy for the political problem of mass poverty, but is likely to have had a favourable impact on the economy as a whole: while population growth in itself is a factor promoting economic growth, this only applies if the number of people does not increase so steeply that it soaks up the growth achieved and more. That is a problem facing the developing countries of the present day, while nineteenth-century Europe, confronted with a similar dilemma, was probably protected by the safety valve of mass emigration.

Of the European emigrants, 41 million, or 70 per cent, went to North America, which after its independence became the New Europe par excellence, thanks not least to its continued geographical expansion. The remaining 20 million or 30 per cent should not, however, be overlooked. South America was the destination for 12 per cent; South Africa, Australia and New Zealand for 9 per cent; and Asian Russia for another 9 per cent. Apart from Russia and Brazil, these nineteenth- and twentieth-century destinations show striking similarities. Argentina, Chile and Uruguay, South Africa, Australia and New Zealand are all located in the southern hemisphere, chiefly in the subtropical to temperate zones with climates more or less in line with what the Europeans were used to. For the most part they were sparsely populated – only southern Chile, the south-east of South Africa and New Zealand were inhabited by substantial pre-European groups of sedentary agriculturalists – and could thus, like North America, be transformed into homelands for white people without too much difficulty. In the nineteenth century it could not have

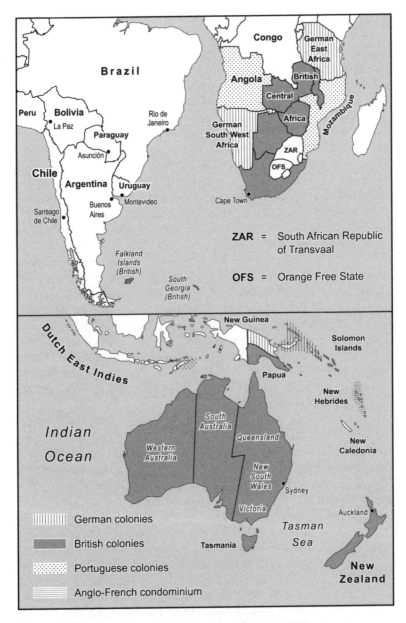

Map 10   The New Europes of the southern hemisphere, *c.* 1890

been predicted that the indigenous inhabitants of New Zealand would not allow themselves to be completely marginalised, and that South Africa would even see the settlement undertaking partially reversed through one of the last decolonisation processes. The settlers' dominant economic form was large-scale agriculture oriented on the world market, mainly using white labour and including livestock farming. The steamship and the invention of refrigeration technology made sea transport faster and cheaper, enabling beef and mutton to take on an increasingly important role. Huge fortunes were made in this process, and even seasonal labourers were sometimes able to make a hand-some living. Where indigenous agriculturalists existed, they were not integrated into the system on equal terms. Their potential competition was eliminated, sometimes violently, and their labour made available for the whites; migratory labour became a way of life. Where there was no indigenous labour to supply a particular demand, contract labourers might be imported, from India, China or the South Sea Islands. This was little more than a contin-uation of slavery by other means, and the coolie trade to South America was known as the 'pig trade'. The growth in demand for labour was particularly intense when, in Chile, South Africa and Australia, the discovery or seizure of mineral deposits shifted the economic focus to the mining sector, to saltpetre and copper, gold and diamonds. Such shifts also necessitated higher invest-ment, which as before still came mainly from Britain – all of these countries being, in one way or another, components of the nineteenth-century British empire of free trade. They owed their development to British-dominated world trade and were in most cases politically dependent, in all cases economically dependent, on Britain. Unlike the tropical colonies, they were also popular targets for the investment activities of British capital. The Latin American countries had become sovereign states, but it was their dependency on Britain that helped them advance from neglected, sparsely populated outposts of the Spanish Empire to thriving participants in the global market and transformed them into countries of white immigration. South Africa, Australia and New Zealand, in contrast, had become parts of the British Empire, an empire that was revitalised after the loss of the United States and the victory over Napoleon and now held a dominant role worldwide. To be sure, just like Latin America these countries were originally mere outposts without economic significance of their own, occupied and maintained chiefly for strategic or other political reasons – but this changed when their economic potential was revealed. They then became little paradises of prosperity for the whites, at least until the crises of the twentieth century. Those that were British colonies tended towards separation, as the United States had done before them, though the accumulated experience of the past meant that this process was handled much more elegantly than it had been the first time around. After the First

World War, this second, exclusively white decolonisation gave birth to the British Commonwealth as a postcolonial organisational form.

The Southern Cone: Argentina, Chile, Uruguay

In the first decades after independence, economic development was rather disappointing, but after the mid nineteenth century the upswing began. European demand was rising due to population growth and an improved standard of living, and this demand could now be supplied using faster and less costly means of transport, the railway and steamship. Alongside its existing exports of leather products and wool, Argentina increasingly exported beef. One indicator of the rise in its pastoral economy is the fact that in 1877–81, the country imported no less than 50,000 tons of barbed wire, recently invented in North America, for its pasture fencing. Then the grain boom began. In 1870 Argentina had still been importing grain; by the First World War its fertile pampas, transformed from grazing to arable land, had made it one of the world's leading exporters of wheat and maize. From 1872 to 1895, the area under cultivation increased fifteenfold. To develop access to the pampas, a railway network was swiftly built, growing from 2,400 to 11,200 km of track in the decade 1880–90 alone. In a way that was typical of the colonies, the rail routes were designed to serve the export harbours, especially Buenos Aires, which sat like a spider in the railway web. Investment for the rail links came principally from Britain, doubling in 1875–85 and quadrupling in 1885–95. By 1913, 60 per cent of all foreign investment in Argentina was still British. Uruguay, too, was dependent on British credit, but its flourishing cattle industry enabled it to build up balance-of-payments surpluses even so. Europeans of the period regarded the meat extract produced from Uruguayan beef by the Anglo-Belgian company Liebig as a miracle tonic. This small country's rail network grew from 705 km to 2,146 km in 1889–1909, remaining in British ownership.

Chile had also substantially increased its grain production by expanding its area of cultivation southwards, but its prosperity arose primarily from mining. In the 1870s it held a 40 per cent share of the world copper market. At that time the majority of what is now the coastal desert of northern Chile still belonged to weak Bolivia, while the desert's nitrate deposits – increasingly in demand as a resource for gunpowder and fertiliser manufacture – were exploited by Peruvian and, especially, Chilean companies. Hoping to solve the problems of the 1870s economic crisis, in 1879–83 Chile waged the 'Saltpetre War', in which Bolivia, tellingly, took almost no part and Peru was crushingly defeated. Nitrate now dominated Chilean exports. In 1890,

70 per cent of it was produced by British companies, although it has not been possible to confirm the truth of the then US secretary of state James G. Blaine's assertion that the Saltpetre War was actually a conflict between Britain and Peru, with Chile playing only an ancillary role. In fact, British capitalism was more inclined to sidestep political risk.

Economic development went hand in hand with white immigration. Immigration was least significant in Chile, though even there Germans were settled as part of the endeavour to gain access to the south against the Indians. Argentina, in contrast, received 5.5 million European immigrants in the 1870–1914 period alone. Despite large numbers returning to Europe, three million of these migrants remained in the country, while Uruguay gained 400,000 people through immigration. That number corresponded exactly to the country's total population in 1870, when Argentina's population numbered only 1.9 million. The consequence was a radical Europeanisation of society; the criollo way of life disappeared, as did the previous physical appearance of the people with its African and indigenous American influences. New Europes had come into being. In 1851–1924, Argentina was the destination of 46 per cent of European immigration to Latin America. Of these immigrants, 38 per cent came from Italy, 28 per cent from Spain and 11 per cent from Portugal; very few originated from non-Latin countries. At times agricultural wages were so high that many Italians came to Argentina as seasonal labourers, moving to Brazil for the coffee harvest and then back home for the European harvest in the northern hemisphere's autumn.

The Europeanisation of the *Cono sur*, or Southern Cone, meant the irrevocable ousting of the Indians, who had up to then been wiped out only in Uruguay. The Araucanians of Chile had held their own, thanks not least to their adoption of horse culture, and in 1612 the Spanish had been forced to accept the Biobío river at Concepción as the Indian frontier. Although both sides continued to make occasional aggressive forays, there were also long periods of peace, especially after the slave trade in Indian prisoners of war was suppressed in 1683. Christian missionary work was possible, if not particularly successful in the face of an intact Indian culture. When the Araucanians crossed the Andes in search of hunting grounds, the Indians there took over the newcomers' cultural technologies, especially horse-riding. Like the Indians of the North American plains, they changed from a hunting and gathering to an equestrian culture, a move that involved not only stockbreeding and engagement in the trans-Andean transport business but sometimes also cattle raids on white farms. But for the process of developing intensive agriculture and expanding the white population, the Indians were a stumbling block. In the 1860s and 1870s both Argentina and Chile pushed back the Indian frontier and built chains of forts, their supply facilitated by the new railway network. In 1879/80 the Argentinian army then 'cleansed' the fertile pampas once and for all in the *Campaña del desierto*, or desert campaign, while deportations, epidemics and alcohol completed the process of destroying the indigenous population. In Chile the advance began in 1878, and although the Saltpetre War provided a period of grace for the Indians and even a chance to counter-attack, by 1883 the Araucanian lands, too, had finally been conquered. In contrast to the Argentinian case, reservations were set up and today are fostering renewed political activity.

South Africa

In order to secure the provisioning of their ships at their base on the Cape of Good Hope, established in 1652, the Dutch East India company had encouraged the settlement of Dutch, Huguenot and German farmers, or *boere*. The demand for meat soon encouraged a large proportion of these people to cease arable farming and build up huge cattle farms in the country's interior instead. These *trekboere* developed a new, semi-nomadic way of life. Land was available in abundance; the non-Bantu Khoisan who had lived in the region were not very numerous and were themselves cattle breeders. They were driven out or taken into service as herdsmen, until a 1713 epidemic drastically reduced their numbers. To the east, the Boers encountered Bantu people, first of all the Xhosa, who combined cattle rearing with tillage and were both more numerous and more militarily powerful than the Khoisan. Here, further Boer advances were bound to lead to large-scale conflict.

The British occupied the Cape in 1795, and in 1815 took possession of it conclusively so as to secure the sea route to India. The British administrators hoped to subject the Boers to legal control, while their missionaries and philanthropists took offence at the Boers' treatment of the Khoisan – this being the period leading up to the 1833 abolition of slavery in the British Empire. The Boers considered the British interventions a curtailment of their way of life and their need for land, and their resentment was exacerbated by the sense that Britain was not supporting them in their battles with the Xhosa on the colony's eastern frontier. They sent scouts to search for land, and in 1835–40 a total of 6,000 white people, around 9 per cent of the Cape Colony's inhabitants, set off in a series of organised convoys on the 'Great Trek', northwards across the Orange River. They were followed by a further 10,000 travelling individually up to 1845.

This white expansion had in fact been preceded by an African equivalent, with which it was to converge in a peculiar way. In the late eighteenth century, probably prompted partly by the thirst for land like the Boers, but also by the extension of trading networks and the gradual increase in colonial influence, the Nguni peoples of eastern South Africa began to form larger-scale communities, culminating in the tightly organised military state headed by the legendary Shaka (c. 1783–1828). Shaka's armies created a new power factor through their conquest and incorporation of other clans, but also triggered the formation of fresh groups. From Shaka's imperial people grew the Zulu, today South Africa's largest ethnic group. From the refugees fleeing the process, Moshoeshoe created his Basotho empire in the mountains, today's Lesotho. From the rebels migrating west and north, finally, the empire of the Ndebele in today's Zimbabwe was formed under the leadership of Mzilikazi.

The *voortrekker* initially settled south of the Zulu empire, on the coast, where they founded their Republic of Natal. They had to face the Zulu in a fierce 1838 battle, where their firearms secured them victory, but in 1845 once again fell under the rule of the British, who were loath to countenance a Boer republic on the sea route to India. Natal was stocked with English settlers and in 1852 became a separate colony, in 1859 beginning to import Indian contract labourers to tend the newly introduced crop of sugar cane. In 1885 there were almost as many Indians as white people in Natal. In the north, the Boers managed to defeat Mzilikazi in 1837 and forced him out of the area. They did not, though, find it easy to form their own state. In 1843 they proclaimed a republic that laid claim to the land between the Orange and its northern tributary the Vaal, but the land was quickly annexed by the British in 1848 after an armed dispute. However, London found the cost of subduing Britain's unwilling subjects too high. In 1852 the British signed an agreement with the Boers north of the Vaal and in 1854 with those to the south, who had already been suppressed. The deal gave the southerners their freedom, so that in the subsequent twenty years the Boers were able to form the Orange Free State and the South African Republic, also known as the Transvaal Republic, as independent entities. The British Cape, in contrast, was granted representative government in 1852, with a parliamentary body alongside its governor and a right to vote for all races – although, just as in Europe, suffrage was restricted by property qualifications. In 1872 this was succeeded by responsible government with its own ministry.

In terms of the global economy, South Africa only became interesting after the discovery of diamond deposits in Kimberley, in the autonomous native territories, in 1867 and of gold on the Witwatersrand, Transvaal, in 1886. The diamond fields were annexed by Britain without delay. The growing expense of mining deep into the earth resulted in a concentration of the companies involved, until De Beers, led by the English entrepreneur and Cape Colony prime minister Cecil John Rhodes (1853–1902), succeeded at the end of the century in establishing a quasi-monopoly on diamond produc-tion, one that has lasted till the present day. The working conditions of the Africans worsened but, as labourers and foodstuff producers, they were still able to benefit from the general boom more than suited the whites, who wanted to take over the land themselves for their now dramatically expanding agriculture and to reduce the Africans to a standing reserve army of cheap workers. By 1899, all South Africa's four colonies had introduced rules that aimed to restrict African arable farming by stopping the unregulated occupa-tion of land, while the British used violence to incorporate the remaining African communities, including the Zulu, into the Cape Colony and Natal. Only Swaziland, Basutoland (now Lesotho) and Bechuanaland (now Botswana) in the north retained semi-autonomy, as protectorates.

At stake in this policy were not only land and population, but also the need to curb the expanding Transvaal in its push towards the sea. The age of imperialism had breathed new life into Britain's interest in controlling all of South Africa, and by 1881 a claim at least to sovereignty over the Boers had been re-established. But the gold boom shifted the balance of power radi-cally. In 1883–95 the state revenue of the Transvaal increased by a factor of twenty-five, and the newly founded Johannesburg on the Witwatersrand rapidly grew into a metropolis, with over a million African labourers living there by 1899. The reservoir of indigenous labour was no longer sufficient, and workers were recruited from Mozambique and even further afield. Mining was expensive, requiring heavy investment, and just as in the case of diamonds this resulted in a concentration of businesses (although this time Cecil Rhodes, again involved in the process, did not succeed in establishing a monopoly). Well over £100 million were invested in the Witwatersrand between 1886 and 1913. The total British assets in South Africa rose from £34 million in 1884 to £351 million in 1911, enormous amounts by the inter-national standards of the day. The white population of South Africa as a whole doubled, even trebled, through immigration. In the Transvaal, tensions arose between the economically powerful 'foreigners' and the Boers, who wanted to retain political control. High demand and high incomes led to the blossoming of all sectors of South Africa's economy. Railways were built, although this time the British were passed over and the Transvaal's President Krüger chose a German-Dutch line starting from the Portuguese-held Delagoa Bay. The 'foreigners', backed by Rhodes and the British Colonial Secretary Joseph Chamberlain, planned a coup in the Transvaal and carried it out in 1895 despite the withdrawal of their sponsors. The coup failed, but control of the Transvaal had now become a vital issue for the British Empire. Tensions continued to escalate, aided by the British High Commissioner, Alfred Milner, and culminated in the Boer War of 1899–1902. Sparked by a conflict over voting rights for 'foreigners', the war resulted in the defeat of the Boers by the numerically superior British. When the British established 'concentration camps' to counter the Boers' guerrilla tactics, these were designed only, literally, to 'concentrate' Boer civilians in one place, not to exterminate them; the 25 per cent death rate among the prisoners was the result of epidemics. The British public reacted with outrage to this 'barbarism' – because its victims were white.

Because they were white, and because their help was needed to create a stable South Africa within the Empire, the Boers lost the war but won the peace. The complaints of mining capital were resolved by changes to the status of the railway and state monopolies, but otherwise the pre-war status quo was largely reinstated. In 1910 the four colonies, now to be known as 'provinces', were combined to form a fairly unitary 'Union of South Africa' with extensive self-government, a land of European settlers in which non-whites had the right to vote only in Cape Province (until it was withdrawn from them there as well, in 1936). The Boers immediately began to regain ground, but the whites of British descent were reluctant to jeopardise white dominance by disputing this trend. In 1913 Africans were forbidden from buying land outside their reservations, and conversely whites from buying reservation land, though this was no great loss to the latter in view of the respective proportions of land and population. Black landowners were not yet being expropriated in 'white' South Africa, but the tendency was clear: rule by the white minority through discrimination against the African majority and systematic exploitation of their cheap labour. South Africa became the promised land of the white man when, after the Boer Nasionale Party's electoral victory in 1948, the existing pattern was carried to its extreme with the methodically planned and rigorously pursued policy of racial segregation called apartheid. The daily harassments of routine racial segregation, 'petty' apartheid, were accompanied by 'macro' apartheid: the aim of making Africans into citizens of autonomous, even sovereign, 'homelands' and thus into foreigners within a South Africa that was purely white in legal terms – foreigners whose cheap labour was always necessary and always available, the homelands being far too small and scantily resourced to feed their own dense populations. At the same time, even after their independence the three British protectorates of Swaziland, Lesotho and Botswana, as well as neighbouring Mozambique and the rest of southern Africa, were to be caught up in the powerful sway of the apartheid state because of its economic and, if necessary, also military power. These nations ultimately held a status not dissimilar to the homelands. This was surely a systematic implementation of a New Europe along the most extreme colonialist lines, a project of demonic grandiosity.

Australia

Australia had no need of such violent means in order to become a land of the whites, a New Europe, its indigenous inhabitants being so few in number and at such a technological disadvantage that as a whole, despite recurrently flaring resistance, they were defenceless in the face of the Europeans – probably the most defenceless of all the victims of colonialism worldwide. The whites could even afford to show them a certain benevolence and justice. Thus in 1838, to the considerable surprise of their fellow citizens, seven white men were hanged for murdering Aborigines. But even Charles Darwin had predicted that the Australian Aborigines would die out inevitably, 'according to a natural law', as their Tasmanian branch did in 1876. Today, their numbers are growing again. The Aborigines are now several hundreds of thousands strong, campaign for their rights and status, have been granted extensive lands and enjoy the benign interest of scholarship and the general public. Yet Australian history is still proceeding without them.

Australia was given its name by its circumnavigator, Matthew Flinders, in the early nineteenth century. It was a kind of substitute for the southern continent of earlier geographers, the non-existence of which had been demonstrated by James Cook, the man who had mapped Australia's eastern coastline. It was there, in 'New South Wales' with Sydney as its hub, that in 1786–88 Britain created an urgently needed substitute for one of the roles previously played by the lost North American possessions: a convict colony. The process started with 757 transported convicts and by 1867, when the transports ceased, 160,000 convicts had been sent to Australia, although some of them returned to Europe after serving out their sentence. In view of the harshness of criminal law at the time, we should certainly not class all these people as criminals in today's terms, especially not all the Irish, who made up a quarter of the transported up to 1823. But by 1810 convicts anyway accounted for only 14 per cent of the 12,000-strong population: the decision had been made to create a real settler colony, in which convicts were deployed as labourers in private agriculture and for government projects. Being free from hostile forces on all sides, Sydney had great potential as a trading base, especially for the seal hunters and whalers of the southern oceans. From 1805, large-scale sheep raising for wool became a further important factor as the expanding British textile industry had developed an insatiable demand for wool, half of which was being supplied by Australia by 1850. As early as 1813 the Blue Mountains had been crossed in search of sheep-grazing land in the interior. In 1810 there were five settlements in New South Wales and two in Tasmania, while Sydney had become a sleek little town. On the urging of respectable citizens, who insisted on their rights as

Englishmen, New South Wales received an appointed legislative council in 1823, as did Tasmania when it became a separate colony in 1825. However, these institutions placed few restrictions on the authority of the governors; the British Empire of the time relied on autocracy. Because the French were making their presence felt on the western Australian coast, the British government acquiesced in the interests of the Asia trade and in 1829 founded a further colony, around today's Perth. The colony was established without convicts, but in 1846 a labour shortage led the settlers themselves to appeal for convicts to be sent. In contrast, the big landowners and merchants who now called the tune in Sydney wanted to attract more cash-rich immigrants by getting rid of the convict population. From 1824, the criminals considered most dangerous were therefore deported, many of them to Moreton Bay near today's Brisbane. These were the beginnings of the Queensland colony. When the colonists of Tasmania had exhausted their grazing land, they founded a settlement on the opposite coast, the germ of the later colony of Victoria. By now more and more free immigrants were flowing into the country, 200,000 of them by 1850, the majority with British government support. To a far greater extent than before, and far more effectively, colonisation and colonial rule were now being politically planned and theoretically underpinned with what can only be called a scientific thoroughness. Colonialism could be counted a branch of the now thriving liberal 'political economy'. Thus, in the establishment of the sixth colony, South Australia, advocates of systematic colonisation (especially Edward Gibbon Wakefield), Protestant philanthropists and speculators all worked together. While the colonial reformer Wilmot Horton was most concerned to find a productive way of removing Britain's poor through government emigration projects, Wakefield initially targeted selected settlers who had sufficient capital to afford the artificially inflated price of land. These purchases were to help fund further emigration, thus simultaneously solving the labour problem. In place of the old, autocratic and aristocratically corrupt empire, argued Wakefield, must come a new, self-governed 'middle-class empire'. In southern Australia this was to be smallholding country offering sanctuary for Dissenters, while in the rest of Australia the Anglicans dominated and the Irish were beginning to set up their own Catholic church. In fact, however, sheep raising and speculation in land could not be halted in South Australia any more than they could in the rest of the country, though a remnant of small-scale food production survived.

In 1850, New South Wales had 265,000 inhabitants, Tasmania 70,000, South Australia 64,000, Western Australia only 4,600. New South Wales was pressing for self-administration and even self-government, the right to legislate on land ownership, immigration and customs – areas that the mother country had reserved for itself – and a responsible ministry as its executive. In the 1850s, after lengthy disputes, constitutions to this effect were worked out for the eastern colonies, which had now grown to five through the separa-tion of Victoria and Queensland, and were passed by English law. The less developed Western Australia had to wait until 1890.

The crucial surge of development occurred on the discovery of gold deposits in various parts of the country after 1851. Between 1851 and 1861, the population grew from 405,000 to 1,146,000. In 1858 there were 155,000 gold diggers working in the mines, and in 1852–70 gold was Australia's most important export. The boom sucked in immigrants and led to growth in agri-culture and manufacturing, although initially with little British investment, so that the railways (the typical magnet for British money), in particular, grew only slowly. The mass immigration from Europe shook up the dominance of the existing oligarchy of merchants and sheep barons. It inaugurated a dynamic move towards universal suffrage with secret ballot, including for women, and the introduction of parliamentary allowances, goals that were achieved earlier here than in the mother country.

Despite London's suggestions of a federation, the individual colonies went their own ways – not even a uniform rail gauge could be introduced without problems. It was only threatening activities by Germany and France in the Pacific that, in 1883, occasioned a federation initiative by Queensland in the north-east, most affected by the situation. This was reinforced by the trade unions' interest in a unified economic policy and especially in a ban on importing Chinese and Melanesian contract labourers. Additionally, by this time a form of Australian patriotism had arisen: whereas in 1861 over half the colonists had been born in Britain, by 1901 82 per cent of them were born in Australia itself. In 1897–1900 a federal constitution was finally drawn up and agreed, clearly oriented on the US model. Britain insisted on the option of Australian federal court decisions being appealed in the mother country, apparently in order to reassure British investors. The Commonwealth of Australia Act was passed in England, and the constitution came into force in 1901. Another New Europe was complete and had eman-cipated itself.

New Zealand

The 'Britain of the South', as New Zealand is sometimes called, is consid-ered the most British of all the colonies and the most European of all the New Europes, despite the fact that its previous population, the light-skinned Polynesian Maori, were sedentary, more numerous, better organised and capable of much more effective resistance than the indigenous peoples of Australia. Concentrated mainly on the northern island, the Maori began trading with Europeans and Australians shortly before 1800. They supplied flax, potatoes, pigs, women and dried human heads, and in return acquired woollen blankets, knives, muskets and the usual infectious diseases. A range of different missionaries arrived, while on the other hand various Europeans who had settled in the country were completely absorbed into Maori culture, allegedly even as far as participating in cannibalism. Maori culture developed a remarkable assimilatory capacity, including the production of syncretistic religious movements some of which survived well into the twentieth century. The arrival of firearms did not necessarily exacerbate the conflicts between individual Maori groups, and in fact may even have mitigated these, since the shooting irons were noisy but ineffective, and thus less dangerous than the traditional weapons of close combat. Either way, the missionaries hoped for a Christian Maori country under their leadership, and skilfully used their considerable political influence in London to undermine every authorised colonisation scheme, although around 2,000 white people were living in the country in 1840 and the New Zealand Company, founded with the help of the colonialist Wakefield, was all set to acquire land for settlement purposes with or without official approval.

In response, London sent a governor charged with treating the Maori chiefs as sovereign and buying the necessary land from them contractually. The resale of that land was, according to the brief, to be carried out via the Crown, while the Maori were to be guaranteed their own possessions and given the status of British subjects. Accordingly, in 1840 a treaty was signed in Waitangi that ceded Maori sovereignty in return for recognition of their ownership of their lands and other property. To fend off the French, who had now appeared in the area, British sovereignty over North Island was proclaimed by virtue of the treaty and over South Island by right of discovery. New Zealand was now a Crown colony – but the question of land remained unresolved. White claims, even such dubious ones as those of the New Zealand Company, proved impossible to suppress, and neither was it possible to stop the Maori from selling their land even when such sales violated their own laws. Because, in line with the foremost principle of all colonial policy, the colony was not to entail any expense for the mother country, the governor had no financial means at his disposal to enforce order. He did, though, with the help of the bishop and chief justice, manage to foil an attempt by the Company and government to suspend the Treaty of Waitangi, declare all unused land Crown property, establish a self-governed settler colony and fence the Maori into reservations.

In 1851 there were 27,000 white people in the settlements (which numbered three each on North and South Island), their livelihood based on 250,000 sheep. In 1853, a new constitution was granted with six provincial councils and a general assembly, which could also decide on the use of unexploited land. Ministerial responsibility was added in 1854; the attempt to reserve native affairs for the governor's authority failed. In 1858 the Maori elected a king for themselves, but real conflict did not yet break out because the focus of white expansion then lay in South Island, where the Maori were less numerous. In 1860 war did begin, when a Maori wanting to sell land was prohibited from doing so by his chief but was given armed support by the British, even though the chief justice had found in favour of the Maori ruler. The Maori were defeated in the ensuing conflict, but London was alarmed at the cost of the operation and withdrew its troops. Despite Maori guerrilla warfare, the New Zealanders were thus able to solve the problem on their own terms and to their own satisfaction, through expropriations and a 'free' land market maintained through violence. Although Maori still owned one sixth of the land in 1892, that sixth was mainly located in barren areas of North Island. By then a policy of reconciliation had prevailed and they received parliamentary seats proportionate to their population; at the same time their cultural integration was proceeding apace, not least through intermarriage – including marriages between aboriginal men and white women, something not tolerated in other colonialist societies. In the twentieth century Maori numbers began to recover, but with 116,000 people in 1951 they no longer had much weight within a population of two million. Today, however, 600,000 of the 4.2 million New Zealanders count themselves as Maori.

After massive immigration in the second half of the nineteenth century, New Zealand became a land of the whites. It has recently been shown that even the plant and animal realm adapted markedly to European influence – a 'New Europe' here arose from what Alfred W. Crosby has called 'ecological imperialism'. The New Zealanders, who from the 1890s made use of modern refrigeration technology to become important suppliers of meat and dairy products to the mother country, saw themselves as British, in some respects more British than the British. The large working class and robust political participation, with liberal and socialist governments from 1891 onwards, built up a welfare state that was far ahead of the mother country's. In 1893, New Zealand became the first country in the world to introduce women's suffrage. It was, then, not only in the United States that the New Europes brought Old Europe's ideals more fully to fruition than Old Europe itself and served as a model for it to follow.

The second decolonisation:
The British Commonwealth of Nations

New Zealand had hardly been settled when, alongside Australian and South African colonies of longer standing, it was granted extensive powers of self-administration, which would grow into full sovereignty during the twentieth century. In the mid nineteenth century, the British regarded the trend towards independence among the white settler colonies in quite a positive light, the closed trading system of mercantilism now having disintegrated. Under the free trade that replaced it, colonies proved to be superfluous – Britain controlled world trade anyway, both inside and outside its colonies, as in Latin America – and merely a burden on the mother country's budget. From the British perspective, thus, self-administration meant above all self-funding, whether the colony wanted it or not. However, developments in colonial policy were initially fuelled not by the new and weak possessions in the southern hemisphere but by the older colony of Canada. Bearing the additional risk factor of its adjacency to the expanding United States, Canada was in a better position than the new colonies to attract the attention of British politicians.

In 1774 Great Britain had allowed Quebec the exercise of French law and equality for Catholics, but ordained an authoritarian system of adminis-tration under a governor with no elected assembly. That might not have worried the French Canadians, accustomed to absolutism, but it did worry the pro-English Loyalists, of whom around 40,000 had moved to Canada, since by this time an elected assembly was felt to be part of the basic equipment of a white British colony. Many of the Loyalists moved to New Brunswick, which in 1784 became a separate colony, as did Nova Scotia, acquired in 1713. Others settled further north, setting the scene for the status of Canada proper to be decided. In 1791 the country was divided into French 'Lower Canada' (Quebec) and British 'Upper Canada' (Ontario), each with a governor and legislative body, but with certain precautionary measures that derived from the US experience. In particular, the governor could dispose over a part of the fiscal revenue independently of the assembly. However, widespread dissatis-faction with this arrangement culminated in rebellions in 1837; in response, the 'Durham Report' was presented in 1839 by the new Governor General of that name. It included the recommendation to rigorously anglicise the French Canadians, which led to a reunification of the two colonies in 1840 so that the now 550,000 English Canadians could assimilate the 450,000 French ones – but its watershed significance for Canada lay in the acceptance that in colonies like Canada, the strict separation of powers, a principle passed down from the eighteenth century and espoused by the United States, was bound to draw the legislature and the executive into constant deadlock. As a result, the system of a parliamentary cabinet was to be adopted, something that had only just been fully implemented in Britain itself. The governor was to entrust policymaking to representatives of the majority in the colonial legislature, and negotiate with them without help from London. Britain would retain responsibility only for constitutional and foreign policy. However, it was only under the influence of free trade that, in 1848, responsible government was granted and the areas of trade and land policy, originally reserved for Westminster, were also transferred to the colony. In 1859 Canada was already able to enforce its own protective tariffs against the mother country – but the alternatives for Britain would have been costly direct rule or annexation by the United States.

In 1867, looking over their shoulder at the expanding United States and guided by their common economic interests, several colonies came together in the 'Canadian Confederation' created by a British law. The confederation combined a British-style cabinet system with US-style federalism, though with a stronger role for the federation than was the case in the United States and later Australia. The original members were Nova Scotia, New Brunswick and the two colonies of Ontario and Quebec, now divided again for this purpose. In 1870 it was possible to acquire the territories of the Hudson's Bay Company, from which the provinces of Manitoba, Saskatchewan and Alberta were separated out by 1912. British Columbia joined in 1871, Prince Edward Island in 1873, the parts of the Arctic claimed by Britain in 1880–1927, and in 1949 Newfoundland became the confederation's tenth and final member.

The confederation was deliberately also labelled a 'Dominion', a term originally referring to England's subject lands, such as Ireland or the Channel Islands, which had their own institutions and limited autonomy but remained subject to British legislation. Just as in the case of the American colonies, an 1865 English law had taken the precaution of explicitly reiterating these conditions. But Canada spearheaded the attempts by the four self-governing white Dominions to change those conditions not only in practice but also in law. Although the British Crown could declare war in 1914 on behalf of the entire Empire without consulting the Dominions, it was the Dominions that decided on the degree of their participation. Their status thus enhanced, they acted as signatories (though still subordinated to the United Kingdom) in the Treaty of Versailles and became members of the League of Nations. In 1921, under pressure from Boer nationalism, the South African premier Jan Smuts finally demanded equal rights with the mother country and ties limited to personal union under the British monarch. The trend was accelerated by Irish independence, won in 1922. Canada declared itself not

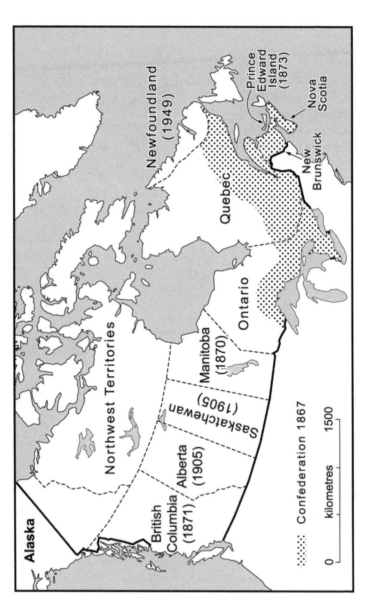

Map 11 Canada up to 1949

bound by Britain's 1923/24 peace agreements with Turkey, and in 1926 it sent its own ambassador to Washington, where an Irish ambassador was already based. For the Imperial Conference of 1926, the Dominions were defined as states independent in domestic and foreign policy, bound to the Empire, or the 'British Commonwealth of Nations', only through the shared monarch; sovereign in the British view but not 'foreign countries' in relation to Britain. Their governors general were now no longer delegates of the British government, but representatives of the British monarch as the head of state of the Dominions. In 1931 the Statute of Westminster set this in law, and by repealing the law of 1865 ended the Dominions' dependence on British legislation and British law. South Africa already considered it appropriate to carry out its own ratification of the Statute of Westminster. In 1961, in the context of its racial policy, it took up the option of withdrawing from the Commonwealth, as Ireland had already done in 1949. Thanks to the experience gained in the first decolonisation, the second round proceeded far more smoothly and unproblematically, although only because it was an internal matter among whites and, for the greater part, Britons. The idea of transferring this model to the 'coloured' colonies was, for the time being, discussed only in India, and there with little success.

The 'whiteness' of the British Dominions and of the New Europes in general is reflected not least in the fact that they picked up and continued the process of expanding Europe in the southern hemisphere. The sub-imperialism of South Africa, Australia and New Zealand, guided by these countries' own interests, often enough conflicted with the policies of the mother country, which shied away from the political and financial costs of further commitments and tried – not always successfully – to curb the initiatives coming from the Dominions. Rhodesia was a product of South African expansion, while Australia and New Zealand cast their eye especially on the Pacific islands. Argentina and Chile quarrelled over Patagonia. But there was now little left to exploit in the southern hemisphere. Was that why the New Europes entered with such vigour into the carving up of the genuine 'southern continent', Antarctica? The process began between the two world wars, Antarctic exploration having only started around 1900. As well as Britain, France and Norway, Argentina, Chile, Australia and New Zealand all laid claim to segments of the Antarctic. As late as 1982, a form of colonial war even broke out between Argentina and Britain over the Falkland Islands, whose only attraction lay in the potential presence of mineral resources.

8 Continental imperialism

In the period when the whites were fanning out across the continent of Australia and the indigenous Americans were being displaced from the Argentinian pampas and Chilean south, a very similar process was unfolding in the northern hemisphere – similar in some cases down to the detail – as the United States appropriated the American West and Russia appropriated Siberia. Colonialism is by no means restricted to activities 'overseas', as is still sometimes asserted: after all, the key criterion, rule arising from the exploitation of a development gap, applies just as well to the American West and Siberia as to Africa or Australia. This would also make the expansion and ascendancy of the Han Chinese and the Chinese Empire a clear case of colonialism, indeed the oldest one of all and the one that has managed to assert itself most tenaciously right into the present day, in Tibet and elsewhere. It is true that the colonialism of the modern era is primarily a European affair – the related phenomena to be found especially in Japan, but also in Egypt and Ethiopia, were reactions to European actions, at times imitating European behaviour and utilising European 'achievements' – but China with its traditional colonialism is an exception which, importantly, can draw on its own traditional ideology of cultural superiority to legitimise its actions. Because the Chinese Empire and the two 'European' continental empires of Russia and the United States all fundamentally rest on settlement, they share with the New Europes the feature of being impossible, or extremely difficult, to decolonise. In fact, America and Russia are perhaps nothing other than huge, long-standing New Europes that are now expanding on their own account, which is why in this case it would be correct to speak not of 'sub-imperialism', like that of the British Dominions, but of 'secondary imperialism' and 'secondary colonialism'. The term 'secondary imperialism' is also useful in that America and Russia have made a seamless transition from continental expansion into overseas expansion, on the model of the naval powers and in rivalry with those powers (here, the United States has been more successful than Russia, no doubt in part because of its more favourable maritime location).

The United States of America

Even as colonists, the Americans were already engaged in westward sub-expansionism, and indeed British attempts to curb these moves after the Seven Years' War played their part in the colonies' alienation from the mother country. It should be remembered that the very first royal charters made territorial claims reaching as far as the Pacific Ocean. In 1780 such claims were ceded to the Union so as to protect the coastal states that could not participate in the claims from unlimited growth by their neighbours. In the 'Northwest Ordinance' of 1787, the Union set out its guiding principles for the ordering of both colonisation and decolonisation. Newly settled areas were to be administered by the centre until they had enough inhabitants to justify a separate legislature and ultimately admission to the Union as a new state. However, in the region between Ohio and the Great Lakes, for which the arrangement was originally designed, it was first necessary to crush the resistance of the Indians. Since the formation of the United States it had been taken for granted by politicians like Jefferson, the author of the Northwest Ordinance, Adams and Monroe that further expansion would spread out across the whole continent of North America. Occasionally sights were also set on Latin America, or even a kind of world domination in the best tradition of Puritan New England. It was thus nothing radically new when the United States' future was defined in 1845 as 'the fulfilment of our manifest destiny to overspread the continent allotted by Providence for the free development of our yearly multiplying millions'.

In 1803 the Union bought Louisiana, which had only reverted to the French in 1800. In 1810 it annexed the then West Florida up to the Mississippi, a territory which originally separated the Union from the Gulf, and in 1819 added the purchase of the Florida peninsula. The writing was on the wall for the Indians of the old South, although (or because) the Cherokee people had integrated very successfully into the cultural and political system of the whites, even holding African slaves. They had rich livestock possessions, workshops of all kinds, churches and schools, a Cherokee having invented a special syllabary for the language in 1819. In 1817 they had even become a republic on the US model. But when gold was discovered on Cherokee land in 1829, the state of Georgia demanded that they be removed. The president at the time was the Indian-hating Andrew Jackson. Although the Cherokee were sufficiently assimilated to take their case to the Supreme Court, the 'Indian Removal Act' pushed them and the other indigenous peoples across the Mississippi into the 'Indian territory' of Oklahoma. Even there the Indians would find no respite: the expansion of the whites caught up with them. The frontier of white settlement advanced only slowly, and came to a halt around 1860 at the 95th meridian, the great plains west of this being regarded as wastelands hostile to settlers. However, there were four western bridgeheads that had links with the east – Texas, Oregon, California and the Mormon settlement in Utah – and this enabled the intermediary space to be gradually taken over and 'filled up'.

1821 saw the opening of the caravan route to Santa Fe in Mexico, the main southern route to the west. In 1823 US citizens were permitted to settle in Texas, then part of Mexico, and their numbers soon outstripped those of the Mexican population there. The new Texans' aspirations for autonomy clashed with the centralism prevailing in Mexico at the time, and after bloody battles an independent Republic of Texas was created in 1836, joining the United States in 1845. On the Pacific north-west coast, claims had already been made in the late eighteenth century, when the Americans reached the area by sea. These claims gathered force once the Louisiana Purchase allowed the United States to inherit the mantle of the Spanish north of the 42nd parallel, where it maintained trading stations for furs and China-bound goods. US settlers gradually arrived in the region via the primary northern route, the Oregon Trail. However, not only was there a competitor presence in the shape of the Russians but, more importantly, the British made claims on the land, the 1818 border between the United States and what would later be Canada, the 49th parallel, applying only as far as the Rocky Mountains. The 'Oregon Territory' between the 42nd parallel and the Russian border at 54°40' was a kind of British-American condominium until, in 1846, the extension of the border along the 49th parallel divided it in two. From the Oregon Trail, a route branched off towards California, which could also be reached via Santa Fe. The Spanish presence there, established only in the late eighteenth century, was sparse and unable to hold out against the Americans who had been arriving in increasing numbers since 1841. Mexico, in the meantime, had failed to fulfil its obligations to American creditors, prompting the United States to call for the Rio Grande boundary and the sale of California and New Mexico – a classic configuration of 'imperialist' policy similar to that adopted by the Europeans only some time later. In the 1846–48 war between Mexico and the United States, the capital Mexico City was captured and California annexed. The peace treaty had Mexico relinquish almost the whole of the south-west of today's United States to the American victors; the matter was rounded off in 1853 with the purchase of land for a planned railway. When gold was discovered in California in 1848, a startlingly rapid development of the area began, enabling it to be admitted as a state of the Union as early as 1850. The Mormons, whose theology was practically a blueprint for an autonomous American salvific history, a kind of historical ideology of this particular New Europe, had retreated westwards from their persecution in Illinois and in 1847 settled in Utah, then still under Mexican rule. Their relations with the United States were amicable, although they did not attain membership of the Union until 1896, when they had officially renounced polygamy. After the admission of Arizona and New Mexico in 1912, the connected territory of the United States of America consisted of forty-eight states.

In other words, in the second half of the nineteenth century the western prairies too were 'opened up' for development and their Indian populations definitively eliminated or displaced. In the seventeenth and eighteenth centuries, the tribes of the Great Plains had taken over the horse from the Spanish to the south and become horse-riding nomads. The culture that most strongly colours our image of North American Indians is thus the most recent one of all. It was a lifestyle based on bison hunting, which required wide and open country. When the price of beaver pelts collapsed around 1840, a fashion for silk hats having supplanted felt, beaver trappers switched to killing bison for hides. This undermined the livelihood of the Plains Indians even before the gold prospectors and settlers arrived and the usual chain reaction set in: violation of a treaty by white interests – futile protests – violent resistance – defeat – a new, less favourable treaty, and so on until the Indians were banished to a reservation on territory that even the whites did not want. An important, and most certainly planned, vanguard role for the penetration of the west was played by the transcontinental railway lines, the first of which was completed in 1869. They were financed in part by land grants from Congress. But the savage days of cattle ranches and cowboys driving out Indians were not to last. In 1874 barbed wire was invented, and adherence to fixed property boundaries could be enforced.

In the 1880s, when the last Indians had been 'pacified', the pioneer era in the west came to a gradual end for the whites as well. The ever-open frontier was permanently closed – only to be re-opened in an ideological form in 1893 by the historian Frederick Jackson Turner and his 'frontier thesis'. According to Turner, it was the simple life at the frontier and its challenges that created the dynamic human type whose congenial form of life is democracy: in short, the American. Once the frontier was closed internally, it could be relocated outwards to great ideological effect. This happened very soon, and the American overseas imperialism of the period around the turn of the twentieth century was by no means, as is often claimed, a temporary aberration of US foreign policy, but rather a continuation along tracks set down in the republic's early days. The exploration and development of the Pacific coastlands and, to a certain degree, also the connection with the coast through the transcontinental railways had been guided by the goal of gaining access to East Asian markets; the project of a US-controlled canal across the

Central American isthmus, successfully completed in 1903, had been pursued vigorously from the 1820s. The advance into Latin America, too, was perfectly predictable, although in this case there was more reluctance to annex land because dark-skinned Catholics were considered inferior and therefore undesirable as potential future fellow citizens. The purchase of Alaska from Russia in 1867 fitted perfectly into the long-term scheme, as did the 1898 annexation of Hawaii, where American settlers had long been an important presence. Above all, however, the war with Spain over Cuba that erupted in 1898 was distinctly expansive in nature. Cuba may have 'only' been made a satellite, but in the process Puerto Rico, Guam and the Philippines were acquired, although in the latter case it was not the land itself but its port, Manila, and its potential for the China trade that attracted US interest. The United States has now relinquished these possessions or integrated them, in the case of Puerto Rico as an associated commonwealth (1952), in that of Alaska and Hawaii as states of the Union (1959). Yet this only implies a return to the concept of building American domination upon economic power and trade – trade not, of course, necessarily meaning free trade. It was on this basis that the United States hoped to achieve worldwide political hegemony in general and the annexation of Canada on the one hand, control over Mexico and the Caribbean on the other.

Russia

Russia, too, saw a continuity of expansion from the sixteenth to the twentieth century, this time eastward. In contrast to all other cases, this had an immediate geographical and historical relationship with the medieval colonisation of Central and Eastern Europe, and the occupation of Siberia may even be regarded as the last stage of that process, most literally as the establishment of a New Europe (with the emphasis on 'New', since otherwise Europe would reach right to the Pacific).

The beginnings of this expansion were founded, as in New Spain and New France, upon plunder, although looting was soon accompanied by settlement if only as a means of securing its continuation. Furs were the treasure at stake. But hunting fur-bearing animals requires an enormous amount of space, as we saw in the case of North America; the stocks of a limited area are soon exhausted. This circumstance tallied neatly with the expansionary aspirations of the tsars in Moscow, who successively conquered the various Tatar principalities into which the western khanate of the former Mongol empire, the 'Golden Horde', had splintered. The capture of Kazan on the Volga in 1552 ushered in an eastward advance, upstream along the Kama and across the Urals to Siberia. In 1573 the enterprising merchants of the Stroganov family, entrusted with this task by the tsars, became embroiled in armed conflicts with the Khan of Sibir. They recruited a troop of 800 Cossacks under Yermak Timofeyevich, who in 1581 defeated the Tatars and conquered Sibir, even if most of the fighters, including Yermak, were killed in the Tatar counter-attacks. The Cossacks traditionally took up the vanguard of the frontier wars, with the usual seamless transition from heroism to plunder; the Russian folk hero Yermak, for example, might equally well be described as a bandit chief. The Cossacks' superiority lay not least in their firearms, against which the Tatars and the Siberian peoples had nothing comparable to offer. In terms of brutality and ruthless exploitation of the indigenous population, their conquest and subsequent rule are indistinguishable from the Spanish *conquista*.

As in the Spanish case, the Crown quickly took up the reins and pursued expansion systematically, using both Cossacks and 'regular' military forces. And as in the Spanish case there were tempting profits to be made: by 1644, 10 per cent of the tsars' income was derived from furs. In 1585–1605 the area of the rivers Ob and Irtysh was subjugated, and in 1604 Tomsk was founded close to the Ob as the seat of administration. By 1628 the Russians had already passed through the lands around the rivers Yenisei, Tunguska and Angara; they had founded Yeniseisk and reached the Lena by 1619. The expansionary movement now forked to the north-east and south-east. In 1632 Yakutsk was founded on the Lena, in 1646 Okhotsk on the Pacific coast, and in 1648 the Russians reached the Kamchatka Peninsula and what would later be called the Bering Strait between Asia and America. At the same time, the Lake Baikal area was subjugated and Irkutsk founded there in 1651. Along with the soldiers, fur hunters and traders, and other adventurers, Russian settlers also trickled in, although well into the twentieth century they headed mainly for the fertile land between the Urals and the Yenisei, so similar to Old Russia, with a preference for the regions of Tobolsk and Tomsk. In 1670 the Tobolsk area had more than 7,500 Russian farmsteads and a farming population of around 34,000. The tsar's officials with their troops were located in the towns and bases, and from there collected *yasak*, the tribute to be paid in furs. Because, as usual in colonial situations, the system was supposed to be self-financing, the officers were given a free hand in the collection of this tax. The consequences can be imagined. The Siberian peoples offered resistance from the beginning, but their small numbers, scattered settlement patterns and hopeless organisational and technological inferiority meant it had little chance of success. Certainly, there are no records of conflicts on the scale of those in North America. The previous population of Siberia was made up of numerous different groups speaking different languages. In the seventeenth century, there are thought to have been sixteen ethnic groups in Siberia as a whole, together numbering around 230,000 people. The most significant were the Buryats, the Tungus and the Yakuts with populations of 30,000 or more.

Although the indigenous peoples' overall numbers rose steeply from the eighteenth century on, they were more and more clearly majoritised by the immigrating Russians. Between 1719 and 1795 their population is thought to have increased from 288,000 to 732,000, but the Russians, who already numbered around 700,000 in 1720, increased at the same pace, so that by the end of the eighteenth century indigenous Siberians made up only 30 per cent of the region's population. In 1897 that figure was 14.4 per cent, with 861,000 of the 5.73 million inhabitants, and by 1989 just 5 per cent, 1.6 million of 32 million. The eighteenth-century tsars worked hard to explore and exploit Siberia, and their efforts were so successful that their appearance on the Pacific caused some consternation among the other colonial powers. The land was divided up into governorates, as in Old Russia, but unlike there, these districts were grouped into governorates general. Settlement proceeded very slowly, a situation not altered even by the systematic transportation of exiles into the region. In 1838–61 the state established 200,000 peasants in Siberia, and these were joined by probably 60,000 illegal immigrants. Not even the abolition of serfdom in 1861 immediately triggered mass migration; this only began towards the end of the nineteenth century, when population growth in European Russia had halved the land available there and a state development policy for the colonies was also in operation. In the period from 1880 to 1913, Russia's population rose from 98 million to 171 million. In 1882, there were 10,000 immigrants to Siberia, in 1894 there were 73,000 and in 1900, 220,000. The increase was inextricably connected with the building of railways, which since 1884 had been considered the foremost political priority in Russian possessions as a whole, including Siberia. The most important was the Trans-Siberian Railway linking Chelyabinsk, Omsk, Novosibirsk, Krasnoyarsk, Irkutsk and Vladivostok, on which construction work continued from 1891 to 1905. The project was driven partly by strategic considerations such as the need to secure the newly acquired Russian Far East, but above all by the deployment of rail links as a mode of economic development under Sergei Witte's leadership of the ministry of finance (1892–1905). Witte's objective was for 'an uninterrupted chain of Russian villages' to arise along the railway, stretching from the Urals to the Pacific Ocean. To this end substantial funds were invested, the necessary infrastructure created, mobility improved, credit distributed and advertising pursued. In 1887–1913, 5.4 million people emigrated to Siberia, the peak being 1908 with 760,000 arrivals. In terms of its population structure, today's Siberia is the most 'Russian' component not only of the former Soviet Union but even of Russia in the narrower sense – a typical result for a New Europe. In the period 1863–1914 the Siberian population rose from 3 million to 10 million, though it was concentrated in the west and the south, where the frontier with Central Asia had now been pushed back. In 1896–1916, 29 per cent of the emigrants were able to settle in the north of what is today Kazakhstan. The Mongols had already provided the link joining the Central Asian region with Russia on the one hand, Iran and northern India on the other, and there had long been well-established trading connections between these countries. Peter the Great fought the Persians successfully, and in 1731/40 Kazakh nomads placed themselves under Russian overlordship as a way of gaining protection from Chinese expansion.

Caucasia was the first region to be incorporated by the Russian empire. Russia had been competing with the Persians and Ottomans there since the eighteenth century, and in 1801–29 took almost all of Caucasia and Transcaucasia from them. Of the many peoples of different Christian and Islamic denominations, the Circassians in the west and the Chechens in the east managed to assert their independence for a while through 'holy wars'. Only in 1864, after the Crimean War, during which these groups had been linked with Russia's enemies, did it prove possible to subjugate them once and for all with a superior force of 200,000 men. Caucasia was a popular settlement area, but until 1917 parts of it remained under a military colonial regime outside the normal administrative structures.

The frontier with the Kazakhs had been secured by Cossack settlements since the eighteenth century. In 1834–54 the Kazakh steppes were encircled, pincer-style, with fortified bases and Cossack villages, a process completed by a military campaign after the Crimean War in 1864, and in 1865 complemented by the seizure of fortified Tashkent. The Kazakhs could now be pacified; there was no thought yet of settlement or further expansion. But interests on the ground, in particular career-minded members of the military who needed conspicuous success stories, often took a different view, and realised they could effectively present the government in far-off St Petersburg with faits accomplis. They put forward the economic arguments of accessing new markets in Central Asia and supplying the Russian textile industry with its own raw cotton, but these points appear to have been of little interest to the government at the time. Instead, they were brought into play retrospectively by the military as a way of legitimising and funding its campaigns. St Petersburg's thinking, in contrast, followed the contours of European power politics. After the Crimean War, it was only in Central Asia that Britain could be defeated. The target was the Uzbek khanates, which used irrigation farming and had created focal points of Islamic culture in their oasis towns. In 1866–76 the khanates of Kokand, Khiva and Bukhara were conquered. This meant that the British and Russian areas of influence had edged closer together, and it was not long before conflicts arose that came close to full-scale war. Russia responded to the extension of British influence into Afghanistan in 1879–81 by annexing the Turkmen area south of Lake Aral. And in Iran, still independent on paper, fierce rivalry developed between the Russian interests in the north and the British in the south, the economic benefits of concessions and loans being, before the exploitation of oil, less important than the gain in prestige that each side aimed to make at the expense of its opponent.

In Central Asia, the military regime at first only permitted settlement sporadically, trying instead to win the loyalty of the subjugated population. The Central Asians became Russian subjects with equal rights; there was neither enforced labour nor military conscription, taxes were not increased and the Muslims' customs and laws were left intact. But in 1896–1916 more than a million immigrants arrived in the steppes of the north, their settlements increasingly hemming in the nomads. Thanks to their faster population growth, the newcomers were in the majority by 1911, though it was only in 1916 that uprisings began, prompted by the conscription of forced labour for the war. In the south, in contrast, there were only 380,000 Russians by 1910, compared to 6.5 million Muslims. Here, not unlike the case of British India, colonialism found expression in the transformation of the land into a source of raw cotton on the one hand, a market for Russian goods on the other. The result was the dissolution of traditional economic forms and the immiseration of the now highly indebted peasants. The Soviet regime then pressed ahead with Russification in the south as well. In 1926–65 the Muslim share of the population fell from 78 per cent to 55 per cent; in towns and cities Muslims even became a minority.

In the Far East, too, Russian imperialism spread into regions of alien culture, originally even beyond the Asian continent: the Russians had already reached the southern coast of Alaska in the mid eighteenth century, in Bering's day. Further journeys followed, especially in search of furs. Finally, in 1799 a group of trading companies joined forces as the Russian-American Company, which in 1818 was operating no less than fifteen Russian stations on American soil, its main location being Novo-Arkhangelsk, today's Sitka. However, the colony faced severe supply difficulties. Among the attempted remedies was the building of Fort Ross, only 150 km north of San Francisco, in 1812. Proving unsuited to the task, in 1841 the station was sold for grain to the Swiss-American Johann Sutter, the founder of California's New Helvetia, which would later be wrecked by

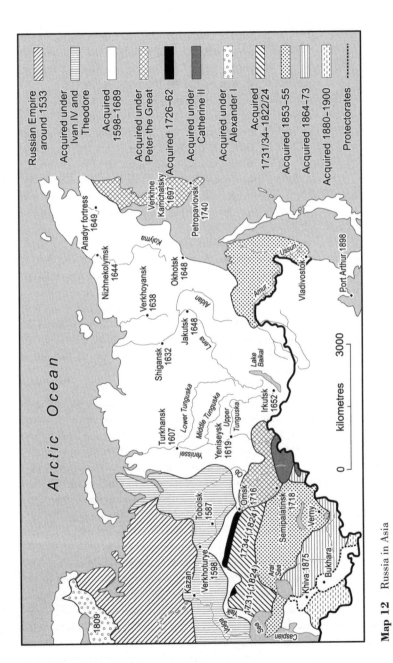

Map 12 Russia in Asia

Legend:
- Russian Empire around 1533
- Acquired under Ivan IV and Theodore
- Acquired 1598–1689
- Acquired under Peter the Great
- Acquired 1726–62
- Acquired under Catherine II
- Acquired under Alexander I
- Acquired 1731/34–1822/24
- Acquired 1853–55
- Acquired 1864–73
- Acquired 1880–1900
- Protectorates

Arctic Ocean

Anadyr fortress 1649
Verkhne Kamchatsky 1697
Petropavlovsk 1740
Nizhnekolymsk 1644
Verkhoyansk 1638
Okhotsk 1648
Kolyma
Aldan
Shigansk 1632
Jakutsk 1648
Lena
Lower Tunguska
Middle Tunguska
Upper Tunguska
Lake Baikal
Ussuri
Amur
Vladivostok
Port Arthur 1898
Turkhansk 1607
Yeniseysk 1619
Irkutsk 1652
Yenissei
Tobolsk 1587
Omsk
Ob
1734 (1824)
1731 (1824)
Semipalatinsk 1718
Verny
Kazan
Verkhoturye 1598
Yaik
Volga
Aral Sea
Khiva 1875
Bukhara
Caspian Sea
1809

0   3000
kilometres

ruthless gold-diggers. Because the Company was not authorised in Canton and therefore had to use the lengthy land route to get its furs to the market on the Russo-Chinese border, it was not financially viable. The problem was exacerbated by the government's lack of interest in its Alaskan outpost, which despite some misgivings was sold to the United States in 1867.

What did interest the Russian government, and had done for a very long time, was the Chinese market. As early as the seventeenth century the Russians had established themselves in the Amur basin, but they were driven out by the Chinese. However, the 1689 border treaty of Nerchinsk, negotiated by Jesuits at the Peking court, permitted regular Russian trading caravans to China. After China's defeat in the First Opium War of 1839–42, St Petersburg watched the growing influence of its British rivals in China with some concern. Russia's 'man on the spot', Governor General Nikolai Muraviev, had high hopes of the mineral resources and developmental potential of the Amur region. Making skilful use of the independence that arose from his faraway location, Muraviev went ahead with projects that St Petersburg hesitated to reverse for fear of losing face. In 1850 he established the town of Nikolayevsk on the Amur estuary. During the Crimean War, in 1855, he succeeded in occupying the left bank of the Amur, but it was only China's defeat in the Second Opium War that won him Peking's cession of the land north of the Amur and east of the Ussuri. This enabled Muraviev, now bearing the title 'Amurski', to establish a warm-water port on the Sea of Japan. It was boldly named Vladivostok, 'master of the east'.

When China was defeated by Japan in 1895, Russia portrayed itself as China's friend and helper. Together with France and Germany it forced Japan to give up the south Manchurian peninsula of Liaodong with its ports, procured French loans for the war reparations now payable, and even formed an alliance with China against Japan. In return, in 1896 the new Russo-Chinese Bank was awarded the concession for a 'Chinese Eastern Railway' from Chita in eastern Siberia right across Manchuria to Vladivostok. The new link was not only a huge shortcut compared to routes within Russian territory along the Amur and Ussuri, but also seemed to open up the possibility of a peaceful economic penetration of, initially, Manchuria on a model not unlike the dreams of the economist Witte. The Chinese market was to be opened for Russian goods that could not compete elsewhere on the world market. This peaceful imperialism foundered economically on the goods supplied by the western competition, and politically when, in 1897, Russia's more bellicose imperialists reacted to the establishment of the German base of Jiaozhou by occupying Liaodong. Russia responded to the Boxer Uprising with the military occupation of Manchuria, which in turn led to confrontation with the resentful Japanese over neighbouring Korea. The Russo-Japanese War of

1904/05 ended with crushing defeats for the Russians on land and at sea; Manchuria had to be relinquished apart from the railway, and Liaodong became Japanese. One consequence of this defeat was the first Russian Revolution in 1905.

China

Even in the seventeenth century Russian imperialism was clashing with Chinese imperialism in the Amur basin, and in the eighteenth a conflict in Central Asia seemed inevitable. At that time China was the stronger party, and in its period of decline in the nineteenth century it was protected from excessive Russian expansion by the interests of other imperialist powers. When China regained its powerful position in the twentieth century, however, new disputes immediately resulted, despite the fact that since 1949 the two countries had both been communist regimes and shared much ideological common ground. There were now even demands for the revision of the Amur-Ussuri border; certainly, in those areas there had been more Chinese than Russian settlers even under Russian rule in the nineteenth century, simply because the population pressure was more intense in China. The indigenous peoples found themselves under attack from both sides. They lost their land to Chinese peasants and were drawn by opium and alcohol into debt bondage with Chinese merchants, indigenous women and girls in some cases being sold by the Chinese as concubines. The Chinese settlers used their connections with secret criminal societies to implement this exploitation through terror. Russian occupation contributed additional aggravations without releasing the inhabitants from Chinese control. Even if here, unlike in European colonialism, colonisers and colonised belonged to the same race, this was clearly a case of colonialism: the rule of one people over another through the exploitation of a development gap.

However, Chinese colonisation and Chinese colonialism exhibit a longevity, a continuity and a structural density that leave the history of European development and expansion in the shade, even taking into account the colonial tradition that reaches back to Europe's emergence from the decline of the Roman Empire. Fundamental to the Chinese case is the expansion of the Han Chinese, which consisted in the spread, by traders and settlers, of a culture that had emerged since the second millennium BCE on the lower Yellow River. Repeatedly interrupted by crises but basically continuous for thousands of years and up to the present, the process has drawn its vitality from two special features. Firstly, China's advanced civilisation is the only one in world history to have remained rooted in its native soil from the start until the present day, and it thus identifies strongly with its territory. The locus of Chinese culture's origins has always remained a core region of China. Secondly, the Han Chinese as an ethnicity define themselves largely in cultural terms, as a group delimited by its identification with the dominant characteristics of Chinese culture. That is, they have always been able to assimilate new groups, which are either willing or forced to subordinate themselves. This does not imply 'tolerance'; if anything, the reverse is true. In contrast to this cultural continuity, Chinese political expansion proceeded very irregularly, with frequent interludes of reversal or even foreign rule. Only occasionally has it converged with the primary cultural expansion, and it has probably arisen less often from an imperial strategy than from the need to fend off the horse nomads of the north or forestall their imminent expansion through preventive strikes. Thus, although the political ideology of the 'Middle Kingdom' was always at hand to legitimise imperial expansion and colonial rule, it was built not on actual political power but on a cosmology of cultural superiority that classifies humanity as either Han Chinese or barbarian and makes the Chinese emperor the pivot of the earthly world. In this sense, there is no 'foreign policy' as such, but rather a range of different ways of regulating relationships with various barbarian peoples, who may in the process partake of the blessings of Chinese culture and thus advance from the status of 'raw' to that of 'cooked' barbarians. For Confucius, the inhabitants of the Yangzi valley were barbarians. Only in historical times were today's southern provinces and the area on the upper reaches of the Yellow River 'colonised', though remnants of linguistic and cultural minorities have survived there to the present day. The south-western province of Yunnan was conquered in the thirteenth century, and successfully sinicised from the seventeenth century on. The Chinese colonisers' and colonial rulers' actual relationships with the colonised there should probably be conceived of as similar to those prevailing in the Ussuri region in the nineteenth century; the Han notion of the barbarian probably did not generate substantially different forms of everyday colonialism than did its European equivalents. However, the fact that the People's Republic of China regards 7 per cent of its population as belonging to ethnic minorities, their settlement areas allegedly constituting no less than 55 per cent of the Republic's area, indicates a modern configuration backed by a still robust Chinese colonialism that resulted from the new political expansion of the Qing dynasty in the seventeenth and eighteenth centuries.

The process was innovatory in its markedly colonialist character, and culminated under the emperors Kangxi (1661–1722) and Qianlong (1736–96/99). Its attention focused primarily on the northern border, which the Ming dynasty (1368–1644), after supplanting the Mongol rulers, was able to defend only with difficulty by means of the Great Wall. In fact, the Qing themselves originally came from Manchuria and brought their ancestral homeland to the empire along with control over the neighbouring Mongol peoples. In the late seventeenth century the inhabitants of Outer Mongolia sought Chinese protection against the expanding Western Mongolians, or Dzungars. Pre-emptive activity to combat this danger furthered the Qing empire's expansion to the north-west (where the Han and Tang dynasties had already maintained a presence). The Dzungars were driven out of Tibet in 1720 and the country was incorporated into the empire as a protectorate in 1751; in 1757 they were defeated once and for all. Chinese estimates say that 30 per cent of them were killed – western authors speak of 'genocide' – while another 40 per cent died of disease and 20 per cent sought refuge with the Russians. The conquered regions were brought together in 1768 as Xinjiang ('new territories'), but only became a regular province in 1884. In the period between 1600 and 1800, China had been enlarged from 4 million km^2 to 11 million km^2.

Although the Qing tried to preserve their own people, they were not able to halt the massive illegal immigration of Han Chinese into Manchuria. Chinese peasants, traders and craftspeople turned this fertile land into a productive agricultural region with strong exports. Under the Japanese and the People's Republic it also became a centre of mining and heavy industry. By the early twentieth century it had been fully sinicised, and today it is divided into three 'normal' Chinese provinces. In Inner and Outer Mongolia the indigenous tribal structures were left intact, but politically the rulers were kept on a short rein and replaced by collaborators if they proved unco-operative. The economy soon fell under the control of Chinese merchants, who used loans to draw the Mongols into complete dependency. In Xinjiang indirect rule was established, based on compromises with the remaining old elites under the control of Chinese garrisons, while in Tibet the significance of the Chinese representative or *amban* (what would in the language of European colonialism be called the 'resident'), with his small garrison in Lhasa, declined; in practice, in the eighteenth and early twentieth centuries this area was under only a loose Chinese overlordship.

The unifying theme in these various strands of Chinese 'colonial policy' was population pressure resulting from the exploding numbers of Han Chinese from the eighteenth century on, which left their mark on the total population of China and experienced only temporary setbacks through the catastrophes of the nineteenth century. The following numbers are cited: 1600: 160 million; 1750: 260 million; 1850: 412 million; 1900: 400 million; 1930: 489 million; 1957: 647 million; 1985: 1,046 million. Population growth has resulted in Han Chinese settlement, economic modernisation and

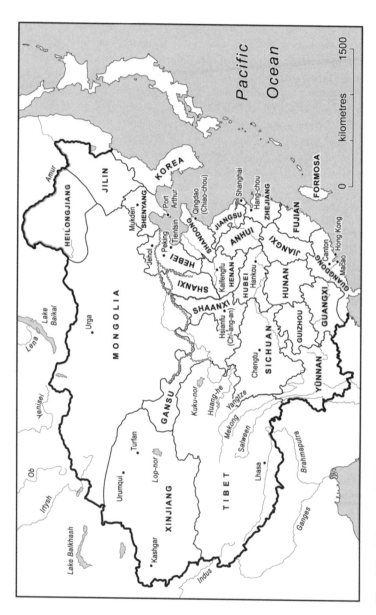

Map 13 China around 1800

when relevant political subjugation proceeding in parallel, especially in the era of the People's Republic. In 1990 the Han Chinese proportion of the population of Inner Mongolia was over 81 per cent, and even in the Tibetan capital, Lhasa, there are now thought to be more Chinese than Tibetans.

Despite the underlying process of sinicisation, the Qing respected the cultures of the subjugated peoples and aimed primarily to integrate their elites into the state. But the modernisation of China under the Republic after 1911 brought with it a modernisation of ideology: the traditional Chinese notion of the barbarian was transformed into modern racism. The Chinese 'race' was now considered to underpin the state, either in the sense that only the Han were viewed as racially fully-fledged Chinese, or in the sense that the Inner Asian peoples were defined as mere subdivisions of the Chinese race for the purposes of integrating the state. In Inner Mongolia, autonomy movements began when the dynasty fell in 1911, destroying the basis of the Mongol princes' personal loyalty to the empire – they owed no obedience to a Chinese republic. China managed to suppress the unrest and divided Inner Mongolia up into provinces, whereas in Outer Mongolia an independent state was established under the integrative leadership of the country's highest Buddhist dignitary. After his death in 1924 there followed, under Soviet influence, the proclamation of the Mongolian People's Republic and the establishment of a communist state based on the Soviet model and standing outside the Chinese imperial union. Xinjiang was held together by an ethnic bond between the various Turkic peoples and the religious bond of Islam, but both splintered into different groups and in the long term were too weak to assure integration. In 1875–77 the Qing had sent a Han army to the protectorate to smash the Islamic rule of Yakub Beg, oriented on the western Muslims. They settled Han Chinese and transformed the protectorate into a province. After 1911, there was a renewed cultural turn towards Islam, while the Chinese provincial government asserted its autonomy in all but name, after 1931 as a Soviet protectorate. In this way, the Chinese and Russians together managed to destroy what had in 1933 been proclaimed a 'Turkish-Islamic Republic of East Turkestan' and kill 200,000 of its population. The Russians, having found a use for Xinjiang's mineral resources, in 1944 tried to back the new 'Republic of East Turkestan' against the Chinese, while at the same time the region was becoming a focus of anti-Russian agitation for autonomy, with some pro-Chinese leanings. However, in 1949–51 the communist People's Liberation Army quashed all such initiatives; 70,000 more Turkestanis were killed and 150,000 fled abroad.

Although the Chinese communists professed a generous policy on ethnic minorities, in practice this was handled more or less arbitrarily in response to the particular power-political requirements of the day. The nation's unity remained the paramount principle, the communists following not a western, ethnically based concept of nation but one shaped by the Chinese tradition, based on historically legitimised territory. Just as before, tolerance extended only to limited variations on a single, Chinese identity. Anything more than that was punished as anti-Chinese 'local nationalism', though this procedure was in fact more likely to provoke ethnically based reactions. Tibet was regarded as a part of China, occupied and, after an agreement signed with the Dalai Lama in 1951, gradually 'modernised'. The east was separated off, made into two Chinese provinces and targeted for Chinese settlement. A rail link and new highways from the north-east and south-east now connected the country with China. New national cadres replaced the old feudal and clerical elite; owing their advancement to the new regime, they showed themselves its reliable advocates. Uprisings in the east in 1956 and in Lhasa in 1959 resulted in the definitive removal of the monastic government and the nobility, and communist economic and social reforms began. Brutal terror was exerted above all during the Chinese Cultural Revolution of 1966–69, which, despite a ruling to the contrary by the Chinese prime minister, also covered Tibet. Everything Tibetan was now to be exterminated: dress, language, script, and especially monasticism. Only thirteen of the 6,500 monasteries remained standing, and of 200,000 monks just a few hundred survived. Paradoxically, the most radical form of communism proved to be also the most radical form of colonialism and sinocentrism.

The liberalisation of recent years has only moderated, not eliminated the colonialist configuration in Tibet, as is shown by repeated protests. In Xinjiang, the mass destruction of mosques by the Red Guards caused many Muslims to flee the province or join the anti-Chinese partisans. The ruthless Chinese exploitation of mineral resources and the ecologically disastrous modernisation of agriculture by the Han settlers, whose numbers have grown since 1949 by a factor of twenty-three, additionally causes resentment and occasionally resistance, in recent times defined as 'terrorism', which was put down with violence as late as 2009. Today, Muslim Uyghurs and Han Chinese each make up around 40 per cent of Xinjiang's population.

Inner Mongolia, too, is an indispensable source of raw materials and a settlement area for the People's Republic. Although it now appears entirely sinicised, the Mongols are experiencing a considerable attraction to the revival of Tibetan Buddhism currently emanating from Outer Mongolia along with, perhaps contradictorily, a cult of Genghis Khan as a historical emblem around which Mongol identity can crystallise. The proximity in the north and west of communities ethnically and culturally related to the colonised minorities, and now independent after the Soviet Union's collapse, may well prove to pose the greatest threat to the perpetuation of Chinese colonialism.

Like its Russian counterpart, Chinese continental imperialism did not to any great extent spill overseas in the way we can observe for the United States. The seven impressive, but still somewhat mysterious, overseas expeditions made by great Chinese fleets in 1405–33 right up to the Red Sea and East Africa remain an isolated episode. Nevertheless, and contrary to the official ideology of a Middle Kingdom sufficient unto itself, large-scale emigration has led to substantial Chinese 'colonies' in all the countries of South-East Asia and beyond, in some cases giving rise to 'New China'-style colonialist phenomena of a type analogous with the 'New Europes'. In Malaya, Chinese made up more than a third of the total population and almost the entire communist partisan movement that unsuccessfully attacked the British colonial power in 1948. Today Malaysia's neighbour Singapore, with its 80 per cent Chinese population, has become a Chinese state. Taiwan was already sinicised in the seventeenth century, and in 1949, after the end of Japanese colonial rule, it was there that the nationalist Kuomintang leadership and a few of its followers retreated after their defeat by the communists.

9   Overseas imperialism in Asia

Along with the first decolonisation in America, the transition from trade with Asian goods to rule over millions of Asians in the course of the eighteenth century was the most important new development since the fifteenth- and sixteenth-century discoveries. It was to give completely new qualitative and quantitative dimensions to the relations between Europe and Asia for the next two centuries. Only from this point on can one speak of European colonialism in Asia including the zones of interest of the naval powers. While European economic, cultural and political influence had previously been rather marginal for Asians, the epoch of western superiority now also began in Asia, and would not end until after the Second World War. Especially in British India, that process gave rise to a new type of colony: the colony of rule, where the primary issue was no longer trade or settlement, but rule exercised by a small number of Europeans – often not even permanently resident in the country – over a huge number of 'natives'. The economic, social and political benefits for the mother country were now derived from this rule. Spanish America had already shown some features of this type, but always in combination with the characteristics of a settlement colony. British India was the first large-scale realisation of the colony of rule. It became not only the most important possession of a European country after the loss of the Americas, but also the model for a new form of European colonial rule that, given its focus on domination, may reasonably be called 'imperialist'. In the nineteenth and twentieth centuries, Indonesia, Indo-China and the larger part of Africa, to name only the most significant areas, were made into colonies of this type. Significantly, Britain's rivals liked to talk of creating a German India, a French or Dutch India in one place or another, and in fact the Dutch succeeded in Indonesia, even down to the choice of name.

This development commenced in the late eighteenth century with the British reaction to American independence, the French Revolution and Napoleon. Around the middle of the nineteenth century there was a certain liberalisation, leaving the settlement colonies more freedom and relying more on free trade than on colonial mastery. This was far from ruling out the use of colonialist force if required, and it anyway applied only minimally to the colonies of rule in India and Indonesia. Additionally, the system was based on Britain's extensive maritime and trading hegemony, the outcome of its wars with France. This made it perfectly feasible for the leading colonial power, unfettered by any meaningful competition, to dispense with formal rule and mercantilist regulation: free trade was the better, because cheaper, form of mercantilism, at least for the monopolists. This interpretation is borne out not only by the persistence of traditional control mechanisms in India even in the era of free trade and the measured doses of violence inflicted in the service of free trade in China and elsewhere, but also, and especially, by Britain's return to formal colonial rule as soon as it began to encounter more effective European competition. The result was the division of Africa that began in the final years of the nineteenth century. This period of increased rivalry between the European powers from 1870 to 1914 is commonly referred to as the 'age of imperialism'. The label may well be justified from the perspective of global politics, but from that of colonial history it is rather misleading, especially when accompanied by the one-sidedly economist reduction of imperialism to the consequences of the international competition between merchants and investors in a setting of high industrialisation. It is indisputable that the style of economic and power politics changed towards the end of the nineteenth century, but that change did not imply a rupture in imperialism's continuity since the late eighteenth century. In Britain the course was already set by then for the annexations that were pursued in the late nineteenth and even the twentieth century. Gallagher and Robinson's 1953 claims for the systematic nature of policy in the British 'imperialism of free trade' may be empirically contestable, but by insisting that the imperialist will to rule showed an underlying continuity despite changes in the precise political instruments, they nevertheless cleared the way for a more accurate view of the history of colonialism.

That new perspective meant rethinking existing explanations of European superiority, which could now no longer be attributed exclusively to the industrial era's technological and political instruments of power. Instead, attention was drawn to the superiority of skilled and disciplined European armies (or armies trained by Europeans) vis-à-vis traditional military forces, a factor particularly salient on the Indian subcontinent. Above all, however, the understanding of European superiority nowadays focuses more strongly on the Asian inferiority that arose from the disintegration of the great empires in the eighteenth and nineteenth centuries. That process unfolded worldwide, largely without the participation of Europeans, and can probably be attributed to the socio-economic shifts triggered by population growth that can be observed across the regions concerned. Commercialisation and large-scale private landholding combined to help regionalise the elites and intensify competition among the new regional powers for resources that were becoming ever more scarce. This also affected European trade, which responded defensively (from its own point of view) and seized the power over those resources for itself.

From trade to rule

It was not the British in India but the Dutch in Java who were the first to attach their trade more firmly to a foundation of political control, learning in the process that political rule too can generate profit. First the sultanate of Bantam in the west, competing with the Dutch and cooperating with the English, was reduced to vassal status in 1684; the Dutch East India company (VOC) took over the pepper monopoly and closed the port to non-Dutch ships. The VOC paid tribute to the overlord of Java, the Sultan of Mataram, in return obtaining the monopoly on maritime trade and free access to trade in the interior. However, in 1677/78, thanks to its assistance during a large-scale rebellion, the VOC was made protector of the sultanate, which at the time was obliged to give up the countryside south-east of Batavia. By taking sides in ever more internal crises, the VOC amassed ever more land and privileges, until after the 1825–30 Java War – an anti-colonial reaction emanating from an Islamic revival movement – the two sultanates of Yogyakarta and Surakarta were reduced to a minimal territory, on which they survived until decolonisation. For reasons of cost, the administration of the newly acquired territories was exercised largely indirectly, by Dutch 'residents' based with the indigenous vassals who, as political and commercial agents of the VOC and backed by VOC troops, were charged with supervising the indigenous government and carrying out the company's business. What the Dutch referred to as 'direct administration', at first introduced mainly in the Priangan area south-east of Batavia, in fact also involved rule by indigenous aristocrats, but without a princely chief. Groups of these 'regents', who imposed a harsh and exploitative rule over their districts, were supervised by Dutch officials. In this case exploitation primarily meant the cheap supply of coffee to the VOC, both without charge as tribute and at fixed prices kept artificially low and additionally reduced by manipulating weights. The system brought about an enforced transition from shifting, slash-and-burn agriculture to terrace cultivation, since this was a way of binding the farmers to the land; more intensive cultivation had also become necessary because the population was rising despite its mistreatment, possibly as a result of the unaccustomed peace under the colonial regime.

On the Indian subcontinent, it was the disintegration of the Mughal Empire into smaller regional states after 1707 that set the scene for change.

The new rulers included both former Islamic court dignitaries, as in Bengal, Awadh and Hyderabad, and the aggressive Hindu princes of the Marathas in the Bombay hinterland. This polycentrism in fact constituted the re-establishment of the political 'normality' on the subcontinent, yet for a long time all those involved, including the Europeans, clung to the Mughal emperor's still formally extant overlordship as a legitimating authority. There were two further factors that pushed developments in India further than those in Indonesia. One was the global political rivalry between Britain and France, including the tendency for each side to take pre-emptive action against real or imputed acts of aggression by its opponent. The other was a breed of political adventurers who skilfully turned the unsettled situation to their advantage in terms of personal gain, military careers and national expansion, often enough in the face of comparatively cautious attitudes from their company management, which was more interested in short-term profits. These 'new conquistadors' thought they knew better what would benefit their company and their country – and, most importantly, themselves. This mode of prosecuting European conflicts on overseas territory, and equally the 'sub-imperialism' of the empire-builders, the 'men on the spot', was among the characteristic features of the 'age of imperialism'. For that reason alone, the beginning of the imperialist age can be located in late eighteenth-century India.

Although the English and French East India companies would have been more than happy to protect their profits by avoiding conflict during the 1741–48 War of the Austrian Succession, the French navy carried out a successful operation against the English, and in 1746, working with the governor of Pondicherry, François Dupleix (1742–54), even captured Madras; the British regained it only in the peace of 1748, and now under the European law of nations. In these conflicts the Indian princes had proved to be no match for the Europeans, and when succession disputes arose in Hyderabad in 1750, Dupleix and his commander Bussy were able to secure the throne for their nominee, subject him to French influence, and have themselves rewarded with rich coastal provinces for Dupleix. The British, in turn, had brought their nominee to the throne in the hinterland of Madras, again a disputed succession. In the Seven Years' War, British naval superiority reversed the French gains, and Pondicherry was returned to France in 1763 only as an unfortified trading base.

As a supplier of fine textiles, Bengal had by now become the most impor-tant part of India for the Europeans. In 1717 the Mughal emperor had granted the English East India Company far-reaching privileges to extend their base at Fort William (Calcutta) and, even more importantly, exemption from all customs duties. For good reason, the Nawab of Bengal considered this unjustified, and he responded in 1756 with an attack on Calcutta. Despite a lack of definitive proof, the story that numerous English prisoners subsequently died after being crammed into a 'Black Hole' was cultivated as a founding myth of British imperialism. In 1757 the British counterattack from Madras led to the recapture of Calcutta and, after some uncertainties, to the battle of Plassey, in which Robert Clive's forces defeated the Nawab in spite of being outnumbered fifteen to one. The Nawab was replaced by a successor chosen by the East India Company, who had to confirm the Company's rights, allocate it a proportion of his tax revenues, and additionally pay it and its officers (especially Clive) several million pounds. The procedure was repeated on several more occasions, and the success of the whole operation was sealed in 1764 by victory at Buxar over one of the former nawabs, the ruler of Awadh and the Mughal emperor. The emperor was obliged to cede *diwani* rights to the Company in Bengal, Bihar and Orissa, allowing it to collect taxes and administer civil justice. The nawab retained control over the military and criminal justice.

The abiding flow of precious metals from Europe to Asia, recorded even in Pliny's day, was now reversed for the first time – an event of great significance for the beginning of colonialist exploitation in Asia. However, the East India Company could not sit back and enjoy its winnings, firstly because it had to transfer £400,000 a year to the British government, and secondly because it had to justify its improved share price by paying out inflated dividends that could only be financed through credit. In the end the Company was forced to ask the government for a rescue loan, which was granted only in return for reforms, word having by then spread of the abuses being perpetrated in Bengal. The Regulating Act of 1773 stabilised the management of the Company, but made it financially accountable to the treasury and politically accountable to the foreign office. The privilege of direct tea export to America, soon to become such a bone of contention there, was intended as an additional measure of support for the Company. The governor of Bengal was made governor-general over Bombay and Madras as well, but his autonomy was limited by a council appointed by the British government. A Crown-controlled supreme court for India was also created. The first governor-general was Warren Hastings (1774–85), a man well versed in Indian languages and cultures, who tried to infuse British rule over India with an enlightened despotism that, while part and parcel of the European trends of the day, also recalled the tradition of the Mughal Empire. Responsibility was now accepted not only for exploitation, but also for the exploited. In Bengal a British district administration and judiciary was created. The equal treatment of English and Indian trade for tax purposes was a great improvement on the previous use of privileges, but – like the unscrupulous financial extortion practised against various Indian principalities to the Company's benefit, misdemeanours for which Hastings was unsuccessfully impeached in 1787–95 – its introduction was motivated by a desperate need for funds. Since 1778/80 the governor-general had needed to fight the French, the Marathas and the expansionist ruler of south Indian Mysore with little idea of how to pay for these conflicts and little support from his council or from his colleagues in Madras and Bombay.

The new system had proved unsuccessful, but giving up India was out of the question: Indian revenues were now funding the flourishing China trade, and it was also evident that the French would be more than happy to take up any position in India left open by a British withdrawal. The time had come for the renewed reforms of the 1784 India Act, on the basis of which India was governed until 1858. The Company shareholders retained the right to elect the directors, but these now only controlled commercial matters and the appointment of officers. When making such appointments they were subject to the supervision (and in political and military issues to the instructions) of a cabinet board for India, the chair of which was in essence a 'minister' for India. Because the role of the governor-general was also strengthened, measures long overdue in India could now be put in place. Firstly, trade and administration were strictly separated in terms of personnel. The officers of the Indian Civil Service (ICS) were well paid and received training in a special college in Haileybury, until in 1857 the ICS was opened up for all applicants, in principle including Indians, when the distribution of offices through the directors' patronage was replaced by an open, competitive entry examination. Offices relating to administration and justice were also separated, and finally the tax system was provided with a firmer basis through the 'permanent settlement' for Bengal, which at a stroke transformed the hereditary tax collectors and police directors of the Mughal era, the *zamindari*, into landlords and the peasants, who had previously been difficult to drive from their land due to customary law, into tenants. Taxes were now fixed in perpetuity and began to arrive punctually, but the improvement in value and productivity benefited only the zamindari, not the tax authorities. The result was the emergence of a web of speculation instead of the hoped-for 'squirearchy', the English system of landed gentry and tenants; it seems that the 'political economy'-oriented planners had overlooked the cultural specificity of the English tradition. The new system was therefore not extended to other parts of India but replaced by tax assessment of the individual cultivator (in *ryotwari*) or the village community (in *mahalwari*).

Although the India Act had expressly forbidden all further expansionism, and many politicians and Company directors kept to that ruling, by 1818 the whole subcontinent had been subjugated, right up to the Indus. The legal basis was a loophole permitting defensive warfare and the fulfilment of the duty of protection of indigenous princes. 'Forward defence' was thus an important component in the inception of British India, as of the British Empire as a whole. This is where we find the specific historical substance behind J. R. Seeley's famous comment that the Empire 'conquered and peopled half the world in a fit of absence of mind'. In India it was initially long-standing enemies among the Indian princes, such as Mysore and the Marathas, that were defeated by the governor-general Richard Wellesley, the brother of the Duke of Wellington, who subsequently annexed the south and the greater part of the northern Indian plains. Such campaigns were motivated partly by the idea that political control would benefit commerce, a notion especially popular in Bombay, which then still lacked a hinterland; partly by the personal ambition of career-minded military men headed by Wellesley; and, up to 1815, partly also by the genuine threat constantly posed by France, which was working with Britain's enemies, and later the more fictitious threat from Russia, against which the north-western frontier was to be secured. When the Netherlands fell under French rule from 1795, their colonial possessions were taken over by Britain. In the negotiations of 1815 the British kept Ceylon, the Cape and Mauritius, but gave back Malacca and Indonesia, in 1819 building the strategically located naval base of Singapore as a substitute. In 1816, armed disputes ended in a lasting modus vivendi with Nepal, while in 1818 the hinterland of Bombay and part of central India was annexed after the conclusive defeat of the Marathas. The remaining Indian principalities became protectorates with British 'residents'. The natural boundaries of the subcontinent had been reached on all sides, and only on the Indus did a border remain open against the kingdom of the Sikhs, a monotheistic and syncretistic religion founded out of Hinduism in the sixteenth century, that had been integrated through stable treaty relations since 1809. It is worth noting that British overseas imperialism started from Bengal and the coasts, and its last port of call was the north-west – the location of the land route to the Indies by which all the previous invaders had arrived.

British India

When the East India Company's charter came up for renewal in 1813, there was some talk of a Crown takeover of India and the opening up of trade. In the event, the Company kept India and the Chinese monopoly but lost its monopoly on Indian trade, consequently abandoning that trade in 1824. From now on the Company could only pay out dividends from its China trade or from fixed grants, most of the Indian revenues having to be spent locally on administrative, military and interest costs. Although a substantial seepage of money to English officials, military men and creditors persisted, the changes put a stop to the unbridled plunder of the early days in Bengal. In fact, even the extraordinary profits of that early period had made up so small a share of British national income that from a macroeconomic point of view they cannot be regarded as a possible cause of British industrialisation, as is often claimed. From a microeconomic point of view it may be added that the 'new conquistadors' were no less conservative in their investment habits than their Spanish predecessors. They tended to put their money into property, gilt-edged stock or their own political careers, seldom into industrial enterprises.

One result – a result, not a cause, as is sometimes assumed – of the transition from trade to rule was a heightening of British ethnocentrism. The older generation of English rulers up to Warren Hastings knew and admired Indian culture, though mainly that of the Muslim elite, which they found more accessible than the complex world of the Hindus, additionally sealed off by its caste system. However, even the immediate successor of Hastings' regarded everything Indian as corrupt, and excluded Indians from the higher ranks of the administration. It became the norm for British officials to dissociate themselves demonstratively from the inferior world of India, especially now that colonial English society had attained greater coherence and self-sufficiency through the increasing presence of English women and families. Indological studies flourished, but in many cases they had turned from an amateurism fuelled by sympathy to bare 'knowledge as power'. The small-minded Christianity of the evangelicals soon gained great influence, followed by the hardly less mean-spirited belief in progress espoused by the utilitarians. For both, Hinduism was a special anathema, something that needed to be overcome through education or liberal economics – in short, through Europeanisation. By around 1850 contempt for everything Indian had virtually become an institution, but the fact that the Indians were, at least in theory, credited with the potential to achieve higher cultural development shows that in this period British ethnocentrism did not yet have the character of racism.

In the first half of the nineteenth century, both liberal and conservative governors-general worked on the 'modernisation' of India. The self-immolation of widows was suppressed, as was human sacrifice by the Kali-worshippers, and slavery was abolished. English became the official language of the higher reaches of justice and administration. The principle of equality before the law – still quite novel in Europe as well – having been introduced at the same time, interest in English education grew, and was catered to by a network of state, private and missionary schools (previously, traditional education had been encouraged and the missionaries kept at arm's length as potential troublemakers). Three Indian universities and a technical college were established; the development of Indian railway, postal and telegraph networks was tackled. A new Indian middle class of businessmen and lawyers found it to their advantage to adapt to British culture, a process reinforced by idealistic attempts to create a spiritual synthesis of western and Indian thinking. Politically, a 'modern' India no longer had any use for the old principalities, which were considered backward and inimical to progress. In cases where there was 'misgovernment' or no natural heir, the princely states were annexed without further ado, very much to the chagrin of the traditional elites, for whom such annexation meant the loss of their status.

In terms of foreign policy, a generally restrained attitude continued to prevail, with occasional expansion through forward defence. In the case of Burma, it seems that Burma itself, reaching out from Assam to Bengal, was the aggressor. After wars in 1824–26 and 1852/53, Assam and the Burmese coastlands were annexed, a fate spared the Burmese interior until 1886, when trading activity had grown and the French threat in neighbouring Indo-China was making its presence felt. A first attempt to bring pro-Russian Afghanistan to heel through a military campaign ended disastrously in 1842; to cover the embarrassment, in 1843 Sind on the lower Indus was annexed unlawfully instead. In 1845 the Sikh kingdom sought a 'social imperialist' escape from an internal crisis by leading its European-trained army against the British. The British won, and did so again in 1848 after an uprising against their resident. In 1849, the Punjab was annexed without instructions from London. When the Russians in Central Asia edged closer and closer to Afghanistan, a second campaign there in 1879–81 succeeded and brought a pro-British prince to the throne. In the course of securing the frontier against Russia, which was also advancing towards Iran, Baluchistan too came under British control, as did various mountainous areas that were combined in 1900 to form the 'North-West Frontier Province'.

The reaction to the policy of modernisation came with the 1857 'Great Mutiny' by units of the Bengali army stationed in the great plains. It was triggered by the violation of cultural taboos. In 1856 the recruits, many of whom were higher-caste Hindus, had had to accept a commitment to serve overseas, something that for Hindus implied exclusion from caste society. Most importantly, rumours circulated that the new rifle cartridges, which had to be bitten open, were greased with beef tallow and pork lard, the cow being sacred to the Hindus and the pig unclean to the Muslims. The arrest of soldiers refusing to use these cartridges led to battles that were cruel on both sides, but which the British finally managed to win: unlike the sepoys, they knew exactly what they wanted and were supported, at least passively, by

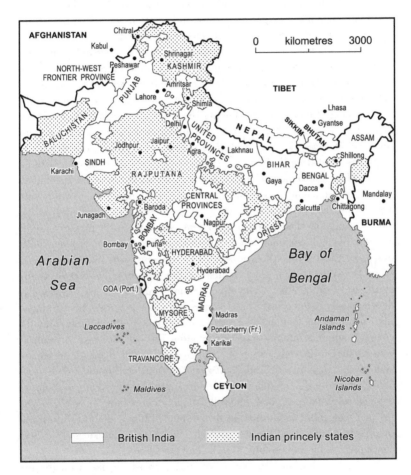

Map 14 British India

large parts of the population. Despite occasional claims to the contrary, the Sepoy Mutiny was by no means India's first war of independence. Rather, it was the last revolt of an old India whose identity was under threat and the role of whose elites had been cast into doubt. On the British side, the mutiny had a shock effect. The East India Company was brought to its knees, and in 1858 India was taken over by the Crown, the governor-general now redefined as the 'viceroy'. The last Mughal emperor was deposed, and in 1876 Queen Victoria herself took on the title of Empress of India. The army was subjected to stricter white control and its Indian troops were in future to be recruited mainly from traditional warrior peoples like the Nepalese and Sikhs. The old lords were now once again considered the more reliable choice, and the modern elites treated with contempt. The policy of annexation against the princes was abandoned and in individual cases, such as that of Mysore, even reversed. In general, a liberal will to improve the world was replaced by doubts as to whether the Indian was even capable of development. Both for India and for the whole of British colonial policy, in fact for western colonialism in general, it is impossible to overstate the significance of this turn towards a system of ruling by 'benevolent despotism', whereby British aristocrats – or middle-class would-be aristocrats – ruled over the masses with the aid of native collaborators, interfering little in their lives yet fundamentally despising them. This system was soon to converge with the emergence of social Darwinist racism, which denied that the 'inferior' races had any future at all. To be sure, this conservative system of rule never corresponded to developments in the economy and society. There the processes of modernisation, once set in motion, proceeded apace, at times inevitably with the colonial administration's own participation, as in the case of railway construction or the codification of law. Driven by Indian demand, the expansion of the western-oriented educational system continued, but Indians educated within that system were often frustrated by the administration. No colonial rule can do without the loyal collaboration of indigenous elites, and the fact that after the Mutiny the British tended to put their faith in traditional elites and neglect the modern ones would not remain without consequences for their empire in India and elsewhere.

If he had not been the most powerful authority in India before, the viceroy became so when the colony's finances were centralised in his hands in 1833. Although theoretically he remained restricted by his council, which gradually evolved into a panel of departmental ministers, this control had no practical relevance in the executive sphere, only in the area of legislature, in which the viceroy appointed additional members to supplement the council. In effect, this meant that the Indian bureaucracy was its own legislator. After 1870 a telegraph connected Calcutta with London, making it possible for the first time in colonial history for the 'men on the spot' to communicate rapidly with the centre, yet this did not stop the viceroy from acting largely on his own account providing he had secured his position through good relations with the currently dominant faction of the oligarchy in London. His superior, or perhaps rather partner, in this process was the secretary of state for India and his ministry, the India Office, but the secretary of state only rarely encountered any parliamentary curbs since the entire Indian government was self-funding and thus not dependent on the parliamentary approval of resource allocations. This was also the reason why the India Office remained separate from the Colonial Office, set up in 1854 with responsibility for the rest of the Empire. Likewise, the more 'gentlemanly' Indian Civil Service kept apart from the gradually emerging class of British colonial officers.

In India, Bengal was now given its own lieutenant-governor and the number of provinces was gradually increased, on rather pragmatic principles, beyond the previous three Presidencies. The governors and their councils were granted limited legislative powers. Ceylon had been a separate Crown colony from the start, and Burma was divided off from India and also made a Crown colony in 1937. Two fifths of the territory belonged to Indian princely states, numbering 562 in 1939 and accounting for one quarter of the total population. These states, ranging in size from Hyderabad with 18 million inhabitants to entities covering only a few villages, had no power to make foreign, customs and transport policy, but otherwise generally stood outside of British legislation and jurisdiction. Their speedy elimination after decolonisation suggests that the continued existence of the princely states, underwritten by the conservative British system of power, had long been an anachronism. Another such anachronism was the capital city of New Delhi, newly built in 1912–31 in an imperial style: by the time it was finished, decolonisation had already begun (though the governments of independent India have always appreciated the city's colonial grandeur). Below the province level, too, the British administrative system was conservative, basically oriented on the traditional administration of the English counties by local gentry. Alongside the judiciary, responsible for British and Indians alike although Indians were not permitted to pass judgement on Britons, there was a 'district officer' with wide-ranging powers of tax collection and law and order in a region between 5,000 and 17,000 km^2 in size. Only gradually were these gentleman administrators – drawn from the ranks of the elite, and almost entirely English, ICS – supplemented by specialists for particular areas of expertise in addition to their subdivisional officers. However, the whole system of rule ultimately rested on the loyalty of innumerable Indian subaltern officers, policemen and soldiers to their few thousand English masters.

Initially half (even at the end, still one third) of the costs of British India were covered by taxing land yield in the tradition of the Mughal Empire. Modern income tax on other earnings gained ground only slowly; revenue from the railways and especially from customs was much more important in 1939. Revenue from the land meant first and foremost grain and export crops: wheat, rice, millet, maize, cotton, sugar cane, oil seed, indigo, jute, tea. Before British rule, taxation had swallowed up between a third and a half of the land yield, but the system had had safety valves that were sealed off by the British. The peasants had previously owned their land by right of use, not as full proprietors, so that it was not possible to impound their holdings if they fell into debt. Because land was not yet scarce, they could move onto new plots. Moreover, taxation was proportional, and dropped automatically in the case of a bad harvest. The British settled fixed amounts of tax and combined the system with the European principles of private property and the liberal market economy. The peasant now had unlimited liability in the case of a bad harvest, and in addition was subject to the creditor-friendly western law instead of the debtor-friendly Hindu law. The result was massive indebtedness, impoverishment and dispossession and the emergence of a social stratum of landless agricultural labourers, especially after 1929, when the world economic crisis set agricultural prices tumbling. Of course, indebtedness does not automatically have to mean dispossession, and recent research suggests that at least the larger-scale peasant farmers in some parts of India may have handled agrarian capitalism rather well. This group, highly influential in the countryside, was nevertheless dissatisfied with the British policy and would later form the core support for the Congress Party. Notwithstanding some successful irrigation projects, the increase in production that can be observed seems to have been achieved mainly through the traditional methods of extending the area of cultivation and deploying more labour.

However, the economic benefits that had been gained were soon reversed by the population explosion and the resultant exhaustion of land reserves. The following population figures are cited: 1845: 130 million; 1871: 255 million; 1911: 303 million; 1941: 389 million; 1988: 1,000 million; 2006: 1,425 million (from 1988: India, Pakistan and Bangladesh combined). Mass emigration was a taboo topic, yet had become common practice by the Second World War, especially from the south-east. Most of the emigrants returned home, but the migration process left Guyana, Mauritius and the Fiji Islands as Indian countries – another form of sub-colonialism. Only from the 1920s did internal migration into the big cities become a more popular alternative. The number of industrial jobs was increasing, and economic historians have recently calculated a modest rise in per-capita income from 1860 to 1920, although this was subsequently eroded again by population growth.

Traditional anti-colonialism like that of Dutt, Marx or Gandhi argues that Britain destroyed the highly developed Indian textile manufacturing sector in the interests of the Lancashire cotton industry, and through 'de-industrialisation' and 're-ruralisation' turned India from an exporter into an importer of finished cotton goods and an exporter of unprocessed cotton. By 1820 exports of Indian textiles had dropped sharply, while Britain exported 818,000 yards of cotton fabric to India in 1814 but 2,038 million yards in 1896. That made up 39 per cent of Britain's cotton exports at the time, its next most important customer, Latin America, buying just 15.7 per cent. The shift was encouraged by tariff policies, although the Lancashire lobby was liable to clash with the fiscal interests of the Indian administration, especially when the Indian government was granted tariff autonomy after the First World War. In 1930 India imposed a 15 per cent tariff on British cotton goods – yet this was a preferential rate in the context of its generally high import duties, and anyway Lancashire's importance for Britain had decreased. But even the enormous scale of English imports could not satisfy Indian demand, so that traditional weaving still had a chance of survival until it was supplanted by an Indian cotton industry and collapsed once and for all.

In 1914, the Indian cotton industry was fourth in the world, ahead of Japan. Bengal jute held something like a global monopoly on packaging materials. Demand from industry and especially from the railways made India the biggest coal producer in Asia after Japan. The iron industry suffered some teething troubles because the material for expanding and operating the railways – in 1914, India's was the biggest network in Asia with 56,300 km of track – was mainly obtained from Britain. Capital, too, came almost exclusively from Britain; an interest guarantee meant that railways were the preferred destination for British investment, absorbing 79 per cent of the £300 million of British capital that was invested in India in 1914 and thus one fifth of all British overseas investment. The routes of the railways, oriented on the ports, followed the colonialist interest in opening up the country for trade. In order to kick-start the development of a domestic Indian industry, strong government investment and not just a half-hearted tariff policy would have been necessary. Politics did, though, make an unintentional contribution to industrial development through the booms of the two world wars, each of which prompted a surge of growth.

India's foreign trade, with its preponderance of raw materials exports and finished goods imports, had a semi-colonial profile but overall a positive trade balance – to be precise, a negative trade balance with Britain and a positive one with other partners. This enabled Britain to use India to compensate for its own trade deficit vis-à-vis third countries, just as the East India Company had done in its trade with China. In addition, Britain received direct payments from India known as 'home charges', especially interest on the railway loans, military expenses and the constantly rising pensions for former Indian civil servants and officers. In 1914 these transfers made up 24 per cent of the outgoings of the Government of India. Invisible earnings from the sea freight and insurance business, which remained strictly in British hands, also contributed to India's massive deficit in the balance of payments with Britain. Military expenses ate into the Indian budget to the tune of a further 40–65 per cent: as well as all the various other benefits it yielded, India paid for itself by maintaining half Britain's total land force without the least cost to the mother country. Indian troops were to prove extremely important for the British in both world wars. The British also knew how to make best use of their control of Indian currency. The high value of the rupee, justified by the silver shortage during the First World War, was sustained after the end of hostilities, amounting to a bonus on British goods and a penalty on Indian ones and leading to an outflow of Indian gold reserves to London. On the other hand, capital exports to India were now less enticing than before. In the Second World War the Indian economy's contribution to the British war effort was carried out on credit, so that by the end of the war Britain owed India 16 billion rupees. Of course, it is a more attractive proposition to grant independence to a creditor, especially if one controls his account, than – as was the case in the United States – to a debtor where there is no guarantee that the loan will ever be repaid. As a whole, then, Dadabhai Naoroji was justified in referring in 1876 to a 'drain of wealth' from India to Britain even if, firstly, the old trade-balance calculations with their fixation on bullion have proved overly naïve and 'mercantilist', while secondly it would be quite wrong to speak of a consistent policy of de-industrialisation. In fact India did experience economic development – but for the benefit of Britain, though that did not always automatically mean the disbenefit of India. Economics is, after all, not the zero sum game the mercantilists believed it to be.

The Dutch East Indies

By the early nineteenth century the British, with an eye to the route to China, had already established themselves on the Malay peninsula, in the hinterland of their new base Singapore, and through a private initiative also on North Borneo. However, Britain gave the Dutch back the core Netherlands possessions in the area, in particular Java, by far the most densely populated of the islands. Given the choice between a strong, aggressive France and a weak though (despite enforced privileges for British trade) unfriendly Netherlands on the Channel coast and in the Malay archipelago, Britain preferred the Dutch. The Netherlands was embroiled in various armed disputes with Indonesian Muslims, the sultanate of Aceh in northern Sumatra even enjoying British protection due to its location across the water from Singapore, and it initially found the colonies costing more than they brought in. This only changed after 1830, with the introduction of the *cultuurstelsel* or 'Cultivation System' that combined the eighteenth-century coffee system with 'modern' land tax on the model of British India. Javanese who had no access to cash to pay their tax could choose, instead of paying out two fifths of their yield, to devote one-fifth of their land and labour to the government's coffers by planting export crops like sugar cane, indigo, tobacco, coffee or tea. If more was produced, it was supposed to be paid for. However, the implementation of the system involved officials creaming off their share and Javanese being subjected to punishments including beatings. By the mid nineteenth century the Cultivation System was occupying around half of the population and one-twentieth of the land. Although it worked to the advantage of the Europeans, the system's consequences for the Javanese do not appear to have been exclusively negative: on the credit side in development-policy terms we might count new employment and the rise of a money economy. Above all, however, in the mother country the Cultivation System became the 'lifebelt' keeping afloat the Dutch economy, which had been considerably weakened by the 1830 loss of the industrialised Belgium. The monopoly distributorship made tidy profits, and could pass on large sums to the Dutch state, peaking in the 1850s. From 1831 to 1877, the treasury took in a total of 823 million guilders. That shrank the Netherlands' national debt, subsidised the development of a Dutch textile industry and laid the financial foundations of the country's railway network. It also boosted shipbuilding and the power of Amsterdam as a trading and financial centre. In short, the Dutch East Indies in the Cultivation System period is one of the few cases where colonialist exploitation was an unequivocal success.

To be sure, the system did not remain unchallenged. As in British India, colonial policy was essentially forged by the governor-general (if anything an even more powerful office than its British equivalent), together with a colonial minister responsible only to the king. The colony thus further underpinned the king's anyway autocratic regime by feeding it revenue that sidestepped parliamentary control. When the minister was made accountable to parliament as well, in 1848, even the liberals had no complaints about the extra profit the system entailed. They did, though, want more freedom for European entrepreneurs and for plantations, and to this end more access to

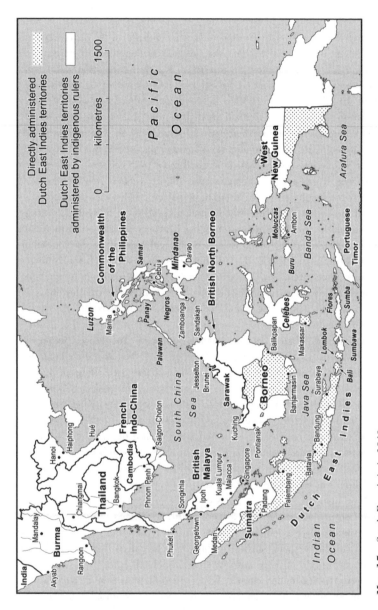

Map 15 South-East Asia in 1940

the land. A series of scandals and the anti-colonial novel *Max Havelaar* by 'Multatuli' (the pen name of E. D. Dekker) thus came right on cue: public opinion could be used to help enforce the dismantling of the Cultivation System, one product at a time, in 1862–1917 and push through a more liberal agriculture legislation. In this process, attention was paid to the protection of the natives, who were not allowed to lease out their land for more than 21.5 years, while rotating leases were subject to authorisation. The government, in contrast, could let state land for seventy-five years. Despite Java's overpopulation, the demand for labour coming from the plantations created some problems, especially when contract labourers had to be brought to the sparsely populated outer islands. At times these labourers were held like slaves; until 1940, it was a criminal offence for them to break their contract. Although the new system did still bring the Dutch considerable profits, those profits' share of the national economy fell sharply, as did the Dutch share of the colony's trade after liberalisation. Neither was it uncommon for the administration's budget to show a deficit. The golden age of the Cultivation System was over and was replaced by the normal conditions of colonialism, in which the state bears the infrastructural costs, if need be at a loss, while private individuals rake in the profits, which do not, however, impact significantly on the economy as a whole.

A further factor in the colonial administration's deficit was the cost of expanding the colony, a process that had returned to the agenda from the 1860s on. The initial aim was to safeguard shipping, which was experiencing phenomenal growth after the opening of the Suez Canal in 1869, against the sultanate of Aceh. Because the British did not want to take on this expensive task themselves, in 1871 they gave the Dutch a free hand in return for equal accreditation for English merchants in Indonesia and the acquisition of Dutch bases on the African Gold Coast (notably Elmina). The war with Aceh lasted from 1873 to 1908 and was only finally won by means of a new strategy, a religious and social policy built on scholarly advice from the Orientalist Christiaan Snouck Hurgronje. Hurgronje was also the source of the suggestion that, in the light of the Aceh experience, a summary declaration of submission should in future be demanded of the indigenous rulers, instead of individual treaties as before. This short declaration, or *Korte Verklaring*, of 1898 contained only three points: a recognition of Dutch sovereignty, a renunciation of their own external relations, and an obligation to obey all instructions from the colonial government's residents. After the pivotal talks between the governor-general, the prime minister and the colonial minister in 1904, the declaration became the basis on which the entire archipelago, including West New Guinea, was subjected to Dutch rule by 1914. One of the motivations was the not entirely unjustified fear that other western powers might become entrenched in the area, in view of Aceh's various attempts to make deals with the Americans, French, Italians and Ottomans. In 1870 the outer islands had contributed 13 per cent of Indonesian exports, but by 1930 that had become more than half, although this growth was due in part to new products such as rubber and petroleum.

However, Dutch imperialism was also characterised by a turn away from the liberalism in colonial policy that generally worked to the disadvantage of the indigenous population, and towards an 'ethical policy' aiming to promote their welfare – if necessary by paternalistic means against their will, or at least against the will of their rulers. The subjugation of the natives in their own best interest: an 'ethical imperialism' of this kind did play a role elsewhere too, to some extent even in the ideology of the Spanish *conquista*, but only in the Netherlands was it raised to the level of a scientific doctrine, drummed into a whole generation of higher colonial officers by Professor Van Vollenhoven at the University of Leiden. In vain did the plantation lobby establish a rival Indological institute in Utrecht; Leiden was the only institution to offer students a foothold in the administrative establishment. In the Indies, relatively few areas were annexed, but unlike in British India, the system of the residents with their white and indigenous bureaucrats, the *priyayi*, who were also expected to undergo training, in practice amounted to direct administration because the almost 300 indigenous rulers were largely deprived of power and financial autonomy. Land grants to white applicants were handled with more reticence, but otherwise the success of the 'ethical policy' appears to have been very limited, no doubt partly because of financial pressures, partly because of a paternalism that often degenerated into repression.

The 'opening' and 'modernisation' of China

Even in the sixteenth century, international law had denied nations the right to stand aloof from international exchange, in practice especially trade and Christian missionary work, as China and Japan had long been doing (with the exception of the Dutch station of Dejima and the licensed businesses in Canton). China was, furthermore, considered a market with a virtually unlimited capacity to absorb the rising tide of western manufactured goods, especially those of the leading industrial power, Britain. For 'free-trade imperialism', opening up these countries was therefore a self-evident objective. Conflict between China and Britain was only to be expected, and it erupted over the rising exports of Indian opium with which the East India Company, having secured itself the Indian opium monopoly, and its business partners were funding their imports from China and the Indies. Opium sales to China grew from around 300 tons in 1810 to around 2,600 tons in 1839, when the outflow of silver and a series of bad harvests triggered unrest and led Peking to send, at last, unbribable officials to Canton to destroy 1,300 tons of opium and try to put a stop to the system. The most important opium traders, equipped with a war chest of £20,000, approached British politicians and public opinion in search of redress for this insult to the British flag. At the same time, 300 Midlands textiles companies were calling for the Chinese market to be opened up. As they pointed out, if each of the 400 million Chinese were to buy just one inch of English cloth, the crisis-buffeted factories would be able to work to capacity for decades. The cabinet decided in favour of war, rejecting criticisms on the grounds that this was a matter not of narcotics trafficking but of making good a wrong and opening a market.

After the British victory – predictable given the progress that had been made in western military technology – the 1842 Treaty of Nanking granted the victors the Crown colony of Hong Kong not far from Canton and Macao, dissolved the monopoly on trade and enforced the opening of four further 'treaty ports' alongside Canton, including Shanghai. British and Chinese officials were henceforth to hold equal rank. There was no mention of opium, but trade in the drug continued to grow until the end of the century. It was halted only in 1911, and from then on was gradually suppressed. Sensing an unfair disadvantage, the United States used the threat of war to obtain the right to establish an American presence in the treaty ports and to extraterritorial consular jurisdiction. Both Britain and the United States also extorted a 'most favoured nation' clause, which laid down that a power in possession of a treaty containing this clause would automatically receive any concessions that China granted to third powers. From the perspective of the West this was an instrument of competition; from that of China it was an incentive to escalate imperialism.

In comparison to their British and American counterparts, the French as yet played only a minor role as merchants. In the rivalry with Britain, the Protestant French minister Guizot put his hopes instead in the Catholic missions that had been banned in 1724 and had only been able to continue their work illegally and under constant threat. As the self-appointed protector of missions (under Church law a role still held by Portugal until 1856), in 1845 France forced China to re-authorise Christianity and return Church property. Up to the present day, modern missionary efforts in China have been discredited by this kind of entanglement with western imperialism: the link between religion and opium was no less explosive here than in the thinking of Karl Marx, until both converged in 1949 with dire consequences for the Christians.

The most important treaty port, Shanghai, was controlled in practice by the consuls of the three powers. Here the customs system became a problem, because western merchants were using bribery to evade the customs duties fixed by the treaty. In response, it was agreed in 1854 that maritime customs should be administered by western inspectors in the service of the Chinese, a system that proved successful and was actually handled in the interests of the Chinese – as far as this was possible given that the three powers could determine the level of tariffs. At the very least it has provided us with reliable data on China's maritime foreign trade. Otherwise, a rather volatile and antagonistic mood prevailed that culminated in a second 'Opium War'. It is said that in the new treaties, imposed after the 1860 invasion of Peking by the British and French, a French missionary working as an interpreter smuggled in a clause that permitted missionaries to purchase land and erect buildings anywhere. The invaders' destruction of the Summer Palace, built in the eighteenth century by Jesuit missionaries in a fusion of European baroque and Chinese styles, may serve as a further symbol of the changed European relationship with China: attempts to open up to the alien culture had been replaced by violence and deception. The new treaties increased the number of treaty ports, opened the Yangtze for trade, provided for tariffs to be set by treaty instead of by the Chinese and imposed the opening of western embassies (in Chinese eyes an inconceivable political equality for 'barbarians'). They also permitted the free practice of Christian religion by Chinese, underwritten by the western powers – something that was to saddle missionary endeavours with numerous opportunistic 'rice Christians' and all sorts of bloody conflicts – and legalised the opium trade and the burgeoning coolie trade. The cessions to Russia in the Amur region have already been mentioned. China's sovereignty was beginning to erode.

Certainly, China's weakness cannot be attributed to exogenous causes alone. These were only able to come to full fruition because of a deep endogenous crisis related to the population explosion, a development that in China's case had to be absorbed by a purely agrarian economy; in other words by increased labour under worsened conditions. Just as this crisis was occurring, the system of rule, which required a strong apex, began to disintegrate. The emperors became ever more incompetent, in part for the simple reason that they were children or youngsters. 'Corruption', anyway common practice, was able to grow to proportions that endangered the state. If previously four to five times the tax revenue actually sent to Peking had been squeezed out of the population, in some areas it was now up to ten times the revenue. The political class of the *shenshi*, also called the 'scholars' or 'gentry', took their cut of the profits. Theoretically, the shenshi were a meritocratic elite who had passed civil service examinations and from whose ranks all the higher offices were to be filled. In practice, however, they included only members of prosperous and well-established families with good connections. Although not identical with the large-scale landowners, the shenshi were closely associated with these. They monopolised the 'classical' Confucian education system and championed the conservative social ethics which underlay that system at the time: an ethics which valued erudition and leisure most highly, placing land cultivation below it and on the lowest rung the occupations of merchant and soldier – that is, the roles that would have been most important in the confrontation with the West. The shenshi saw the existing, labour-intensive economic system as being on a human scale and therefore preferable to inhuman western technology. When labour became cheaper and capital more expensive, their interest in innovation declined even further. In short, China's political class did not 'modernise' because it saw no need for modernisation. In economic terms, China was caught in a 'high-level equilibrium trap'.

The convergence of the underlying economic crisis with western aggression and the crisis in the system of rule did not, however, necessarily mean the end of the line; according to Chinese historiography it indicated that one dynastic cycle was coming to an end because the 'mandate of heaven' had run out for the ruling dynasty and it was ripe for replacement. Just as in the fourteenth century the Ming dynasty had seized power and in the seventeenth the Qing, a revolutionary movement in the south now proclaimed *Taiping Tianguo*, the 'Heavenly Kingdom of Great Peace', as an alternative dynasty led by a charismatic visionary. Between 1850 and 1864 the Taiping rebellion affected more than 100 million people and cost 20 to 30 million of them their lives. What was new was the fact that this movement used a synthesis of Chinese ideas and elements of Protestant Christianity to cast radical doubt on the traditional order. Instead of the customary hierarchy, the rebels proclaimed the abolition of private property, land allocation based on need and radical equality even for women, along with a Puritan rigorism and the replacement of Mandarin, the official language monopolised by the gentry, with the spoken language of the people. The gentry saw its interests better served by the old dynasty, and managed to destroy the Taiping. In the process, no role at all was played by the Manchu troops and only a minor one by the western intervention under Charles Gordon, later to be the hero of Khartoum. The decisive contribution was made by Chinese armed forces, recruited in part through the exploitation of regional differences. Having once granted authority to these warlords, Peking was not in a position to rescind their regionally based powers, and it was at this time that the political disintegration of China into spheres of influence of regional military commanders began.

These men were, however, very much inclined to 'modernise' in their own way, which meant Chinese education for the fundamentals and western teachings for the practical applications, or, more concretely, grafting new achievements in armaments, shipbuilding and other technologies onto the old China and becoming rich in the process. In greater or lesser coordination with Peking, the 'provincial lords' built armaments factories and cloth mills, shipyards and steamer lines, coalmines and arsenals, railways and telegraph networks. To this purpose *compradors*, the Chinese middlemen of western companies based in the treaty ports, assembled expertise and capital for the future. Around 1870 China may have been no less ripe for successful modernisation than was Japan. But the real reins of power between 1862 and 1908 were held by the Empress Dowager Cixi, who had no appreciation of the need to modernise or to respond to international politics. Most importantly, the majority of the gentry opposed the process. In a certain sense they were even justified in their rejection of the valueless barbarian arts: appropriating western technologies to any large degree, as the reformers wanted, was indeed not possible without also adopting something of their cultural assumptions, as both reformers and gentry disdained to do. It was only defeat by Japan, and the escalating western pressure associated with that defeat, which resulted in the political class formulating radical plans for modernisation, in line with Kang Youwei's observation that since it was impossible to save the ancestors' empire, their institutions were no longer of much use. The young emperor was persuaded to introduce important reform edicts during the 'Hundred Days' of summer 1898, until his aunt Cixi had him locked up for the rest of his life and ordered the execution of some of the reformers. Instead, the court supported the xenophobic excesses of the popular 'Boxer' movement in 1899/1900, the suppression of which through a western and Japanese intervention brought China yet more humiliation. By this time, the court had nothing left to hope for. Making deals with rebels against foreigners had resulted in just as much loss of face as making deals with foreigners against rebels. In the end even Cixi was obliged to agree to reforms, a move that did not suffice to prevent the collapse of the dynasty and the proclamation of the republic in 1911. One further attempt was made to found a new dynasty, but by then the reformers had become revolutionaries. The 'May Fourth' student movement of 1919, responding to fresh indignities imposed by the Treaty of Versailles, was determined to make a radical break with China's past. It was the starting point for both the Kuomintang and the Chinese communists, even if each group re-established traditional patterns of behaviour as soon as it came to power.

The 'opening' and 'modernisation' of Japan

At first sight, the point of departure in Japan seems similar to that in China. The country had been closed off since 1637 and foreign trade highly restricted. The 'opening' of Japan in the mid nineteenth century, too, initially seemed to be a matter only of internal turmoil and external threat. However, there were significant differences from China that contributed to the success of 'modernisation' at the first attempt. The country was smaller and therefore easier to control. More importantly, government and society were organised not only on bureaucratic but also on feudal lines, with a double apex: the institution of the Japanese emperor, as in China based on cosmological myths, was politically powerless, since military and political power lay with the *shogun* and his government, the *bakufu*. The shogun controlled one quarter of the country directly and the rest as the feudal liege lord of the 260–270 *daimyo* who exercised almost unfettered power in their local domains. They were the lords of the approximately 570,000 samurai or military nobility that made up around 6 per cent of the population. Unlike the Chinese 'gentry', the samurai were guided not by abstract social morality and the values of civil culture but by the ties of personal loyalty and warrior virtues. However, the lasting peace had largely robbed them of their function, while the merchants, just as in China the despised lowest estate, played a greater role in practice than in the social theory of the day, due in part to the commercialisation of agriculture. Commerce, credit and the money economy were more highly developed than in China, and despite extreme pressures on small farmers the land had become prosperous, thanks to economic growth accompanied by a population rate kept artificially stable. Japan embarked on 'modernisation' from a relatively high level of development. As it proceeded, regional disparities led to a shift in the balance towards the southern daimyo at the expense of the bakufu. In these southern domains, the key part had long been played by the samurai.

From the late eighteenth century on, Russian, American and European ships had recurrently appeared on the waters before Japan – indeed, it was to forestall the Russians that the Japanese colonised and Japanised their northern island, Hokkaido. Otherwise they were able to keep the foreigners at bay until, after acquiring California, the Americans launched a massive push into East Asia. In 1853/54 an American fleet imposed a treaty that was followed by further agreements with the other powers and ever more comprehensive concessions: the opening of ports, the right to establish businesses, consulates, fixed customs tariffs, most-favoured-nation clauses. In the course of just a few years, Japan like China was caught up in a web of unequal treaties. The bakufu's readiness to compromise went hand in hand with a readiness to adopt western technologies as a way of strengthening its own position. This met with fierce resistance from some samurai groups, who elevated the almost forgotten emperor to the figurehead of a new national ideology and began to fight the foreigners under the banner 'Honour the Emperor, expel the barbarians'. In 1863/64, the barbarians thereupon bombarded two Japanese ports. For the competing samurai elites of the opposition, the implication of the attacks was that the country's westernisation must be rapidly advanced, especially in the military sector, something that could only be achieved through strong and unified political leadership. The samurai of the south defeated the shogun and seized control over the young emperor Mutsuhito, who in 1868 abolished the shogunate, moved his residence from Kyoto to Edo (hitherto the seat of the bakufu, now renamed Tokyo), and took power with his own government made up of young samurai bureaucrats from the south. This was the 'Meiji Restoration', so called after Mutsuhito's imperial name.

Alongside the usual empty phrases, the government's programme included an appeal to collect knowledge from all over the world in order to reinforce the emperor's rule, a rule which was to be established first of all through internal centralisation. In 1870–73 the feudal system was abolished and replaced politically by prefectures on the French model. The estate-based society fell; the daimyo and samurai received compensation but had to renounce their privileges, and became completely redundant when general conscription was introduced. Commoners were allowed to choose a family name and to decide freely on their profession and place of residence, inevitably triggering mobility and with it a further potential for modernisation. In 1871 a currency reform introduced the decimal system and, following the pattern of the Mexican silver dollar, the yen. The system's financial foundation was secured by a new land tax with fixed rates based on individual property. The government showed careful restraint with respect to foreign loans, but it had soon accumulated so much confidence that it was able to obtain credit within Japan. Although the peasants had to bear the initial costs of modernisation, their lives were more tolerable than the desperate situation under the shogunate because of new safety valves: not only the availability of industrial jobs, but also a mass army, trained along Prussian lines from the 1880s onwards. The army was the instrument of a subsequent politics of imperialism that probably contributed to the political integration of the masses.

The promotion of industry and technology also took place under the wing of the military, and consequently began with iron and steel production and shipbuilding. The first Japanese steamship was launched in 1866. In the area of textiles, the ministry of industry did not, in fact, limit its interest to clothing the army, but also attended to import substitution when the imports favoured by the treaties threatened the Japanese balance of payments and currency. Private capital was slow to materialise, the first entrepreneurs coming primarily not from conservative merchant circles but from the samurai milieu and the middle classes: of Japan's later financial and industrial giants, Mitsui is descended from rice-wine traders, Mitsubishi from a samurai family that took up shipping and shipbuilding. But the starting level of capital formation was so high that in the 1880s private businesses were able to take over the state concerns. The 1890s brought the great surge in growth, an important contribution coming from the war booms of 1894/95 and 1904/05 and the war reparations that Japan imposed on defeated China and Russia. Inspired by its first victory, Japan was able to rid itself of the unequal treaties in 1898 in bilateral negotiations, and achieved equal international status. Between 1889 and 1913 its foreign trade volume doubled every ten years; coal consumption rose from 2 to 15 million tons, food production grew by a third and the railway network trebled in size. The Japanese merchant fleet grew to 1.5 million gross register tons, and the shipyards were building 100 new ships every year.

However, these successes were accompanied by a conservative political turn. In the 1870s the enthusiastic adoption of western lifestyles had reached its peak, and there was talk of popular sovereignty and parliamentarianism. But after a regime crisis, from the 1880s on it was drummed into the Japanese that while western technology was useful, Japan with its own moral values was far superior to the rest of the world. In school classrooms, western content was once again subordinated to the 'classical' Japanese virtues of obedience, harmony and the fulfilment of duty. A revival of Shintoism facilitated the creation of the new national myth of *kokutai*, imperial rule as a national essence. The notion survived up to 1945 and beyond, and found expression in the constitution, also in place until 1945, which was promulgated in 1889. Based on a Prussian model after research missions and lengthy collaboration with German jurists, the constitution placed all three branches of government in the hands of the emperor, although he was to issue laws with the consent of a two-chamber parliament holding budgetary rights, while jurisdiction was carried out in his name by independent judges. The ministers were accountable to the emperor alone. The electorate for the lower chamber was initially restricted by census to around 1 per cent of the population. Against the backdrop of the previous system of rule, this constitution was by no means reactionary, since parliamentarianism and the principle of the rule of law laid the groundwork for further innovations. To be sure, the military was accountable to the emperor alone, although it could also influence the government via the minister of war. Most importantly, the emperor held political leadership without political responsibility. Incapable of fulfilling this onerous task, the emperors became the tools of unaccountable oligarchies.

The role of German jurists and Prussian officers in Japan reveals one of the secrets of Japanese modernisation's success: a willingness to learn combined with control over the material and teachers. Whereas China turned its back on western culture for the time being, Japan had long made a habit of selectively adopting foreign ideas and technologies. This process of reception had continued even during the country's isolation, through the mediation of the Dutch. While a Chinese traveller to the west could expect trouble when he returned home, the Japanese specifically sent their student and civil-servant elites abroad. Above all, however, Japan made optimum use of its 'development aid workers', around 4,000 of them in state service and two to three times as many in the private sector. They remained merely advisers, and were replaced as quickly as possible by Japanese, if only for reasons of cost. A third of the foreigners were English, the rest mainly French, American and German. The different nationalities were deployed in different spheres so as to keep their rivalry alive and get the best from each group. Thus Britons were brought in for the navy, railways, telegraph and public construction works; Americans for diplomacy, postal services, elementary schooling and agriculture; Germans for the military and law and for higher education and medicine.

This system allowed Japan to retain its distinctiveness, at least until 1945, and even the most assiduous reception of foreign ideas never compromised the nation's cultural identity. In fact, it has always been part of the essence of Japanese culture to receive and adapt foreign influences, not least from China, which itself had traditionally rejected such influences. Whereas China always saw openness and closedness only as mutually exclusive alternatives, Japan's remarkable blend of the two aspects was probably the main source of its success. Openness will have been fostered by the dynamic economic development that was already under way, closedness by the political system's assertiveness and its inauguration of a new nationalism. But this was only possible because Japan had a dual apex with emperor and shogun. Where China had no alternative to its hamstrung dynasty, determined nationalists in Japan were able to replace the shogunate with the politically fresh institution of the emperor, in whose name they partially modernised the country and prepared it to compete politically on the world stage.

High-imperialist power rivalry in China

With its victories in the Sino-Japanese War of 1894–95 and the Russo-Japanese War of 1904–5, Japan had successfully gained a seat at the table of the great powers. Notably, even in the case of the Russo-Japanese War this victory came at the expense of the Middle Kingdom, since Manchuria, the object of the dispute, did not belong to either of the belligerents but to a third power, the non-participating China. More generally, the escalation of international rivalry during the decades around 1900, which are referred to as the 'age of imperialism' and culminated in the First World War, was marked by the principle of 'convenance' and compensation. That is, two opponents would come to an agreement at the expense of a powerless third, and if one state managed to make a territorial gain there was a self-evident claim to compensation for all the others. This tried and tested recipe of European balance-of-power diplomacy was excellently suited to resolving the increasingly frequent conflicts that arose when not only the United States and Japan, but also more and more European countries elbowed their way into the arena of colonialist politics. Since China was considered the richest prize, it was there that the jostling was fiercest. It was obvious that China had reached the limits of its power to resist, and that its division was only a matter of time.

The catalyst came from the German Empire. The unequal treaties with China and Japan that the Prussian East Asian expedition had signed in 1861 had included the plan, as yet unrealised, to establish an East Asian naval station. German trade with China was developing well, thanks in part to the armaments that the busily re-arming 'provincial lords' were buying from Krupp. A 'German-Asiatic Bank', founded in Shanghai in 1889 by a consortium of large German banks on a government initiative, was intended to serve commerce but also to pave the way into the Chinese railway business. In the view of Wilhelm II's aggressive foreign policy, Prussia had earned China's gratitude by lending it diplomatic support against Japan in 1895, and this gratitude should take the form of granting Prussia the port of Qingdao in Jiaozhou Bay, Shandong Peninsula. When China refused, the Germans began to keep an eye out for any Chinese provocation, and they did not have to wait long. Two Catholic missionaries were murdered in 1897 and Wilhelm was able, as he put it, to show 'with the most brutal ruthlessness' that 'the German Kaiser is not to be trifled with, and that it is a bad thing to have him as an enemy'. Germany imposed a treaty whereby the Chinese leased out Jiaozhou for ninety-nine years, renouncing Chinese sovereignty, and granted the Germans the right to build railways and exploit the mineral deposits in Shandong. Qingdao flourished, but only with the help of subsidies from the Reich; otherwise only railway construction was economically successful.

Seeking compensation for the German gains, Russia occupied the Liaodong Peninsula as part of its imperialist eastwards expansion. It obtained the right to build the South Manchurian Railway. France demanded and received a base on Guangzhou Bay, along with railway concessions in

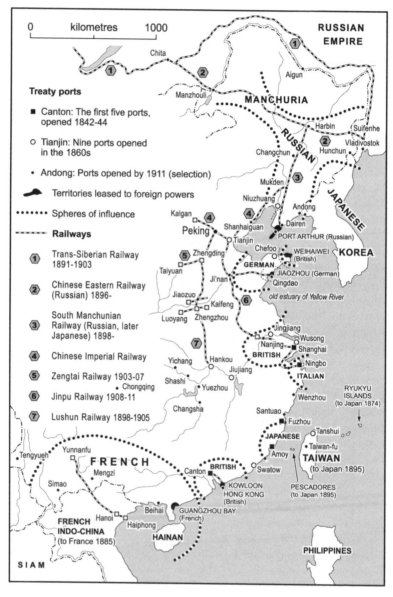

Map 16   China in the era of high imperialism

southern China and the assurance that the provinces of Guangdong, Guangxi and Yunnan would not be ceded to a third power. Japan obtained a similar assurance for the province of Fujian. Demonstratively flaunting its power to the Russians, Britain had Weihaiwei, opposite Port Arthur, ceded to it and took the opportunity to extend Hong Kong by adding the 'New Territories' on a lease of ninety-nine years (ending, of course, in 1997).

The Yangtze basin was also 'reserved' for Britain, which maintained a gunship flotilla on the river until 1941. But apart from Russia and Japan, nobody had an interest in dividing China up into zones of exclusive influence, and the US 'Open Door' policy met with approval from all the other powers. The intention of the policy was for no country to disadvantage another economically within its own Chinese sphere of influence; to this end, the customs system was to remain under Chinese authority. This cooperation between the powers – occasionally precarious, but as a whole solidly grounded in common interests – proved its worth again during the anti-foreign Boxer movement. The Boxer Protocol of 1901 imposed enormous indemnities and established what was virtually a 'supra-government' in the shape of the ambassadors of the powers. The protocol brought China to the high point of its career as a 'semi-colony', but its transition into a 'full colony', or division up into several such colonies, would have offered no benefits to the powers: their economic interests were too closely intertwined for that. The system of the treaty ports, now numbering forty-eight, was international in its conception, even if the leading trading power Britain drew the greatest profits from it. Railway construction, which since the 1880s had promised to become a business similar in scale to that in British India, was handled by consortia more or less unified in national origin and concentrating on particular regions. It was rare for railways to be built by foreigners under exclusion of China, exceptions being the Chinese Eastern Railway built by the Russians, the Yunnan Railway by the French or the Shandong Railway by the Germans. For the most part the railways formally belonged to the Chinese state but remained in the hands of foreign consortia until China had paid back the associated loans, the conditions of which were usually very unfavourable to the Chinese as a result of political pressure. However, being creditors of the Chinese state, these consortia had an interest in the continued existence of China irrespective of their own national make-up.

There were thus many different reasons to favour the continued unity of the Chinese empire and, with it, continued access to all China's markets. This is not to say that the interplay of business and politics was always harmonious or international cooperation never contradictory. At times political allies might compete economically in China while political opponents worked in unison, as was the case for Britain, France and Germany after

1905. China was left to foot the bill. If some historians claim that western intervention remained marginal and incapable of impacting decisively on the huge empire's socioeconomic development, others note that the massive western interventions of 1897–1911 thwarted Chinese efforts to modernise, by skimming off the income needed for capital formation and sapping the authority of government. One thing is certain: the western powers may have kept China's existing regime alive in the short term, but in the long term they thoroughly undermined it.

From free-trade imperialism to high imperialism

Along with the carving up of Africa that took place in the same period, the escalating power rivalry around China is the epitome of high imperialism. The characteristics of high imperialism are the ambition to open up and control markets as a way of accessing raw materials and ensuring sales for domestic industry; the endeavours by powerbrokers and military policy-makers to tighten the informal control required for this purpose, up to and including the establishment of formal colonial rule; great powers suspiciously watching each other's every move and taking every gain by another power as grounds to seek an immediate compensatory gain for themselves, international politics now being regarded as a social Darwinist struggle of the nations in which only the strongest will survive; and finally an international commonality of investor interests that may at times actually defuse this political conflict potential. Interest originally focused on markets, as is shown by the history of the 'opening' of China and Japan. But the later history of China also demonstrates that increasing international competition and political rivalry fostered a tendency towards formal colonial rule that distinguishes multinational 'high imperialism' from the previous, British-dominated 'free-trade imperialism'. The case of China does also indicate that this tendency could be obstructed by the combination of competing power interests and interwoven economic interests, enabling the country in question to maintain its formal independence. As well as formal colonial rule along the lines of British India, the era of high imperialism also saw informal control of a country by a single colonial power – like British rule in Egypt – and thirdly the 'semi-colony', in which the presence of several competing powers made it possible or even necessary for a remnant of effective political independence to survive. Alongside China, the Ottoman Empire is a prime example of this third type. It is notable that as soon as the First World War reduced the number of powers competing for influence there, the Ottoman Empire was divided up. In Iran, it was only the rivalry between the two world powers

Britain and Russia that, by keeping them both in check, sustained the rule of the Shah, although they did divide the country into a Russian sphere of interest in the north and a British one in the south in 1907. In that same year a treaty between Britain and France laid down that Siam (as Thailand was called until 1939) would be maintained as a neutral buffer state between French Laos and British Burma. In this case the rivalry of the great powers exceptionally left the affected country plenty of room for manoeuvre, enabling autonomous policymaking and a successful, independent modernisation, if one that bears only limited comparison with its Japanese counterpart. Like Japan's, Siam's modernisation initially proceeded under the hand of a powerful national monarchy, but the persistence of earlier power and property relations and the traditional mentality hampered agricultural and industrial success, as did the relative weakness of the country, which unlike Japan was not able to prevent its markets being flooded with western goods. Less powerful countries that did not have this kind of niche in international politics found even political self-determination impossible. The Madagascan monarchy's efforts to modernise, for example, were not sufficient to preserve the country from French colonial rule.

High imperialism is thus distinguished not so much qualitatively as quantitatively from the preceding European expansionism, starting with the quantitative increase in the participating powers, which now included newcomers like Germany and Italy as well as non-European states like the United States and Japan. What was novel was only the more energetic state intervention in economic policy and the nervous, occasionally even hysterical, tone of international politics. What remained unchanged was the imperialist nations' quest for ever larger economic and political spheres of influence, driven by increasing industrialisation in all the western countries. In this process, different actors made rather haphazard use of very different instruments: economic interests co-opting the power of the state was by no means the norm, and the reverse also occurred. It should be remembered that 'the' economy rarely shared a common set of interests. Textiles, heavy industry, 'modern' industries in the chemicals and electrical sectors, banking, commercial and transport enterprises rarely acted in concert, and the much-cited concentration of economic power was also very unevenly developed. But in times of accelerating international competition accompanied by decelerating economic growth, concern for the nation's prosperity took on a more prominent role within a politician's duties, particularly when increasing parliamentarisation made that politician increasingly dependent on the feelings of his or her voters. Because the scope for action overseas was becoming more restricted and, where separate spheres of influence existed, borders were rapidly moving closer together, the opportunities for expansion no longer seemed limitless. A kind of last-minute panic arose; the powers tried to secure the maximum range of options for the future by consolidating their possessions while there was still something to be had.

Britain's economic and political advantage was shrinking at a time when the electoral reforms of 1867 and 1884 ushered in an age of mass politics. Needing to appeal to a mass public, politicians now sometimes found themselves the prisoners of their own populism, which would also define their later image in the history books. In reality, the alleged dispute over colonial policy between the Liberal prime minister Gladstone (1868–74, 1880–85) and the Conservative Disraeli (1874–80) was largely for show: Gladstone was not really in favour of dissolving the Empire any more than Disraeli was really interested in systematically expanding it. Anyway, the debate still applied almost solely to the white settler colonies and India – and even this only marginally, since relationships with other powers and domestic policy were both far more important. Thus, it was the Irish question that split the Liberal party and led to a Conservative regime in 1885–92 and 1895–1905, under the premiership of Salisbury from 1885 to 1902. This was the period when imperialist, racist, social Darwinist thinking began to dominate both elites and masses, with politicians of both parties loudly proclaiming a new-found faith in imperialism. The colonial secretary Joseph Chamberlain (1895–1903), whose office now acquired its first real political clout, and the prime minister were fully aware of the public impact of economic arguments. Imperialist policy was represented as a necessary component of the struggle of the nations, especially as Britain's share of the world economy was falling dramatically. In the Boer War of 1899–1902 the Empire's popularity intensified into nationalistic excess, but soon afterwards the imperialist fever passed and the 'normal' list of political priorities was restored.

The experience of the Boer War also brought forth the first coherent, critical analysis of imperialism, a seminal text even today. John A. Hobson argued that imperialism was bad for the nation but good for 'certain classes and certain trades' such as the military, bureaucrats, the armaments industry and, especially, the mainly Jewish investors and finance capitalists he claimed to have observed in South Africa. Because of the overproduction and underconsumption of goods and capital due to insufficient demand on the domestic market, sales or investment opportunities had to be sought abroad, something that imperialist policies aimed to promote. It would, wrote Hobson, be unnecessary if domestic demand were boosted by means of a dynamic wages policy and tax-funded reform policies. Instead, imperialism distracted the attention of the masses onto foreign policy, despite the flimsiness of the justifications for imperialist policies. The point has long been upheld against Hobson that British investments were actually not made in those colonies acquired in the imperialist age but in the white colonies, in India, in Latin America and in Europe. It is also clear that colonial expansion anyway often emanates not directly from the mother country but rather from interests in the colonies themselves, the 'men on the spot'. However, P. J. Cain and A. G. Hopkins have come back to the idea that British imperialism since the seventeenth century can be explained by the continuous interest of a certain, politically crucial group. For them this group is not the industrial capitalism of the north of England, for example the Lancashire textiles industry, but the politically powerful rent-seeking 'gentlemanly capitalism' of the south, leadership of which shifted in the mid nineteenth century from large landowners to the finance and service capitalism of the City of London.

In France there was no such continuity. After 1871 it had been possible to revile colonial expansion as tantamount to a betrayal of the goals of revanchism. This was the grounds for the French premier Jules Ferry to be ousted in 1881, over Tunisia, and in 1885, over Tonkin. Although the final decade of the nineteenth century saw the establishment of an official expansion programme, its implementation by influential politicians and the founding of a parliamentary *groupe colonial*, that 'colonial party' was always a minority, and business interests in expansion were limited to individual groups, remaining weak overall. The colonies only became economically important for France after the First World War.

In Germany, media discussion of all the usual imperialist arguments began at an early stage, but under Bismarck practical colonial policy was a short episode that arose when a range of domestic-policy needs coincided with a favourable foreign-policy moment, Britain being paralysed by conflicts with Russia and France. Bismarck probably used colonial policy to outmanoeuvre the anglophile crown prince, win elections, deflect domestic conflicts outwards and possibly also stimulate the faltering export economy through a countercyclical trade policy, the latter two points serving to stabilise the system of rule. But it remained a temporary crutch, whereas under Wilhelm II from 1897, imperialist 'world policy' was a firm part of the programme, if mainly on paper after 1906. China and the Ottoman Empire were anyway more economically important than the German possessions in Africa and the South Seas.

The overseas imperialist expansion of the United States stood somewhat in contradiction to the nation's anti-colonial origins. In its continental expansion, the Indians could simply be driven out and the territories, once settled with white immigrants, made members of the Union. That was not an option for dark-skinned Catholic or heathen Latin Americans or Asians, and at least in Asia, US imperialism was limited to the establishment of bases as a means of opening up market access. As a rule, the United States remained true to this imperialism of free trade and free investment, which comfortably coupled ideology with vested interests. However, the long-term programme, with its high expectations of foreign markets, did not rule out recurrent military interventions and occupations, and in the Spanish-American War of 1898 these even led to the temporary acquisition of genuine colonies. In its racist doctrine of social Darwinism, too, the United States paid tribute to the imperialist spirit of the age.

When the imperialist fever of the turn of the century had broken and the world had been carved up, a debate flared within German-speaking socialism on why capitalism had not long since collapsed, as Marx had predicted. For Rudolf Hilferding in 1910, Rosa Luxemburg in 1913 and Lenin's immensely popular summary *Imperialism, the Highest Stage of Capitalism* of 1917, the division of the globe between giant finance-capitalist concerns using imperialist expansion was the last resort of 'decaying' capitalism, which would ultimately perish through self-destruction as in the First World War or, as Lenin's later acolytes took particular pains to elaborate, through the resistance of the colonised. However, by this point capitalism had achieved such stability through the development of domestic markets – the path demanded by Hobson and declared impossible by the Marxists – that it now no longer had much need of the former colonies' markets and commodities, aside from a few strategic products such as petroleum. Under these circumstances, anti-colonial critique after the Second World War took a 'turn to the periphery'. On the one hand, the significance of local processes and the activities of the 'men on the spot' were examined and the indispensable role of indigenous collaboration in colonial rule was emphasised; on the other, there was a general move to consider less the causes than the consequences of western expansion in the colonies. According to the 'dependency' theories that emerged from the late 1950s onwards, these consequences consisted in irremediable underdevelopment and lasting dependence on the centres of the world economy. Today these theories, too, have been largely falsified by the extremely divergent and in some cases very successful development of particular ex-colonies – and it has even become possible to proclaim the end of 'big theory' as such, as Ulrich Menzel showed in 1992.

High-imperialist colonies in Asia and the Pacific

Through its missionaries, France had already upheld links with *Indochine*, as the French called the eastern half of the South-East Asian peninsula, since the seventeenth century. Tonkin in the north and Cochinchina in the south, connected by the coastal Annam, formed the Annam empire under Chinese suzerainty and Chinese cultural influence. Cambodia and Laos, to the west, were under Siamese rule and Indian cultural influence. In 1859, Napoleon III occupied Saigon in response to persecutions of Christians in Annam, in consideration of the Catholics at home. Vietnam had to cede the city to France in 1862 along with the east of Cochinchina, not least at the behest of the navy. By 1867 the remainder of Cochinchina was conquered and neighbouring Cambodia secured by making it a protectorate. The French now sought a route to southern China's markets and raw silk, so that in 1885 China's neighbour Tonkin was annexed and Annam reduced to a kind of protectorate. China had to give up its suzerainty over the area. Siam's expansion towards Laos, suspected by the French of being fuelled by Britain, was halted when the Siamese were forced to cede Laos in 1893; the spheres of influence were sealed against Britain in 1896 (finalised in 1907).

The colony called the *Union indochinoise* consisted of five unequal parts: the regular colony of Cochinchina, the French inhabitants of which enjoyed limited participation in the administration and sent parliamentary deputies to Paris, and the four protectorates of Annam, Tonkin, Cambodia and Laos, which had *Résidents supérieurs* as French representatives. Although France's penetration of the region was more thorough than Britain's in India, the role of the residents in Laos and Cambodia was more or less similar to that of the British residents posted with Indian rulers, while in Tonkin the resident system was expanded to form a kind of direct colonial administration. Annam's ruler was weakened by the fact that his council of ministers was presided over by the French resident. However, the crucial role was that of the governor-general and his central administration in Hanoi, funded from customs receipts. The coastal and delta lands were densely settled rice-growing areas with a tendency to large-scale land ownership. Development policy focused primarily on rail construction and the link to China via the Yunnan Railway; otherwise, Tonkin was to remain a producer of raw materials and a market for the mother country's goods. Coal from Tonkin was exported as far afield as Japan. While imports from third countries were subject to French tariffs, commerce between the colony and the mother country was duty-free, enabling France to achieve dominance of the colonial market. Yet Indo-China never in fact became a goldmine, a 'French India'.

Of the tiny British Straits Settlements on the Malay peninsula, only the port of Singapore was significant at first, but when, in 1867, the settlements were separated from India and subordinated to the Colonial Office, a local lobby began a campaign to influence policy in London. The lobbyists were looking for British investment in the tin mines operated by Chinese entrepreneurs and labourers, as global demand for tin was now on the rise. London only responded when it became clear that the investors and the notoriously combative Malay states might otherwise put themselves under the protection of a different power. However, the pace was dictated by a dynamic governor on the ground, who began by placing the tin-rich states under the authority of his residents. He reacted to French expansion in Indo-China by advancing to the eastern coast, and to German activities by acquiring the north from Siam by 1909. The colony now also included four Federated Malay states and a further five Unfederated ones. The conditions were in place for an enormous surge in tin mining, and by 1890 Malaya was already producing more than all other countries put together. The necessary shift of production from surface to deep mining, with its greater demands on investment, enabled the British to edge the capital-poor Chinese gradually out of the business: in 1906 Chinese entrepreneurs were producing 90 per cent of the tin, by 1936 only 36 per cent. The rubber plantations established from 1895 on became an entirely white business. They benefited from the demand of the fledgling automobile industry, and attracted so many investors that in 1914 more capital was invested in Malaya than in any other colony outside of India and the white Dominions. If the tin mines continued to be operated with Chinese labour, the rubber plantations used imported Indian labour, resulting in a tense triangular relationship between Malays, Chinese and Indians.

The Philippines were originally not a high-imperialist colony but a sub-colony of Spanish Mexico, established in the sixteenth century. This prolonged period of rule led to a degree of cultural assimilation unique in Asia, the Filipinos becoming Asia's only Christian majority people. Direct rule by Spain after the loss of Latin America brought the Philippines free trade and with it economic modernisation, through the cultivation of export crops such as sugar cane, tobacco, Manila hemp and indigo, though mainly on large estates and under the control of British and Chinese companies. A modern indigenous elite aspired to independence on the Latin American model – as, indeed, everywhere the existence of modern elites appears to trigger decolonisation processes. A war of independence ended in 1897 with defeat by Spain, and another in 1902 with defeat by the United States. During the Spanish-American War and as part of its imperialist turn, the United States had occupied Manila in 1898, making it an 'American Hong Kong'. This made it necessary to seize the whole archipelago at the same time, since a Spanish or independent Philippines would have posed a contin-ual threat to Manila. Thus the Philippines too were drawn into the spate of high-imperialist expansion around 1900. However, the Americans immedi-ately introduced civil administration and a comprehensive policy of reform that included land reform. The latter, at least, remained largely ineffectual, because the supremacy of free-trade policy and a liberal market economy meant that although production of cane sugar, coconut oil, hemp, tobacco and rubber soared, this only led to a further consolidation of large-scale land-holding. The pattern has been common in cases where modern market economy conditions collide with premodern social ones.

In the Pacific, the wide expanses seemed at first to offer plenty of space for many different interests: whalers; sandalwood and trepang traders hoping to supply these Fijian products to the Chinese market; harmless and criminal adventurers of all kinds; missionaries of diverse denominations and – equally important at the time – diverse national origins. From the mid nine-teenth century these were joined by white planters producing commercial crops, primarily sugar cane, cotton and copra, the crushed and dried coconut meat that was increasingly in demand in the west as a raw material for oil extraction. Just as in New Zealand, the white presence triggered processes of transformation that were bound to culminate in white hegemony, given the environment of imperialist power rivalry. After all, the reasoning ran, one could hardly accept an enemy power annexing the island in question.

The process began innocuously enough. By around 1840 American Puritan missionaries had made Hawaii an educated and Christian nation under its existing indigenous monarchy. In Tonga, Australian Methodist missionaries contributed to the stabilisation of the indigenous monarchy, which gave itself a constitution in 1875 and has survived until the present day, although it was placed under British protectorate in 1900 in the wake of the great imperialist clean-up. In other parts of the region, events unfurled less smoothly. On the Tahitian islands, British Congregationalists had been able to win over the monarchy to a somewhat straitlaced 'kingdom of God' in the early nineteenth century, but committed the error of having the French Catholic competition expelled. Looking for a base and a boost in their pres-tige against Britain, in 1842 the French established a protectorate over the island group by force of arms. In 1847, the French protectorate finally received the blessing of a Britain disaffected by its experiences in New Zealand. When Napoleon III occupied New Caledonia in 1853 and set up a convict colony, soon to grow into a flourishing mining economy (nickel, chrome, phosphate), Britain acceded because it needed French support in the Crimean War. In Samoa, the expansion of plantation operations after the mid-century profoundly shook the political system, but did not culminate in annexation because here the competing Americans, Germans and Britons kept each other in check. For a time the three consuls exercised a kind of suzerainty not unlike that in other 'semi-colonies'. On the Fiji Islands, too, rivalry existed between American, Australian, British and French planters, but in this case the Australians managed to induce a hesitant Britain to annex the islands in 1874 – for the time being as a way of creating a base for infor-mal control over the Pacific.

However, from the 1880s the western presence had been growing to such density that the powers began to feel threatened by each other and tried to secure their positions through pre-emptive annexations. When German plantation companies propagated the establishment of a colony of New Guinea, at first unsuccessfully, Queensland became nervous and in 1883 annexed eastern New Guinea; the Germans followed suit in 1884, now having obtained imperial protection for the lands. Finally, in 1885/86 Berlin and London came to an agreement that divided eastern New Guinea into a German northern and a British-Australian southern half including the neighbouring Melanesian island groups. Melanesia was a source of contract labour – in practice a form of slavery – not only for the northern Australians and the Germans, but also for the thriving mines of French New Caledonia. At the same time, the emerging sub-imperialism of Australia and New Zealand in Polynesia was getting in the way of the French westwards advance from Tahiti. The participants hurriedly entrenched their power over various island groups, while the New Hebrides, a favoured source of Melanesian contract labourers, was transformed into an Anglo-French condominium in 1906. Samoa's informal condominium was brought down by shifts in interests and influence between the parties involved. For Germany, economic ascendancy in the region made the islands a prestige project at home, so that in 1899, against the backdrop of the new US imperialism, Britain was paid off with concessions in Africa and the island group divided up between Germany and the United States. The German Empire also purchased the Caroline and Mariana Islands from defeated Spain. Finally, Hawaii's independence fell victim to American imperialism. First the United States acquired the naval base of Pearl Harbor in 1884. Then, in 1890, American protective tariffs were introduced that threatened American-operated sugar production on the islands; annexation by the United States would eliminate the tariff disadvantage. When the situation was exacerbated by a crisis in the monarchy, the American settlers seized power and in 1894 founded a Republic of Hawaii that was to become a US territory in 1898 and a federal state in 1959. The Pacific, too, was now fully in the hands of the imperialist powers of the west.

10   Imperialism in Africa

Africa had played a role in the history of European colonialism as early as the fifteenth century, but it was only in the nineteenth century that the continent was subjugated. Africa was Europe's third and last colonial empire, after America and the lands of Asia and Australasia. It was the last to be colonised and the last to be decolonised, and still suffers most severely today from the consequences of colonialism. Asia and America had more to offer the Europeans, while Africa supplied mainly slaves, which could for the most part be bought from indigenous intermediaries. There was thus little occasion for Europeans to advance into the interior of this anything but inviting continent. Africa's coasts are naturally forbidding and possess few good harbours; its rivers are difficult to navigate, their estuaries often interrupted by rapids. Large parts of Africa are relatively dry, and the luxuriance of its tropical rainforests is an illusion, arising from rapid turnover, not fertile soils. Finally, Africa is home to a variety of infectious diseases that have frequently been fatal for Europeans.

The once customary description of the inhabitants of sub-Saharan Africa as peoples without letters or history has proved to be a prejudice of European writing-based culture and of a historiography rooted in that culture. Aside from the fact that the Arabic script was widespread in Sudan and that Ethiopia had long been using a script of its own, an absence of writing is anyway far from signifying an absence of history. Alongside its remarkable politically acephalous lineage systems, sub-Saharan Africa has brought forth an abundance of imperial formations, quite apart from the north's Ancient Egypt and the kingdoms of the Europid Arabs and Berbers of Muslim North Africa. The continent has given rise to a further three races in addition to the dominant Negrids and the Europids of the north: the Aethiopids in the east, who combine features of black and white races but today are no longer viewed as 'mixed-race' but rather as descending from shared ancestors of those two major groups; then the longer-standing inhabitants of the south, the Khoisanids, in pejorative European usage called 'Hottentots' or 'Bushmen', who have a paler, yellower skin and other features distinct from the Negrids; and finally, on Madagascar, the descendants of prehistoric Malay immigrants who brought their language with them. The Khoisanids, with their hunting and gathering way of life, and the Negrid rainforest farmers, thinly settled and impoverished, are the only ones not to have developed any large-scale political entities.

Not only eastern Madagascar but the whole of eastern Africa has formed part of the Indian Ocean oecumene since ancient times. Long before Islam, Ethiopia received influences from the Arabian peninsula; its black Jews, the 'Falasha' community now resettled in Israel, are a particularly remarkable legacy of that history. Above all, however, the trade in gold, slaves and ivory on the eastern coast between Mogadishu in the north and Sofala in the south enabled migrants from Arabia and Persia to create an urban culture of mainly black Muslims (erroneously referred to in later sources from German East Africa as 'Arabs'). Their language, Kiswahili, is a Bantu idiom enriched with Arab vocabulary, and was originally written in Arabic script. It is still the area's language of common use today. The Portuguese conquered the coast in pursuit of their trading empire, but were driven out in the seventeenth century by the Sultanate of Oman, which in 1840 moved its residence to the island of Zanzibar off the East African coast. Only Mozambique remained Portuguese.

In comparison to Arab influence, the European presence in Africa was initially only marginal. It was mainly oriented on trade, the only exception being the Boer population of the colony founded at the Cape of Good Hope in 1652, who by 1800 made up around 87 per cent of the approximately 25,000 Europeans living in Africa. But the impact of Europeans was greater than these figures might suggest, especially because of the slave trade that was pursued for three centuries in the west, where 5,000 kilometres of coast from Senegal to Angola were studded with slave-trading stations, most densely on the Guinea coast covering today's Ghana, Togo, Benin and Nigeria. In this region, the slave trade shaped the economy and society probably more strongly than anywhere else except Angola. The Europeans were mainly kept away from the country's interior by their African business partners. In 1787, a time when slavery was beginning to fall into disrepute in Britain, an attempt was made to create a new home for former slaves in Sierra Leone, but this had to be taken into British government hands as a colony in 1808. Experiments like that in Sierra Leone were repeated several times, with limited success. The most important of them was the colony of Liberia, established in 1822, where the United States hoped to divest itself of its liberated slaves. In 1847 Liberia became an independent republic, although one where African Americans exercised the same kind of colonial rule over autochthonous Africans as whites did elsewhere on the continent. In contrast to the Portuguese coastal bases of Angola, in Mozambique Portuguese adventurers (including mixed-race and even Asian people) advanced inland along

the Zambezi and built themselves large estates, or *prazos*, that were in practice independent fiefdoms. Portugal having ceded some islands in the Gulf of
Guinea to Spain in 1778 (Spain had previously held only its old fortified
bases, or *presídios*, on the north coast of Morocco), by around 1800 all five
of Europe's long-standing colonial powers had possessions on the edges
of Africa.

European free-trade imperialism and African expansion

Recent research agrees that Africa was certainly not drawn into the European
world system only after its subjection to formal colonial rule in the era of high
imperialism: European penetration had already begun in earnest by around
1830, in the shape of free-trade imperialism. Europe's status changed from a
source of demand, especially for slaves, to a source of supply, especially of
textiles and metal goods, that was constantly in search of new markets. In
Africa this economic expansionism was attended by scientific and religious
expansionism to a particularly striking extent. Geographers and ethnologists
proposed to tackle the last 'blank spots' on the map of Africa, and the evangelical revival movement prompted the first energetic efforts by Protestants to
convert the heathen; at the same time, the Catholics were beginning to
recover from the collapse of their missionary institutions, so closely associated with the defunct ancien régime, and turned to new, more successful
forms of organisation. All three expansionary tendencies were combined in
the person of the Scot David Livingstone (1813–73), whose exploration of
Central Africa in 1854–56 took him right across the continent from Luanda
to the eastern coast. Livingstone was a missionary, explorer and textile-
industry promoter all in one. When his contact with the outside world broke
down during his travels west of Lake Malawi and Lake Tanganyika in 1866–
71, he was sought and found by the American journalist Henry Morton
Stanley, who marked the start of a new breed of power- and media-conscious
explorers. High imperialism was on its way.

On the other side of the equation, Africans were instigating intense
political activity at this time. The nineteenth century saw a rise in religious
movements and African trading systems, including the emergence of an
African capitalism, and the founding of new dominions and empires. Some of
these were themselves colonial in character, especially the Egyptian
conquest of Sudan but also the later Amharic conquest of southern Ethiopia
that took place during the age of high imperialism. In many cases these
developments were driven by new kinds of warrior groups, such as the

'military states' of southern Africa, the 'commandos' of south-west Africa or the large armed caravans of the Swahili in East and Central Africa. Much of this may have been a reaction to the European presence and demand, and some of it was only made possible by the adoption of European ideas and technologies, especially in military affairs. But it would certainly be wrong to explain the entire African dynamic in terms of European stimuli. The Muslim revival movements emerging from the late eighteenth century, at least, had nothing to do with Europe.

In the Ottoman province of Egypt, Napoleon's attempted invasion shook up the status quo. In 1805 the Albanian officer Muhammad Ali seized power and was finally confirmed by the hard-pressed Sultan as a virtually independent hereditary governor (a post later to be known as the Khedive). To shore up his power, and focusing on reforming the army along western lines, Muhammad Ali initiated a modernisation process that can fairly be compared with Japan's. Modern educational institutions were created in all domains, semi-feudal structures of rule replaced by a bureaucratic hierarchy, European (especially French) experts enlisted and study groups sent to Europe. A new land tax paid for the system. The economy, especially foreign trade, was to be stimulated by monopoly companies. This was the context of Egypt's conquest of Sudan in 1820–42, which originally aimed to acquire supplies of gold, ivory, slaves and cotton from the country, but in the end proved an economic disappointment. Muhammad Ali also temporarily subjugated parts of Arabia, and the Red Sea seemed destined to become an Egyptian inland water. He advanced towards Syria, even towards Istanbul itself, and had to be halted by the European powers.

Under Muhammad Ali's successors, the British were able to take control of railway construction, but it was the French who obtained the contract for the Suez Canal in 1854 and built it in 1859–69. In the 1860s and 1870s Muhammad Ali's grandson Ismail tried in vain to extend his power from Sudan out to the Nile sources in the Great Lakes region (modern Burundi, Rwanda, Uganda) and to Ethiopia, in cooperation with European explorers and adventurers. The liberalisation of land law and foreign trade, along with continuing modernisation measures, drew tens of thousands of western experts and businessmen into the country – resulting in a backlash against the foreigners. In southern Sudan, Levantines, Egyptians and northern Sudanese, with their fortified bases and armed helpers, had become the masters and terrorisers of the country, although they were more interested in ivory than in black slaves. The American Civil War of 1861–65 had endangered European industry's supply of raw cotton and quadrupled prices, and the resulting cotton boom enabled Ismail to fund his schemes with massive loans from western banks. Accordingly, the end of the Civil War brought him

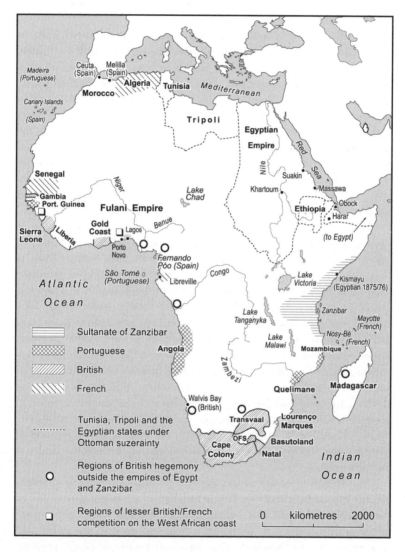

Map 17 Africa up to *c.* 1878

disaster. The outcome of Ismail's ambitious but incautious policy of modernisation and integration into the European world economy was that Egypt's state revenue no longer covered the interest and repayment of its loans. It was facing bankruptcy.

Christian Ethiopia initially proved unable to attain either unity or modernisation. Tewodros II was brought down by a conflict with the British, who cornered him and drove him to suicide with an Anglo-Indian invasion force in 1868. His successor had to share power with rivals including King Menelik of Shewa, who maintained his own relations with the West and in 1869 established a consulate in British-occupied Aden – European activity in the countries around the Red Sea was increasing at the time due to the imminent opening of the Suez Canal. The British strengthened their relationship with the Somalis of Berbera, the French acquired Obock (the heart of what would later become French Somaliland and today's Djibouti) in 1862, and in 1869 an Italian shipping line bought Assab from a local prince.

In North African Tunisia, the configuration of power was similar to Egypt's. The Tunisian beys found it useful to make overtures to European powers as a way of gaining leverage against the Ottoman Sultan's plans to strengthen his suzerainty. Since the 1850s Europeans had been permitted to purchase land in Tunisia, so there were no further obstacles to a penetration of the country. Additionally, the rulers of Tunisia needed to pay for a range of costly policies, especially a relatively large army, and took out loans in Europe at unfavourable conditions, which they were unable to repay. Britain concluded that a state bankruptcy was most likely to result in French intervention, and in 1869 instead arranged for Tunisia's finances to be placed under the control of an international commission. After the French defeat of 1871, the newly unified Italy – the source of the greatest number of immigrants to Tunisia – tried to gain control of its Mediterranean neighbour. Britain responded by issuing a guarantee for Tunisia, whose remnant of independence was thus, once again, maintained only through the rivalry of the western powers.

The French involvement was partly a result of its conquest of neighbouring Algeria from 1830 on. This in turn had arisen from a provocation by the Algerian ruler, the *Dey*, which Charles X's restoration government turned to its own domestic purposes: a victorious invasion was to help the government win the French elections, specially postponed for the purpose, and to stabilise the floundering monarchy. The plan came to nothing, but the new regime of the 'citizen king' Louis-Philippe remained in Algiers, not wanting to show any sign of weakness. It was only successful indigenous resistance, framed as a 'holy war' by a Muslim brotherhood led by Abd al-Qadir, that prompted the French to take over the entire, hitherto politically disunified country in the 1840s to 1860s. They did so systematically, with heavy deployment of resources and a high degree of brutality. The Second Republic of 1848 left only the south to the military administration, establishing the three départements of Algiers, Oran and Constantine in the north. From now on these were regarded as integrative components of the mother country, despite various phases when Algeria was once again given an additional, special status with a joint governor-general, for example under Napoleon III in 1860–71. The associated improvement in the position of the Arabs, Berbers and Jews was, however, limited. They were entitled to become French citizens, soldiers and civil servants, but only at the price of giving up their Islamic or Jewish law – that is, their cultural identity. Suffrage and civil rights were restricted to the 'French', almost half of whom in fact originated from Spain and Italy. Only a minority practised agriculture, but this sector expanded thanks to the government's systematic policy of expropriation in the fertile regions of the north. First the enemy princes and Muslim foundations were expropriated, then the rebellious tribes, which were pushed into the interior (*refoulement*), and finally the allegedly surplus property of a tribe could be confiscated (*cantonnement*). Uprisings after the regime change of 1871 offered a welcome pretext for further large-scale land confiscations. In the end, laws were passed in 1873 enabling collective land ownership to be dissolved and the land to be privatised upon the application of a single participant. It was always possible to find straw men, and the small-scale landowners could then be bought out, most easily when times were hard. At the end of the century, around 3 million indigenous Algerians faced 500,000 French settlers, or *colons*, of whom around 200,000 were now living on at least 800,000 ha of expropriated land.

In Tripolitania, a dynastic crisis resulted in Ottoman provincial administration being reimposed in 1835 – the very fate that the Bey of Tunis had feared. Its eastern neighbour Cyrenaica fell more and more completely under the control of the Senussi, a rigorist Islamic order founded in 1833. In western Sudan, a tradition of Islamic revival movements like this went back to the eleventh century. Now black Muslims, the Negrid Tukulor in today's Senegal and the Ethiopid Fulbe or Fulani, nomads who had spread between Senegal and the north of today's Nigeria, became the proponents of that revivalism. In 1804 the Fulani Usman dan Fodio (1754–1817) unleashed jihad against the Islam of the trading Hausa people, which he considered to be contaminated by African polytheism. The conflict gave rise to the Sokoto Caliphate, a league of emirs authorised by the caliph or sultan that reached from Bornu to the Niger and from the desert to the Benue. In

the west, El Hadj Umar Tall (1794–1864), a son-in-law of the Caliph of
Sokoto, took up the holy cause and founded his Tukulor theocracy between
Senegal and the Niger. The later Mahdi of the eastern Sudan was part of the
same trend. But in the west these movements for the most part were still
fighting the black unbelievers, not the Europeans, despite the fact that the
French governor of Senegal, Louis Faidherbe (1854–65), was already
preparing the ground for an Algeria-style conquest of the entire Senegal
region. In 1857 Dakar was founded.

On the Guinea coast, increased British activity motivated the French to
proliferate their own bases; in 1842 they established themselves on the
Ivory Coast and in Gabon. The suppression of the slave trade (enforced
since 1807 by the British navy) and indigenous suppliers' move into new
commodities, especially vegetable oils for European industry, required
uninterrupted control of the coastline. The prime principle of colonialism
being that colonies must not entail any cost but only create profit, the bases
established to this end had to finance themselves through customs revenue
– and for sufficient revenue to be collected, control of the coast had to be
absolute. As a result, in 1851 the British took over the Danish coastal
stations, in 1871 the Dutch ones. When it came to the French posts, this
proved impossible; on the contrary, Britain's growing rivalry with the French
and with the newly arriving Germans would soon result in a race for acquisitions in the interior.

That time had not yet come, and in fact at this stage there were many
indications of a successful African defence. Although Britain was able to
thwart the attempt by its partners, the Fante on the coast of today's Ghana, to
build themselves a modern political organisation, it was defeated by the
Ashanti Empire of the interior in 1863, just as it had been in 1824. Only in
1873 did Britain capture the Ashanti capital, Kumasi, and in 1874 the
coastal strip was proclaimed a colony. Britain's intentions did not go further
than that, but the expedition to Kumasi, like the campaign in Magdala,
Ethiopia, in 1868, had demonstrated British muscle. It was a dress rehearsal
for the imperialism of the future.

On the Guinea coast a milieu emerged, reaching wider than the traditional business partners of European trade, that was partially modernised on
a European pattern. The collective and individual remigration of free African
Americans played an additional stimulating role: more than 3,000 African
Brazilians are thought to have been living in Lagos after 1800, and they
wielded considerable influence. In this way, multiple processes of social
modernisation began among the Fante of the Gold Coast, the Egba, the
Yoruba, the peoples of the Niger Delta and the Duala in Cameroon. For example, Abeokuta had its own newspaper as early as 1859, something not

matched by British Lagos until 1863. Particularly notable are the attempts by former slaves to Christianise Africa, culminating in the 1864 appointment of a black Anglican bishop for the mission in the Niger region. In the 1870s the influence of Europe was still rather minor from an African perspective. That was due to the prosperity and diversity of the African economy and the skill of African businesspeople. When the Europeans finally resorted to violence in order to secure control over West Africa, therefore, this may have resulted not only from intra-European power rivalry but also from a sense of their weakness vis-à-vis the Africans.

Either way, the Europeans now began to succeed in parting the veil that the Africans had hitherto kept carefully closed over the continent's interior. Between 1778 and 1830 they finally solved the puzzle of the Niger's course; because of its change of direction, the river's upper and lower reaches had previously been attributed to two separate systems. The Sahara was crossed several times, a special contribution being made in the 1850s by the German explorer Heinrich Barth in the service of the British. For the first time, the Europeans were now in a position to understand the workings of the trans-Sudan and trans-Saharan trading networks. On the southern side, in Sudan, those networks were controlled by black Muslim merchants, the Dyula in the west, the Hausa in the centre, the Jallaba (mainly arabised Nubians) in the east. In the desert interior the Tuareg participated, in the north the oasis inhabitants from Tripolitania to Morocco, while further east the Senussi had brought the desert trade under their control – in 1895 they moved their head-quarters to the oases of Kufra, and in 1899 even into the Tibesti mountains. From the south came ivory, leather, ostrich feathers and especially slaves. Although the Ottoman Empire had formally abolished slave trading in 1857, Morocco only agreed to accede to that ruling in 1912. From the north came cotton goods and other textiles, armaments, metal goods, perfumes, tea, sugar, porcelain, paper: for the most part items that were produced or sold by Europe. At this time cotton goods from Manchester were finding their way to Kano in northern Nigeria from both the south and the north. In 1850, Barth had estimated the British share of cotton goods at just one eighth, but by 1891 the British consul in Tripoli claimed that Manchester goods made up 70 per cent of the Saharan trade.

Further south along the West African coast, the trading systems were more modest in scale. Portuguese Angola remained a slave-trading colony well into the second half of the nineteenth century. Experiments with sugar production, cotton cultivation and coastal fishery met with only limited success, and the advance into the interior failed, as did the creation of a land bridge to Mozambique. The old and new empires of the Central African savannah were too strong and too shrewd.

In East Africa, the trading system of the Swahili merchants was expanding, especially after the Sultan of Oman transferred his residence to Zanzibar in 1840 and, with the help of capital from Indian merchants, made the island the world's biggest producer of cloves. Western trading partners were attracted by the tariffs policy, trade agreements with Britain, France and the United States, and a range of commodities now enriched by the products of the African mainland. The foot caravans sent by the 'Arabs' took such goods as glass beads, copper wire and firearms into the interior, returning with ivory for trade and slaves for the plantations. Today's Tanzania, especially, profited from these transactions. Its African population even participated in them directly, sending out its own large, armed caravans. Others made money from supplying food and salt; the rise of Buganda is thought to have been based on the control of salt lakes. Buganda's king even came close to converting to Islam but then, alarmed by Egyptian expansionism, turned to Christianity instead. A cultural shift of considerable proportions had begun, as can be deduced from such changes as the spread of Swahili as a second language and of the rectangular house at the expense of the round hut. In the core grounds of the ivory and slave hunters in the south, and west of the Great Lakes in the eastern Congo basin, a very different picture emerges. In these areas there were no African communities capable of protecting themselves and participating in the business, and the caravans wrought terrible devastation. When the explorer Stanley arrived, the East African trading system in the Congo basin had already advanced to a point just 450 km from its West African counterpart, because its key commodities, ivory and slaves, were no longer to be found further east.

In Madagascar, the old rivalry between Britain and France on the Indian Ocean persisted into the nineteenth century, while an indigenous dynasty had made use of firearms and a professional army built up by various Europeans to subjugate almost the entire island by 1828. This development was accompanied by a remarkable degree of technological modernisation driven in part by missionaries from the London Missionary Society, admitted in 1818. A fierce xenophobic reaction temporarily replaced the British 'development aid workers' with French ones, but the prime minister Rainilaiarivony, who ruled the country as the spouse of three successive queens in 1864–95, put his hopes in the British, since France refused to dissociate itself from the order once issued by Louis XIV to annex the island. When Rainilaiarivony and his wife, along with the entire elite, became Protestants, the now downgraded Catholics became advocates of a French intervention. However, there was neither opportunity nor occasion for such action, and it seemed possible that Madagascar would be able to carve out a power-political niche for itself between the two great colonial powers.

The 'Scramble for Africa' in high imperialism: The transition to rule

The imperialist division of Africa may have seemed quite redundant not only to the Africans but also to the British; after all, in the mid 1870s free-trade imperialism was giving the world's then greatest trading power an informal hegemony over Africa that appeared to rest on very firm foundations. French areas seemed like enclaves in British-controlled Africa, and the remaining three coastal powers could be regarded as clients of Britain – not only Egypt and Zanzibar but also Portugal, which in 1846 and 1857 had watched the British ride roughshod over its claims to the Congo. A political doctrine of British 'paramountcy' was developed, involving not so much the possession of a region but the power to keep other powers out of it. However, in 1871 the German Empire and Italy entered the political arena as new powers with considerable national aspirations; the old colonial powers Portugal and Spain were likewise gripped by national ambition and, above all, Britain's arch-rival France was making substantial gains in strength. The scene was set for what *The Times* in 1884 labelled the 'Scramble for Africa', a process that resulted in the continent being almost completely carved up in the course of just a few years. In the era of high industrialisation, industrial and trade policy became more important for European countries than ever before, and a phase of decelerating growth brought an immediate return to neo-mercantilist protectionist tariff policies, in Germany in 1879, in France in 1881. Under these circumstances it seemed sensible to secure trading partners through annexation, as a form of forward defence for the British and offensive territorial gains for the others. The gaining or safeguarding of raw material supplies and markets was promulgated, a claim that for critical observers like Hobson concealed the need to secure capital investment opportunities. Certainly, these economic programmes were rarely realised in practice – but that was immaterial in an age of mass politics and mass media where economic expectations alone were quite enough to trigger nervous political action. Hence the hastily acquired options, the many unsecured mortgages on the economic future that typify the era of high imperialism.

This Europe-centred global perspective does not, however, by any means suffice to explain high imperialism. Factors on the African side must also be taken into account, both Europeans and Africans having participated in the process. Where interests were in such close proximity and edging ever closer, as in West Africa, action by one party or nation was bound to provoke a reaction by the others. Events of this kind did not necessarily occur with the knowledge and agreement of the European leadership, but for reasons of national prestige that leadership was rarely willing to disavow its sub-imperialists in Africa or elsewhere. The Europeans on the ground were in many cases traders, but also often military officers who, as in British India or Russian Central Asia, were pursuing personal agendas in the service of national honour and private ambition. To this extent, Joseph A. Schumpeter was justified in viewing imperialism as the outgrowth of an already outdated warrior-class mentality. It also appears that the first generation of adventurers were disproportionately afflicted with psychological and sexual problems, making their behaviour all the more liable to elicit strong reactions from the Africans. African uprisings – whether 'primary' resistance against the establishment of foreign rule or 'secondary' resistance against the increasing pressure exerted by such rule – galvanised the colonial masters into harsher repression, since giving way was not an option if national prestige was to be preserved. When a slur seemed to have been cast on national honour, an exception was made to the usual skimping with resources from the mother country. By these means, many a military campaign mutated from a temporary measure into a permanent conquest. The Africans involved had no insight into these mechanisms of European politics, so that their resistance frequently proved counterproductive, starting with Algeria in the 1830s and 1840s. But anyway the Africans were not always in a position to perceive what was at stake. Early imperialism, especially, often seemed barely distinguishable from the other conflicts to which they were accustomed. Furthermore, unlike the Europeans they lacked a notion of 'Africa' as such. The Europeans knew they were in the process of dividing up Africa, while the geographical consciousness of the Africans as a rule remained restricted to their immediate environment. Many Africans did not even realise at first that their rulers had changed, since there was little alteration to everyday life and they may not have actually seen any white people face to face – early colonial rule was weak, and saved money by deploying as little personnel as possible. It may have been only the ecological crises associated with colonial rule that gave Africans a sense of the catastrophically altered situation. By the 1880s and 1890s, the rinderpest virus introduced from Europe had killed three quarters of Africa's cattle population, severely weakening the cattle-breeding societies. There was also an epidemic of sleeping sickness unprecedented in scale; smallpox and famine. It seems that half the population of the lower Congo died in this period. Some Africans believed that a kind of 'biological warfare' was being waged by the Europeans, or in their terms that witchcraft was at work.

A clear distinction can be drawn between a first, contingent and coastally oriented phase lasting till the 1884/85 Berlin Conference and a second phase in which the interior was systematically penetrated on the basis of the conference's General Act. Penetration was complete by the turn of the twentieth century, but was followed by all sorts of conflicts, consolidations and amendments. Morocco and Tripolitania also fell into European hands; after the First World War the German colonies were redistributed and in 1935/36, finally, Ethiopia too was conquered, by the Italians.

In Algeria, France's defeat in 1871 meant the victory of the settlers who controlled the three départements and their politically disadvantaged Muslim populations. Once the *Code de l'indigénat* was introduced in 1881, Muslims could be sentenced to fines and prison terms by the administration without trial. By 1890, only 736 Algerians had made use of the option of giving up their cultural identity and becoming French citizens. In fact, assimilation of this kind was not in the interest of the *colons*. Thus, the general schooling system was introduced more or less solely for the French; there was no money left for the Muslims. The *colons*' vineyards prospered when the great phylloxera epidemic blighted vines in France. Algeria was a blend of a settlement colony and a colony of rule, as Spanish America had once been and until recently South Africa was as well; we might also describe it as a case of internal colonialism similar to that in Israel or, again, South Africa.

Now that shifts in global politics had rendered the previous balance of power obsolete, Algeria's neighbour Tunisia also fell under French control. At the Congress of Berlin, held in 1878 to resolve the latest Balkan crisis, Britain had appropriated Cyprus as the key to the Middle East and the Suez Canal. France was now owed compensation and Tunisia seemed the obvious choice, though this was only put into practice when the Tunisians threatened to turn to Italy. In 1881 an invading army arrived, and the Treaty of Bardo established French rule. After the suppression of the usual uprisings of primary resistance, the treaty was supplemented in 1883 by the Convention of Al-Marsa. The word 'protectorate' was not mentioned anywhere in the convention, and formally the absolute monarchy of the Bey remained in place, but the French resident became his prime minister and minister of foreign affairs, without whose signature no ordinance could take effect. The administration and finances were now overhauled, an education and health system established along European lines, and the exploitation of the mineral resources phosphate and iron ore was initiated through the construction of ports and railways. Agricultural development was left to European private initiatives. However, there was no mass French immigration; the majority of the Europeans in the country were Italians, forming a state within the state that held the potential to become a threat.

At this time Egypt, with its 1,500 km of railways, 8,000 km of telegraph lines and 4,500 elementary schools, was the most highly developed country in Africa. However, in 1876 it was forced to declare bankruptcy, having been

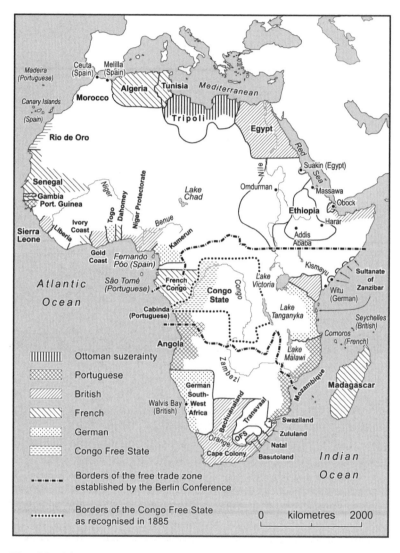

Map 18   Africa *c.* 1887

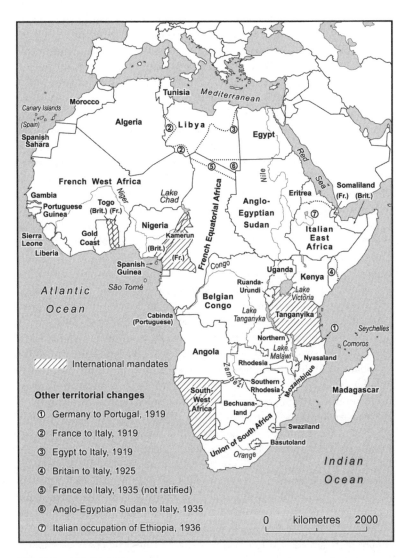

Map 19   Africa in 1939

unable to prevent collapse by selling its shares in the Suez Canal to the British government in 1875. The situation was further exacerbated by natural disasters and the consequent breakdown of agriculture. France and Britain acted in the interests of the creditor banks, first having the Ottoman sultan replace the Khedive by his son, whose ministers managed to draw up a practicable compromise solution in 1881: state revenues were to be rescued, and interest and repayments safeguarded, in return for a lowering of the interest rate to 5 per cent plus supervision by an international debt commission under joint Anglo-French leadership. But however successful this solution was in financial terms, it failed politically, provoking a military coup against the foreigners. Britain and France responded in 1882 with a military intervention that was carried to its conclusion by the British alone. Cairo was occupied and reforms began. The railway administration became British, the army was dissolved and replaced by a British-controlled gendarmerie, and the fiscal administration taken into British hands. Although the Khedive was permitted to appoint a new government, he was very clearly given to understand that it would take 'advice' from the British consul Evelyn Baring, from 1901 the Earl of Cromer, who was the real ruler of Egypt from 1883 to 1907. Hydraulic engineering projects, including the Old Aswan Dam, and the modernisation of the bureaucracy, including a new land registry, were the most important achievements and contributed substantially to an agriculturally based prosperity, though this also drew on the renewed rise in the price of cotton.

The British were actually ready to leave Egypt again as early as 1885. The fact that they did not is related to the defeat inflicted on the British-led Egyptians by Muhammad Ahmad, the Sudanese Mahdi, in 1883: the British found it necessary to avert the threat to the route to India arising from unexpected events on the Nile. In 1885 Charles Gordon, sent to Sudan again as governor-general, was killed during the Mahdi's capture of the capital, Khartoum. Unlike developments in western Sudan, here the millennialist Islamic revival movement led by the Mahdi, 'rightly guided' by God, should be viewed as a nativist reaction to the European advances. For Muhammad Ahmad the issue was not, as for many of his followers, resistance to Egyptian taxation and the abolition of that vital source of income, the slave trade, but a fundamental rejection of the Egyptian policy of modernisation, which took unbelievers into its service and mimicked their customs. However, the Mahdi cannot be regarded as a forerunner of the Sudanese independence movement. For one thing, his movement saw itself as the kernel of a world domination, not of a Sudanese 'nation' (something that was not yet thinkable at this time), and for another, Mahdism brought about a schism in Sudanese Islam that still persists today, if in a discreetly muted form. Seeing that the Mahdi could not be beaten with the resources of Egypt, Britain initially abandoned Sudan. It was in a position to do so because the Mahdi's successor in 1885, the Khalifa Abdallahi, reacted to the failure of his attempts at expansion by moving to a policy of, in practice, 'Mahdism in one country' that aimed to stabilise the new empire.

The British did, however, commit themselves on the Red Sea, since here a threat was posed not only by the Mahdists but also by Britain's European rivals. The Red Sea port of Suakin was held and the British position on the northern coast of Somalia, opposite Aden, stabilised through treaties. France had finally made Obock a colony in 1884/85, and the Italian state, after taking over the private colony of Assab in the wake of the 1885 occupation of Massawa, had begun to push into Eritrea.

Obock was of interest to France because it lay on the sea route both to Indo-China and to Madagascar, where Britain had now accepted French claims despite the London Missionary Society's important role in the country's successful modernisation. A first French attack in 1883 ended in a treaty that left foreign policy to a French resident but guaranteed the sovereignty of the queen in internal affairs. France also obtained a base on the northern tip of the island and lavish war reparations.

Unlike in the continent's north and north-east, in West Africa it was economic interests that dominated, fuel for purely political conflict being largely absent. But the West Africa trade was of only minor significance in the context of the European economies, so that its representatives had little access to substantial political influence. The companies involved also tended to loosen their ties with the mother country, focusing on the more saleable foreign-produced goods or docking at ports controlled by other powers where the customs duties were lower. The advent of the steamer in place of the sailing ship had given them greater flexibility and reduced their dependence on the winds and currents of these difficult waters. They could now head for quite new harbours and even advance upriver. That meant an expansion of the European trading systems, which were bound to run up against each other at more and more different points. It also meant a destabilisation of African intermediary trade and thus of the relationships between Africans and Europeans.

Britain would very much have liked to secure its hegemony through the discreet tool of the paramountcy doctrine, and hoped for French compliance. That compliance came to an end when France was universally courted at the 1878 Congress of Berlin and when, in 1879, more aggressive leftwing forces came to power in Paris. Starting from Senegal, the peanut-growing regions were annexed, then links were created on the one hand with Algeria, on the other with the Niger bend and the Niger Delta. French troops pursued these objectives from the upper part of Senegal from 1879 until Britain halted their eastwards expansion on the Niger in 1897. During their advance, the French encountered not only the declining Tukulor empire of El Hadj Umar Tall but also the new empire of Samory Touré, originally a Malinke trader, who controlled large areas of the upper Niger in the mid 1880s. Battling for pure Islam against African opponents, he went about demarcating the spheres of influence by means of treaties with the French, which the latter interpreted as implying a protectorate. For them, the only remaining goal was to forestall the British.

On the Guinea coast itself, competition was increasingly fierce, French merchants there feeling squeezed by the British and Germans, though due less to British and German gains than to the consequences of the explosion of their own trade. British exports were still higher than French exports, but in the period 1854–80 the British increased theirs by only 41.6 per cent, compared to a French increase of 405 per cent. Britain's annexation of Lagos in 1861, then of Gold Coast in 1874, and subsequently the appearance of the Germans all seemed to indicate that the French were being edged out. They responded by proclaiming their protectorate over the coast of eastern Togo in 1883, while in 1885 the British used treaties to establish a protectorate over the area of the Niger Delta, where a private colonial company was operating on a royal charter. The working principle that those who profited from colonialism should bear its costs was also followed elsewhere at this time, by the Germans and in the Congo.

Britain had prevented Portugal from gaining control over the Congo River estuary, but in 1879/80 two new competitors unexpectedly appeared: King Leopold II of Belgium, who proposed to enter the colonial business in a personal capacity, and the French explorer Pierre Savorgnan de Brazza. Leopold set up a joint stock company to explore and develop the Congo basin, in the service of which Henry Morton Stanley in 1879–83 created treaties and established stations between what would later be called Leopoldville/Kinshasa and Elisabethville/Lubumbashi. At first, economic and not political control seemed to be at stake. However, in 1880 de Brazza signed a treaty of cession north of the river that was ratified by the French parliament in 1882 during a – temporary – surge of national enthusiasm. Leopold thereupon had the recognition of his sovereignty inserted into the treaties and from 1884 laid claim to possession of the Congo basin for his company, while Britain now recognised the Portuguese claims it had so recently suppressed, and set about stretching them to their limit. This seems to have been the occasion for the British cabinet to acknowledge the end of the era of informal hegemony, especially since Bismarck recognised Leopold's claims and made use of the muddled situation to arrange for an international conference on the Congo to be held in Berlin in 1884/85.

By this time Bismarck too had started acquiring African possessions for the German Empire. In Germany, as elsewhere, an organised colonial lobby had long existed. It was no coincidence that this lobby's spokesman, Friedrich Fabri, had previously been director of the Rhenish Missionary Society, active in German South West Africa, which between 1868 and 1880 had applied in vain for Prussian (later German) protection during the danger-ous escalation of the notorious conflicts between the Herero, a Bantu pastoral people of the central highlands, and the Nama and Orlam, Khoikhoi groups known pejoratively as 'Hottentots', in the inhospitable south of the region. The National Liberals and parts of the Catholic-oriented Centre Party supported colonial policy, whereas conservatives along with left-liberals and socialists were initially opposed, though in the era of Wilhelm's 'world policy' they converted to the idea almost without exception, including the right wing of the Social Democratic Party. However, the impetus for action was provided not by the Empire but by trading interests and political adven-turers on the ground.

In 1883 Adolph Lüderitz, a tobacco dealer from Bremen, signed a treaty with a Nama chieftain that ceded the port of Angra Pequena, along with a twenty-mile-deep strip of land at the mouth of the Orange River. Whether due to misunderstanding or deception, the Nama ended up calculating that area in English miles of 1.6 km, while the Germans used geographical miles of 7.4 km. After further treaties concluded by other individuals, along with the demarcation from Portuguese Angola and from the British protectorate of Bechuanaland (today's Botswana), established as a precaution against German expansion, German control now covered more than 800,000 km^2. Lüderitz turned out, though, to have been overly ambitious, and by 1885 he had been forced to sell his holdings to the new German 'Colonial Society for South West Africa'. This company was established not on the basis of economic interests – large-scale capital in Germany showed little interest in the colonies – but as a favour to the chancellor: Bismarck did not want 'colonies' as such but only what, translating the English 'protectorates', he named *Schutzgebiete*, which were to be administered and exploited by private chartered companies. The aim was not only to save the Empire money, but also to prevent parliament from holding influence over the colonies through its budgetary rights, the real lever of further democratisation in Germany. But that was exactly what happened when the charter idea foundered and the Empire had to take over responsibility, a development already looming in South West Africa when an imperial commissioner was posted there in 1885.

In East Africa, Carl Peters, the representative of the 'Society for German Colonisation', had signed the first treaties in 1884/85 as nothing more than a minor irritant in the smoothly functioning relations between Britain,

Zanzibar, the Swahili and the European trading houses; the Hamburg companies involved thought little of the initiative. But although, or perhaps because, conflicts with Britain seemed imminent – in East Africa, too, Britain had hitherto deliberately kept to informal hegemony – Peters received political backing from Berlin. A 'German East African Company' was formed with the Emperor as its largest shareholder, other sources of capital again being reluctant to invest. As the imperial commissioner, Peters was able to conclude further treaties and show the Africans what a member of the German master-race really looked like. In 1886 Britain, under pressure, had to agree to a treaty that guaranteed Zanzibar control of the coast and divided up the spheres of influence into a British Kenya and a German Tanganyika, as these colonies were later called.

In West Africa, in contrast, there were genuine trading interests at stake. As protective tariff policies proliferated, the companies of the German Hanseatic cities that maintained trading posts and plantations between Liberia and the Congo River estuary saw the increasingly dense web of British and French control and developments in the Congo region as threats to their business. Their representations succeeded in inducing Bismarck to dispatch the explorer and Tunisian consul-general Gustav Nachtigal to West Africa as an imperial commissioner. His brief was originally only to ensure fair treatment of the Germans, but he was subsequently required to make claims to German sovereignty in the areas of interest to German companies by hoisting the imperial flag. This was done in Togoland and Kamerun in summer 1884, pre-empting the British by a mere matter of days. Characteristically, the canny Hanseatic businessmen rejected all plans for a chartered company, so that by 1885 the first imperial governor already had to be sent to Togoland and Kamerun.

Britain's tractability in all these cases can be explained by its difficult foreign-policy circumstances, which were ruthlessly exploited by Bismarck. In 1884, after the Anglo-French split over the financial administration of Egypt, he reacted to London's stalling by obtaining French agreement to hold the international Congo conference in Berlin. Because Leopold had shrewdly accorded France the option to buy his Congo company if it were to collapse, Paris was very interested in the issue. The Berlin Conference of November 1884 to February 1885 did not in fact carve up Africa, the demarcation of boundaries actually taking place in a series of two-page agreements. Rather, it first of all officially recognised Leopold's acquisitions as a neutral state, on condition that the expanded Congo region and all of East Africa remained a free-trade zone accessible to all the powers. It then, however, established a new principle of international law, namely that for the possession of overseas territories to be recognised, their officially notified and effective occupation was necessary; 'effectivity' here meant the maintenance of law and order, particularly for the benefit of trade. This was the end of the era of vague Portuguese claims and informal British hegemony. Unasked, Africa had been integrated into the western law of nations, with the result that precise boundary lines were now required. In Berlin, high imperialism gave itself a set of procedural principles – division could now begin in earnest.

The 'Scramble for Africa' in high imperialism: The division of the continent

King Leopold continued to exhibit an insatiable appetite for more and more land – more land meaning more profit for its absolute ruler. An army of Africans was created, and deployed to demolish the Swahili trading system. Leopold then attempted to extend the Congo Free State as far as the Nile. A rudimentary administration was established with 440 indigenous chieftains appointed as the lowest rung of authority. The main objective was earning profit, since at first the enterprise found itself under repeated threat of bankruptcy and was only rescued by loans from the Belgian government. The rubber boom turned the situation around, though only with the help of some highly dubious methods. In 1891/92 Leopold violated the General Act of the Berlin Conference by introducing the principle that all land not occupied by Africans was state property and could only be exploited by the state or its licensed entrepreneurs: in practice a monopoly on ivory and wild rubber. Because the agents of the state received a bonus for their consignments, while the subjected population was coerced into labour by means of taxation and military force, an exploitative system arose that was, at times, nothing less than criminal. Nevertheless, in 1901 the Congo was supplying one tenth of the world's entire rubber production. Leopold used the opulent profits to fund extensive building projects in Belgium. When the first information began to trickle through about the atrocities being committed in the Congo – deeds that have been used as ammunition against imperialism right up to the present – Leopold and the Belgian public feigned deafness or claimed to suspect malicious slander by the British competition. In 1904, however, the appointment of an international commission of inquiry could no longer be avoided, and its shocking report finally led the Belgian state to take over the colony along regulated administrative lines in 1908. In neighbouring French Congo and Gabon, and in the south of German Kamerun, the colonial powers had also handed the territories over for purely economic exploitation to various companies, under whose rule similar brutalities were perpetrated. But when de Brazza was sent back to the French Congo to report on the situation there, his unsparing comments remained unpublished in France. Instead of reforms there were cost-free manoeuvres.

For Portugal, the Berlin Conference's humiliating resolutions spurred the colonial lobby to new efforts. Their objective now was to implement effective occupation by linking up Angola and Mozambique into one big continental empire, which would draw in today's Malawi, Zambia, Zimbabwe and the southern DRC on the principle of the *contra costa*, the 'coast-to-coast' ideal. Expeditions were dispatched to gather information and make treaties. Germany, France and in the end even King Leopold were willing to recognise the Portuguese claims, but Britain already had its advance guard on Lake Malawi, while its South African sub-imperialists were pushing forward to the Zambezi. Believing there was gold to be had north of the Transvaal, Cecil Rhodes set up a capitalist extraction company, the British South Africa Company (BSAC), on the familiar pattern and had London grant it a royal charter to administer Central Africa. In 1890 troops, prospectors and settlers began to advance into the land of the Ndebele and Shona. Violent conflicts resulted, especially when it emerged that there was no gold in the area after all and the attention of the whites turned to land acquisition instead. Rhodes lost interest in the country later named Rhodesia in his honour, but the British government took on supervision of the BSAC in the interests of the natives. Even before this, the Shire Highlands had become attractive in British eyes with the discovery of a navigable tributary of the Zambezi, and were occupied. The Highlands formed the core of British Nyasaland, today's Malawi. Portugal was harshly forced to renounce its hopes, for a land connection between its colonies was now out of the question. In fact, it was difficult enough for Portugal to develop the enormous territories it had already gained: the poverty of the migrants to Angola meant that a plantation economy was slow to become established there. Mozambique was prosperous in comparison, but only because it was largely left to international corporations under strong British influence. Among other things, the construction of railways to the Transvaal and Rhodesia brought jobs and tax revenue as well as a boom for the ports of Lourenço Marques (modern Maputo) and Beira.

Because Britain had recognised the French protectorate over Madagascar in 1886 in return for France keeping its hands off East Africa, France faced no obstacles in violently reducing the island to colony status by 1897, after a series of brutal ultimatums. The prime minister and queen were deported to Algiers and recalcitrant aristocrats shot. But as well as his successful campaign of pacification, the governor-general Joseph Simon Gallieni (1896–1905) also pursued a remarkable development policy which, surprisingly, he even managed to induce Paris to fund. Transport links were built, agriculture promoted and regulated by a modern property law, a French education system established. However, the language of the ruling Merina still remained the country's second official tongue, so that Madagascar is one of the few African countries that was able to make an indigenous language the basis of its national language after independence.

In East Africa, Britain regarded control of the Nile as vital to ensure the security of Egypt (which, in turn, was to underpin the security of India), especially as Sudan was still in the hands of the Mahdists. The chartered Imperial British East Africa Company (IBEAC) was thus asked to build a rail link to Uganda. German interests were paid off in 1890 with the Heligoland-Zanzibar Treaty: in return for giving up parts of East Africa and accepting the British protectorate over Zanzibar, Germany received the North Sea island of Heligoland (under British control since 1814), those parts of the East African coast that had previously belonged to Zanzibar, and the Caprivi Strip, named after the German chancellor of the day, as a land connection from German South West Africa to the allegedly navigable Zambezi. By 1892 the IBEAC had already collapsed, and Britain was even considering withdrawal from East Africa – but the imperialist turning-point of 1895 brought in a forward strategy. At this time there was also talk of a 'Cape to Cairo' line of continuous British colonial rule from Egypt to the Cape. British East Africa, later Kenya, was transferred to the Crown in 1895. White planters established themselves in its highlands, thanks not least to the improved access provided by the Uganda Railway that was built in 1895–1911. When a protectorate agreement was signed with the king of Buganda, it initially made the British look like a troop of mercenaries in the service of Bugandan imperialism. However, by 1908 Britain had succeeded in establishing a system of indirect rule in Uganda, with partial autonomy for the African kings.

In German East Africa, attempts to transform informal control into formalised rule rapidly caused uprisings that were beyond the German East Africa Company's capacity to handle. The Empire had to take over the colony in 1891, but the turbulence persisted, probably because the process of European conquest coincided with an ecological crisis. In 1891–97 the German *Schutztruppe*, or 'protection force', carried out sixty-one campaigns of punishment and repression. Labour enforced through taxation, together with the obligation to grow cotton, paved the way for the Maji Maji rebellion that devastated the south of the colony in 1905–7 and probably cost 130,000 people their lives. Overall, though, the Germans made quite skilful use of indigenous assistance, even to the extent that their support for the Muslims and for Swahili as a language of common use aroused indignation among the missionaries.

Elsewhere, the implementation of German rule was likewise a lengthy and arduous affair. In German South West Africa (modern Namibia) the Herero had found a modus vivendi with the Germans, but among the Nama Hendrik Witbooi sustained resistance for many years, a process that he recorded in his diary – one of the very rare early written sources of African origin. Only the astute governor Theodor Leutwein (1894–1905) was able to defeat him and to establish a quasi-feudal system of government via the chiefs, although the loss of land to white settlers, malpractice by white traders and the general legal insecurity of the Africans soon undermined the whole edifice. In 1904 the Herero and Nama rebelled against the Germans. By 1907 it had been necessary to deploy 14,000 German soldiers against the two peoples, and more than half of each group are thought to have lost their lives. In the German parliament the war's enormous cost, at 600 million marks, led to angry opposition attacks on the government's colonial policy, especially as there had also been conflicts in Togoland and Kamerun due to the administration's excesses and an uprising in the brutally exploited southern Kamerun. Although what was dubbed the 'Hottentot election' of 1907 ended in defeat for the critics of colonialism and a belated conversion to imperialism for some of them, the government was nevertheless forced to alter the course of its colonial policy. From now on the natives and their labour were considered a colony's most valuable commodity and were, accordingly, to be handled with care. This made it possible to rein in the East African settler interests to the benefit of autonomous African production. In South West Africa, in contrast, the settlers were in such a strong position that they were able to maintain the formal status of the defeated Africans as forced labourers virtually devoid of rights.

In Somaliland, Britain used Italy as a kind of proxy, allowing it to set up a protectorate over the southern Somali coast in 1889. Italy's continued advance into Eritrea brought it into conflict with the emperor of Ethiopia. He was fighting the Mahdists at the same time, and was also unable to rely on the loyalty of his most powerful prince, Menelik of Shewa, who was making secret deals with Italy. When the emperor was killed by the Mahdists in 1889, Menelik succeeded to the throne. He initially gave Italy carte blanche in the north, an area dominated by his predecessor's people, and concentrated on his own imperialist expansion southwards against the Oromo and Somalis. Menelik's treaty with the Italians included an article that in the Amharic version offered Ethiopia Italy's services in the diplomatic arena, but in the Italian version established Italy's protectorate over Ethiopia. Desperate for foreign-policy success, the Italian prime minister Crispi wanted to put the Italian interpretation into practice, but Menelik in the end renounced the treaty, though not without making peaceful overtures.

Italy planned on resolving the 'Abyssinian question' through military force. However, in 1896 Ethiopia crushingly defeated the Italians, who were now obliged to recognise Menelik's sovereignty but remained in possession of Eritrea and Somaliland. France, too, now had to content itself with narrow boundaries for Obock-Djibouti. Menelik maintained good relations with the European powers, but kept up secret contact with the Khalifa Abdallahi in Sudan, knowing full well that all Europeans were the enemies of all Africans. He himself, however, exercised an untrammelled imperialism towards other Africans, creating both the frontiers of today's Ethiopia and its ethnic problems. To be sure, if they accepted Christianity and the Amharic language and way of life, those conquered by Menelik were able to become equal subjects, which certainly helped to stabilise Ethiopian rule. The country's modernisation was limited to technological resources, such as firearms and telephones, and 'cosmetic' measures intended to emphasise Ethiopia's equality of rank with the whites.

In 1897, the Khalifa Abdallahi was harried by Leopold's Congo Army in the south. France intervened, forcing Leopold's troops to retreat in order to keep open its own route to advance from central Sudan to the Nile. But the British decision to move into Sudan starting from Egypt was not directed against France; it was designed to counter the growing anglophobia in Egypt by providing a trophy for the Khedive. In 1898 the main force of the Khalifa was mown down with modern rapid-fire weaponry, and in the autumn the British reached Fashoda on the upper Nile, where a French mission had raised its flag but was now forced to retreat by the balance of numbers. At this time only a lack of support for France prevented the eruption of an Anglo-French war. Conquered Sudan was made an Anglo-Egyptian condominium, in practice a further British colony: the all-powerful governor-general was appointed by the Khedive but on the recommendation of London, and was always British. He initially ruled with British provincial governors and inspectors and Egyptian district commissioners, but was soon able to build up a broad consensus by means of a cautious promotion of Islam, a Sudanese-friendly land policy and low taxes. The price was paid by Egypt, which had to cover military, administrative and infrastructural costs – a variant of British colonial rule that was nothing if not economical.

It was in West Africa that the roots of the 1898/99 Fashoda crisis lay, its ferocity arising from the collision of the two great colonial powers' expansionism at the intersection there of their respective axes of advance, north–south (Cairo to the Cape) and west–east (Senegal via Lake Chad to the Nile). At first the colonial powers found the implementation of effective occupation in West Africa quite simply too expensive. In agreement with France and Germany, in 1889/90 Britain drew deliberately narrow borders for Sierra

Leone and Gambia, and kept the hinterland open only in Gold Coast and Nigeria. Nevertheless, both Europeans and Africans began to prepare for armed conflict. When the 1890 anti-slavery conference in Brussels reserved modern weaponry for Europeans, this was – not unjustifiably – regarded by the Africans (including Witbooi in South West Africa) as a conspiracy against them. In 1891 the storm broke when the French attacked Samory Touré in pursuit of the colonial empire that imperialists were propagating at home: an entity supposed to gather up for France all the land west of a line from Tunisia to Lake Chad and the Congo, aside from a few coastal enclaves left to other powers. In 1898 Samory, who had hoped in vain for British protection, fell into French hands and was deported to Gabon. In 1892–94 the march continued across Dahomey. By now the Germans had advanced into the north of Togoland and Kamerun, so that in agreement with Britain in 1893 and France in 1894 they were able to fix the borders of the colonies there. In Britain, too, a turn towards imperialism was taking place, and in 1892–94 British troops captured the African cities of south-west Nigeria, imposing a resident on the Ashanti in 1895 and answering their rebellion with annexation in 1901. On the Niger a force was put up against the French, who reacted by agreeing to recognise the borders of Nigeria in 1898. In the Sokoto Caliphate and its emirates in the north, Frederick Lugard now established indirect British rule, a system that was developed for pragmatic reasons of cost and only retrospectively worked up into colonial-policy dogma. It would be several more years before the French had secured command of the Lake Chad region, longer still before they controlled the Saharan interior.

Of the parts of Africa still independent at the beginning of the twentieth century, Morocco had long been attracting the covetous eye of the Europeans as a supplier of raw materials, a market for manufactured goods and a field for investment. At first it seemed that the rivalries between the powers would enable the country to remain independent, as had been the case in China and the Ottoman Empire. Furthermore, Britain saw no benefit in having potential European enemies on the sea route to India, directly across from Gibraltar. It was only a change of government in Morocco with subsequent unrest that stirred up the situation. France accorded Spain a zone of influence in the north, and was given a free hand in the rest of Morocco by Britain in the *Entente cordiale* of 1904. French penetration and the establishment of a protectorate was now supposed to go ahead, but this was hindered on two occasions by the German Empire, which in 1905 and 1911 provoked the first and second Moroccan Crises. In the end, the international control resolved in 1906 as a way of weakening France had little impact, and Germany's attempt to compensate for the establishment of the French protectorate by extorting the concession of the French Congo culminated in 1911 with the acquisition of a rather paltry strip of land between Kamerun and the Congo River. In Morocco Louis Hubert Lyautey, schooled by Gallieni, took on the task of transforming the country as its resident (1912–25).

Once again an African country had been divided up without the participation of Italy. As a change of power was occurring in Istanbul, Italy took the opportunity to occupy Libya, a country it had long since penetrated economically and which the Ottoman Empire was obliged to cede in 1912. However, the struggle with indigenous resistance, especially that of the Senussi, lasted until 1932. Its brutality demonstrated an unmistakeable continuity between the pre-Fascist and Fascist eras.

When the German colonies were distributed among the victors of the First World War, Italy felt cheated once again, having received almost nothing. The German war aims had included a large German 'Central Africa' that would connect up their existing possessions by the addition of Angola, Mozambique and the two Congo colonies. In the event, Germany was speedily deprived of all its possessions except for German East Africa, and even there the partially successful resistance did the Germans more harm than good. Under the pretext of League of Nations mandates, South West Africa was transferred to the Union of South Africa; Togoland and Kamerun were divided between Britain and France; and Tanganyika fell to Britain, which was thus able to bridge the gap in its Cape-to-Cairo line. Only Ruanda-Urundi, where the Germans had exercised a loose indirect rule, was passed to Belgium.

Mussolini turned Italian resentment to skilful use for an imperialist policy that ostentatiously claimed to pick up the thread of the Imperium Romanum – initially an elaborate enterprise with sparse results, for the Italian possessions of Libya, Eritrea and Somaliland were simply too poor. Ethiopia, led from 1930 by Emperor Haile Selassie, tried to further its development with the help of various different powers, including ones then quite innocent of imperialism such as Sweden or the United States. Italy was also on Ethiopia's list, even though it had been plotting an invasion since 1925. In 1934 Rome decided to invade: Libya had been successfully pacified and relations with Britain and France, which expressly gave Italy a free hand in Ethiopia, were excellent, partly due to the threat posed by developments in Germany. In 1935/36, under Badoglio and Graziani, the Ethiopian resistance was systematically destroyed in a pincer movement from north and south, using the most modern materials, including poison gas. After the fall of Addis Ababa, the Italian king adopted the additional title 'Emperor of Ethiopia'. Italy had achieved its goal, and with this last exploit of European imperialism Africa had come completely under colonial rule – or at least had been put through such rule, for in Ethiopia it would last only a few years.

Colonial rule in Africa

At this time, Britain and France each had control of 36 per cent of Africa's surface; 47 per cent of the population were British subjects and 27 per cent were French subjects. Africa had thus become a British and French continent. Of the remaining five colonial powers, Germany and Italy played only a temporary role, while Spain was a political dwarf in colonial terms. Belgium and Portugal, as junior partners of the two great powers, evinced a Latin culture related to the French and with similar ideals of assimilation. In the case of Belgium, the similarity was reinforced by the shared French language. To simplify, one might thus contrast a British and a Franco-Latin system of rule. Certainly, the surrounding colonial situation meant that these systems, if opposite in theory, shared much common ground in practice, and indeed their differences may have resulted less from distinctions of principle than from the fact that the British generally held richer and more densely populated lands. Although the bulk of the French possessions formed a gigantic expanse, between half and two thirds of their economic value was concentrated in the densely settled countries of the northern margin, the Maghreb. The two large colonial federations *Afrique occidentale française* (AOF) and *Afrique équatoriale française* (AEF) lagged behind, especially the latter: the mandate territory Cameroun alone brought in more profit than the whole of AEF. The West African possessions of Britain were far better off. Nigeria is Africa's most populous country, and the four West African colonies supplied palm oil, peanuts, cotton, minerals and half the world's cocoa, as well as becoming important consumers of British manufactured goods. British East Africa was no treasure chest, but the copper mines of Northern Rhodesia were important assets, as was Southern Rhodesian agriculture. The Belgian Congo was eminently prosperous thanks to its mineral resources.

In terms of legal status, the British colonies – apart from the special cases of the Dominion of South Africa and the League of Nations mandates – included on the one hand Crown colonies with degrees of political participation by the population, which ranged from parliamentary responsible government with a cabinet alongside the governor, to representative government with a solely legislative assembly, to rule exercised by the governor alone; and, on the other, protectorates under indirect rule. Some colonies included several different types, for example Nigeria with its colonies in the south, protectorates in the north and a mandate in the east. Equal legal treatment could be conferred by the British parliament, but was avoided because while the inhabitants of Crown colonies were British subjects, those of protectorates were not. As long as no British interests were affected, the colonies (or rather their governors) were allowed considerable freedom of action, especially if they were able to pay for themselves.

For a long time the French colonies made a loss. In fact, their financial autonomy was minimal because, as a matter of principle, all financial and other decisions of any significance were made in Paris. Apart from some protectorates, such as Morocco and Tunisia, the colonies were components of the one and indivisible French Republic. For those that had come under French sovereignty through protectorate treaties, France unilaterally abolished this status in 1904. Key figures in the process were the governors-general of AOF and AEF, who as representatives of the French government possessed more or less unlimited powers, including that of justice. The governors of the individual colonies in theory had similarly comprehensive authority, but because finance was mainly controlled from the centre, the central administrations were able to disempower their regional governors to a large degree. In Algeria specific conditions applied, and the residents in Tunisia and Morocco had to work with the still extant indigenous institutions.

The Belgian and Portuguese systems were closely related to the French one. However, neither white nor black inhabitants of the Congo had any decision-making rights, whereas in the Portuguese colonies, as in some French ones, there was a right to vote in the mother country's parliament and a local self-administration, though only for French or Portuguese citizens. Germany came late and had no experience, resulting in serious errors but also in attempts to make good use of the other powers' experience. Its system had not matured before it collapsed. In legal terms the German colonies were part of Germany, but the German constitution did not apply there and German law applied exclusively for German nationals, a status which Africans could only achieve through formal naturalisation. The sole ruler and legislator was the Emperor; parliament only came into play if a law was to be passed for German citizens or if funding had to be approved. Settlers' claims to participation in power played a limited role in German South West and East Africa.

For reasons of cost, colonial governments made do with only small numbers of whites, who thus tended to enjoy a considerable degree of power. Shortly before 1940 in Nigeria, there were still just 386 white administrators for a population of 20 million. As ever, the system here functioned only with the help of indigenous collaborators: on the one hand the chiefs, on the other the auxiliary personnel of policemen, clerks, nursing assistants and so on. For this reason, it is important to consider the role of the African in the respective colonialist doctrines. After the First World War, both the great colonial powers pledged themselves to the idea of trusteeship, in line with the 'dual mandate' set out by Lord Lugard in 1922: responsibility for the civilisational advancement of the people, and responsibility for the development of the land's resources to benefit humanity as a whole. However, the routes by which the two powers proposed to reach this goal seem to embody two almost diametrically opposed models of colonial rule. The assimilation favoured on the Franco-Latin side appears to be a progressive doctrine and has, accordingly, been preferred by the left. It aims to make the colonies into equal members of the Republic, its inhabitants into French people in terms of language, education and culture, of clothing and behaviour, of political mentality and political rights. In contrast, the British system of 'indirect rule' appears more conservative, in that it allows the conventional structures of indigenous communities and the indigenous culture to remain in place as long they do not controvert British morality and British interests too dramatically. At bottom, however, both doctrines tell us more about the mentality of the colonial masters than about colonial reality, where the pressures of everyday politics led to a considerable degree of adaptation and evened out the differences. Systematic assimilation was not an option because the size of the respective populations meant it would have made France a 'colony of its colonies', as deputy Edouard Herriot worried in 1946. Indirect rule, in turn, could not be fully realised because European government and economics inevitably generated changes in the traditional structure of society and politics.

Indirect rule was nothing new; it had been practised by the ancient Romans, and the British had long been applying it successfully in the Indian princely states. Lugard adopted it in northern Nigeria mainly to save money. He established a set of principles for the purpose: continuation of the existing system of rule with its methods of succession and recruitment, but with the option of British intervention in a crisis; continued practice of Islamic law, but with supervision by the British resident and confirmation by him of any death sentence, and discontinuation of inhumane punishments such as amputation; taxation by both the British and the emir, but with British control over the scale of taxation and tax exemption for trade; continued keeping of house slaves, but abolition of slave-trading and propaganda for the virtues of free wage labour; the Crown's right to dispose over land and mineral resources, but expropriation only in urgent cases; disarmament of the Fulani and military monopoly for the British; prohibition of spirits and the unrestricted practice of Islam. In other words, a British resident was supposed not only to enforce the Crown's authority but also to accomplish economic and social progress. It was only Lugard's successors that sidelined this dynamic aspect and set their sights on protecting the 'idyll' of the Fulani aristocracy from capitalism, individualism and democracy. They thus conserved archaic political structures that might otherwise not have survived – as became clear on the advent of modern, western-educated African elites who detested this feudalism no less than the colonial power that made cosy deals with it at their expense. Because indirect rule did not envisage political modernisation, it offered less scope for modern elites than the French system did. The British system made no provision either for these elites or for the African masses now streaming into the cities. Those Africans who did not draw immediate profit from it probably rejected the system of indirect rule. They wanted to take on modern ways of life, not to have to listen to the colonial power prescribing what was 'African'.

It was also the case that in substantial territories there were no indigenous rulers who could act as partners in this system. In the south of Nigeria and in East Africa, the British had to create their own indigenous chiefs, just as the Belgians did in the Congo. There is thus some justice in the assertion that the much-cited African 'tribes' were to a certain degree not African in origin at all, but products of colonial rule.

To the extent that the French doctrine of assimilation had not already been abandoned in favour of a doctrine of 'association' rather similar to indirect rule, it was in practice applied only to people of French descent and to a few privileged areas like the 'four communes' in Senegal. These, along with northern Algeria, had the right to elect deputies for the national assembly in France. As a rule, however, full French civil rights could only be attained by individuals agreeing to give up their own culture and adopt French customs. Specifically, this meant French schooling and usually the abandonment of Islam. The colonies were parts of the Republic, yet in 1939 *citoyens* made up only 0.5 per cent of the population in AOF. The rest remained *sujets*, with few political rights and an inferior legal status as laid down by the *indigénat* laws. Although not citizens, they could be conscripted for military service and, especially, for compulsory labour, a very important factor in the French colonies but hardly existent in the British ones. The legal system was French, but for native 'subjects' justice could be carried out without trial through the administrative structure, which could impose penalties of up to two weeks' imprisonment.

In both British and French colonies, the decisive role was played by the indigenous official chiefs. Their function was similar in the two contexts, but the different importance they were accorded clearly illustrates the practical distinction between the systems. The British made a habit of respecting a chief – even one they had installed themselves – as an authority on his own law, enabled to pass legal judgement and to raise taxes which he shared with the colonial government, although if supervision was weak it was quite possible for him to line his own pockets and build himself a personal following. Among the French, in contrast, the chief remained the creature and executor of the colonial government. He too could raise taxes, but he had to pass them on in full and drew a salary that was docked if he failed to observe the correct behaviour. Furthermore, he not infrequently lacked traditional legitimation: whereas the British preferred to keep on the old elites and at most replaced individuals, the French, though also following this principle, additionally promoted reliable native auxiliaries or soldiers, sometimes even women, to the status of *chef* as long as they seemed trustworthy. Accordingly, after the end of colonial rule the British chiefs often retained their power while the position of the French ones largely collapsed.

But what was the objective in governing the African? He was to be governed for his own good, naturally – to 'civilise' him, although this was not intended to mean putting him on an equal basis with the European, at least not immediately. He did have to learn two basic forms of civilised behaviour very quickly if he was to be useful to humanity and especially to his masters: working, and paying taxes. The two were inextricably linked, since taxation was purposefully deployed as a way of pressurising Africans into giving up their 'lazy' life and earning the money required for taxes through wage labour or production for the market. No less important, however, was the contribution this made to funding colonial rule. The German colonies were in deficit apart from Togoland, whose solvency earned it the label 'model country' in Germany. The richer colonies of West Africa were in a better position. AOF was able to sustain itself because the governor-general implemented a kind of fiscal equalisation balancing out richer and poorer colonies, a scheme regarded by the wealthier ones as robbery. AEF, in contrast, depended on constant subsidies from Paris. The whites were enlisted to pay customs and also income taxes along French lines, although at times taxes were either lower than those at home or payable in the mother country – another form of profit transfer. Under these circumstances, the importance of the poll tax or 'hut tax' collected by the government-appointed chiefs should not be underestimated. It was sometimes so high that it ate up the Africans' cash income alarmingly or even completely. In Senegal during the Great Depression, tax revenues from the whites fell by two thirds while those from the Africans remained the same – that is, the African taxpayers had to bear the brunt of the crisis. In AOF, the tax burden was still at 40 per cent in 1940.

Finally, most colonies made use of compulsory labour for public works such as railway construction. Between 1921 and 1934, work on the Congo-Ocean Railway from Brazzaville cost 20,000 forced labourers from AEF their lives. Added to this was compulsory production of export crops on government-owned land. Corvée labour of this kind, being for 'public purposes', was exempt from the international ban on forced labour resolved in 1926. The French and Portuguese spheres of power also continued the practice of the administration recruiting cheap and not entirely voluntary labour for

European companies. In contrast to British Africa – trade unions were founded in Nigeria as early as 1905 – labour organisations were prohibited in the French colonies until 1937. In Portugal, the legally enforced obligation on subjects to work for six months of every year meant in practice that forced labour was recruited for the administration and private companies, under conditions that for the most part remained catastrophic until after the Second World War.

In Africa as elsewhere, the encroachments of fully fledged colonialism no longer met with any large-scale armed resistance. That kind of struggle characterises the phase of colonialism's introduction and then, under new circumstances, its decline and fall during decolonisation. This is not to say that those subjects unwilling to collaborate had accepted their fate with resignation. Africans skilfully practised a wide range of everyday, by no means always passive, resistance. They could evade taxes and conscription by absconding and react to the colonial rulers' projects with boycotts or even sabotage; at the very least they could protest symbolically, through demonstratively wearing certain garments or colours or participating in 'leisure activities' within organisations that would later become the pace-makers of decolonisation.

The colonial economy in Africa

As in other colonial contexts, in Africa the colonial economy started out as a pillage economy, a form of plundering on a grand scale that reached its zenith in the Congo colonies. The principle there was to exploit the natural products of ivory and wild rubber as rapidly as possible through brutal abuse of the natives, without making the slightest investment in the land. In this way concessionary companies were able at times to achieve profits of up to 1,400 per cent. But even before the First World War, the crises mentioned above, along with the collapse of the wild rubber boom in 1910, led to the realisation that the development of the colonies – what Albert Sarraut in the 1920s named their *mise en valeur* – and taking better care of African labour was actually in Europe's interest. However, such development was primarily to mean the mass-scale, cheap production of goods required by the mother country, at least in the French case: Britain only turned systematically to this kind of economic policy after the Great Depression or even after the Second World War.

In Africa, the control over the production factor of land was crucial. As in most non-European cultures, unrestricted private ownership of land on the model of Roman law was unknown, but rather than unappropriated land there was a plethora of complicated ownership claims by groups and individuals. When required, colonial administrators would declare land that seemed 'unowned' by European standards to be state property and pass it on to white settlers or corporations. Private ownership of land might be introduced for Africans, but this was associated with registration, taxation and other inconveniences and often resulted in the land finally being lost to white creditors and purchasers. There were, however, also cases of African ownership structures being respected to the disadvantage of the Europeans. As a rule, the older the colony was and the more white people had settled there, the more land was lost to Europeans. Algeria and South Africa may stand as extreme examples of land loss, but generally conditions varied from one colony to the next. In Uganda the British accepted indigenous land ownership, whereas in Kenya they promoted white settlement so energetically that in 1930, when protection for the Africans was introduced here as well, a white person owned on average seventy-three times as much land as an African. In contrast, in British West Africa white land ownership was discouraged as a general principle, and the alienation of land was very rare. AOF and Madagascar remained countries of smallholders, while AEF and the Belgian Congo continued generously allocating concessions, though not full property rights, to capital companies. In Togoland and Kamerun conflicts arose because the plantation owners were able to appropriate particularly fertile land for themselves, while German East Africa operated a reasonably successful smallholding policy. In South West Africa, almost all the land was expropriated after the great rebellion and thus became available for settlers and corporations.

Land-policy strategy was closely intertwined with the prevalent form of agricultural use. The preservation of African land ownership was not intended to protect purely subsistence farming but to have African farmers produce cash crops for the global market. In contrast, the white settlers' operations and the plantations owned by the capital companies, which might be cattle farms or themselves produce cash crops, were well served by a policy of expropriation or the more subtle procedure of using reservations to reduce African land ownership so far that Africans had no choice but to work for the Europeans. As a whole, the production of cash crops by African farmers gained in significance, whether through the policies of the colonial administration, as in AOF and German East Africa, or through African initiatives as in Senegal, Gold Coast and Uganda. In Senegal African farmers, with the important participation of a Muslim brotherhood, considerably extended the area of peanut cultivation; soil exhaustion ensued. In the Gold Coast colony, Africans began cultivating the cocoa tree and, through private and cooperative initiatives independent of both the colonial power and the traditional authorities, acquired the necessary land to make Gold Coast/Ghana the world's prime cocoa producer. In Uganda, African cotton cultivation led to an economic symbiosis between African farmers, British wholesalers and Indian retailers. African cash-crop smallholding is a primitive economic form involving low costs but also little opportunity for marketing, a combination that may lead to the dominance of large trading companies. Added to that are the dependence on world market conditions and vulnerability to crisis that typify monocultures. Attempts to improve the situation through irrigation systems were successful in the case of the Gezira scheme in Sudan, but less so in the Niger project above Timbuktu. Such efforts can anyway not alleviate the consequences of dependence on the world market.

However, cotton, wool, rubber, maize, palm oil, cocoa and peanuts made up only 20.2 per cent of African exports in 1913 and 25.14 per cent in 1935, whereas in the same years 55.9 per cent and 53.5 per cent of export revenue came from gold, diamonds and copper. In global economic terms Africa was a mining colony, with leading roles for South Africa and soon also Northern Rhodesia (copper) and Katanga in the southern Congo (copper, gold, diamonds). In the British colonies of West Africa, too, mining gained in importance. While most companies operated their mines with qualified white workers and unqualified, rapidly replaced and therefore cheap black labour – that is, migrant workers – the *Union minière du Haut Katanga* found the white workers too expensive and the black migrants too unproductive. It chose instead to create a well trained and well cared-for team of black skilled workers, and reaped notable rewards.

The distribution of investment reflects the geography of production. State investment, of which there was almost as much as private investment overall, was unable to remedy the problem that investment did not flow into areas where a lack of capital was hindering urgently needed development. The reason was that during the colonial period both public and private investors put their money primarily into the export sector in its broader sense. As a result, development was lopsidedly oriented on foreign trade, thus on the economic interests of the European economy and not on those of the African economy – it was, precisely, colonial economic development. This can still be seen today by looking at the maps of the most important state investment, rail transport. In Africa even more clearly than in India and with very few exceptions, rail construction had created a system of branch lines leading to the ports, a pattern that served not the needs of the continent but its exploitation by Europe.

If foreign trade was the big business offered by Africa, this applies less to the colonial powers taken as a whole, since Africa's share of their trade balance remained mainly rather modest until the period of the Second World

War. Rather, particular sectors and particular companies were the major beneficiaries not only of trade but also of state infrastructural projects. If Africa was probably a loss-maker for European state budgets across the board, private individuals made enormous profits, though little is known about the exact extent and economic impact of those earnings in the mother countries. That is partly the result of company structures: the African side of the trade retained an element of barter, whereby the companies or their employees could make extra profits by setting off goods against goods, using truck systems or advances, and on the European side some companies were no longer purely national concerns – in the Africa trade, the era of multi-nationals dawned early. Alongside the South African diamond monopoly and the gold oligopoly, a further example would be the margarine and soap corporation Unilever operating in tropical Africa, originally an English firm but soon a multinational one that used French subsidiaries to gradually penetrate the market of the French colonies. Africa was most important to Unilever for its supply of raw materials. In the Belgian Congo, for example, the company had access to 750,000 ha for oil-palm plantations. Two other giants were the *Compagnie française de l'Afrique occidentale*, based in Marseilles, and the *Société commerciale de l'Ouest africain*, founded by Swiss merchants. The Belgian *Société Générale* was a holding company that controlled the crucial *Union minière* in the Congo along with three dozen other companies from a wide range of sectors. In the field of banking, concentration was if anything even more pronounced, resulting in further under-capitalisation of Africa because the big banks tended to invest their money not in Africa but in Europe.

Social change in Africa

Whether intentionally or not, colonial rule and the colonial economy gave rise to massive social change. New social strata and groups arose: alongside wage labourers, there were now also new, western-style elites in the service of the colonial government and in the liberal professions. In some places colonial rule also set in motion a rapid growth in the African population. The reduction of mortality appears not to have been the decisive factor, as previously thought, since medical care remained mediocre until the middle of the twentieth century. Probably more important was an increased birth rate, which, as in nineteenth-century Java, may have been related to the more optimistic attitudes to the future fostered by better life prospects, in spite or even because of foreign rule – an interesting corrective to some overly simple anti-colonial views of history. Against a backdrop of political and economic change, population pressure and hopes for better opportunities increased horizontal mobility. A new economic geography now prevailed: instead of being relatively evenly distributed according to the requirements of subsistence farming, the population became concentrated at those points where work and sustenance beckoned, on plantations, in mines, at rail hubs, in administrative centres and ports. Seasonal workers may have taken the first steps, their families soon moving to join them. The new towns and cities became the major destinations of migration, and between 1850 and 1950 Africa experienced an urbanisation far above the global average, resulting in conditions that today no longer differ much from those in Europe. There is one substantial distinction, however: many African cities do not offer immigrants regular employment but at best casual labour. The settlement form that corresponds to this improvised form of livelihood is the huge shanty town, in Francophone regions named *bidonvilles* after the sheet metal from old oil drums, *bidons*, that is their most popular building material. The inhabitants of these slums are by no means 'uprooted' victims of social anomie; they have often developed forms of social organisation adapted to their new way of life, not least with recourse to shared ethnic identities.

Even where the more upmarket neighbourhoods of Africa's cities are now inhabited by black elites, the city maps still preserve a fundamental feature of colonialism: the racial stratification of African colonial society with the 'whites' at the top, the 'blacks' at the bottom and the 'Arabs', Indians and 'coloureds' in the middle. Such stratification may be the norm not only in colonial history but in world history as a whole, yet unlike in other colonies the visible characteristics of the 'black' races, especially skin colour, ensured that the boundaries were difficult to cross. European racism was at its sharpest in the settlement colonies, in South Africa, Algeria (here not even directed at 'blacks'), Rhodesia, Kenya, German South West Africa. In general, and in other regions too, the social Darwinism dominant in the era of imperialism further aggravated the situation. Thus, for example, around 1890 the Niger mission with its black bishop was racially 'cleansed' by white missionaries.

To be sure, European missionaries were not only the agents of imperialist expansionism and partners in the colonial project, but also acted as committed advocates of the Africans. However, they rarely had any doubt that colonial rule was justified by the cultural superiority of the whites. At this time Christianity was not proclaimed as being compatible with all cultures (a claim that can, indeed, be disputed even today); rather, the introduction of European culture was to take place in concert with the process of Christianisation. In fact, in quantitative terms alone missionary and imperialist activities went hand in hand: the nineteenth century was not only the pinnacle of European expansion, but also the great century of missionary work, which unlike before was now borne along by mass religious movements, just as high imperialism was borne along by mass political ones. Before the First World War, Protestants and Catholics each maintained more than 500 missionary stations in Africa. Cooperation with the colonial governments normally ran smoothly, each side needing the other's help. In the Belgian and Portuguese colonies especially, there was certainly no separation of church and state. Conflicts did arise over the treatment of the natives or when missionaries were reluctant to share control over the population with administrators, particularly if economic interests – such as missionary-owned plantations – were at stake. The Catholic missions were geographically more evenly spread, while Protestant missions were less common under the Latin colonial powers, but this had to do less with denominational differences than with national concerns that missions might conceal agents of the powerful British or aggressive German rivals. A further point of conflict was the missionaries' accusation that the British, French and German administrations were giving unfair preference to Islam – but then, in AOF 70 per cent of the population professed Islam and only 8.5 per cent Christianity.

Overall, however, the work of the missionaries did yield substantial successes. In 1984 it seems that 45.4 per cent of all Africans were Christians and 41.5 per cent Muslims, with only a small remnant practising traditional religions. Today the figures are 48 per cent and 41 per cent. Since they include Muslim North Africa, immune to Christian missionary efforts, the proportion of Christians among sub-Saharan Africans is even higher, and today Africa south of the Sahara is more Christian than Europe is. It must, on the other hand, be borne in mind that only three quarters of these Christians belong to what used to be the missionary churches, 9.5 per cent being Ethiopians and Copts and 14.4 per cent belonging to the numerous African churches. Even when, between the world wars, the churches began a systematic Africanisation of their personnel – in 1930 the Catholic Church consecrated its first black African bishop since 1512 – for some time it remained the case that the older Christian brothers, the whites, took charge while the younger ones, the Africans, had to defer. Islam in Africa presented a less racist face. Even where it did not become the epitome of anti-colonial resistance, as in the north, it defined itself as a religion of Africans for Africans. African Christians too soon followed that route, founding their own, purely African churches (easily done in the Protestant and Evangelical areas) or developing influential syncretistic movements that merged Christian with traditional African elements, such as the Zionist churches of South Africa or Kimbanguism in the Congo. Sometimes that culminated in a distinctly anti-colonial millennialism, as was the case in the Central African Kitawala ('kingdom') movement. The much-posed question of whether such syncretisms still constitute authentic Christianity can only be answered if one defines what 'authentic Christianity' is to be – European Christianity?

11 Late imperialism and the great decolonisation

In many respects, modern colonialism reached its zenith only in the twentieth century. The colonial empires of Britain and France achieved their widest extent when the German colonies and the Ottoman Empire were parcelled out after the First World War, and some of the colonies only became really economically valuable for their owners during the interwar period or even after the Second World War. Italy and Japan distinguished themselves as particularly aggressive and, at least temporarily, highly successful imperialist powers. The Portuguese colonial empire was not fully developed until after 1945. And with Jewish settlement in Palestine in the wake of British imperialism, the establishment of the State of Israel and its self-assertion, a community based on the combination of colonisation and colonialism came into existence for the last time. On the other hand, by this point the end of colonialism was already looming. The process began with Japan's achievements in the international arena around the turn of the century, regardless of the fact that these successes were themselves a form of imperialism and colonialism. Many colonies gained significantly in status through their contributions to the two world wars, which, conversely, demonstrated to the colonised world the disunity, vulnerability and ultimately the weakness of the white man. In the India of the interwar period, a mass movement for decolonisation arose and had a global impact that can hardly be overstated. Churchill was probably right to claim that no single individual contributed more to the fall of the British Empire than Mahatma Gandhi. In 1932 Moritz Bonn, a German emigrant teaching in London, coined a name for the coming events: 'All over the world a period of counter-colonization began, and *decolonization* is rapidly proceeding'. After the Second World War, further change was generated by the new authority of the two world powers, the United States and the USSR, who both took a firm stand against conventional colonialism. The unified global politics of international interpenetration that European expansionism had created now also reached its highest point. So it was that in just a few years around 1950 almost all the Asian colonies, and around 1960 most of the African colonies, succeeded in gaining political independence. Two further waves followed: the Portuguese colonies in 1974/75 and finally, largely due to the altered global role of Russia, Namibia in 1989 and the 'internal' colonies of Russia and South Africa in the 1990s, cases that had previously appeared invulnerable to decolonisation. This great decolonisation was not a painless process; the political legacy of colonialism played an important part in generating new trouble spots, up to and including bloody wars between the liberated peoples.

The Oriental question and the First World War

The 'Oriental question', apparently first described as such in 1822, asked what was to become of the collapsing 'semi-colony' of the Ottoman Empire. The answer offered after the First World War would turn out to be a provisional one, for the Middle East remained a prime flashpoint of global political unrest with only a partial change in the actors. Its old and new problems have not been fully resolved even today. The Ottoman Empire had struck fear into Europe's heart as late as the seventeenth century, but in 1774, when Russian protectorate was imposed over the sultan's Orthodox subjects, a process of decline began which would drag on until 1923. It was marked by both the interference of the great powers and the awakening nationalism of a multi-ethnic empire. This first made itself felt in the Balkans, from Serbia's autonomy in 1812 to Albania's independence in 1913. The original Ottoman system of rule had been based on expansionism and plunder, but when both land and booty failed to materialise, the Ottoman elites turned instead to internal exploitation, for the most part without any recognition of the necessity of modernisation. The economy remained focused on agricultural exports, while manufacturing suffered due to cheap European imports. As a result, the empire was overtaken by its European opponents not only politically, but also economically in the mobilisation of resources.

At first the political, cultural and economic influence of France was dominant, and would probably have culminated in a hegemony in alliance with Muhammad Ali's Egypt if the sultan had not been rescued by a Russian intervention in 1832 and a British one in 1839. For Russia, a vulnerable Ottoman Empire under Russian influence was preferable to the empire's dissolution, which would only mean gains for Britain and France; Britain, in contrast, wanted to keep Russia on a short leash in the region, as everywhere else. In 1841 the five powers agreed on the peace-time closure of the Turkish Straits. Although this came at the expense of the sultan's sovereignty, it also indirectly guaranteed the continued existence of his empire. British imports now prevailed, three quarters of them cotton goods. In 1838 the British imposed general customs tariffs of 3 per cent for imports, 12 per cent for exports and 2 per cent for transit trade. Privileging western merchants in this way was a practice that went back to the 'capitulations' common since the sixteenth century. Originally marks of favour handed out by an all-powerful sultan to useful foreigners, their function was now reversed, as a system of unequal treaties that enabled the penetration of the country by free-trade imperialism without consideration of that country's own interests. As well as tariff privileges, tax exemption and freedom for foreigners to establish themselves and practise their religion, a particularly important point was that foreigners were subject solely to the jurisdiction of their consuls and, in cases of conflict with the indigenous population, could only be prosecuted with the consuls' cooperation.

Enjoyment of these privileges could also be extended to particular protégés, people originally subjects of the Ottoman Empire but now genuine or fictitious employees of the consulate or else members of groups of foreign origin, such as Greeks, Jews or Armenians. This was supplemented by the Ottoman *millet* system, the traditional self-government of the Christian and Jewish religious communities to the benefit of the Ottoman taxman, which was now also transformed into a protectorate by foreign powers. The Catholics came under the protection of France, the Orthodox under that of Russia, while Britain was responsible for the Protestants. The background to this development was the fact that a large number of western missionaries, under western protection, were now setting their sights less on the Muslims than on the Eastern Christians, a focus that would turn out to offer important leverage for imperialism, especially in Lebanon and Palestine. In the Holy Land, where the Christian denominations were in fierce competition, Russia responded to the French-backed Catholic gains by issuing far-reaching demands on behalf of the Orthodox. In the context of the contemporary configuration of power, the rejection of those demands eventually led to the Crimean War of 1854–56.

As a supporter of the victorious western powers, the Ottoman Empire received recognition as a European state in the peace treaty along with a guarantee for its existing possessions, after an 1856 decree had promised its Christian and Jewish subjects full legal equality and announced a programme of modernisation in justice, administration and finance. This dovetailed with the internal Ottoman modernisation process of *Tanzimat* that unfolded in 1836–76, first steps having already been taken in the late eighteenth century. Initially Tanzimat involved only the construction of a modern military, with a new education system to flank it. Istanbul's rival Muhammad Ali proceeded in exactly the same way. However, these measures were soon followed by administrative reforms: a ministry system, in which the grand vizier was nothing more than a prime minister, and a professional civil service were created, a penal code and a commercial code drawn up, and higher schooling for boys and even for girls was established under a specialised ministry for education. Ottoman lifestyles became increasingly westernised, with more and more men wearing western-style clothes. Finally, in 1876, a constitution was drawn up that provided for proportional representation of the different nationalities – but in 1878 was, like the parliament itself, abolished during a conservative backlash.

The realisation of the reforms anyway left much to be desired, mainly because the state's finances were in a disastrous condition. The gaps were stopped with western loans, which were only to be had at extremely unfavourable conditions. In 1854–74, nominally 242 million Turkish pounds were borrowed at 5–6 per cent; however, because only 128 million of this was actually paid out, the interest rate in practice came to more than 10 per cent. New loans were taken out in order to redeem the debt, and a carousel of debt restructuring to the benefit of the western banks ensued. When ministers demurred, political pressure was applied to persuade them. After the state bankruptcy of 1875, in 1881 an international public debt commission, the *Administration de la dette publique ottomane*, was established and given permanent charge of a segment of state revenues to administer through its own apparatus. It did good work, prompting various developmental initiatives and acquiring new loans for the empire at better conditions, but notwithstanding that, the Administration was the perfect instrument of classic finance-capital imperialism, which in this case had no need to intervene militarily and establish political rule as it had done in Tunisia and Egypt. The Public Debt Administration collaborated closely with the French-dominated *Banque impériale Ottomane*, the *Deutsche Bank* and the British-influenced National Bank of Turkey (originally intended as a means of breaking the monopoly of the former two). These banks offered short-term loans and, counting on later consolidation in cooperation with the Administration, issued bonds – though these were often tied to particular projects or used to extort concessions for the partner companies.

The real money was to be made in railway construction. Only the Hejaz railway link from Damascus to Medina was built by the Ottomans on their own account. The remaining lines were constructed mainly by French and German firms, backed by an Ottoman state guarantee of profitability and in many cases by additional concessions such as the mining rights for mineral resources on either side of the track. By 1910, two thirds of coal, chrome and copper production was in foreign hands. Added to this were further concessions for public works such as tramways, telephones, gas, water and electricity in the big cities. French capital dominated, but German investment had overtaken British by 1914, due not least to the German-financed Baghdad Railway. In 1888, a consortium led by the Deutsche Bank had taken over the rail link from Istanbul to Vienna and in 1889 had obtained a concession to build the Istanbul–Ankara line. Determined scheming by the competition immediately threatened to undermine the arrangement, but Wilhelm II managed to have the contract finalised in 1902. French capital did, though, remain involved, and in 1914 an agreement was also reached with the British, despite their feeling that Germany's advance into Iraq threatened not only their Indian empire but now also their Middle Eastern oil interests. During a journey through the Orient in 1898, Wilhelm II had declared himself a friend of the sultan and all Muslims, while simultaneously practising Christian imperialism in Jerusalem. The consecration of the imposing Lutheran church in Jerusalem was intended primarily as an affront to the British, whose 1841 treaty agreement to maintain a joint Anglican and German Protestant bishopric in Jerusalem Wilhelm had cancelled in 1886. As a consolation prize, the Catholics received the supposed house of the Virgin Mary. One important reason to keep the Catholics happy was that the French government, rigorously anticlerical in internal affairs, liked to act the generous sponsor of Catholicism when it came to foreign policy. The Pope was forced to accept a continuing French protectorate in order to avoid inflaming French anticlericalism even further.

All this, however, seems innocuous in the context of the problems with minority nationalities that were now plaguing the Ottoman Empire in Asia as well, initially under the banner of religion until language, ethnicity and culture became the new vehicles of nation-building. Bloody conflicts between the Catholic Maronites and the quasi-Muslim Druze of Lebanon had been resolved in 1861 with the help of an intervention by the powers, establishing a semi-autonomous province with proportional representation of the different religions. What seemed more threatening was the stance of the Armenians, in the east of Anatolia near the heart of the empire, who had fallen under Russian and British influence. Their rebellious spirit would be broken by Turkish and Kurdish terror in 1894–97; it is thought that more than 100,000 Armenians lost their lives in this period. The national awakening of the Arabs, in contrast, at first appeared to be harmless or even useful: in the case of Jamal ad-Din al-Afghani and Muhammad Abduh it was originally limited to a pan-Islamic programme of religious renewal in combination with the adoption of western science and technology. During and after the First World War the sultan, in his capacity as caliph, tried to make pan-Islamism into grist for his own mill – and not without success.

In 1908 a group of officers known as the 'Young Turks' managed to have the constitution reinstated. The composition of the parliament, nearly half of whose members were Arabs and other non-Turkish nationalities, initially seemed to herald the emergence of a neo-Ottoman Empire as a federation or

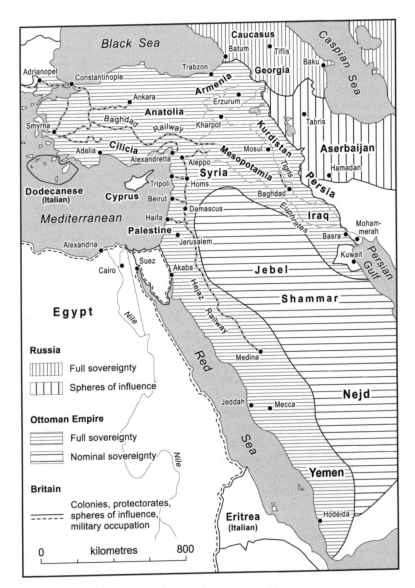

Map 20   The Ottoman Empire before the First World War

else on the model of Austro-Hungarian dualism. Instead, however, the 'national' idea of Turkifying the entire empire gained ground among the Young Turks; there was even talk of a racist 'pan-Turanism' of all the Turkic peoples. Defeats in the Balkans and by Italy only heightened Turkish nationalist aggression, as the Armenians found to their particular cost during the First World War. When the Armenians aligned themselves with Russia, and Britain advocated the plan of an Armenian 'national home', the government responded with brutal 'resettlement' campaigns during which 600,000–1,000,000 people died. Among the Arabs, too, the First World War revealed the extent of the antipathy to the Ottomans that had accumulated.

By no means all the Young Turks favoured Germany, but the pro-German faction succeeded in pushing Turkey into the war on the side of the Central Powers. An Allied attack on the Dardanelles failed, and in the Caucasus the situation remained undecided right to the end. In the Arab parts of the empire, in contrast, the British eventually achieved results, with considerable support from India and the Dominions. Egypt was immediately turned into an independent monarchy under British protectorate; attacks on the Suez Canal were deflected and Iraq with its oil resources was successfully captured at the second attempt. Arab ambitions were mobilised in the catchment area of the Hejaz railway from Damascus to Medina, albeit with the help of some highly dubious diplomatic manoeuvres. In 1916, the high commissioner in Egypt, Henry McMahon, wrote to the Sharif Hussein of Mecca about a future Arab kingdom, but with nebulous reservations regarding Iraq and French interests in Syria. Shortly before this, there had been secret discussions with France over the war objectives, in which Russia and Italy were later involved. In the resulting 'Sykes-Picot' agreement, Russia was to be allocated the Turkish Straits and Armenia, while Italy was to receive southern Anatolia, France would receive south-east Anatolia including Kurdistan, and Britain would receive the seaports of Akka (Acre) and Haifa, southern Iraq and the Gulf coast. Because of its holy sites, Palestine was to come under international administration. However, in 1917 the British foreign secretary wrote to a representative of the Jewish Zionist movement that the British government viewed 'with favour the establishment in Palestine of a national home for the Jewish people, and will use their best endeavours to facilitate the achievement of this object', with the proviso that there must be no prejudice to the Arabs' civil and religious rights (they had no political rights) or to the legal status of such non-Zionist Jews in third countries as preferred to assimilate there. This document, which came to be known as the Balfour Declaration, was designed to win the support of US and Russian Jews and to counter German overtures. It was a successful strategy: by the end of the war, and with the help of an Arab revolt, almost the whole of the Arab Middle East was in British hands.

In East Asia the weakness of the German possessions meant that the war was over in a matter of weeks. Australia took and kept New Guinea with its neighbouring islands, New Zealand acquired Samoa, while Japan – to the dissatisfaction of the Dominions – received English approval to appropriate Qingdao and the island groups north of the equator.

The distribution of the booty of the German colonies and the Ottoman Empire took place after the war in the legal framework of mandates issued by the newly formed League of Nations. The 'Class A' mandates that were applied in the Middle East differed from the Class B and Class C mandates for former colonies in providing for an imminent introduction of independence. France received Syria, and was able to hive off the Greater Lebanon that had been demanded by the Maronites and their French associates. This extension of Lebanese borders meant the inclusion of Sunni and Shiite minorities as well as the already existing Druze minority, thus laying the foundations of later conflicts in Lebanon. An intensive French penetration of both countries began, but independence, planned for 1936 after some disputes, was delayed as a result of the Second World War until the post-war period.

The kingdom established by the Arabs in Damascus had been crushed, and King Faisal, a son of Hussein's, was relocated by the British into the new kingdom of Iraq, which remained a British satellite even after the end of the mandate. Another new kingdom, Transjordan, was created for Faisal's brother Abdullah. As part of the British mandate of Palestine, Transjordan could be kept on a short rein, and by this means the oil pipeline from Mosul to the Mediterranean remained completely inside British-controlled territory. Hussein was left to himself – that is, to a 1924 conquest of Hejaz with its lucrative pilgrimage business by Saudi Arabia, at that time still lacking oil. The aim of uninterrupted British control of the Suez Canal and of the sea and air routes to India had been achieved, thanks above all to the directly exercised mandate in Palestine itself. There, however, the colonial power had saddled itself with the task of keeping the Arabs reasonably satisfied while simultaneously enabling the Jews to attain the home they had been promised. A zigzag course was pursued, adapting to whatever seemed to serve British interests better at any one time.

As for the rest of the Ottoman Empire, the peace dictated at Sèvres in 1920 provided for further forfeitures to Greece, France and Italy, along with an independent Armenia and an autonomous Kurdistan with the option of independence. Furthermore, the international Public Debt Administration was now to take over the whole of economic and fiscal policy. However, Mustafa Kemal managed to exploit the considerable conflicts among the powers involved, and used his still intact army to defeat the various invaders one by one. Armenian independence was crushed with the help of the Bolsheviks and Armenia's Russian component was reduced to a Soviet Republic. Kurdistan was carved up among the newly formed countries; as Muslims, the Kurds did not even have a claim to protection as a religious minority. In the Treaty of Lausanne in 1923, the Aegean Islands were ceded to Italy and Greece, but Anatolia and Thrace were retained and, except for the demilitarisation of the Straits, full sovereignty was regained. The defunct empire's debts were distributed among the creditor countries and the Debt Administration dissolved. The national assembly abolished the sultanate in 1922, the caliphate in 1924. The Ottoman Empire became Turkey, defined as a nation state. The founder of that state, Mustafa Kemal 'Atatürk', was now able to set to work on his energetic modernisation policy – in a fiercely nationalistic vein determined by the circumstances.

Israel: Colonisation and colonialism

Although traditionally defined in religious and cultural terms, under the pressure of the nineteenth-century pogroms (especially in Russia) the Jewish people fell into line with contemporary trends by coming to regard themselves as a nation. At a conference in Basel in 1897, the Zionist movement made a 'publicly and legally assured home in Palestine' part of its manifesto. Theodor Herzl, author of the programmatic *The Jewish State* (1896), even tried to attract Wilhelm II's interest in the project. During the First World War, with the help of the influential Zionist Chaim Weizmann, the Zionists managed to effect the Balfour Declaration. Since 1882, the Jews who had always lived in the towns of Palestine had been joined by ever more waves of immigrants making *aliyah* from Eastern Europe, and by 1914 the Jewish community, at 85,000 people, had grown to form 12.3 per cent of Palestine's population. Although most immigrants settled in towns, it was nevertheless the militant socialists who set the tone. In 1909/10 they founded the first kibbutz, a form of strictly collectivist agricultural settlement, and by 1986 kibbutzim numbered 269, compared with 720 co-operatively organised or 'normal' villages. Backed up by the Jewish National Fund's systematic policy of land acquisition and the reclamation of desert land, along with the development of citrus farming, the Jewish settlement of Palestine became the last case of large-scale colonisation – not always, but frequently enough, at the expense of the Arabs. Following the principle that colonies must not entail costs, the mandatory authorities invested practically nothing in development assistance for Arab Palestinians, while the Jewish population, in addition to their head start in modernisation, had around $400 million at their disposal for development between 1919 and 1939. The increasingly well organised Jewish community, or *Yishuv*, with the Jewish Agency as its western partner, gradually began to encounter organised Arab resistance. However, the Jewish defence organisations that had been assembled since 1907 were also deployed against the mandatory power if need be.

The crux of the problem was continued Jewish immigration, soon to gain further momentum through National Socialist persecution and the Second World War. The British project for a shared constitution foundered on Arab resistance in 1922 and on Jewish resistance in 1935. Civil war then prevailed, with terrorist campaigns between the two groups and the mandatory power. In 1937 the Zionists might have accepted a proposal for partition, but the Arabs rejected it, as they did the renewed plan for a jointly governed state that was tabled in 1939. Talks between the adversaries petered out, both parties finding it unnecessary to consider any compromise and retreating into increasingly entrenched positions. After the Second World War, Britain, with an eye to its interests in the Middle East, pursued a clearly pro-Arab policy including restrictions on Jewish immigration; the Jews now put their hopes in the United States, where a 1942 conference of Jewish organisations had resolved 'that Palestine be established as a Jewish commonwealth' (the Biltmore declaration). In 1946, the Jews began to use guerrilla tactics against the British, and in 1947, under American pressure, the British finally handed their mandate back to the United Nations, which now worked out a complicated partition plan. However, the British withdrawal led to an escalation in armed hostilities. On 14 May 1948 the leader of the Jewish Labour Party, David Ben-Gurion, proclaimed the state of Israel. It was recognised within minutes by the United States, but on 15 May already found itself under attack from the members of the newly established Arab League. Israel proved the superior force; additionally, its most dangerous opponent, Abdullah of Transjordan, had no interest in a Palestinian state and held secret talks with Israel to appropriate for his kingdom those territories on the west bank of the River Jordan, including East Jerusalem, that Israel had not been able to conquer.

The subsequent mass exodus of the Arabs suited the Israelis. They systematically promoted it: in place of the 369 abandoned Arab settlements, they were able to create 186 new Jewish ones. If in 1946 there had been 608,000 Jews and 1.35 million Arabs in the area, by 1948 there were 650,000 Jews and only 160,000 Arabs. Israel subsequently took in 600,000–800,000 Jews expelled from the oriental lands, the largest wave of immigrants until the post-1990 period when hundreds of thousands of Jews were allowed to emigrate from the former Soviet Union. Israeli colonisation could now be pursued with impressive effectiveness, even if more Israelis

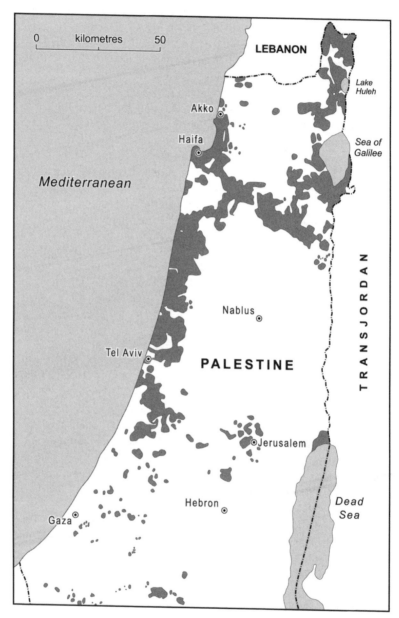

Map 21   Jewish-owned land in 1944

Map 22   Israel 1947–1967

than ever lived in towns and cities. The great water conduit from the Sea of Galilee into the Negev Desert deserves special attention, as the battle for water was to play a continued and important role in the conflicts with the Arabs both inside and outside Israel. In 1980, Israel had 3.28 million Jewish and 600,000 Arab inhabitants, but added to these were 700,000 Arabs in the West Bank and 442,000 in the Gaza Strip. During its pre-emptive strike against the threat from Egypt, the Six-Day War of June 1967, Israel had occupied and retained Jerusalem, the Jordanian part of Palestine, the strategically important Golan Heights beyond the Sea of Galilee and the Gaza Strip. This made it a colonial power, for while the Arab inhabitants of Israel were (despite a theoretically high degree of equality) in practice at least second-class citizens, the new Arab population remained merely the subjects of a repressive military administration and served to provide cheap migrant labour. In addition, colonisation and colonialism were deliberately combined in the systematic establishment of new Jewish settlements inside the captured territories, a total of 144 settlements with 120,000 inhabitants. The constant threat to Israel, for example in the First Gulf War of 1990/91, inevitably led to a further hardening of Israeli attitudes, so that this last colony of the West, like South Africa and the Soviet Union, appeared impermeable to decolonisation.

Japanese imperialism and the Second World War

In terms of both domestic and foreign policy, the regime of the regenerated Japan was under pressure to succeed. But in the period around 1900, the only way to achieve an equal seat at the table of the great powers seemed to be imperialist expansion – a perspective shared by the Germans. First of all Japan's neighbour Korea was 'opened up' in 1876 following the pattern established by the western powers in China. China laid claim to sovereignty over Korea, and although Japan initially accepted the situation, in 1894 a war erupted over the issue. It was won with surprising ease by Japan. In 1895, China was forced to cede both Taiwan and the Liaodong Peninsula in southern Manchuria, though the latter gain was reversed under western and Russian duress and had to be supplemented by a Japanese declaration guaranteeing Korean independence. When its chief rival, Russia, was defeated in 1905, Japan acquired not only Liaodong (with a sphere of influence in southern Manchuria), but also the southern half of the island of Sakhalin. Japan was also able to make Korea a protectorate, and annexed it in 1910; Korea, like Taiwan, remained a Japanese colony until 1945. Japanese ambitions now turned towards China, where Japanese trade and investment was growing at a breathtaking speed. Japan is a country poor in raw materials, and by 1920 China had become its main supplier of coal, iron and raw cotton, while also providing a market for 50 per cent of Japanese textile production. That was a prize worth fighting for, especially as Japan had good starting positions in Liaodong and, as the heir of the Germans, Qingdao. Although Japan had supported the republican movement that eliminated the Chinese imperial system in 1911, the confirmation of its conquests in Shandong by the Versailles treaty in 1919 precipitated a violent anti-Japanese reaction in China. It became the nucleus of a movement of cultural renewal among the Chinese elites, which had now begun to aspire to systematic modernisation by means of westernisation. In 1922 the powers proved willing to recognise China's sovereignty and integrity, but not to abolish the unequal treaties or to reinstate tariff autonomy.

The army of the Chinese nationalist party, the Kuomintang, recaptured the north including Peking in 1928, in the course of its successful campaign against the quarrelling provincial 'war lords' who had divided China up among themselves. This was followed by the first clashes with the Japanese, who dominated Manchuria. The Japanese governments of the 1920s, under the influence of economic leaders, did not succeed in getting to grips with the radical nationalist and anti-parliamentarian movement, which was driven mainly by the military and aimed to bring the Meiji Restoration closer to its objective of internal harmony and external hegemony. The global economic crisis exacerbated Japan's potential for aggression, the view being widespread that territorial expansion was the only route to effective self-assertion for the Japanese, crowded as they were on resource-poor islands and facing the worldwide erection of tariff walls and restrictive US immigration laws. This was the setting in which the government accepted the army's unauthorised occupation of the whole of Manchuria and of the adjacent Chinese province of Jehol (Hebei) in 1931–33. Over the next few years the Japanese puppet state of Manchukuo, led by the last emperor of the Manchu dynasty, experienced a great economic upturn to the benefit of Japan. In China, however, the gradual reintegration of the country under Chiang Kai-shek was making itself felt; tariff autonomy was also regained and the privileging of foreigners through the unequal treaties gradually dismantled, although this goal was only fully achieved in 1943–46. But whereas China was striving for equality of status, Japan was staking out a claim for hegemony to the exclusion of third powers. The incident at the Marco Polo Bridge was enough to trigger the Sino-Japanese War of 1937–45, and in Japan military officers and other specialists took the reins of power. The Japanese goal was not to conquer China but to establish an unassailable hegemony over it, but although the Chinese lost battles due to inferior training and weaponry and

Chiang Kai-shek had to retreat to Chongqing in the south-west, China's huge expanse and population meant the war was impossible for Japan to win. Entrenched in Chongqing, Chiang Kai-shek was still able to obtain supplies via Tonkin and Burma.

Parts of South-East Asia had long since been drawn into the Japanese sphere of interest as markets and as suppliers of raw materials. In the 1930s Japan was buying most of the chrome, manganese, copper and iron produced in the Philippines; the entire Malaysian production of iron, bauxite and manganese; half the coal mined by Indo-China and large quantities of rubber. The Dutch East Indies supplied one-quarter of Japan's oil requirements, British Borneo one-eighth. Japanese immigrated to the various locations and ran their own companies there. But what gave the colonial powers most cause for concern was the flood of cheap Japanese textiles and other export goods that threatened to squeeze their own exports out of the South-East Asian markets. Everywhere, tariff barriers were constructed against Japanese imports.

The defeats suffered by the western powers in 1940 put new wind in the sails of Japanese enthusiasm for a 'Greater East Asia Co-Prosperity Sphere'. As well as the existing Japanese empire and China, this was to embrace the Philippines, Siam, Malaya, Indonesia, Indo-China, Burma and if possible also British India; as good colonialists, the Japanese planned to devote the south to raw materials' production and Japan, Manchukuo and China to industry. Japan anticipated war with Britain, but not war with the United States, from whose economic dominance it was trying to free itself.

In 1940 France was obliged to accept the Japanese occupation of Tonkin, and yielded to Japanese pressure to cede parts of Laos and Cambodia to Siam. Britain, on the other hand, could only temporarily be forced to close the Burma Road in 1941. But the Burmese nationalists saw the chance offered by the Japanese: the British (just like the Dutch for those Indonesian leaders they had not yet arrested) had left them in no doubt that the 1941 Atlantic Charter's right of peoples to choose their own form of government applied only to those oppressed by the Nazis, not to them. After all, the argument ran, they had never been oppressed. The attitude of the western colonial powers could only work to the Japanese advantage, although Japan was not yet able to push through its objectives in its negotiations with the Dutch. Politically isolated Indo-China, in contrast, was completely occupied in 1941 and subjugated to Japanese economic control. This step would lead to a fateful rupture with the United States, which had up to now only hesitantly curbed its supply of scrap metal and oil (US oil covered 75 per cent of Japanese demand). The two different positions now proved to be irreconcilable: Japan expected the recognition of its hegemony in Asia, while the

United States demanded withdrawal from China and respect for the integrity of third countries. The more the United States considered itself forced to adopt repressive measures such as partial embargoes, the more Japan considered itself forced to seek substitutes in South-East Asia in order to escape the US stranglehold. When President Roosevelt responded to the occupation of Indo-China by imposing a total oil embargo and freezing Japanese assets, Britain and the Netherlands followed suit with trade restrictions, so that Japan was able to vindicate its use of violence as a way of breaking free from economic blockade. With the Japanese attack on the US fleet in Pearl Harbor on 7 December 1941, the Second World War in the Pacific began.

Japan now rapidly overran the whole of South-East Asia. In quick succession Indo-China and Thailand were forced to join Japan; Guam, Wake and Hong Kong were occupied and Malaya was attacked. Fortress Singapore fell on 15 February 1942, causing such consternation that some have named this date as the beginning of the end of the British Empire and European colonialism. Shortly afterwards, the Dutch East Indies also had to surrender; the Americans in the Philippines followed, while in the same period the conquest of Burma was completed, British troops there only just managing to escape to India. The expected advances into British India and Australia did not occur, because in August 1942 the American counter-attack in the Pacific had begun. Even so, South-East Asia remained Japanese for two years.

Despite Japan's success in capitalising on anti-western and pan-Asian ideas, and the fact that both rulers and ruled were Asians (even belonging to related groups in the case of Korea and China), Japanese colonial rule did not differ substantially from its European counterpart. It too was foreign domination for the benefit of another nation; it too was founded on development differentials, and it too included an element of racism. There were differences, such as the targeted economic development in Korea, Manchukuo and Taiwan on the one hand and the unrestrained exploitation of South-East Asia on the other, but these arose only from the specific needs of Japan (the latter also from the critical turn taken by the war). Japan's pursuit of economic exploitation revealed its rule to be colonialism of the usual kind. After all, South-East Asia had not been occupied for the sake of its liberation but for the sake of its raw materials. Economic relationships were limited to links with the Japanese Empire. Although Japan needed certain commodities such as oil and cotton, it could by no means absorb the entirety of raw-materials' production and could certainly no longer supply all the necessary manufactured goods, despite the activities of Japanese companies that in some cases, like Mitsui and Mitsubishi, had directly appropriated

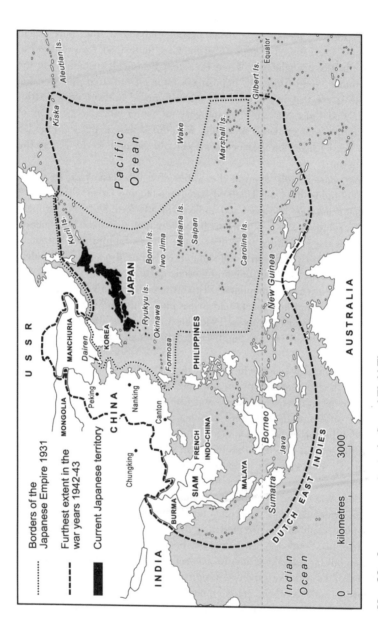

Map 23 Japanese expansion in the Second World War

Borders of the
Japanese Empire 1931

Furthest extent in the
war years 1942-43

Current Japanese territory

previously European firms. Japan paid for all deliveries, but with worthless paper money, thus obtaining the goods at no cost while provoking inflation in South-East Asia. Inter-regional trade largely collapsed as well, and the general impoverishment culminated in famines that are said to have killed millions of people. The brutal Japanese persecution of the ethnic Chinese, who were rather disliked in many areas, may not have concerned other South-East Asians to any great extent, but the recruitment of forced labour certainly did not enhance Japan's popularity.

At first, only the Filipinos took up a clearly anti-Japanese stance. In the Philippines the anti-Japanese guerrilla campaign became a mass movement and was if anything strengthened by the answering Japanese terror. The 'People's Army against the Japanese', or *Hukbalahap*, even undertook land reform within the country. The other South-East Asians appear to have taken a largely neutral or indifferent attitude. Although there were always collaborators to be found in the ranks of the indigenous independence movements, these pursued their own objectives, while in turn the Japanese were rather reserved in their promises of independence, having initially hoped to annex Malaya and Indonesia. Only in 1943/44, their backs to the wall, did they show themselves willing to accede to demands of this kind, and not until the end of the war did it become clear that they had themselves been outwitted. In Indo-China, the Vichy French remained partners, permitted to continue governing the country under Japanese supervision, and were able to establish a rigorously fascist regime. Only with the attempt by French colonists to approach de Gaulle's 'Free France' did the Japanese stage a last-minute intervention, taking over the country and promising independence to the indigenous population. By this point Japan had already lost the war in the Pacific. In 1944 the battle for the Philippines had begun, and on 6 and 9 August 1945 nuclear bombs exploded over Hiroshima and Nagasaki; on 8 August the Soviet Union declared war and invaded Manchuria, and on 2 September the formal surrender was signed. Japanese imperialism was over.

Decolonisation in Asia

The fact that decolonisation in Asia began immediately upon the end of the Second World War cannot, however, be explained by Japan's galvanising role alone. Just as important was the presence of an independence movement in British India, one that had existed in an early form since the turn of the century and grew into a powerful nationalist movement during the interwar period. This is another illustration of the triangle of forces that has always been required for decolonisation to succeed: a strong indigenous nationalist movement, an acquiescent colonial power, and an international configuration conducive to decolonisation. Even a nationalist movement as powerful as India's would not have been in a position to achieve independence on its own if the colonial rulers had been determined to pursue a consistently repressive line and had not been prevented from doing so by the international political environment. It was only changes in the two latter conditions during and after the Second World War that enabled India to achieve its independence in 1947. The picture was similar in all the other countries, including the stragglers Russia and South Africa; Israel may serve as a cross-check.

There is also a dialectical relationship between decolonisation and colonialism, in that colonialism cannot avoid building the basis for decolonisation and thus initiating its own destruction. That basis consisted of, firstly, modern elites which, although in principle were perfectly prepared to cooperate with the colonial power, turned against that power when their claims were frustrated, and secondly the creation of a new political and geographical entity out of which an independent nation could emerge. Colonial rule was what made the Indian subcontinent into a political unit; few could have predicted that in 1947 this unit would disaggregate again into two hostile nations and in 1971 into three: India, Pakistan and Bangladesh.

When the Indian National Congress was founded in 1885, it was a collection of westernised elite notables who saw all-Indian national solidarity primarily in terms of their own access to equal participation in the colonial rulers' power. A different kind of nationalism evolved under the wing of the Hindu religion. Whereas Ram Mohan Roy (1772–1833) had reinterpreted Hinduism into a 'modern' and rational religion, Swami Vivekananda (1863–1902) and others now propagated variants that also drew on western thinking, but were more mystical in orientation. The crucial point became the identification – based on readings of the ambiguous didactic epic *Bhagavad Gita* – of a third path of perfection alongside the path of knowledge and the path of devotion: the path of selfless action. Around 1900 this was used to legitimise Hindu terrorism, but it would later inspire Gandhi's policy of nonviolent action. The prospect of political participation based on majority democracy meant that the Muslim minority perceived the new Hindu activism as a potential threat. Muslims began to align themselves more closely with the colonial power, and in 1906 founded the All-India Muslim League. In ideological terms Hindu religions are extremely tolerant, but that very fact makes it possible for them to assimilate everything, a feature bound to be unacceptable to the Muslim devotees of a single, jealous God. A situation developed where the Hindu nationalist movement, invoking its universalist tolerance, interpreted the Muslims' theologically inspired resistance to integration as wilful separatism, while the Muslims regarded the comprehensiveness of Hindu claims as a particularly insidious attack on their identity. To this extent, the revival of Hinduism paved the way not only for the nationalist movement's burgeoning success, but also for its later split. A further factor was the new British policy of communalism, giving special treatment both to the Muslims and to other specified communities. It is a moot point whether this was a malicious strategy of *divide et impera* or rather an attempt to find fair ways of managing the problems of law and order.

Either way, the Morley-Minto Reforms of 1909 – liberal in intent but diluted into a conservative outcome – remained modest. They involved a minor extension of the powers and composition of the central and provincial legislative councils, where appointed members still made up the majority. During and after the First World War, the British clash with the Ottoman sultan, the caliph, encouraged cooperation between the National Congress and the Muslim League. A shared constitutional plan was developed, with the important participation of Mohammed Ali Jinnah (1867–1948), a member of both Congress and the Muslim League who was not, however, a devout Muslim but a fully westernised lawyer. During the First World War Britain had deployed twelve divisions from the Dominions and sixteen from India; 62,000 Indians were killed, quite apart from India's financial contributions. As well as providing the crucial impetus for the decolonisation of the white settlement colonies, the war therefore also led to a promise of responsible government for India. Such government would ultimately have led to Dominion status, but the Montagu-Chelmsford Reforms of 1919 turned out to be very far from fulfilling such expectations. They gave the central and provincial legislative assemblies a parliamentary character, albeit subject to a strictly limited franchise, but left the viceroy and his governors extensive 'emergency powers', as well as restricting the establishment of parliamentary ministries to the provinces and introducing a diarchy whereby, from the outset, the Indian ministers were allocated only the less important responsibilities while the crucial areas remained in British hands. Indian resentment was further fanned by the continuation of the discriminatory emergency laws during peacetime.

When the reaction set in, it was already under the leadership of Mohandas Karamchand Gandhi (1869–1947), who in this period transformed the Indian nationalist movement from a local dignitaries' club into a mass cause that also embraced the lowlands. This process made him the father of modern India and, indeed, the most important protagonist of the decolonisation process worldwide. Its basis was a profound intellectual engagement with the West that began during his legal studies in London.

Gandhi remained a representative of Indian culture through and through –
that was, after all, the cornerstone of his authority with the masses – but far
from ignoring western culture, he was permeated by its influence to such an
extent that his career would have been unthinkable without it. This background was what enabled him to give his people back their cultural
self-confidence and to lay the groundwork for India to cut itself free from the
metropolis. His methods ultimately impacted back onto the West, and found
admirers and imitators worldwide. As a result of his traumatic experience of
South African racism, Gandhi became a pioneering advocate for the rights of
the Indian minority there in 1893–1915, developing his method of nonviolent struggle and leading it to a successful conclusion, if only temporarily.
His strategy combined the carefully planned but peaceful provocation of the
adversary, which had to be accompanied by an unconditional willingness to
suffer, with an absolute regard for fairness in the conflict, the objective being
to shame one's opponents into changing their position and retreating. This
form of action requires not only great self-control, but also an adversary
susceptible to such methods – as were the British, with their constant
concern for political morality. In tactical terms, however, it suits the situation
of an oppressed minority with clearly delimited objectives better than a
majority with the general, nebulous goal of 'independence'.

After a series of spectacular campaigns, in 1920 Gandhi was able to take
on leadership of the Congress at a critical juncture and began a joint nonviolent campaign for *Swaraj* or self-rule with the Muslims, who at this stage
were still willing to work together with the Hindus. The Congress was
restructured into linguistic provinces (the forerunners of today's Indian
federal states) and provided with a tight, authoritarian leadership. 'Non-
cooperation' – that is, the boycott of the English legal system and educational
institutions, the new constitution and the elections – was intended to bring
the British system of rule, so dependent on the cooperation of Indians, crashing down. A further element was the introduction of the hand spinning wheel
to help free India from its dependence on British cotton textiles. However,
the hoped-for British collapse did not materialise, because whereas a minority would have been possible to unite, the majority by its very nature did not
enter the conflict as a unified whole.

At a time when the Great Depression was looming and promised to hit
India hard by pushing down commodity prices, a new British 'statutory
commission' (without a single Indian member) arrived in India. The Congress
demanded Dominion status by the end of 1929, threatening that otherwise it
would take up the battle for complete independence. Here, the radical influence of Jawaharlal Nehru (1889–1964) was already evident. When the British
promised Dominion status at some unspecified point in the future, the reaction

was a substantially more aggressive campaign of 'civil disobedience', that is, the targeted, nonviolent infraction of British laws. Gandhi once again devised a campaign rich in symbolism and propaganda value: the extraction of sea salt to evade oppressive British salt taxes. Gandhi's negotiations with Britain – in themselves an enormous achievement of the nationalist movement, which as such understandably aroused the ire of Churchill – foundered on Gandhi's refusal to accept the government's policy of communalism. The campaign was successfully crushed and Gandhi withdrew from politics.

The new constitution of 1935 was far removed from the goal of Dominion status. Its provisions included diarchy at the highest level and the integration of the Indian princely states, but neither of these plans came to fruition and for central government the 1919 situation remained in place until 1947. In the provinces, however, a full parliamentary system was now introduced, strengthening the Congress and weakening the League, which now retreated more and more into the idea of a separate nation for Muslims. When, in 1939, the viceroy declared war on Germany without the slightest consultation with Indian politicians and Britain refused to apply to India the democratic principles for which the West was fighting, the Congress politicians resigned. League politicians remained in office and were able to consolidate their position. Under pressure from his powerful ally Roosevelt, Churchill reluctantly dispatched a constitutional policy mission led by the Labour politician Stafford Cripps, a friend of Nehru's, and was greatly relieved when it failed. Congress campaigns were brutally and successfully suppressed, while 2.46 million Indians fought for Britain on various fronts and 180,000 were killed, wounded or taken prisoner.

After the war, it became obvious that the introduction of a parliamentary system was now inevitable, and the new British Labour cabinet therefore decided to accelerate the process in the hope of pressurising India's politicians to come to agreement – the Congress still wanted a strong, all-Indian central government, while the League was working for a separate Pakistan in one or another form. In 1947 partition was finally accepted, and in August the independence of India and Pakistan within the British Commonwealth was proclaimed. Burma (today's Myanmar) and Ceylon (today's Sri Lanka) followed India into independence in 1948; Burma also left the Commonwealth. However, on the Indian subcontinent independence was immediately attended by new problems, as partition drove millions of Hindus and Muslims from their homes and hundreds of thousands of people were slaughtered on both sides. Added to that, the first war between the two countries, over the possession of Kashmir, erupted straight away. Gandhi once more managed to curb the killing and exert a settling influence; the result was that in 1948 he was murdered at his prayers by a Hindu. But if the new

India differed from Gandhi's vision, this was not due to partition alone. Once the princely states had been integrated – a surprisingly trouble-free process, probably indicating how obsolete they were – and a rather authoritarian constitution had been created, the stage was set for a western-oriented modernisation policy of precisely the kind that Gandhi had hoped to avoid. As regards foreign policy, the remaining French possessions were taken over and in 1961 the Portuguese territories were occupied. Although in cases like these the long-standing prime minister Nehru was anything but squeamish in his use of violence, he always took good care to represent Indian politics as morally superior to the imperialist West. Under the rulers of India since then, especially those from Nehru's family, conditions have undergone even further 'normalisation'.

Unlike the European colonial powers, President Roosevelt had always emphasised that the freedom-loving slogans of the Atlantic Charter of 1941 were intended to apply to all peoples, and he put special pressure on Britain to this effect in the case of India. In 1943, the United States drew up a system of trusteeship according to which the planned United Nations Organisation, established in 1944, would decide on the timing of independence for all colonies. However, this resolute line was soon to be replaced by a less credible, erratic course on the part of the newly leading world power, which was trying to find a balance between its programme of decolonisation (including the desire to become a spearhead of the 'younger nations') and its own strategic and economic interests without upsetting its allies, especially once the Cold War began.

In the Philippines, the United States had worked towards autonomy, ruling out the full membership of the Union that was the goal of many Filipinos. However, the indigenous elite was well aware that it needed to remain close to the United States, in view of the latent Japanese threat and the Philippines' dependence on the American sugar market. During the Great Depression, the argument was won by those US interests that wanted to be rid of the islands: the Cuban sugar lobby, the sugar-beet lobby and the trade unions, fearful of cheap labour. In 1933 the US Congress passed legislation for the autonomy of the Philippines and its complete independence within ten years, although the date by which it was to become foreign territory for the purposes of tariffs was pushed back again when the Depression came to an end. After the war American military bases were established and in 1945 the constitution of 1933 was restored, but the left-wing popular movement was mercilessly stamped out. In 1946 the Philippines was granted a further eight years of free trade with the United States and war reparations, in return for agreeing to tie the peso to the dollar and to permit Americans equal rights with Filipinos regarding land use. On this foundation, the

Philippines formally achieved the status of an independent republic as early as 1946.

In his 1944 plans, Roosevelt had already had to exempt strategically important Pacific islands such as Guam and Wake from the manifesto of freedom, and when the United Nations was founded, the US trusteeship idea was severely truncated after lengthy debates. In the end it was no longer all colonies that were to be subject to United Nations trusteeship, but only the mandates of the former League of Nations and the territories liberated from Axis rule. For other areas the stated objective was no longer 'independence' but 'self-government', leaving plenty of scope for the invention of new forms of dependence like the *Union française* ('French Union'). Although the colonial powers retained complete power of control, they had to submit annual reports to the United Nations. Added to this, the Trusteeship Council could receive petitions from its trust territories and appoint commissions of enquiry. A further factor was the anti-colonialist activity of the Security Council and, especially, the UN General Assembly, in which former colonies made up a majority from the start. As for the hostility of the USSR and the socialist bloc to the colonial powers, this was probably counterproductive once the Cold War began – for example, if the United States had refused to support French attempts to recolonialise Vietnam in 1945, in 1949 it was already willing to change its mind. Overall, however, the climate of international relations had now altered in favour of decolonisation.

The Dutch in Indonesia would be the first to feel that change. After the war, their response to the nationalist movement there remained limited to the usual repressive measures. In Indonesia, Islam had taken on an integrating function at an early stage, and in 1912 a Muslim mass organisation was founded. As early as 1920 a communist party also came into being, and in 1926 it risked an attempted revolution. In subsequent years the nationalist idea was nurtured in a range of different groupings, continually suppressed and re-formed, that recruited their members in large part from the frustrated modern elite. Achmed Sukarno (1901–70), a gifted speaker who combined an Islamic and a western education, played an important role in this process, and like the other leaders was repeatedly arrested and exiled. In 1942 the Japanese, in search of allies, fetched him home and had him build up a national mass movement with territorial defence forces. This movement was finally, with some reluctance, promised independence by the Japanese. Sukarno proclaimed the Republic of Indonesia on 17 August 1945 based on the five principles – the *pancasila* – of nationalism, internationalism, representative government, social justice and belief in God. The Dutch troops rapidly succeeded in driving the new republic into a corner, so that in 1946, on the urging of the British and the United Nations, a United States of

Indonesia was created in union with the Netherlands. It was supposed to consist of the Republic with the densely settled Java and the smaller states that had been busily created by the Netherlands on the Dutch-controlled outer islands. After a swing to the right in the Dutch elections, conflicts in 1947 were answered by a Dutch 'police action' against the Republic. Despite early successes, a UN intervention prompted by India and Australia forced the Dutch to cease hostilities and accept mediation by a US-chaired committee. Because the beleaguered republic nevertheless managed to put down a communist rebellion in 1948, the United States, under pressure from its own public opinion, moved from a pro-Netherlands to a pro-Indonesian policy. This was evidently just as good a way of securing US oil and commercial interests. As a result, a second and very successful 'police action' by the Dutch against the Republic starting in late 1948 provoked not only a vigorous reaction from the United Nations and international public opinion, but also an indication by the United States that the Netherlands was putting its Marshall Plan aid in jeopardy. The outcome, in 1949, was the establishment of an independent federal republic, which as early as 1950 had become unitary and in 1956 withdrew from the previously agreed union with the Netherlands after the Dutch refused to hand over West New Guinea (West Irian, today's West Papua). That handover was enforced in 1963 with the help of US pressure. It was not the only case where liberated Indonesia pursued its own national imperialism. In 1963–66 an attempt was made to capture the formerly British North Borneo, and in 1975 the formerly Portuguese East Timor was annexed. What the respective populations thought of this remains dubious to say the least. In East Timor repression and resistance prompted a referendum in 1999 and independence as a separate state in 2002.

In French Indo-China, too, a modern elite emerged, although France abandoned the ideals of assimilation early enough to prevent that elite from gaining access to real social and political influence. Resentment at this fact combined explosively with the immense hardship that followed the collapse of the rubber and rice markets during the Great Depression, and in 1930 both the Vietnam National Party and the communist party attempted uprisings. In the communist rebellion, Ho Chi Minh (1890–1969) already figured importantly. The electoral victory of the left in France in 1936 brought some improvement in the situation and the introduction of the mother country's labour and social legislation, but attempts to establish a National Congress along Indian lines continued to be answered with repression. The nationalist movement Viet Minh, driven underground during the Second World War, fell under the control of the well organised and determined communists, and Vo Nguyen Giap built a successful guerrilla campaign that carved out 'liberated zones' in Tonkin in 1944. But however bitter the feuds between the French of various different political persuasions, they were united on one issue: their intention to recolonialise Indo-China. Even the French communists, unwilling to tread on toes at home, failed to support their Vietnamese comrades. On 2 September 1945, the Viet Minh proclaimed the Democratic Republic of Vietnam, based in the north. It was recognised as a component of the *Fédération indochinoise* within the French Union. However, France put paid to the new republic's hopes of achieving a unified independent Vietnam, not only by subjugating Cochinchina but in the end also by attacking the north and sabotaging negotiations. Giap thereupon, in late 1946, declared war.

Although the French secured the most important locations and connecting lines, this barely impacted on Giap's underground strategy. That strategy, which would prove effective despite some setbacks right up to 1975, took its cue from the Chinese communists in their struggle against the Kuomintang and Japan. It included carefully targeted intimidation of the civilian population, and operated in three phases: 1. guerrilla warfare to cut the enemy off from the population and draw the population onto the 'correct' side by means of terror from both the enemy and Giap's forces; 2. establishment of its own power within a demarcated area and the creation of a regular army; 3. attacks on the enemy's remaining enclaves. The Chinese communists by now having driven the corrupt Kuomintang regime to Taiwan in 1948/49 and taken over power in China, the Viet Minh had, for the time being, a friendly neighbour in the north. On the other hand, the United States, which had previously taken a rather distanced view of French colonialism, now proved willing to act in support of the French, especially after Chinese intervention dangerously escalated the Korean war that erupted in 1950. But the considerable success of the French campaign was broken by a disastrous defeat at the battle for Dien Bien Phu in 1954, due among other things to Giap's use of weaponry captured by the Chinese in Korea, and the Geneva Conference on Indo-China agreed on an independent Vietnam 'provisionally' partitioned at the 17th parallel. However, the South Vietnamese regime, now supported by the United States in place of France, refused to allow nationwide elections, while the North supported the guerrilla campaign being waged by the southern 'liberation front', the Viet Cong. In 1964, finally, the United States moved to attack North Vietnam. This second Vietnam war was, like the first one, impossible to win against the will of a hostile population. It ended in 1975, after the retreat of American politics, with the collapse of South Vietnam and reunification under Hanoi. This victory over American neocolonialism caused as much of a sensation as the victory over French colonialism.

Contemporaneously with the French, the British in Malaya were waging a similarly 'dirty war' against the communist Malayan Races Liberation Army

(MRLA) – and winning it. The methods were the same; the crucial difference was that the MRLA was an almost wholly Chinese movement, lacking any substantial support from the rest of the population. Originally Britain had aided this partisan movement in fighting the Japanese, but after the war, when (unlike in India) it energetically set about re-establishing its rule in pursuit of trade, tin and rubber, it turned to a one-sided reliance on the Malays and their princes. Britain's fear of a communist world conspiracy, along with its adversaries' disgust at anti-Chinese discrimination and the miserable conditions of Chinese mine and plantation workers, culminated in the outbreak of hostilities in 1948. But by 1960 the partisans had been defeated, and it had proved possible to forge a conservative alliance of Malay, Chinese and Indian parties with the pivotal participation of the Malay sultans, one of whom became the head of state for each five-year term. In 1957 the Federation of Malaya became independent within the Commonwealth. When the communist danger appeared to have been banished and global strategy had changed, Singapore was also able to obtain autonomy in 1958/59. In 1963 it was combined with Malaya and the British possessions on North Borneo (except for Brunei, which gained independence separately in 1984) to form the new federal state of Malaysia. In 1965 Singapore left the federation due to conflicts over the role of the Chinese. This time, Britain was not even consulted; its colonial domination was now history.

Today, most of the British, Australian, New Zealand, French and US colonies in and around the Indian and Pacific Oceans have likewise been able to attain independence or at least internal self-government, although in many cases their small size or complex internal circumstances have made decolonisation and independence difficult and conflicted. Mauritius and the Fiji Islands, for example, have a population majority of Indian immigrants as a result of British colonial rule.

In 1955, the representatives of twenty-nine Asian and African nations of western, communist and neutral political alignment met in Bandung, Sumatra, for a conference whose final communiqué attacked continued colonialism as the enemy of progress and a violation of the UN-defined right of nations to self-determination, and called for its speedy eradication. These were only words, but words which had an explosive effect – especially in Africa, where colonialism was anything but a thing of the past.

Decolonisation in Africa

Whereas in Asia the colonial powers more or less rapidly resigned themselves to defeat, in Africa they hoped to assert their position, and even set about building up their African possessions into economic substitutes for the lost Asian ones. The substantial participation of Africans in both world wars had increased African self-confidence, just as the battles between the whites and the humiliating defeats of colonial powers had damaged those powers' prestige – but, at least in sub-Saharan Africa, there were as yet no mass movements for independence, only limited initiatives by the modern elites to gain a foothold in the existing political system. Even pan-Africanism had done little to change that. Soon after the Fifth Pan-African Congress in 1945, western-trained figures like Kwame Nkrumah (1909–72) of Gold Coast and Jomo Kenyatta (1891–1978) of Kenya returned to Africa full of the will to achieve independence, but at first they met with little success. In North Africa, however, the picture was different, among other things because here modern nationalist movements could tap into historical communities, whereas state formation in sub-Saharan Africa generally had to work with colonies that had often arisen by chance, and needed to be completed before a nation could be built.

When the self-appointed leader of 'Free France', Charles de Gaulle, called the governors of the African colonies to a conference in Brazzaville in 1944, he announced the introduction of a more humane colonial policy, but ruled out future self-government in the sense propounded by the United Nations. The new French constitution of 1946 created the French Union structure to encompass Indo-China, yet the African colonies were once again made integrative components of the mother country's republic, although their inhabitants were promoted from the status of *indigènes* to that of *autochtones*. Belgium, Portugal and Spain saw no need for any action at all. Only in Britain did it slowly dawn on some that if Africa's independence was not yet ripe for implementation, this could only be a matter of time.

For now, however, economic development in Africa was on the agenda in what has been described as nothing less than a 'second colonisation'. In the French case, some have considered the period 1945–52 the zenith of its colonialism in Africa. New officials and experts streamed into the colonies. In 1929 Britain had begun to approve funding for the development of the colonies, and in 1940 and 1945 it increased those sums significantly. Certainly, such development was to be pursued strictly in the interests of the mother country, which found itself in dire economic straits at the time. Purchase prices were kept artificially low, and the foreign currency earned through exports to third countries such as the United States was skimmed off, so that the colonies earned Britain valuable dollars. It is thought that between 1945 and 1951, Britain put £40 million of development aid into the colonies, but received £140 million in return. In France, too, a development fund was established in 1946 in order to safeguard the supply of goods to the metropolis. When the Korean War boom of 1952 ended Europe's post-war crisis, the colonies lost some of their attraction and in some cases even became a burden. There is, though, no evidence that decolonisation was planned as a means of offloading them as unprofitable encumbrances. In fact, carefully planned decolonisation was anyway extremely rare. Even Britain did not lead its Asian or its African colonies into independence with deliberate care – the wise guiding hand of British decolonisation was a propaganda myth designed to add the finishing touch to a generally positive historical image of the British Empire and Commonwealth.

Egypt had pushed through its independence as early as 1922, and by 1936 had rid itself of most of the special privileges still held by Britain at that time. British troops only remained on the Suez Canal. But the turmoil of war, economic crises, Islamic revivalism and finally the humiliating defeat by the young Israeli state prepared the ground for the disintegration of the monarchy, which was ousted in 1952 by a military coup. The coup's leader, Gamal Abdel Nasser (1918–70), took over power himself in 1954, establishing a presidential single-party regime and trying to make Egypt the nucleus of an 'Arab nation' through development policies framed by an 'Arab socialism'. However, the United Arab Republic formed by unification treaties with Syria and other countries from 1958 onwards was short-lived. Nasser's greatest foreign-policy success actually arose from his military defeat during the Suez Crisis of 1956. When Egypt refused to join the Baghdad Pact created by the West in 1955, and was duly refused western loans to finance the new Aswan Dam, Nasser turned to the communist bloc and nationalised the Suez Canal Company, 44 per cent of whose shares were owned by the British government. France, Britain and Israel thereupon launched a successful military attack in the old imperialist style – but pressure from the two world powers forced them into an embarrassing retreat, while Nasser rose to became a respected leader of the anti-colonial 'Third World'.

In Sudan, the new administrative cadres of the *effendiyya* class had become the sponsors of the nationalist movement, which was, however, split into pro-British and pro-Egyptian factions and two different strands of Islam. In 1946, in a move not unrelated to its difficulties in Egypt, Britain decided in favour of the right to self-determination within twenty years, and now tried hastily to revise its policy of separation between the Muslim north and the black African, largely Christian, south of the country. The result was a series of bloody conflicts that has continued until the present day. When Egypt abrogated the condominium agreement in 1951 and proclaimed its king the ruler of Sudan, Britain reacted by proclaiming self-government. The new Egypt relinquished its claims and, in cooperation with the British, the leader of the previously pro-Egyptian group led Sudan into independence in 1956.

At the end of the war, Italy's possessions were almost completely in British hands. Haile Selassie could not be prevented from returning to Ethiopia in 1942 to reign for a further thirty-three years, while numerous powers were registering an interest in the strategically important Libya. Italy tried to get its colonies back in the form of United Nations trust territories, a move that was supported by the Soviet Union in view of the promising state of the Italian communist party. When a UN partition plan collapsed, the Senussi leader Sayyid Idris, with British backing, declared independence for Libya. This was accepted by the United Nations for 1951, although Tripolitania was by no means enamoured of the Senussi monarchy and the country, still impoverished before the discovery of oil, was facing substantial social conflicts. However, Italy managed to regain its former Somaliland colony for ten years as a trust territory. In 1960 it proved possible to unite Italian Somaliland with British Somaliland – deliberately politicised by the British – and form the independent Republic of Somalia, one of the few new states of Africa that had an ethnically and linguistically unified population, although that has not prevented it from having largely split apart today. The former British Somaliland on the northern coast has now become a separate entity again. The smaller French Somaliland had been so successfully sealed off from events that it did not have to be granted independence until 1977, as the Republic of Djibouti. The most complicated case was that of Eritrea, where even a UN commission was unable to determine the will of the population, since there were movements both for independence and for federation with Ethiopia. In the end federation was the option chosen, although Eritrea retained an autonomous status. By 1962 the Ethiopian government had managed to transform the territory into a 'normal' province, provoking rebellion by the Eritrean Liberation Front, which in 1993 finally achieved its goal of independence after the collapse of the Ethiopian revolutionary regime in 1991.

In the French Maghreb, the will for emancipation had taken on sharper contours since the interwar period; at the same time, by 1955 the area was home to 1.7 million French settlers with considerable influence in Paris, and Algeria was legally part of France. It became the battleground of the bloodiest and most protracted of all the independence wars apart from Indo-China's.

After the Second World War, Tunisia's Neo Destour party (*destour* meaning constitution) continued to suffer repression by the French, as did the Istiqlal ('independence') party in Morocco. The Tunisian leader, Habib Bourguiba, was locked up; Sultan Muhammad V of Morocco was deposed with the help of conservative Berber leaders and banished to Madagascar. Seeing, however, that this did not halt the spiral of terror and counter-terror, after the end of the Indo-China war in 1954 the French government decided to clarify conditions in North Africa as well. In 1955 Bourguiba was able to return home and by 1959, after deposing the Bey, changed Tunisia into a single-party state with a strong presidential regime. The Sultan of Morocco, too, was called back and in 1956 separated the country from France, replacing his legitimist title of sultan by the populist one of king.

The Moroccan monarchy proceeded to break the power of the parties and trade unions, making skilful use of 'social imperialism' to underpin its authoritarian regime through an expansionist foreign policy. Although Spain had given up its Moroccan possessions except for Ceuta and Melilla in 1956, Morocco now used historical arguments to stake a claim not only to the Spanish Saharan colony Río de Oro (Western Sahara) but also to French Mauritania and parts of the Algerian Sahara. These territories hold rich deposits of phosphate and iron ore. When Spain withdrew from Río de Oro after the death of the dictator Franco in 1975, Morocco divided up the territory with the now independent Mauritania, while the United Nations ordered a referendum. Since 1976 the independence movement Polisario has been fighting for a separate Western Sahara – now only against Morocco, Mauritania having withdrawn in 1979. A ceasefire in 1991 enabled an agreement to implement the referendum, although the result will depend on who is allowed to vote in this sparsely populated area. The plebiscite has still not taken place.

In Algeria there was no bilingual compromise for modernisation as had been the case in Tunisia and Morocco. Instead, modernity continued to mean abandoning one's own culture and becoming French. In the interwar period an opportunity for such integration might still have existed, since at that stage very few alternatives were available. But the French settlers remained unaccommodating: integration would have meant a threat to their own privileged position. Denied access to the French *patrie*, the Algerians began to create one of their own instead. Islamic, bourgeois and – among the Algerian workers in France – proletarian organisations emerged, and in 1943 a popular 'Manifesto of the Algerian People' called for equal rights, self-determination and, at the very least, autonomy. The French response was repression, and a wave of ferocious excesses on both sides during the German surrender in 1945 opened what was probably already an unbridgeable rift between the two parties. Furthermore, a new Statute of Algeria in 1947 introduced limited autonomy for Algeria but allowed Muslims only a minor share in this. Newly formed Algerian parties achieved little, and in 1954 a radical group launched an armed uprising. Thanks to broad-based support among the population, it was successful enough for its *Front de libération nationale* or FLN to assert a political monopoly in 1956 and to establish a Tunis-based government in exile in 1958.

For France, François Mitterrand declared: 'Algeria is France [...]. The only negotiation is war.' But the FLN's war consisted not only in guerrilla campaigns against the hugely enlarged French army presence, but also in selective terrorism against French civilians and those Algerians labelled 'friends of France', as well as generalised terrorism, for example through bombing post offices and cafes. This was intended to sever the population psychologically from the existing rulers, since it predicated a willingness to obey FLN instructions to avoid particular locations. However, the disproportionately resource-intensive French campaigns of repression were also not without success. Large-scale forced resettlement improved control over the country, and France succeeded in crushing the Algerian general strike that had begun on the occasion of the UN debate on Algeria and initially attracted complete compliance from the population. Subsequently, the French used systematic mass torture to gain intelligence on the FLN organisation in the capital and destroy it. The use of torture cannot be laid at the door of army despotism; it took place with the knowledge and endorsement of the politicians in Paris. Furthermore, a section of the Algerian leadership was imprisoned after the French pilot of a Moroccan passenger plane turned them in to the French government. Despite all this, the FLN managed to hold its ground due to support from the population, Arab neighbours and international opinion, with the Swiss connection and the international arms trade playing the usual discreet role. In 1958, the French government's flirtation with Algerian offers of talks led to a coup by the settlers and the army, bringing de Gaulle and his Fifth Republic to power in France. In the interests of a renewed national resplendence, de Gaulle wanted to discard France's ballast and, despite bitter and sometimes violent resistance from the settlers and the army, betrayed his 'kingmakers' to bring about Algerian independence in 1962. Bloody power struggles among the victors and the mass exodus of the settlers resulted, but for the time being it was possible to secure French interests in Saharan oil and natural gas. For the first time, a colony with a strong settler component had been decolonised.

In British East and Central Africa, too, the presence of settlers hampered and delayed decolonisation, but could not ultimately prevent it. In West Africa, the absence of settler interests meant that once decolonisation began to gather momentum it was achieved everywhere within just a few years. At first the British hoped to stabilise their rule by extending consensus through increased political participation for the Africans. However, the newly emerging parties and mass movements quickly proceeded to demand autonomy and independence. In the context of economic crisis in Gold Coast (soon renamed Ghana after an ancient African empire, if not with complete historical accuracy), Nkrumah made his party a collection point for radical nationalism and established himself as a charismatic leader by combining the methods of Gandhi with those of an American electoral campaign. At first this put him behind bars, but as early as 1951 he became prime minister after his party's electoral victory. Nkrumah was able to centralise the country at the expense of the traditional chiefs and, in 1957, to attain complete independence. By 1958 this had already degenerated into a form of one-party – in fact, one-man – rule that turned the once flourishing country into a quagmire of inefficiency and corruption, though on the international stage Nkrumah continued to play the role of the revered pioneer of independence and pan-Africanism.

The British division of Nigeria into the three regions of the North, West and East in 1946 promptly resulted in the emergence of regional parties and, in 1960, independence on the basis of a federalist constitution with three strong regional states and a weak centre. That not only meant an unstable equilibrium between the three parts, but also established the dominance of the Fulani, the Yoruba and the Igbo in their respective regions – areas that were in fact still inhabited by numerous other peoples. In the course of attempts to contain these problems through military regimes and experiments in redivision, one outcome was the secession of the Igbo land of Biafra in the south-east, quashed by the central government in 1967–70. At this stage international oil interests had already begun to figure, and subsequently brought the country what would prove to be an ill-fated economic boom.

It was Sierra Leone's turn to reach independence in 1961, and Gambia's in 1965. Gambia's planned unification with formerly French Senegal foundered on the linguistic splits inherited from colonial rule. Even in Liberia, the term decolonisation can be applied to the process by which the African Americans at last began to cede a share in power to the 'savages' of the hinterland, who managed to seize the presidency in a 1980 coup.

For historical reasons, aspirations to independence in Madagascar had triggered an uprising as early as 1947, although it was violently quelled by the French army. Otherwise, the long overdue changes in French Africa (AOF and AEF) occurred if not without conflict, then at least in a fairly evolutionary manner. The participation of emancipated Africans in arrangements that were normally decided exclusively in Paris was already beginning to play a role, the policy of integration having gradually brought about notable reform legislation. Forced labour was abolished, and the Africans were granted French citizenship with the social and political rights of full French citizens. French party politics now became relevant, although considerable success was also garnered by an inter-territorial African party, the *Rassemblement démocratique africain* led by the Ivorian Félix Houphouët-Boigny. The Africans could vote for the national assembly and many other bodies, but most importantly, each colony now had its own assembly. In order to forestall developments like those in Indo-China and Algeria, in 1956 the colonies were granted universal suffrage and a parliamentary government, only minor rights now being reserved to the governors. In this way, the colonies became potential states, but on the level of AOF and AEF nothing changed: the 'federations' were destined to disappear. This 'Balkanisation' of Africa prevented the emergence of strong federal states with diversified economies. African opinion was divided on the issue. Léopold Sédar Senghor, the most prominent of the Francophone African intellectuals, the herald of *négritude* and member of the Académie française, controlled Senegal via his own mass party, but rejected Balkanisation quite as energetically as did his rival Ahmed Sékou Touré (1922–84), a grandson of Samory Touré who had brought French Guinea under the rule of his party. But faced with the prospect of falling under Senegal's influence and having to finance the deficit of the poorer countries, Houphouët-Boigny preferred his prosperous Ivory Coast to remain separate with good connections to Paris. This was how matters rested.

In 1958, again in Brazzaville, de Gaulle invited the colonies to choose between independence and a *Communauté* of autonomous states under French leadership, the choice to be based on referendums. Only Guinea chose independence, and found itself cast out without support. The others proceeded more cautiously, but finally reached their goal through treaties initiated by Senegal, Sudan and Madagascar. In 1960, thus, all the remaining eleven colonies of AOF and AEF, together with Madagascar and the mandates of Cameroon and Togo, became independent at a stroke. Today some of these countries are among the world's poorest, and others have inherited considerable internal tensions occasionally culminating in armed conflicts, for example in Chad between the Ethiopid Muslims and nomads of the north, backed by Libya, and the western-influenced Negrid farmers of the south, backed by France. Everywhere there have been single-party regimes and military coups, and Central Africa even saw emperor-style rule in the shape of the would-be Napoleon, Jean-Bédel Bokassa.

Belgian Congo (1971–97, Zaire; from 1997 the Democratic Republic of Congo) was not able to resist the pull of events in its neighbouring countries. However, when the rudimentary modern elites of the *évolués* coalesced, with the support of the colonial administration, this occurred primarily along ethnic lines, the only exception being the national party of Patrice Lumumba (1925–61). After a change of government in Belgium in 1958, the hope was to avoid France's mistakes in Algeria by taking the wind out of the sails of nationalism through accommodation and thus creating a willingness to cooperate and safeguard Belgian economic interests. The Africans themselves were astonished when their independence was announced for 1960, with a strong federal republic composed of six provinces. However, in the prosperous region of Katanga Moïse Tshombe (1919–69) entrenched himself and his regional party, backed by business in the area. The elections revealed a tremendous degree of division: Lumumba became prime minister with just under one third of the votes, but the army rebelled after just a few days, feeling cheated of the bonus it had hoped to gain from independence. Katanga seceded, whites fled in panic and Belgian troops intervened. The government called for UN help against the Belgians, and UN troops were immediately dispatched. Lumumba was dismissed by the country's president, escaped, was captured, and was finally killed in Katanga; Zaire began to fall apart. The United Nations established a weak central government and reversed the secession of Katanga, enabling Tshombe to become the federal premier in 1964 and, with the help of white mercenaries, to suppress the remaining 'rebels' sufficiently for the centre to turn its attention back to its own internal power struggles. In 1965, the army chief of staff, General Mobutu, emerged as the victor from these battles. Until his overthrow in 1997, he worked towards integration of the state of Zaire by combining controversial methods and substantial self-enrichment with an ongoing impoverishment of the country. In the end, the outcome of his kleptocracy was actually to fragment the country. In 1961 Ruanda-Urundi became the two new states of Rwanda and Burundi, which have been riven ever since by conflicts between the previously ruling Tutsi and the now emancipated Hutu, culminating in several waves of genocide.

In East Africa, legislative and executive councils for the three colonies of Kenya, Tanganyika and Uganda were composed according to the principle of 'racial partnership' with fixed proportions of Europeans, Indians (who were numerous and economically influential in this region) and Africans, but placing the Africans at a substantial disadvantage. The result was an upswell of support for the independence movement. In Tanganyika, this movement gained an overwhelming electoral victory in 1957 under Julius Nyerere, and in 1961 it was able to achieve independence after London had made the decision to give up Africa. In 1964 the United Republic of Tanzania was formed through unification with Zanzibar, whose monarchy had not long outlived the independence gained in 1963. In Uganda, the kingdom of Buganda tried to assert its privileged position, and the country finally became independent in 1962 with a compromise whereby Buganda retained an autonomous status and its king was head of the shared state, while the leader of the anti-Bugandan coalition movement was prime minister. Conflict was inevitable, and in 1966 led to the elimination of the monarchy with the military's help. The unified state soon fell under a regime of terror and experienced a lengthy period of chaos.

In Kenya, from 1952 onwards the Kikuyu people, who had been most seriously affected by the land policy favouring the numerous white settlers, reacted to their economic and social plight with sabotage and terrorist killings, which is not to say that they were not pursuing internal ethnic agendas at the same time. This nativist 'Mau Mau' uprising was successfully suppressed by 1960, but the moment had now come to make concessions to the Africans. In 1961 they at last received a majority of seats in the legislative council, and in 1963 Kenyatta, imprisoned up to that point as allegedly responsible for the rebellion, was able to lead the country into independence. Those white settlers who did not wish to stay were bought out with the help of British and World Bank loans – though not by African farmers.

In 1923, when the charter of the British South Africa Company expired, the settlers in Rhodesia decided against joining forces with the Boers, whom they regarded with suspicion, and in favour of self-government. Despite the special rights reserved by London, the settlers were able to create legislation that placed Africans at a severe disadvantage, especially in terms of land ownership. As a result, 5 per cent of the population owned 49 per cent of the land. The white Rhodesians had been agitating for union with copper-rich Northern Rhodesia and the labour reservoir Nyasaland (in neither area were there many whites) since 1936, and in 1948 Britain began to give way, not least in the hope of creating a British-controlled counterbalance to the alarming vigour of South Africa. In 1953 the Federation of Rhodesia and Nyasaland was established, and very quickly experienced a considerable economic upturn. Nevertheless, opposition to the federal government grew among the whites, as did the active resistance of the Africans in all three countries, so that the British doubted the federation could remain politically viable. In 1960 the Conservative but pragmatic British premier Harold Macmillan travelled through Africa and spoke of the 'wind of change' that had prompted him to yield to aspirations for independence in East and Central Africa. By virtue of the remaining British rights, Northern Rhodesia (now Zambia), and Nyasaland (now Malawi) received their independence under African leadership in 1963; the federation was dissolved.

The residue, Southern Rhodesia, now aggravated its racist policies in the interests of the settlers, while Britain made independence conditional on the dismantling of discrimination and transition to African majority government. In 1965 the Rhodesians responded with a unilateral declaration of independence in the style of 1776 – colonists rising up against an unjust mother country. In 1970 the Republic was proclaimed. There could be no question of a British intervention, economic sanctions were fruitless, and the African opposition was split into three separate movements, partially on ethnic grounds. However, from 1972 the Shona organisation Zimbabwe

National Union (ZANU) launched a guerrilla war from Mozambique that was ultimately successful and achieved control of large parts of the north-east. With the added factors of an economic crisis and pressure from abroad, including from South Africa, a solution was reached at the 1979 Commonwealth conference in Lusaka, Zambia. In 1980 Zimbabwe was founded under the ZANU leader Robert Mugabe, whose policies have since led the country into misery. However, what was once British Africa was now completely independent. As early as 1970, London had made the institutional changes logically implied by decolonisation: the former Colonial Office (integrated into the Commonwealth Relations Office in 1964) and the Ministry of Overseas Development were dissolved, or rather incorporated into what was now known as the Foreign and Commonwealth Office.

Neocolonialism and Portuguese decolonisation

In his 1965 book *Neo-colonialism. The Last Stage of Imperialism*, the gifted propagandist Kwame Nkrumah attached a newly coined expression to a deliberate echo of Lenin's old definition of imperialism. Certainly, there is no doubt that the actual substance of independence (particularly in Africa) left much to be desired. While the British Commonwealth entered by the new states had an occasionally useful but generally rather noncommittal character and the sterling bloc was beginning to disintegrate, in the Francophone states of Africa the currency for the most part remained tied to the franc and the meetings of the heads of state with the French president still had considerable political significance. France used targeted development aid to hold most of its former colonies on a short leash, and even to keep alive the colonial model of an area of economic complementarity for the metropolis. The proportion of non-repayable financial aid was very high. Educational development was particularly prioritised: thousands of Africans were trained in France and two-thirds of the French development aid workers were teachers, who as before regarded themselves as missionaries of French language and culture. The term 'cultural neo-imperialism' would not be unjustified here. After the founding of the European Economic Community (EEC) in 1958, the former French colonies were 'associated' and received access to preferential tariffs and further development aid. When the Commonwealth states were added with Britain's entry into the EEC, criticism began to be voiced about the existing system's neocolonial character. In its place, the Europeans made agreements with the 'ACP' group of states in Africa, the Caribbean and the Pacific that favoured their exports, although these arrangements ran into difficulty because of competition between the members (for example between African and Latin American banana producers) and, especially, because the EEC was not genuinely prepared to question its notorious agricultural and industrial protectionism.

In many cases the Africans had been relying on a small number of export products since the colonial era, and they now remained dependent on the world market and the large, often multinational or American companies that controlled it. The increasing tendency for US trade, investment and economic aid to target Africa seemed, indeed, to amount to a new form of colonialism – or rather a very old one: the free-trade imperialism of indirect economic control and political hegemony that has no need of costly direct colonial rule and can confine itself to occasional strategic interventions, possibly even with the useful pretext of the United Nations. The dependency theories flourishing at this time originated in Latin America, but were easy to transfer to Africa. After all, it was argued, in Africa just as in Latin America the colonial powers had, in their own interests, transformed undeveloped economies into underdeveloped ones that neocolonialism could keep permanently in that condition by means of their dependency on the world market and foreign investment. To be sure, high commodity prices meant that this indisputable dependency of the former colonies probably worked to their advantage up to around 1975. Neither can responsibility for the subsequent undesirable developments in Africa be borne by changes in the global economy alone; the new African governments' alleged dependence did not prevent them from making bad economic policy decisions such as industrialisation policies that ignored demand patterns, money wasted on vanity projects and the military and state apparatus, artificially overvalued currencies combining with artificially depressed agricultural prices to undermine a neglected agricultural sector, or high foreign debt to cover deficit spending. Choices like these, however, arose not so much from the new politicians' incompetence as from the overblown optimism of the new dawn and boom years and from the need to achieve consensus by satisfying the population's expectations of the new regime.

These developments were further favoured by the rivalry of the two world powers, the United States and the USSR (even at this stage, the People's Republic of China also occasionally made an appearance), for influence in the former colonies of Asia and Africa. US economic aid came as a package with political and military interests, for example when Egypt, Sudan and Somalia began to receive the lion's share of aid as soon as Ethiopia turned to the Soviet Union in the wake of its 1977 revolution. US military aid, too, could be legitimated as a defensive measure against the Soviet advance into Africa, which in the 1970s and 1980s acquired surprisingly large dimensions through military aid, military advisers and even military bases as well as targeted economic assistance, at times with the important participation of Soviet satellites such as Cuba or East Germany.

The eastern bloc's preferred partners were, on the one hand, the South West African people's movement SWAPO, fighting against South Africa, and on the other the former Portuguese colonies that became independent in 1974/75. After the Second World War these territories had become a notable theatre of late colonialism and neocolonialism. Politically, the authoritarian regime in Lisbon had made its colonies into overseas provinces, promoting emigration and, above all, a fast-track development policy to the benefit of Portugal. The cultivation of coffee in Angola and cotton in Mozambique was greatly boosted using official and unofficial forced labour; the mining sector was developed by means of American, South African and West German investment; and the construction of irrigation and energy systems was taken in hand. The overseas territories' trade rose rapidly, and in the 1960s Angola is said to have experienced growth of 17 per cent in its industry alone.

The African resistance movement also took shape only in the late 1950s and early 1960s. Brutal repression by the police provoked a violent response, and uprisings began in Angola in 1961, in Portuguese Guinea in 1963 and in Mozambique in 1964. Unlike before, these movements were able to draw extensively on bases in allied neighbouring countries and help both from other African states and from the communist bloc. In Guinea-Bissau the Portuguese were forced back into their military bases, and in 1973 the nationalist movement declared an independent republic after elections on a single list. The United Nations immediately stepped in to protest against Portugal's illegal occupation of parts of this republic. In Mozambique, the liberation front claimed control of the north of the country, while in Angola rivalry between three liberation organisations with different ethnic bases and different African and international backers allowed the Portuguese a little more room for manoeuvre. However, even in this decolonisation process the decision was ultimately made in the mother country, where the revolution of 1974 called for 'democracy at home – decolonisation in Africa'. In Guinea-Bissau, Portugal could simply recognise the government when the revolution came. In Mozambique, the Cape Verde islands and São Tomé and Príncipe, the transition of power to the new republics in 1975 also went smoothly, even if Mozambique was to face several more years of civil war against a movement backed by white South Africa. In Angola, however, the three movements failed to form a coalition as previously agreed and already began fighting each other in 1975, the Marxist MPLA receiving support from Soviet arms supplies and East German expertise, as well as at least 13,000 Cuban combat troops. Its opponents were initially able to access help from Zaire, the United States and China, but UNITA then began to cooperate mainly with

South Africa, whose troops repeatedly raided Angola because SWAPO was using the country as a base for its struggle against its South African masters. In South Africa and South West Africa, the internal colonialism of the apartheid regime continued to hold its ground as an apparently unshakeable bloc. Unlike the French settlers in Algeria, the white 'Afrikaners', as their name suggested, no longer had a mother country to which they could retreat.

Decolonisation in Russia and South Africa, blocked decolonisation in Israel, non-decolonised territories

The impetus for this final step, with its completely unforeseeable results, this time arose directly from changes in the global political arena: from the internal crisis and dissolution of the Soviet Union and the communist bloc. The general secretary of the Communist Party of the USSR elected in 1985, Mikhail Gorbachev, launched an energetic renewal of domestic and foreign policy. Because the USSR's worldwide political commitments and the costly arms race was siphoning off energies urgently required at home, Gorbachev set about implementing a policy of disengagement and disarmament that in 1987 led to the first, epoch-making disarmament treaty with the United States. The USSR withdrew its troops not only from Afghanistan, fought over for so many years, but also from Eastern Europe, and agreed to Germany's reunification. Internally, a course of reform promising openness and transparency aimed to improve efficiency for industry through greater independence and, for the state, to boost consensus and renew the elites through greater popular participation in politics. However, the consequence was that the Communist Party's monopoly on power was increasingly questioned, and in 1990 finally had to be abandoned in favour of a multi-party democracy. At the same time, the new policies were accompanied almost from the start by an 'explosion of ethnicity' in Russia's multi-ethnic empire, with unrest and secessionist aspirations appearing on all fronts. Gorbachev, now elected president in accordance with a new constitution, was unable to halt the fragmentation of the USSR. A failed coup in 1991 set the seal on the system's collapse. Gorbachev was forced to step down and the USSR split into its fifteen union republics, which laid claim to unrestricted sovereignty. The majority of them, including the five Central Asian republics, recombined to create the loose league known as the Commonwealth of Independent States, but the Baltic states were no longer willing to join such an arrangement, and neither, initially, was Georgia.

To the degree that this process of ethnic and nationalist disaggregation unfolded in the Caucasus and Central Asia, from a historical point of view we must describe it as decolonisation, since these were territories that Russia had once subjugated in a clearly colonialist manner. In this sense, the attainment of unrestricted sovereignty by Armenia, Azerbaijan, Georgia, Kazakhstan, Kyrgyzstan, Tajikistan, Turkmenistan and Uzbekistan is no different from the independence of Vietnam, Algeria or Tanganyika. However, a significant distinction lies in the fact that because, like the colonies in other parts of the world, many of the new states gained independence within their existing frontiers, they have themselves remained multi-ethnic entities within which minorities feel colonised and aspire to decolonisation. This is true most of all for the still enormous 'rump' Russia, the former Russian Soviet Federative Socialist Republic, which even in the past encompassed sixteen autonomous republics, five autonomous territories and ten autonomous districts, some of which are also located in the once colonially ruled Caucasus. In 1991 a separatist Chechen movement won elections in the Chechen-Ingush Autonomous Soviet Socialist Republic and immediately declared independence for Chechnya, to which Russia responded, after some hesitation, with an invasion. It is worth remembering that the Chechens were one of the Caucasian peoples who vigorously resisted nineteenth-century Russian encroachments until the bitter end. The decolonisation of the former Russian empire is thus by no means concluded, although of course there are cases, especially in Siberia, where it may even be doubted whether decolonisation is feasible at all – but then, those doubts applied in Central Asia and South Africa as well.

The consequences of the Soviet disengagement from Africa were felt first in Namibia, as the United Nations named the formerly German South West Africa (now occupied by South Africa) in 1966 when trying to terminate South Africa's mandate. Shortly before the Soviet withdrawal, the liberation organisation SWAPO had taken up arms against South African troops. Because SWAPO recruited mainly from the country's largest population group, the Ovambo, and always insisted on the principle of 'one man, one vote', South Africa was able to mobilise the other ethnic groups' fears of being majoritised and to channel those concerns into the South West African version of its apartheid and 'homeland' policy. The end of the Portuguese colonies in 1974 meant South Africa no longer had a cooperative partner beyond its northern border. Instead, SWAPO, also supported by the communist bloc, was now able (with Cuban cover) to operate from the north, especially as the Ovambo were at home not only in South West Africa but also in southern Angola. Negotiations with South Africa foundered on SWAPO's claim to a national monopoly, while South Africa acted the generous protector of minorities and on this basis twice tried to initiate elections and a form of South West African self-rule tailored to South African interests, discreetly

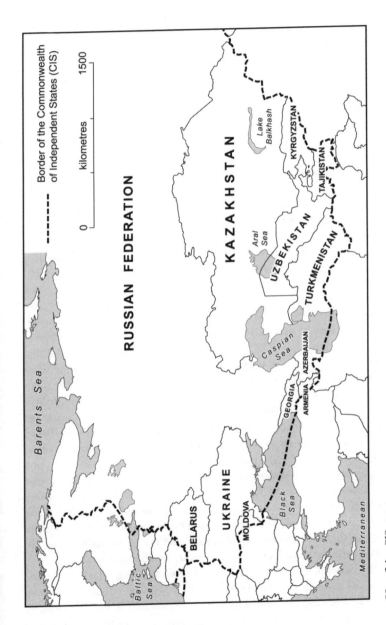

Map 24 CIS states

setting aside the principles of apartheid to some extent. Mediation attempts by the United States and a 'contact group' of other western powers failed; so did initiatives by the United Nations, which had pinned its colours to SWAPO and thus alienated South Africa. It was only the disengagement of the Soviet Union in 1988 that made possible the success of talks between Angola, Cuba and South Africa, paving the way for the Cubans to withdraw from Angola and the South Africans from Namibia and for free elections to be held at last under UN supervision. SWAPO renounced its monopoly status and in 1989 took up the challenge of free elections, which it won by a large margin. Namibia became independent that same year, and led by its SWAPO government it has, despite all its economic and political weaknesses, evolved in a peaceful and orderly way.

However, the causes for the later spread of decolonisation into South Africa itself are not to be sought only in these external developments, which among other things robbed South Africa of the 'communist' enemy on which its repressive system was discursively and emotionally fixated, but also in political changes within the country itself. In the 1970s, massive opposition and alarming unrest was already indicating that apartheid policy in its existing form had led South Africa into a cul-de-sac that could only be escaped through reforms. Under Pieter Willem Botha as prime minister and later president in 1978–89, the Namibia problem was resolved and some amelioration of apartheid was introduced, although the rigorous rejection of majority, 'one man, one vote' democracy remained untouched, as did that epitome of repression, the permanent state of emergency. But during these years an important shift occurred within the ruling National Party. The influence of the white working-class component – the always and everywhere particularly racist white 'little man', the hard-done-by Boer – declined as the party moved more and more towards becoming an interest group of the upper middle class of businesspeople, professionals and high-level civil servants. This group 'converted', like most of the political elites of those years, to a vulgar liberalism for which apartheid seemed to be a straitjacket detrimental to the economy. The move from primary to secondary industry meant that instead of huge numbers of cheap, unskilled labourers, qualified black labour and its mass spending capacity would in future be required. A further factor was the 'Americanisation' of culture and the elites' retreat from the Calvinist orthodoxy that had, at the very least, an affinity with racism.

This was the context within which the new party chairman and president, F. W. de Klerk, could relatively quickly instigate a radical change of course. In 1989 talks were held with the African leader Nelson Mandela, by that time imprisoned for more than twenty years, who was finally released in 1990 and immediately spoke out for a peaceful solution to the racial conflict.

The government ended the state of emergency and 'petty apartheid', the daily harassment of racial segregation in everyday life, while the most important organisation of the Africans, the African National Congress (ANC), of whom Mandela was the vice-president, proclaimed an end to armed struggle against the apartheid regime. In 1991 the government began to contemplate the reincorporation of the homelands into a new South Africa, but declared the return of all previously African land to be unrealistic. The major apartheid laws were repealed (the Land Act, the Group Areas Act, the Population Registration Act, the Internal Security Act), and on 14 September an agreement was signed by de Klerk, Mandela (by then the ANC's president) and more than twenty other organisations, rejecting violence and calling for negotiations held on democratic principles. By the end of the year, the Convention for a Democratic South Africa (CODESA) began talks and, although repeatedly interrupted by conflicts and acts of violence in the country, in late 1993 ratified an interim constitution, a 1992 referendum among the white population having shown 68.7 per cent support for de Klerk's reform course. In April 1994, parliamentary elections were held with the participation of all the country's inhabitants for the first time. The ANC won a majority of 62.65 per cent; the National Party (NP) obtained 20.39 per cent. In the nine newly formed provinces into which the homelands had been absorbed, the results were similar, and only in the Western Cape did the NP manage to reach 53.2 per cent. The bicameral parliament elected Mandela as the country's president and de Klerk as one of the two vice-presidents, in line with the constitution – his party having obtained more than 20 per cent of the vote. The interim constitution, which now came into force for a period of five years, placed the cabinet under an obligation to reach consensus, while the two chambers of parliament took up their shared task as a constitutive assembly. The government's statement focused on the black population's pent-up demand for social and political change. In 1995, the newly created constitutional court abolished capital punishment (the apartheid regime had held the world record for legal death sentences). Since then, however, the new unitary state with its exemplary democratic constitution of 1996 has been threatened not only by the understandable social impatience of the Africans, but also by ethnic divisions – and not only those that the apartheid regime itself produced as part of its principle of divide and rule.

Israel at first seemed immune to the changed climate of global politics. Certainly, the conservative government of the Likud bloc agreed peace with Egypt in 1979, but this was done mainly in order to underpin its aggressive policy vis-à-vis the Palestinians and safeguard the settlers in the occupied territories. In late 1987 the *Intifada* (literally 'shaking off') began, a long-term uprising against the occupation power which was driven not least by

Arab youngsters devoid of prospects. The uprising and Israel's harsh response to it proved to be extraordinarily telegenic, and attracted violent criticism of Israel from the international public sphere. The fact that in 1988 the Palestinian Liberation Organisation (PLO), proclaiming a Palestinian state, simultaneously acknowledged the existence of the State of Israel for the first time was ignored in this coverage, as was the US pressure in that period to halt the promotion of Jewish settlement in the West Bank. By intensifying the threat to Israel and undermining the position of the radical Arabs, the first Gulf War in 1990/91 if anything helped harden the Jewish stance. But the pressure of global politics had grown substantially, because from this point on the United States and the Soviet Union, which now permitted hundreds of thousands of Soviet Jews to emigrate to Israel, were acting in concert. In 1991 Israel agreed to participate in talks with Arab countries under the aegis of the two world powers, although these talks began to stagnate even before the formalities had been settled.

However, the Labour Party's electoral victory in 1992 could be interpreted as a popular vote for a negotiated peace. In 1993, therefore, after secret negotiations with the PLO in Norway, accords were signed on 13 September agreeing mutual recognition, an autonomous status for the Palestinians within Israel with the election of a representative body mandated until 1999, and in any case the continuation of negotiations, even those on the most sensitive problem of all, the status of East Jerusalem. A substantially enlarged 'Greater' Jerusalem, now wholly integrating the eastern half captured in 1967, has been Israel's inviolable capital since 1950, but the Arabs have not abandoned their claims in view of their own sacred sites in the city. Another particularly explosive issue is the existence of 144 Israeli settlements in the occupied territories, whose inhabitants consider themselves betrayed by their government at the least sign of concession to the Palestinians. Nonetheless, in 1995 an agreement was reached and implemented to establish an autonomous Palestinian regime in the Gaza Strip and in Jericho, and the gradual transfer of civil administration in parts of the West Bank began. This was far from indicating that Israel had renounced colonial rule. Nothing had changed with respect to the economic dependence of the Palestinians, afflicted by mass unemployment. Furthermore, their autonomous authority was responsible for only 27 per cent of the West Bank, disconnected islands in the 73 per cent of the area which was still controlled by Israel and on which the building and extension of Jewish settlements proceeded undeterred. The Palestinian Authority suffered from internal political structural problems and was also, given the circumstances, unable to cast itself in the role of an equal partner to Israel. Instead, it remained subject to Israel's informal colonialism; that is, it was left more or less entirely vulnerable to coercive measures and military or secret-service attacks. Acts of violence against Israel that had formerly been defined as political resistance were now reimagined by both parties in a religious framework. On the Palestinian side, an ever more important role in that process was played by the Muslim organisation Hamas, which had originally been backed by Israel as an alternative to the secular PLO. Thanks to extensive support from the United States, Israel's conservative-led coalition governments have been able to delay further negotiations since 1996.

General Sharon's 'visit' to the Temple Mount in 2000, escorted by more than a thousand armed officers, ignited the second Intifada, marked by a greater use of violence than the first. On becoming prime minister, Sharon immediately began to build a border wall for the protection of Israel, pushing far into the West Bank. The replacement of the Palestinian president Arafat, who had died in early 2004, by a more pragmatic successor and Sharon's evacuation of the few Jewish settlements in the Gaza Strip in 2005 seemed to open up a new opportunity for the peace process; Hamas also agreed to a ceasefire. However, the overwhelming electoral victory of Hamas in early 2006 provoked not only fierce reactions from Israel and the West, but also an armed power struggle with Fatah, the military wing of the PLO. In the Gaza Strip that struggle ended in the victory of Hamas, while Fatah just managed to cling to power in the West Bank. The existence of two separate and mutually hostile Palestinian regimes reinforces the position of the Israeli rulers even further, and the decolonisation of Palestine that was hoped for in 1993 has receded even further into the distance: in view of the continuing threat of Palestinian attacks, Israel cannot contemplate respecting the territorial integrity of the Gaza Strip, while in the West Bank such integrity is anyway impossible due to the scattered nature of the Palestinian areas. Added to this is the problem of the annexation and systematic Judaisation of East Jerusalem, which at present seems irreversible. The West is embroiled in this continued colonialism not only diplomatically but also financially, since Israel relies on aid from the United States, the PLO on aid from the European Union.

Israel currently has 7 million inhabitants, 5.4 million of them Jews (77 per cent) and 1.26 million Arabs (18 per cent). The country recently received more than a million immigrants from the former Soviet Union, 750,000 of them in the period from 1989 to 1999 alone. Towns and cities are home to 91 per cent of Israelis; 224,000 of Jewish Israelis live in the settlements of the West Bank among the 2.5 million Arabs there, 30 per cent of whom are refugees from today's Israel or descendants of those refugees. In the much smaller Gaza Strip there are thought to be 1.5 million Palestinians, 60 per cent of them refugees or the descendants of refugees. The Gaza Strip has the population density of a metropolis and the highest birth rate in the world. Economic hardship, especially the extremely high level of unemployment, and the possibility of attributing responsibility for this wholesale to the Israeli rulers, have made the Gaza Strip a political powder keg.

The developments of the 1990s triggered by Gorbachev at first seemed likely to bring decolonisation closer to its conclusion right across the world. However, in Palestine those expectations have not been fulfilled. The other remnants of the former colonial empires still to be found worldwide are probably less troublesome: there are few candidates for decolonisation left, but plenty of problems regarding how to deal with them in view of their small size and minor economic significance. Many have been, or are in the process of being, integrated into the metropolitan centres despite the great distances involved, and their inhabitants appear to be happy with that situation. Only the nickel-rich French territory of New Caledonia is still awaiting a referendum on independence, after an uprising of the Melanesian minority was suppressed and an interim arrangement reached. British Bermuda, in contrast, one of the very oldest of the English colonies, rejected independence in a 1995 referendum and has remained a British overseas territory, along with St Helena, the Falkland Islands, Gibraltar and others. French Guiana, Guadeloupe and Martinique in the Caribbean, as well as Réunion and Mayotte in the Indian Ocean, are overseas départements (simultaneously regions) of the French republic, Mayotte with certain restrictions. It is still unclear what will become of the semi-autonomous *Collectivité d'outre-mer* of French Polynesia, a group of 130 islands with Tahiti at its heart. In the Caribbean, particularly, alongside the independent islands (all attempts to build a federation here having failed) there are also several British, French and US islands and island groups which appear impervious to decolonisation. Of the islands of the Netherlands Antilles, referendums decided that three would become 'normal' Dutch municipalities and the other two would take on an autonomous status as constituent parts of the Kingdom of the Netherlands alongside the 'mother country'. The sectors and islands of Antarctica to which various countries lay claim are almost entirely uninhabited.

Despite all the remaining problems, however, it is possible to speak of a worldwide end to colonialism in practice. This is far from implying that a line has been drawn under its historical significance. In many respects, the process of dealing with colonialism's historical legacy has only just begun.

12   A balance-sheet of colonialism

Since Francisco López de Gómara in 1552, it has been common practice to declare the discovery of America and of the sea route to East India the most important events in human history. Adam Smith repeated the assertion in 1776, as did Karl Marx in 1848, although each of the three thinkers had different notions of the consequences of these events for humanity's destiny: religious, economic or anti-capitalist – but never other than political. And indeed, European expansion can ultimately claim to have forged the many worlds of human beings into the single world in which we live today. Certainly, this kind of perspective is Eurocentric, but Eurocentrism can hardly be avoided in a case where the matter itself is centred on Europe. Such Eurocentrism is defensible in that it involves no value judgement. It does not intend to glorify the cause of European unification by arguing that historically Europe did its job well. Strictly speaking, we cannot know whether Europe did its job well or not.

For both theoretical and empirical reasons, it is impossible to make academically rigorous – that is, verifiable – statements about whether European colonialism was good or bad for the world as a whole or even for just one part of it, even in the unlikely event that everyone agreed completely on what to consider good and what bad. Even for a phenomenon as obviously negative as the Europeans' trade with African slaves, the dispassionate perspective of economic and social history has identified possible positive aspects, such as the relief of Africa from excess population and the better nutrition available in parts of America. To be sure, such detachment appears cynical in that people's condition is determined not only by their being but also, and primarily, by their consciousness. The historian must take account of this and understand, for example, that in some circumstances people prefer to be governed badly by their own kind than well by foreigners.

It is thus not possible to make a precise quantitative calculation of what the Europeans gave and what they took, drawing up accounts which would enable each country to demand reparations from the former colonial powers or the European Union. But if we are content to accept purely qualitative observations, then there is much that can be said – with a degree of plausibility sufficient for historical statements – about what colonialism gave the colonisers and what it gave the colonised, and about its continuing impact today. I will address these points initially for Europe, then for the colonies, along the four dimensions of the environment, the economy, politics, and society and culture. These domains cannot, of course, always be neatly demarcated. Moreover, such general observations clearly cannot apply equally for all European countries or for all colonies. They are nevertheless useful as a means of orientation.

The environment in Europe changed only slightly and slowly as a result of colonialism, through the introduction of American crops, especially potatoes, maize, tomatoes and tobacco, which (with the exception of tobacco) only achieved broad-based acceptance during the eighteenth and nineteenth centuries. Farm animals like the turkey, pests like the Colorado beetle and infections like syphilis and AIDS were and remain relatively insignificant. After all, Europe has been exposed to the diseases of Asia from time immemorial; when the plague disappeared in the eighteenth century, cholera took its place in the nineteenth.

The new crops, especially the potato, would in some places attain enormous economic significance for mass nutrition and thus for population growth. Only in the nineteenth century did emigration come to serve as an economic safety-valve for the exploding population, but most of the approximately 61 million Europeans who found a new home overseas went to an ex-colony, the United States. The critical economic question remains how far the profits of colonialism – initially the precious metals imported from Latin America, then trading profits, and finally the transfer of profits from the colonial economy – contributed to Europe's economic upturn and made industrialisation possible. Overall, we should only assume a limited significance. American precious metals facilitated European world trading and the finance business, but certainly did not form its foundations. The sixteenth century's 'price revolution', too, was already under way before colonialism began. As for the other kinds of colonial profits from trading and investment, these were often handsome, yet it was only in exceptional cases that they directly benefited the state and society of the colonial powers, one such exception being the Netherlands in the nineteenth century. Instead, they mainly fell to individuals and specific companies. All the model calculations suggest that their macro-economic significance was rather marginal, even if at some points (interestingly enough, towards the end of colonialism) they became important for a limited time. It should be borne in mind that the colonial trade possessed an influential lobby from a very early stage and for this reason, along with the fiscal importance of customs duties, has left us disproportionately abundant sources. As a result, the trade's significance for the economy as a whole has sometimes been overestimated. Of genuine importance, however, are 'linkages', especially the stimuli exerted indirectly by the colonial trade on other sectors of the economy. Examples would be its impact on various parts of the transportation system, beginning with shipping, maritime insurance, and so on. Fundamentally, though, the colonial business was never the one pivotal sector of Europe's economy. And the fact that the greatest role was played by the white settlement colonies and ex-colonies like the United States only extends the geographical reach of the basic economic-history observation that the Europeans' best customers have always been other Europeans. In short, colonialism favoured the rise of the European economy and industrialisation in many different ways, but was probably not a necessary, and certainly not a sufficient, condition for it.

Politically, colonialism led to shifts in the distribution of power. Without its colonial empire, England would not have achieved its long-standing primacy as a maritime and global power, while Russia and the United States derived their power from the colonisation of their continents. Earlier colonial powers, in contrast, may have drawn more harm than benefit from their empires. Spain's power really rested on its possessions inside Europe, and revenues from its colonial empire may well only have tempted it into the exaggerated superpower politics that would accelerate its decline in the seventeenth century. On the other hand, colonialism meant that European politics became world politics; the European state system became a world state system. Even from the seventeenth century it would be fair to speak of 'world wars', and international law received new impulses from the debate over Spanish titles in America. Yet, at a deeper level, the political picture still parallels that of the economy: the crucial factors were always the relationships between the European (later, western) powers, while the colonies were seldom – perhaps in the case of British India – more than pawns in that game. And it was a long time before the new players brought forth by colonialism, such as the United States and Japan, were given the attention they deserved.

The same point can be made for the domain of society and culture, where Europe was most convinced of its superiority to all 'heathens' and 'barbarians'. Characteristically, López de Gómara's realisation of the enormous historical significance of the new worlds was not broadly accepted for a very long time. Basic knowledge of the new countries and European perceptions of them long remained surprisingly sketchy. The scholarly study of Asia, America and Africa developed very slowly, and was originally pursued almost exclusively by missionaries, who required this kind of knowledge for their work. An intellectual dialogue with foreign cultures ensued only in exceptional, transient cases like that of China in the seventeenth and eighteenth centuries. In fact, the enthusiasm for China indicates with particular clarity that the Europeans were less interested in the Other than in themselves. Thus, the much-admired Noble Savage is ultimately nothing other than a dressed-up – or rather undressed – European. Here as elsewhere, colonialism's repercussions on Europe turn out to have been more or less marginal; apparently, colonialism was a rather one-sided affair. Yet that very fact had far-reaching psychological consequences for the Europeans and the world. Colonialism brought people of the most diverse origins into contact worldwide and mixed them as never before in history, and one result was the new, or at least intensified, perception and instrumentalisation of racial differences. Whereas in the past conflicts had been explained in religious, social or regional terms, they could now be grounded on distinctions of 'race'. The growth of ethnic consciousness and the emergence of racial criteria are a heavy burden left by colonialism. For Europeans, it has meant on the one hand a reinforcement of their superiority complex, on the other the birth of a guilt complex. Incidentally, these cannot be sharply distinguished and attributed unambiguously to 'the right' and 'the left': one may remember, for example, the sense of a civilising mission felt by the French left or the taken-for-granted assumption that a sense of guilt attests more to a refined political sensibility.

In the colonised world – not surprisingly, in view of the distribution of power – colonialism had far more profound consequences. Often enough, European rule precipitated, intentionally or not, a revolutionary transformation of ecological systems, and the global spread of the western economic system and economic thinking continues to cause further environmental harm even after the end of colonialism, damage that has now begun to ricochet back on the Old World. New plants and animals along with new economic forms radically changed entire countries, as in the case of the savannahs of central North America, which today are one of the world's breadbaskets. Deep ploughing and monocultures have brought serious environmental problems. Above all, the introduction of completely unknown European domestic animals to America, Australia or New Zealand signified an ecological revolution with far-reaching effects on the nutrition and lifestyle of human beings, as can be seen in the transformation of the Plains and Pampas Indians into horse-riding hunter nomads. At the same time, imported infectious diseases had a catastrophic impact on the previously isolated inhabitants of America, Australia and the Pacific Islands, in America ultimately leading to a complete replacement of the human population of particular regions through the forced migration of Africans. Later migrations of 'free' labourers had similar results, as in the case of Indian Mauritius or Chinese Singapore.

In economic terms, colonialism first of all meant the spread of European crops, later American crops mediated by Europe, across the entire world.

Regions that had previously been exploited extensively only by hunters and nomads could now be turned over to intensive agricultural use by sedentary populations. What the potato was for Europe, maize and cassava were for Africa, maize and sweet potato for China, and so on. The outcome was increased food production for humanity. Secondly came the exploitation of mineral resources, from the silver of Spanish America, via the gold, diamonds and mineral ores of Africa, to today's most important primary commodity, oil. The third pillar of the colonial economy was the production of high-value tropical agricultural products such as sugar, coffee or tea by capital-intensive, large-scale businesses. Innovations of this kind were frequently accompanied by the brutal exploitation of non-European labourers; the slave trade was supplanted by a global trade in contract labour that was little better, quite apart from the use of forced labour in Africa. However, a fourth possibility in Asia and Africa was production for the world market by indigenous smallholders: cocoa in Ghana, peanuts in Senegal, copra in New Guinea. In all these cases, integration into a world market controlled by Europe and North America became the crucial factor. Because the colonial rulers generally neglected to develop industry in their colonies, a one-sided dependence of raw-materials producers on the world market arose and has only been reversed temporarily in the strategically important case of oil.

However, dependence and undesirable structural trends should not be interpreted sweepingly as irreversible underdevelopment, in the style of dependency theories. The colonised were anything but the helpless victims of colonialism: they often turned the given circumstances to their own advantage with considerable skill and success. The postcolonial economic triumphs of Korea and Taiwan can be attributed not least to entrepreneurs who had successfully established themselves in economic niches under Japanese colonial rule. Furthermore, the very phenomenon of bad economic-policy decisions in the postcolonial states demonstrates that – despite their structural dependence – they have retained substantial room for manoeuvre, even if while exercising this they have fallen prey to imported misconceptions of development policy and paid for their catch-up industrialisation with an irresponsible neglect of agriculture.

In the domain of politics, the crucial legacy of colonialism is the modern state on the western pattern, with its legislature, executive and judiciary, its military and its education system. It would be wrong to place excessive emphasis on the relative lack of success enjoyed by the state's democratic variant in the postcolonial world – after all, in Europe itself the state remained far from democratic for a very long time. It is more important to note that the postcolonial states were rarely able to pick up on existing pre-colonial communities, and much more often inherited colonial frontiers and forms of rule. As a result, the new ruling elite is confronted not with a mature civil society but with one fragmented by long-term oppression and more or less artificially divided along ethnic lines; the elite still treats society with as much authoritarianism as did the old colonial rulers. Democratic institutions have been adopted in too unquestioning and formalistic a way, and they lack the social infrastructure to create the basis of a functioning opposition and changes of government. It becomes all too tempting to revert to indigenous traditions that are alien to modern statehood. This explains much of what the West denounces as 'corruption'. In other cases, military government may seem to offer the only alternative to rule by the postcolonial state elite. Here, it is worth asking whether the 'Caesarism' of a Bokassa in Central Africa or a Mobutu in Zaire is European or African in origin, or is a synthesis of the two. Or to what extent the various African and Arab 'socialisms' are African and Arab, how far they correspond with what is called 'socialism' in Europe, and whether the synthesis is a successful one. Indeed, how should a successful synthesis be defined?

This brings us to what is, in my view, the most important legacy of colonialism, the sociocultural one. Everywhere colonialism gave rise to new societal groups on a western model – workers and managers, teachers and lawyers, civil servants and professional soldiers – and, as their shared environment, the modern city with a western-style transport and communication system. Added to that are new roles for women, often associated with emancipation from existing conditions. Western lifestyles in terms of clothing, food and entertainment are now widely taken for granted. The demonstration of authenticity by wearing traditional robes often conceals assimilation in the form of western underwear. Bread has replaced porridge, and knives and forks instead of fingers are used for eating. McDonald's is omnipresent, television is the standard form of entertainment and football is the national sport. All this rests on western science, technology, medicine and economics, and on ideas and ideologies such as rationalism and individualism, the rule of law and human rights, Christianity and socialism – ideas that are more or less western in origin, but have now become the common, and indispensable, property of humanity. For in the long term, colonialism did not only bring repression, but also liberation from what Ali A. Mazrui has called the shackles of tradition.

The 'postcolonialists' assert that such liberation in reality amounted only to a renewed psychological subjugation by the West, because it took place through the medium of the West's institutions and languages. Political decolonisation may be completed to a certain degree and economic decolonisation is well under way, at least in some countries, but in the postcolonialists' view cultural decolonisation has hardly begun, the West still holding the unchallenged mastery of discourse. This circumstance is, they argue, a result of the western-based education system, the most lasting legacy of colonialism, which was taken over wholesale by the new states after alternative models failed. Even parents critical of the West send their children to western-oriented schools to avoid depriving them of opportunities. As a result, the postcolonial elites still look at the world from the perspective of the former colonial rulers, something legitimated by western culture's claim to universality. The modern nation state of European origin and the western-oriented educational system reinforce each other, and still mould the discursive practices of the postcolonial world.

While western historians can continue to write their own history without taking the least account of the rest of the world, historians from former colonies have no choice but to keep writing European history, because even while studying the history of their own countries they remain reliant on the European-style modern nation state as their 'master narrative'. Tellingly, it is above all literary scholars of the postmodern confession, mainly of Indian origin, who are working on the decolonisation of thought. Using the philosophical toolbox of Michel Foucault and Jacques Derrida, they continue to rely not only on western thinking, but also on the western – especially US – universities where they have found positions: a dilemma of which they are perfectly well aware and which underpins their special emphasis on the creativity of the border-crossing existence and cultural hybridity.

We have this school of thought to thank for valuable initiatives towards a critical investigation of colonialism's legacy. Nevertheless, its underlying assumptions are untenable and, indeed, are even refuted by its own findings. After colonialism, it is no longer possible to speak of binary oppositions between unambiguously western institutions and languages on the one hand and a series of distinct, genuinely autochthonous cultural inheritances on the other, but only of a multiplicity of mixed forms, 'hybrids', the importance of which the postcolonialists are the first to underline. This is because everywhere in the colonies, 'appropriation' has been at work. It therefore makes no sense to defend a non-western culture by demonstrating historically that particular achievements, for example human rights, already existed in a certain place before the Europeans arrived, although this line of argument is a popular technique of intercultural assimilation. After the end of colonialism, the 'others' have well and truly appropriated all these things, so that while it is correct to speak of the 'Europeanisation of the world' as the epitome of the colonial legacy, this must be understood only in a historical sense. The concept of the world's 'Europeanisation' can now only be used in the same way as the 'Romanisation' of France, which does not imply that today's France has anything 'Roman' about it except for ruins. And if today

the English language is increasingly becoming the medium of global communication, the monopoly of the 'Queen's English' has long since been broken
by an American or Australian, an Indian or Nigerian English joining it on
equal terms. The rule of English now has only a historical relationship with
the one-time rule of England; on the contrary, decolonisation has led to the
English being expropriated of their language. The fact that one of the new
proprietors has now become a global empire of a new kind is not unrelated to
historical colonialism, but it is most certainly another story.

Bibliography

This bibliography is designed to facilitate further research, and is therefore restricted mainly to publications in English and secondarily in German, to general standard works and overviews that contain references to further sources, and to studies outstanding in terms of their content and methodology. If no references are given for a particular sub-chapter, the general publications should be consulted.

General publications
D. H. Abernethy, *The Dynamics of Global Dominance. European Overseas Empires, 1415–1980* (New Haven 2000).
R. von Albertini and A. Wirz (eds), *European Colonial Rule 1880–1940: The impact of the West on India, Southeast Asia and Africa* (Westport 1982).
L'aventure coloniale de la France, 4 vols in 5 parts (Paris 1987–90). From 1789.
P. Bakewell, *A History of Latin America, c. 1450–1930* (Oxford 1997).
D. G. Boyce, *Decolonization and the British Empire, 1775–1997* (Basingstoke 1999).
D. A. Brading, *The First America. The Spanish Monarchy, Creole Patriots and the Liberal State, 1492–1867* (Cambridge 1991).
P. J. Cain and A. G. Hopkins, *British Imperialism*, 2 vols (London 1993).
The Cambridge Economic History of the United States, 3 vols (Cambridge 1996–2000). Vol. 1, the colonial era.
The Cambridge History of Africa, 8 vols (Cambridge 1975–86). Vols 4–8, 1600–1975.
The Cambridge History of the British Empire, 8 vols in 9 parts (Cambridge 1929–59). Vols 1–3, general; vols 4 and 5, India before and after 1858; vol. 6, Canada; vol. 7:1–2, Australia and New Zealand; vol. 8, South Africa. Dated, but still informative and rich in material.
The Cambridge History of China, 15 vols (Cambridge 1978 ff.)
The Cambridge History of Iran, vols 6–7 (Cambridge 1986–91). 1335–1750 and 1722–1979.
The Cambridge History of Japan, 6 vols (Cambridge 1988 ff.). Vol. 4, early modern Japan; vol. 5, nineteenth century; vol. 6, twentieth century.
The Cambridge History of Latin America, 9 vols (Cambridge 1984 ff.). Vols 1–2 on the colonial period.
The Cambridge History of the Native Peoples of America, 3 vols in 6 parts (Cambridge 1997–2000).
The Cambridge History of Southeast Asia, 2 vols (Cambridge 1992). Before and after 1800.
W. L. Cleveland, *A History of the Modern Middle East*, 3rd ed. (Westport 2004).
L. E. Davis and R. A. Huttenback, *Mammon and the Pursuit of Empire. The Economics of Imperialism 1869–1912* (New York 1988).

B. W. Diffie and G. D. Winius, *Foundations of the Portuguese Empire, 1415–1580* (Minneapolis 1977).

A. T. Embree (ed.), *Encyclopedia of Asian History*, 4 vols (London 1988).

N. Etherington (ed.), *Missions and Empire* (Oxford 2005).

F. Fernández-Armesto, *Pathfinders. A Global History of Exploration* (Oxford 2006).

M. Fröhlich, *Imperialismus. Deutsche Kolonial- und Weltpolitik 1880–1914* (Munich 1994).

General History of Africa, 8 vols (Oxford/Paris 1990–99). The UNESCO history.

H. Gründer, *Welteroberung und Christentum. Ein Handbuch zur Geschichte der Neuzeit* (Gütersloh 1992).

H. Gründer, *Geschichte der deutschen Kolonien*, 5th ed. (Paderborn 2004).

Hakluyt Society. Three series containing several hundred volumes of sources on the history of expansion from the Middle Ages to the nineteenth century in English translation; quality varies.

Handbuch der Geschichte Lateinamerikas, 3 vols (Stuttgart 1992–96). Vol. 1 also deals with the Atlantic discoveries and spans the period up to 1760; vol. 2, 1760–1900.

L. Harding, *Geschichte Afrikas im 19. und 20. Jahrhundert*, 2nd ed. (Munich 2006).

M. Havinden and D. Meredith, *Colonialism and Development. Britain and its Tropical Colonies, 1850–1960* (London 1993).

D. Henze, *Enzyklopädie der Entdecker und Erforscher der Erde*, 5 vols (Graz 1978–2004).

Histoire de la colonisation française, 2 vols (Paris 1991). Before and after 1815.

Histoire de la France coloniale, 2 vols (Paris 1990–91). Before and after 1914.

J. Iliffe, *Africans. The History of a Continent*, 2nd ed. (Cambridge 2007).

K. F. Kiple (ed.), *The Cambridge World History of Human Diseases* (Cambridge 1993).

T. Klein and F. Schuhmacher (eds), *Kolonialkriege. Militärische Gewalt im Zeichen des Imperialismus* (Hamburg 2006).

K. Koschorke, F. Ludwig and M. Delgado (eds), *A History of Christianity in Asia, Africa, and Latin America, 1450–1990: A Documentary Sourcebook* (Grand Rapids 2007). Textual sources with often excellent commentaries and references.

T. O. Lloyd, *The British Empire 1558–1983* (Oxford 1984).

F. Madden and D. Fieldhouse (eds), *Selected Documents on the Constitutional History of the British Empire and Commonwealth*, vol. 1 ff. (London 1985 ff.).

M. Mann, *Geschichte Indiens. Vom 18. bis zum 20. Jahrhundert* (Paderborn 2005). Events, economy, society, technology; little on culture.

P. J. Marshall, *The Making and Unmaking of Empires: Britain, India, and America c. 1750-1783* (Oxford 2005).

C. Marx, *Geschichte Afrikas. Von 1800 bis zur Gegenwart* (Paderborn 2004).

The New Cambridge History of India, vol. 1:1 ff. (Cambridge 1988 ff.). Four series of thematic volumes; see individual titles.

J. S. Olson (ed.), *Historical Dictionary of European Imperialism* (New York/Westport 1991).

The Oxford History of the British Empire, 5 vols (Oxford 1998–99). Vol. 1, beginnings; vol. 2, eighteenth century; vol. 3, nineteenth century; vol. 4, twentieth century; vol. 5, historiography.

Periplus. Jahrbuch für außereuropäische Geschichte 1 (1991).

W. Reinhard, *Geschichte der europäischen Expansion*, 4 vols (Stuttgart 1983–90). Overview organised by geographical region 1415–1989, with abundant sources and references.

S. H. Roberts, *The History of French Colonial Policy, 1870–1925*, 2nd ed. (London 1963).

A. J. R. Russell-Wood (ed.), *An Expanding World. The European Impact on World History, 1450-1800* (Aldershot 1995 ff.). 31-vol. series of essay collections on individual themes.

E. Schmitt (ed.), *Dokumente zur Geschichte der europäischen Expansion*, 5 vols (Munich/Wiesbaden 1984–2003). Annotated German translations, Middle Ages to c.1800.

J. E. Schwartzberg (ed.), *A Historical Atlas of South Asia*, 2nd ed. (New York/Oxford 1993).

B. Sundkler and C. Steed, *A History of the Church in Africa* (Cambridge 2000).

J. D. Tracy (ed.), *The Rise of Merchant Empires. Long Distance Trade in the Early Modern World, 1350–1750* (Cambridge 1990).

J. D. Tracy (ed.), *The Political Economy of Merchant Empires, 1450–1750* (Cambridge 1991).

U. Van der Heyden and H. Stoecker (eds), *Mission und Macht im Wandel politischer Orientierungen. Europäische Missionsgesellschaften in politischen Spannungsfeldern in Afrika und Asien zwischen 1800 und 1945* (Stuttgart 2005).

R. Zöllner, *Geschichte Japans. Von 1800 bis zur Gegenwart* (Paderborn 2006). Pleasingly idiosyncratic.

1. Colonies and colonialism

D. Fieldhouse, *Colonialism 1870–1945. An Introduction* (London 1981).

H. Fischer-Tiné (ed.), *Handeln und Verhandeln. Kolonialismus, transkulturelle Prozesse und Handlungskompetenz* (Münster 2002).

M. Hechter, *Internal Colonialism. The Celtic Fringe in British National Development, 1536–1966* (London 1975). Controversial, but stimulating.

Kolonisierung als weltgeschichtliches Phänomen (Stuttgart 1990). Privately printed by the Breuninger Kolleg.

H.-H. Nolte (ed.), *Internal Peripheries in European History* (Göttingen 1991). Colonialism-related cases among dependent countries in Europe.

J. Osterhammel, *Kolonialismus: Geschichte, Formen, Folgen*, 5th ed. (Munich 2006). An excellent taxonomy.

D. Rothermund (ed.), *Aneignung und Selbstbehauptung. Antworten auf die europäische Expansion* (Munich 1999).

J. Vogt, 'Kolonie, Kolonisation, Dekolonisation: Umriß einer Fragestellung', *Saeculum* 30 (1979), 240–50. An ancient historian discusses the history of the concept.

2. The European Atlantic

H. Afflerbach, *Das entfesselte Meer. Die Geschichte des Atlantik* (Munich 2001).

U. Bitterli, *Die Entdeckung Amerikas von Kolumbus bis Alexander von Humboldt* (Munich 1991).

F. Fernández-Armesto, *Before Columbus. Exploration and Colonization from the Mediterranean to the Atlantic, 1229–1492* (Basingstoke/London 1987).

D. Henige, *In Search of Columbus. The Sources for the First Voyage* (Tucson 1991).

K. Herbers, 'Die Eroberung der Kanarischen Inseln, ein Modell für die spätere Expansion Portugals und Spaniens nach Afrika und Amerika?' in H. Duchhardt (ed.), *Afrika. Entdeckung und Erforschung eines Kontinents* (Cologne 1989), 51–95.

H. Pietschmann (ed.), *Atlantic History. History of the Atlantic System, 1580-1830* (Göttingen 2002).

P. E. Taviani, *Columbus, the Great Adventure. His Life, his Times, and his Voyages* (New York 1991). The Italian standard 1989 biography in English translation.

3. Europeans and Asians

R. J. Barendse, *The Arabian Sea. The Indian Ocean World of the Seventeenth Century* (New York/London 2002).

J. R. Bruijn (ed.), *Ships, Sailors and Spices. East India Companies and their Shipping in the 16th, 17th and 18th Centuries* (Amsterdam 1993).

K. N. Chaudhuri, *Trade and Civilization in the Indian Ocean. An Economic History from the Rise of Islam to 1750* (Cambridge 1985).

S. Diller, *Die Dänen in Indien, Südostasien und China (1620–1845)* (Wiesbaden 1999).

M. Dunn, *Kampf um Malakka. Eine wirtschaftshistorische Studie über den portugiesischen und niederländischen Kolonialismus in Südostasien* (Wiesbaden 1984).

H. Furber, *Rival Empires of Trade in the Orient, 1600–1800* (Minneapolis 1976). Sequel to Diffie and Winius.

M. Krieger, 'Konkurrenz und Kooperation in Ostasien. Der europäische Country-Trade auf dem Indischen Ozean zwischen dem 16. und dem 18. Jahrhundert', *Vierteljahrschrift für Sozial- und Wirtschaftsgeschichte* 84 (1997), 322–55.

M. N. Pearson and A. Dasgupta (eds), *India and the Indian Ocean 1500–1800* (New Delhi 1987).

Portuguese 'Crown capitalism'

J. C. Boyajian, *Portuguese Trade in Asia under the Habsburgs, 1580–1640* (Baltimore/London 1993).

J. Correia-Afonso (ed.), *Indo-Portuguese History. Sources and Problems* (Bombay 1981).

V. Magalhães Godinho, *Os descobrimentos e a economia mundial*, 4 vols, 2nd ed. (Lisbon 1984–86). The Portuguese standard work of economic history; abridged French edition: *L'Économie de l'empire Portugais aux 15. et 16. Siècles* (Paris 1969).

M. Newitt, *A History of Portuguese Overseas Expansion, 1440–1668* (London 2005).

M. N. Pearson, *The Portuguese in India* (Cambridge 1988). Vol. I:1 of *The New Cambridge History of India*.

S. Subrahmanyam, *The Portuguese Empire in Asia, 1500–1700* (London 1993).

S. Subrahmanyam, *The Career and Legend of Vasco da Gama* (Cambridge 1997). Essential.

Dutch mercantile capitalism

F. S. Gaastra, *The Dutch East India Company. Expansion and Decline* (Zutphen 2003).

G. D. Winius and M. P. Vink, *The Merchant-Warrior Pacified* (New Delhi 1991).

English mercantile capitalism, its European competitors and the Asian commodity cycles

C. A. Bayly, *Indian Society and the Making of the British Empire* (Cambridge 1988). Vol. II:1 of *The New Cambridge History of India*.

K. N. Chaudhuri, *The English East India Company, 1600–1640* (London 1965).

K. N. Chaudhuri, *The Trading World of Asia and the English East India Company, 1660–1760* (Cambridge 1978). A comprehensive quantitative study.

P. Haudrère, *La Compagnie Française des Indes au XVIIIe siècle (1719–1795)*, 4 vols (Paris 1989).

P. Lawson, *The East India Company. A History* (London 1993).

J. F. Richards, *The Mughal Empire* (Cambridge 1992). Vol. I:5 of *The New Cambridge History of India*.

European mission, mutual perceptions of Europeans and Asians, new discoveries

C. R. Boxer, *The Christian Century in Japan, 1549–1650* (1951; reprint Berkeley 1974). A classic.

G. Elison, *Deus Destroyed. The Image of Christianity in Early Modern Japan* (Cambridge, MA 1973). Critique of Christianity.

I. Kern, *Buddhistische Kritik am Christentum im China des 17. Jahrhunderts* (Frankfurt 1992).

D. F. Lach and E. J. Van Kley, *Asia in the Making of Europe*, 3 vols in 10 parts (Chicago 1965–99). Monumental history of European perceptions of Asia, up to the eighteenth century.

W. Li, *Die christliche Chinamission im 17. Jahrhundert* (Stuttgart 2000).

D. Mungello, *The Great Encounter of China and the West, 1500–1800* (Lanham 1999).

C. Totman, *Early Modern Japan* (Berkeley 1993).

4. The Iberian Atlantic

L. N. McAlister, *Spain and Portugal in the New World, 1492–1700* (Minneapolis 1984).

M. Morineau, *Incroyables gazettes et fabuleux métaux* (Paris/Cambridge 1978).

Spanish conquest and rule/Economy and society of Spanish America

J. Denzer, *Die Konquista der Welser-Gesellschaft in Südamerika (1528–56)* (Munich 2005). Corrects previous views.

B. Hausberger, *Für Gott und König. Die Mission der Jesuiten im kolonialen Mexiko* (Vienna/Munich 2000). Detailed and critical; missionary work as subjugation.

R. Himmerich y Valencia, *The Encomenderos of New Spain, 1521–1555* (Austin 1991). Prosopographical study.

G. D. Jones, *Maya Resistance to Spanish Rule. Time and History on a Colonial Frontier* (Albuquerque 1989).

B. de Las Casas, *Werkauswahl*, ed. M. Delgado, 3 vols in 4 parts (Paderborn 1994–97). German translation from Spanish.

P. Mai and W. Reinhard (eds), *Die alltägliche Conquista. Zwölf Briefe des Pedro de Valdivia von der Eroberung Chiles 1545–1552* (Frankfurt 1995). German translation with a commentary.

J. L. Martinez, *Hernán Cortés* (Mexico 1993).

J. H. Parry and R. G. Keith (eds), *New Iberian World*, 5 vols (New York 1984). Collection of sources translated into English.

K.-P. Starke, *Der spanisch-amerikanische Kolonialhandel. Die Entwicklung der neueren Historiographie und künftige Forschungsperspektiven* (Münster 1995).

E. Tandeter, *Coercion and Market. Silver Mining in Colonial Potosí, 1692–1826* (Albuquerque 1993). Also covers free labourers.

H. Thomas, *Conquest: Montezuma, Cortés, and the Fall of Old Mexico* (New York 1993). A comprehensive study.

C. Wurm, *Doña Marina, la Malinche. Eine historische Figur und ihre literarische Rezeption* (Frankfurt 1996).

Brazil and its gold cycle

T. Pinheiro, *Aneignung und Erstarrung. Die Konstruktion Brasiliens und seiner Bewohner in portugiesischen Augenzeugenberichten 1500–95* (Stuttgart 2004). Argues that both 'Noble Savage' and cannibals are European modes of appropriation.

5. Plantation America and the African Atlantic

Portuguese and Dutch Brazil in the sugar cycle

G. Böhm, *Los sefardíes en los dominios holandeses de America del Sur y del Caribe, 1630–1750* (Frankfurt 1992). Detailed study of Jews in the Dutch colonies.

H. Den Heijer, *De geschiedenis van de WIC* (Zutphen 1994). The most recent overview.

J. I. Israel, *The Dutch Republic and the Hispanic World, 1606–1661* (Oxford 1982).

J. I. Israel, *Dutch Primacy in World Trade 1585–1740* (Oxford 1989).

Sugar and new powers in the Caribbean

C. C. Goslinga, *The Dutch in the Caribbean*, 3 vols (Assen 1971–90).

R. B. Sheridan, *Sugar and Slaves. An Economic History of the British West Indies, 1623–1775* (Bridgetown 1974).

R. L. Stein, *The French Sugar Business in the Eighteenth Century* (Baton Rouge/London 1988).

The African Atlantic

R. Anstey, *The Atlantic Slave Trade and British Abolition, 1760–1810* (London 1975).

P. Curtin, *The Atlantic Slave Trade: A Census* (Madison 1969). The foundational quantitative study for more recent discussions of the slave trade.

C. Degn, *Die Schimmelmanns im atlantischen Dreieckshandel* (Neumünster 1984). A German-Danish trading (and slave-trading) company.

D. Eltis, D. Richardson, S. D. Berendt and H. Klein (eds), *The Atlantic Slave Trade. A Database on CD-ROM* (Cambridge 1999).

J. K. Inikori and S. Engerman (eds), *The Atlantic Slave Trade. Effects on Economies, Societies, and Peoples in Africa, the Americas and Europe* (Durham/London 1992).

J. K. Inikori, *Africans and the Industrial Revolution in England. A Study in International Trade and Economic Development* (Cambridge 2002). The key role of slaves in the creation of economic value.

H. Klein, *The Atlantic Slave Trade* (Cambridge 1999). An authoritative survey.

P. E. Lovejoy, 'The volume of the Atlantic slave trade. A synthesis', *Journal of African History* 23/24 (1982), 473–501.

P. Manning, 'The demography of African slavery: A global model', *Social Science History* 14 (1990), 225–79.

D. Northrup, *Africa's Discovery of Europe, 1450–1850* (Oxford 2002).

A. Reuter, *Voodoo und andere afroamerikanische Religionen* (Munich 2003).

B. Solow and S. Engerman (eds), *British Capitalism and Caribbean Slavery. The Legacy of Eric Williams* (Cambridge 1987).

J. Thornton, *Africa and Africans in the Making of the Atlantic World, 1400–1680* (Cambridge 1992).

E. Williams, *Capitalism and Slavery* (Chapel Hill 1944). The book offering the provocative hypotheses on the connection between slavery and English industrialisation.

A. Wirz, *Sklaverei und kapitalistisches Weltsystem* (Frankfurt 1984).

6. New Europes on the North Atlantic and the first decolonisation

M. Egnal, *New World Economies. The Growth of the Thirteen Colonies and Early Canada* (Oxford 1998).

H. Wellenreuther, *Niedergang und Aufstieg. Geschichte Nordamerikas vom Beginn der Besiedlung bis zum Ausgang des 17. Jahrhunderts* (Münster 2000).

H. Wellenreuther, *Ausbildung und Neubildung. Die Geschichte Nordamerikas vom Ausgang des 17. Jahrhunderts bis zum Ausbruch der Amerikanischen Revolution* (Münster 2001).

New France in Canada and New Netherland on the Hudson

K. Anderson, *Chain Her by One Foot. The Subjugation of Native Women in Seventeenth-Century New France* (London 1991).

O. A. Rink, *Holland on the Hudson. An Economic and Social History of Dutch New York* (Ithaca 1986).

U. Sautter, *Geschichte Kanadas*, 2nd ed. (Munich 1992).

B. G. Trigger, *Natives and Newcomers, Canada's 'Heroic Age' Reconsidered* (Kingston 1985).

G. Vidale and C. Vidale, *Histoire de l'Amerique Française*, 2nd ed. (Paris 2006).

New England and the building of British North America

D. Armitage and M. Braddick (eds), *The British Atlantic World, 1500–1800* (Houndmills 2002).

J. Grenier, *The First Way of War. American War Making on the Frontier, 1607–1814* (Cambridge 2005).

M. Jensen (ed.), *American Colonial Documents to 1776* (London 1955) (*English Historical Documents* 9).

R. Middleton, *Colonial America. A History, 1607–1760* (Oxford 1992).

W. Nester, *The Great Frontier War. Britain, France, and the Imperial Struggle for North America, 1607–1755* (Westport 2000).

W. Nester, *The First Global War. Britain, France, and the Fate of North America, 1756–1775* (Westport 2000).

D. B. Quinn (ed.), *New American World. A Documentary History of North America to 1612*, 5 vols (London 1979).

The economy and society of British North America
V. D. Anderson, *New England's Generation. The Great Migration and the Formation of Society and Culture in the Seventeenth Century* (Cambridge 1991).
B. Bailyn, *Voyagers to the West. Emigration from Britain to America on the Eve of the Revolution* (London 1987).
E. R. Ekirch, *Bound for America. The Transportation of British Convicts to the Colonies, 1718–75* (Oxford 1987).
J. McCusker and R. R. Menard, *The Economy of British America, 1607–1789* (Chapel Hill/London 1991).
R. Nichols, *Indians in the United States and Canada. A Comparative History* (Lincoln 1998).

The first decolonisation
N. Canny and A. Pagden (eds), *Colonial Identity in the Atlantic World, 1500–1800* (Princeton 1987).
L. J. Cappon, B. B. Petchenik and J. H. Long, *Atlas of Early American History. The Revolutionary Era 1760–1790* (Princeton 1976).
H. Dippel, *Die amerikanische Revolution* (Frankfurt 1985). Brief but informative.
L. Dubois, *Avengers of the New World. The Story of the Haitian Revolution* (Cambridge, MA 2004).
J. P. Greene and J. R. Pole (eds), *A Companion to the American Revolution* (Oxford 2000). Authoritative handbook.
J. E. Rodriguez, *The Independence of Spanish America* (Cambridge 1998).

7. New Europes in the southern hemisphere and the second decolonisation
D. Denoon, *Settler Capitalism. The Dynamics of Dependent Development in the Southern Hemisphere* (Oxford 1983). A first attempt to offer a theoretically informed overview.
J. Evans, P. Grimshaw, D. Philips and S. Swain, *Equal Subjects, Unequal Rights. Indigenous Peoples in British Settler Colonies* (Manchester 2003).

The Southern Cone: Argentina, Chile, Uruguay
W. Bernecker, H. Pietschmann and R. Zoller, *Eine kleine Geschichte Brasiliens* (Frankfurt 2000).
G. Beyhaut, *Süd- und Mittelamerika II: Von der Unabhängigkeit bis zur Krise der Gegenwart*, 12th ed. (Frankfurt 1991). Vol. 23 of *Fischer Weltgeschichte*.
D. Bushnell and N. Macaulay, *The Emergence of Latin America in the Nineteenth Century*, 2nd ed. (New York 1993).
V. Fifer, *United States Perceptions of Latin America, 1850–1930* (Manchester 1991). Argentina and Chile during the gradual detachment of England.
R. Miller, 'British investment in Latin America, 1850-1950. A reappraisal', *Itinerario* 19:3 (1995), 21–52.
T. E. Skidmore and P. Smith, *Modern Latin America*, 5th ed. (Oxford 2001).

South Africa
J. Fisch, *Geschichte Südafrikas* (Munich 1990).
L. Thompson, *A History of South Africa*, 2nd ed. (New Haven 1995).

Australia
A. Hagemann, *Kleine Geschichte Australiens* (Munich 2004).
J. Matthäus, *Nationsbildung in Australien von den Anfängen weißer Besiedlung bis zum Ersten Weltkrieg (1788–1914)* (Frankfurt 1993).
The Oxford History of Australia, 5 vols (Melbourne 1989 ff.). Vol. 2 (1770–1860) to vol. 5 (1942–88) have appeared.
J. H. Voigt, *Geschichte Australiens* (Stuttgart 1988).

New Zealand
G. W. Rice (ed.) *The Oxford History of New Zealand*, 2nd ed. (Oxford 1992).
P. M. Smith, *A Concise History of New Zealand* (Cambridge 2005).

The second decolonisation: The British Commonwealth of Nations
W. D. McIntyre, *The Commonwealth of Nations. Origins and Impact, 1869–1971* (Minneapolis 1977).
N. Mansergh, *The Commonwealth Experience* (London 1969).

8. Continental imperialism

The United States of America
W. P. Adams, *Die USA vor 1900* (Munich 2000).
W. P. Adams, *Die USA im 20. Jahrhundert* (Munich 2000).
The Cambridge History of American Foreign Relations, 4 vols (Cambridge 1993). Up to 1865; from 1865; from 1913; from 1945.
J. Heideking and C. Mauch, *Geschichte der USA*, 4th ed. (Tübingen 2004).
J. Heideking and V. Nünning, *Einführung in die amerikanische Geschichte* (Munich 1998). Title is misleading; an excellent introduction to the historiography.
H. Keil, 'Die Vereinigten Staaten von Amerika zwischen kontinentaler Expansion und Imperialismus', in W. Reinhard (ed.), *Imperialistische Kontinuität und nationale Ungeduld im 19. Jhdt.* (Frankfurt 1991), 68–86.
C. A. Milner, C. A. O'Connor and M. A. Sandweiss (eds), *The Oxford History of the American West* (New York 1994. Richly illustrated, serious study with extensive references.
H. Schambeck, H. Widder and M. Bergmann (eds), *Dokumente zur Geschichte der Vereinigten Staaten von Amerika*, 2nd ed. (Berlin 2007). 1492–2006, documents in German translation.

Russia
J. Baddeley, *The Russian Conquest of the Caucasus* (1908; reprint Richmond 1999).
D. Dahlmann, *Sibirien. Vom 16. Jahrhundert bis zur Gegenwart* (Paderborn 2007).
J. Forsyth, *A History of the Peoples of Siberia: Russia's North Asian Colony, 1581–1990* (Cambridge 1992). An outstanding, pioneering work.
A. Kappeler, *The Russian Empire. A Multiethnic History* (Harlow 2001).
M. Khodarkovsky, *Russia's Steppe Frontier: The Making of a Colonial Empire, 1500–1800* (Bloomington 2002).
M. Rywkin (ed.), *Russian Colonial Expansion to 1917* (London 1988). Uneven; nothing on Siberia after 1689 or the Caucasus after 1813.
S. F. Starr (ed.), *Russia's American Colony* (Durham, NC 1987).

China

C. Blunden and M. Elvin, *Cultural Atlas of China* (Oxford 1983).

S. Dabringhaus, 'Ethnische Identitäten im modernen China' in W. Reinhard (ed.), *Die fundamentalistische Revolution* (Freiburg 1995), 69–110.

S. Dabringhaus, *Territorialer Nationalismus in China. Historisch-geographisches Denken 1900–49* (Cologne 2006).

C. P. Fitzgerald, *The Southern Expansion of the Chinese People* (London 1972).

A. T. Grunfeld, *The Making of Modern Tibet* (London 1987).

P. Perdue, *China Marches West. The Qing Conquest of Central Eurasia* (Cambridge, MA 2005).

9. Overseas imperialism in Asia

C. Clarke, C. Peach and S. Vertovec (eds), *South Asians Overseas. Migration and Ethnicity* (Cambridge 1990).

R. P. T. Davenport-Hines and G. Jones (eds), *British Business in Asia since 1860* (Cambridge 1989).

J. Gallagher and R. Robinson, 'The imperialism of free trade', *The Economic History Review* VI:1 (1953), 1–15.

From trade to rule

C. A. Bayly, *Imperial Meridian. The British Empire and the World, 1780–1830* (London 1989).

H. V. Bowen, *Revenue and Reform. The Indian Problem in British Politics, 1757–73* (Cambridge 1991).

S. Förster, *Die mächtigen Diener der East India Company. Ursachen und Hintergründe der britischen Expansionspolitik in Südasien, 1793–1819* (Stuttgart 1992).

British India

C. A. Bayly, *Indian Society and the Making of the British Empire* (Cambridge 1988). Vol. II:1 of *The New Cambridge History of India*.

C. A. Bayly, *Empire and Information. Intelligence Gathering and Social Communication in India, 1780–1870* (Cambridge 1996). Among other things, criticises the Orientalism hypothesis.

S. Bose, *Peasant Labour and Colonial Capital. Rural Bengal since 1770* (Cambridge 1993). Vol. III:2 of *The New Cambridge History of India*.

B. Chatterji, *Trade, Tariffs and Empire. Lancashire and British Policy in India 1919–1939* (New Delhi 1992).

N. B. Dirk, *Castes of Mind. Colonialism and the Making of Modern India* (Princeton 2001). On the concept of caste.

H. Fischer Tiné and M. Mann (eds), *Colonialism as Civilizing Mission. Cultural Ideology in British India* (London 2004).

P. J. Marshall, *Bengal: The British Bridgehead. Eastern India 1740–1828* (Cambridge 1988). Vol. II:2 of *The New Cambridge History of India*.

B. N. Ramusack, *The Indian Princes and their States* (Cambridge 2004). Vol. III:3 of *The New Cambridge History of India*.

D. Rothermund, *Indiens wirtschaftliche Entwicklung. Von der Kolonialherrschaft bis zur Gegenwart* (Paderborn 1985).

B. R. Tomlinson, *The Economy of Modern India, 1860–1970* (Cambridge 1993). Vol. III:3 of *The New Cambridge History of India.*

The Dutch East Indies
Itinerario. A Leiden-based journal of the history of European expansion; especially useful regarding research on the Dutch colonies.
M. Kuitenbrouwer, *The Netherlands and the Rise of Modern Imperialism. Colonies and Foreign Policy, 1870–1902* (New York/Oxford 1991).
S. Wedema, '*Ethiek' und Macht. Die niederländisch-indische Kolonialverwaltung und indonesische Emanzipationsbestrebungen 1901–1927* (Stuttgart 1998).

The 'opening' and 'modernisation' of China
P. A. Cohen, *History in Three Keys. The Boxers as Event, Experience and Myth* (New York 1997).
K. Mühlhahn, *Herrschaft und Widerstand in der Musterkolonie Kiautschou. Interaktionen zwischen China und Deutschland 1897–1914* (Munich 2000).
J. Osterhammel, *China und die Weltgesellschaft. Vom 18. Jhdt. bis in unsere Zeit* (Munich 1989). Essential.
C. A. Trocki, *Opium, Empire and the Global Political Economy. A Study of the Asian Opium Trade, 1750–1950* (London 1999).

The 'opening' and 'modernisation' of Japan
J. Ando, *Die Entstehung der Meiji-Verfassung. Zur Rolle des deutschen Konstitutionalismus im modernen japanischen Staatswesen* (Munich 2000).
O. Checkland, *Britain's Encounter with Meiji Japan, 1868–1912* (Basingstoke 1989).
B. Martin (ed.), *Japans Weg in die Moderne. Ein Sonderweg nach deutschem Vorbild?* (Frankfurt 1987).
W. Schwentker, 'Modernisierung von oben. Japan im 19. Jhdt.', in J. Osterhammel (ed.), *Asien in der Neuzeit 1500–1950* (Frankfurt 1994), 101–24.

From free-trade imperialism to high imperialism
I. Brown, *The Elite and the Economy in Siam, c. 1890–1920* (Oxford 1988). Partial modernisation in the shadow of the great powers' rivalry.
D. Fieldhouse, *Economics and Empire, 1830–1914* (London 1973). Empirical research turns to the 'periphery'.
J. A. Hobson, *Imperialism: A Study* (London 1902). The groundbreaking theoretical study.
U. Menzel, *Das Ende der Dritten Welt und das Scheitern der großen Theorie* (Frankfurt 1992). A stimulating collection of critical essays.
W. J. Mommsen, *Theories of Imperialism* (London 1980). Overview of theories.
W. J. Mommsen and J. Osterhammel (eds), *Imperialism and After. Continuities and Discontinuities* (London 1986).
W. Reinhard (ed.), *Imperialistische Kontinuität und nationale Ungeduld im 19. Jahrhundert* (Frankfurt 1991).

High-imperialist colonies in Asia and the Pacific
P. Brocheux and D. Hémery, *Indochine: la colonisation ambiguë 1858–1954*, 2nd ed. (Paris 2001).

D. Brötel, *Frankreich im Fernen Osten. Imperialistische Expansion and Aspiration in Siam und Malaya, Laos und China, 1880–1904* (Stuttgart 1996).
H. Hiery (ed.), *Die deutsche Südsee 1884–1914. Ein Handbuch*, 2nd ed. (Darmstadt 2002).

10. Imperialism in Africa

J. Middleton, *The World of the Swahili. An African Mercantile Civilization* (New Haven 1992).

European free-trade imperialism and African expansion
G. Campbell, *The Rise and Fall of the Merina Empire. An Economic History of Imperial Madagascar, 1750–1895* (Münster 2002).
C. Hamilton, *Terrific Majesty. The Powers of Shaka Zulu and the Limits of Historical Invention* (Cambridge 1998).

The 'Scramble for Africa' in high imperialism: The transition to rule
J. Andall and D. Duncan (eds), *Italian Colonialism. Legacy and Memory* (Frankfurt 2005).
S. Förster, W. J. Mommsen and R. Robinson (eds), *Bismarck, Europe and Africa. The Berlin Africa Conference 1884–1885 and the Onset of Partition* (Oxford 1988).
A. Jalata, *Oromia and Ethiopia. State Formation and Ethnonational Conflict, 1868–1992* (Boulder 1993). On the question of Amharic colonialism.
M. Lyons, *A Colonial Disease. A Social History of Sleeping Sickness in Northern Zaire, 1900–1940* (Cambridge 1992).
T. Pakenham, *The Scramble for Africa* (London 1991).
K.-M. Seeberg, *Der Maji-Maji-Krieg gegen die deutsche Kolonialherrschaft* (Berlin 1989).
H. L. Wesseling, *Divide and Rule. The Partition of Africa, 1880–1914* (Westport/London 1996).
H. Witbooi, *The Hendrik Witbooi Papers*, ed. B. Lau (Windhoek 1989). An African source.

Colonial rule in Africa
W. U. Eckart, *Medizin und Kolonialimperialismus: Deutschland 1884–1945* (Paderborn 1997).
P. Sebald, *Togo 1884–1914* (Berlin 1988). Thanks to this and the following book, German Togoland is particularly well researched.
T. von Trotha, *Koloniale Herrschaft. Zur soziologischen Theorie der Staatsentstehung am Beispiel des 'Schutzgebietes Togo'* (Tübingen 1994). Wide-ranging study grounded in the history of administration.
J. Zimmerer, *Deutsche Herrschaft über Afrikaner. Staatlicher Machtanspruch und koloniale Wirklichkeit im kolonialen Namibia* (Münster 2001). German rule after the Herero and Nama wars.

The colonial economy in Africa
A. Eckert, *Grundbesitz, Landkonflikte und kolonialer Wandel: Douala 1880–1960* (Stuttgart 1999).
S. Kanfer, *The Last Empire. De Beers, Diamonds and the World* (London 1993).

Social change in Africa
S. Abun-Nasr, *Afrikaner und Missionar. Die Lebensgeschichte von David Asante* (Basle 2003).
J. E. Genova, *Colonial Ambivalence, Cultural Authenticity, and the Limitation of Mimicry in French-Ruled West Africa, 1914–56* (New York 2004). Assimilated Africans.
J. Higginson, *A Working Class in the Making. Belgian Colonial Labour Policy and the African Mineworker, 1907–1951* (Madison 1990).
J. Iliffe, *East African Doctors. A History of the Modern Profession* (Cambridge 1998).

11. Late imperialism and the great decolonisation

C.-R. Ageron, *La décolonisation française* (Paris 1991).
R. von Albertini, *Decolonization. The Administration and Future of the Colonies, 1919–1960* (New York 1971).
G. Altmann, *Abschied vom Empire. Die innere Dekolonisation Großbritanniens 1945–85* (Göttingen 2005).
F. Ansprenger, *The Dissolution of the Colonial Empires* (London 1989).
G. Balfour-Paul, *The End of Empire in the Middle East. Britain's Relinquishment of Power in her Last Three Arab Dependencies* (Cambridge 1991): *Sudan, South West Arabia, the Gulf.*
British Documents on the End of Empire (London 1992 ff.). Three series, each including numerous volumes.
G. Brogini-Künzi, *Italien und der Abessinienkrieg 1935/36. Kolonialkrieg oder totaler Krieg?* (Paderborn 2006).
A. Clayton, *The Wars of French Decolonization* (London 1994).
J. Darwin, *The End of the British Empire. The Historical Debate* (Oxford 1991).
B. Digre, *Imperialism's New Clothes. The Repartition of Tropical Africa, 1914–19* (New York 1990).
F. Füredi, *Colonial Wars and the Politics of Third World Nationalism* (London 1994).
H. Grimal, *La décolonisation de 1919 à nos jours*, 3rd ed. (Brussels 1996).
D. Rothermund, *The Routledge Companion to Decolonization* (London 2006).

The Oriental question and the First World War
S. N. Faroqui (ed.) *The Later Ottoman Empire, 1603–1839* (Cambridge 2006). Vol. 3 of *The Cambridge History of Turkey.*
H. Inalcik and D. Quataert (eds), *An Economic and Social History of the Ottoman Empire, 1300–1914* (Cambridge 1994).
A. L. Macfie, *The End of the Ottoman Empire, 1908–23* (London 1998).
R. Mantran (ed.), *Histoire de l'Empire Ottoman* (Paris 1989).
J. Matuz, *Das Osmanische Reich. Grundlinien seiner Geschichte* (Darmstadt 1985).
M. Reinkowski, *Die Dinge der Ordnung. Eine vergleichende Untersuchung über die osmanische Reformpolitik im 19. Jahrhundert* (Munich 2005). Compares regions and examines terminology.
M. E. Yapp, *The Making of the Modern Near East, 1792 to 1923* (London 1987).

Israel: Colonisation and colonialism
N. Caplan, *Futile Diplomacy*, 2 vols (London 1983–88). Negotiations between Arabs and Zionists, 1913–48.

Y. Hazony, *The Jewish State. The Struggle for Israel's Soul* (New York 2000). The debate on Zionism.

Y. Karmon, *Israel. Eine geographische Landeskunde* (Darmstadt 1983).

G. Krämer, *A History of Palestine. From the Ottoman Conquest to the Founding of the State of Israel* (Princeton 2008). Includes the foundation of Israel.

W. Lehn and U. Davis, *The Jewish National Fund* (London 1988).

H. Mejcher (ed.), *Die Palästina-Frage 1917–1948*, 2nd ed. (Paderborn 1993).

J. N. Moore (ed.), *The Arab-Israeli Conflict*, 4 vols in 5 parts (Princeton 1974–91).

H. Near, *The Kibbutz Movement. A History*, 2 vols (Oxford 1992–97).

C. C. O'Brien, *The Siege. The Saga of Israel and Zionism* (New York 1986).

I. Pappe, *The Ethnic Cleansing of Palestine* (Oxford 2006). Controversial portrayal of the founding of the state.

M. Rodinson, *Israel: A Colonial Settler State?* (New York 1973).

A. Shlaim, *The Politics of Partition. King Abdullah, the Zionists and Palestine, 1921–1951* (New York/Oxford 1990). Abridged second edition of the 1988 book on collusion with Transjordan.

Japanese imperialism and the Second World War
W. G. Beasley, *Japanese Imperialism, 1894–1945* (Oxford 1987).

R. H. Myers and M. R. Peattie (eds), *The Japanese Colonial Empire, 1895–1945* (Princeton 1984).

Decolonisation in Asia
P. R. Brass, *The Politics of India since Independence* (Cambridge 1990). Vol. IV:1 of *The New Cambridge History of India*.

J. Brown, *Nehru* (London 1999).

M. Frey, *Dekolonisierung in Südostasien. Die Vereinigten Staaten und die Auflösung der europäischen Kolonialreiche* (Munich 2006).

H. Mejcher, *Die Politik und das Öl im Nahen Osten*, 2 vols (Stuttgart 1980–90). Before 1938; 1938–1950.

R. Schulze, *A Modern History of the Islamic World* (New York 2000).

M. E. Yapp, *The Near East since the First World War* (London 1991).

Decolonisation in Africa/Neocolonialism and Portuguese decolonisation
M. Bennoune, *The Making of Contemporary Algeria, 1830–1987. Colonial Upheavals and Post-independence Development* (Cambridge 1988).

T. Chafer, *The End of Empire in French West Africa. France's Successful Decolonization?* (Oxford 2002).

A. Des Forges, 'Leave None to Tell the Story'. Genocide in Rwanda (New York 1999).

R. B. Edgerton, *Mau Mau. An African Crucible* (London 1989).

J. D. Hargreaves, *Decolonization in Africa* (London 1988).

N. MacQueen, *The Decolonization of Portuguese Africa. Metropolitan Revolution and the Dissolution of Empire* (London 1997).

G. T. Mollin, *Die USA und der Kolonialismus. Amerika als Partner und Nachfolger der belgischen Macht in Afrika 1939–65* (Berlin 1996).

Decolonisation in Russia and South Africa, blocked decolonisation in Israel, non-decolonised territories
Afrika-Jahrbuch 1 (1987) ff.

R. Götz and U. Halbach, *Politisches Lexikon GUS*, 2nd ed. (Munich 1993).
R. Götz and U. Halbach, *Politisches Lexikon Rußland* (Munich 1994).
Jahrbuch Internationale Politik 21, 1993/94 (1996) ff.: *previous title* Die internationale Politik.
Nahost-Jahrbuch 1 (1987) ff.

12. A balance-sheet of colonialism
P. Chabal, *Power in Africa: An Essay in Political Interpretation* (London 1992).
P. Childs and R. J. P. Williams, *An Introduction to Post-Colonial Theory* (New York 1997).
A. W. Crosby, *Ecological Imperialism. The Biological Expansion of Europe, 900–1900*, 2nd ed. (Cambridge 2004).
D. Fieldhouse, *Black Africa, 1945–1980. Economic Decolonization and Arrested Development* (London 1986).
D. Fieldhouse, *The West and the Third World* (Oxford 1999).
Y. Kachru and C. L. Nelson, *World Englishes in Asian Contexts* (Hong Kong 2006).
D. L. McNamara, *The Colonial Origins of Korean Enterprise, 1910–1945* (Cambridge 1990).
P. K. O'Brien and L. Prados de la Escosura, 'Balance sheet for the acquisition, retention and loss of European empires overseas', *Itinerario* 23:3–4 (1999), 25–53.
J. Osterhammel and N. P. Petersson, *Globalization. A Short History* (Princeton/Oxford 2005).
W. Reinhard, *Parasit oder Partner? Europäische Wirtschaft und Neue Welt 1500–1800* (Münster 1997).
W. Reinhard (ed.), *Verstaatlichung der Welt? Europäische Staatsmodelle und außereuropäische Machtprozesse* (Munich 1999).
J. L. Watson (ed.), *Golden Arches East. McDonald's in East Asia*, 2nd ed. (Stanford 2006).
C. Young, *The African Colonial State in Comparative Perspective* (New Haven 1995).

Index